Prehistoric Patterns
of Human Behavior

A Case Study
in the Mississippi Valley

Plate I. Research personnel of the Powers Phase Project: summer of 1974. *First row, left to right:* Bruce Smith, Kathy Parrent, Mary Petruchius, Oscar Richardson (landowner of the Gypsy Joint site), Dennis Grega. *Second row, left to right:* John Cox, Leslie Harrison Fedota, Virginia Balnius, Kathy Mastricola, Linda Anderson, Kevin Monahan. *Third row, left to right:* James Perren, Russel Bailon, James Krakker, Charles Hastings, James E. Price, Cynthia Price, Bill Messina, Jay Sperber. *Not shown:* Neil Sonenklar.

Prehistoric Patterns
of Human Behavior

A Case Study in the Mississippi Valley

BRUCE D. SMITH

Department of Anthropology
National Museum of Natural History
Smithsonian Institution
Washington, D.C.

With a contribution by

WILMA WETTERSTROM

Department of Humanities
Massachusetts Institute of Technology

ACADEMIC PRESS   New York   San Francisco   London

A Subsidiary of Harcourt Brace Jovanovich, Publishers

This is a volume in

Studies in Archeology

A complete list of titles in this series appears at the end of this volume.

ACADEMIC PRESS, INC.
111 Fifth Avenue, New York, New York 10003

United Kingdom Edition published by
ACADEMIC PRESS, INC. (LONDON) LTD.
24/28 Oval Road, London NW1

Library of Congress Cataloging in Publication Data

Smith, Bruce D
    Prehistoric patterns of human behavior.

    (Studies in archeology series)
    Bibliography: p.
    1. Gypsy Joint site, Mo.   2. Mississippian culture.
3. Missouri––Antiquities. I. Title.
E78.M8S62   977.8'894   77–11222
ISBN 0–12–650650–7

For Martha

Contents

Contents

List of Plates

List of Figures

List of Tables

Preface

Although archaeologists are interested in gaining an understanding of the cultural systems of prehistoric human populations, they obviously cannot directly observe the patterns of behavior of those populations. Rather, they must induce such prehistoric patterns of human behavior indirectly, by recording and analyzing the spatial and contextual patterns of material remains resulting from such behavior.

The basic scientific puzzle that confronts every archaeologist, then, is how to identify accurately and correctly the human behavior patterns that produced archaeologically evidenced patterns of material remains. This process of translating resultant patterning of material remains into causative patterns of human behavior would appear to be a rather simple and straightforward task, judging from much of the archaeological literature of the last decade. Unfortunately, the apparent ease with which some archaeologists can make the jump from material remains to human behavior is largely illusory, a product of their strong desire to identify such causative patterns of human behavior, combined with a lack of understanding of the complexity of the reasoning process involved in making such a logical jump.

One of the primary aims of this book is to present a detailed consideration of the logical structure of the reasoning process that should be employed in attempting to identify causative patterns of human behavior. In order to deal specifically with the logical problems inherent in archaeological reasoning (Smith 1977), the *Hypothetico-Analog (H-A)* method of inductive confirmation, a supplemented version of the *Hypothetico-Deductive* method, was developed. The article just cited presents a detailed discussion of the logical structure of the *H-A* method, and how it differs from other versions of the scientific method that have been proposed for archaeology, whereas this book represents an attempt to articulate the *H-A* method with reality, in the form of an archaeological data set. Above all, then, this book is a methodological case study—a demonstration that a specific method of inductive confirmation can be successfully employed in an archaeological context.

In addition to employing the scientific method in archaeological reasoning, this book is a methodological case study in a number of other respects. The archaeological project to be described was carried out within a problem-oriented research framework, with five general problem areas explicitly identified and pursued. The excavation and recovery strategies that were subsequently implemented to gain information relevant to each of the stated research questions are also explicitly detailed, as are the methods of recording and quantitative analysis employed.

Finally, an attempt was made to present the total archaeological data set in a format that would allow reanalysis and replication studies to be carried out by other archaeologists. Coded locational and identification information for every item recovered during the research project is presented in appendixes.

The archaeological data set employed in this methodological case study was recovered during the total excavation of a relatively small Powers Phase (Middle Mississippi) site consisting of two habitation structures and a series of nine pits, four of which had associated activity areas. Based upon completed analysis and interpretation of the data set recovered from the site, it appears to have been a settlement occupied by a nuclear—minimally extended—family group on a year-round basis for less than 3 years. A relatively wide range of both male and female domestic and subsistence activities were carried out during occupation of the settlement. Such small homestead settlements, representing the lower end of Mississippian settlement systems, have rarely been excavated, and until now, none has ever been described or analyzed in any detail. Thus, in addition to functioning as a methodological case study, this book presents a detailed description of a previously little-known component of Mississippian settlement systems.

Chapter 1 provides background information concerning the Powers Phase, and would be of interest to all readers. Chapter 2 describes the site selection, data recovery, and data processing methods employed during the excavation of the Gypsy Joint site, along with a discussion of the problem orientation that structured the research strategy. It too is of interest to most readers. Chapter 3 contains detailed descriptions of the cultural features and artifactual materials uncovered at the Gypsy Joint site, and is directed primarily to those readers with a specific interest in Mississippian archaeology. Chapter 4 deals with the description and analysis of ecofactual materials recovered from the Gypsy Joint site, and includes a contribution by Dr. Wilma Wetterstrom. Chapter 5 analyzes the spatial patterning of material remains at the site, providing nearest neighbor analysis for data sets from the major features. Chapter 6 contains the interpretive core of the research monograph, with research goals more specifically articulated in the form of alternative hypotheses and associated observational predictions. The relative strength of each of these hypotheses is then evaluated by comparing its set of observational predictions with the material remains recovered from the site. For the reader primarily interested in the application of the scientific method to archaeological inference, this final chapter, along with Chapter 2, should provide interesting reading.

Acknowledgments

Although the final published results of an archaeological research project usually carry the name of a single individual or a limited number of individuals, there is always a larger group of people who have been directly involved with the field and laboratory phases of the project and have contributed in many important ways to the final product. This monograph is no exception.

The field crew that excavated the Gypsy Joint site under my direction consisted of undergraduate and graduate students from a number of universities and colleges (Plate I). Russell Bailon, Virginia Balnius, Leslie Harrison Fedota, Kathy Mastricola, William Messina, Mary Petruchius, and Jay Sperber were undergraduate and graduate students at Loyola University of Chicago. Charles Hastings, James Krakker, and Neil Sonenklar were graduate students at the University of Michigan, and John Cox and Kathy Parrent were students at the University of Missouri—Columbia and Southeast Missouri State College, respectively. All of these individuals contributed in a variety of ways to the excavation of the Gypsy Joint site, and their long hours of enthusiastic and conscientious work are greatly appreciated.

James and Cynthia Price provided logistical support and laboratory facilities for the Gypsy Joint crew, and contributed to the success of the field season in a great number of ways. They also took time out from their own research activities toward the end of the field season to direct the excavation of Structure 2 at the Gypsy Joint site. Their many efforts toward making the summer field season of 1974 an interesting and successful one are gratefully acknowledged.

Analysis of much of the Gypsy Joint materials was carried out at the University of Georgia Laboratory of Archaeology. My sincere thanks go to William Mitchell and Janet Morris, who spent many long hours identifying and analyzing materials recovered from the Gypsy Joint site.

Dr. Wilma Wetterstrom of the Massachusetts Institute of Technology identified and analyzed the ethnobotanical materials recovered from the Gypsy Joint site. In addition, a small quantity of maize recovered from the site was analyzed by Hugh Cutler and Leonard Blake of the Missouri Botanical Gardens. The efforts and expertise of these individuals is recognized and appreciated.

Spatial analysis of a number of point data sets from the Gypsy Joint site was carried out by Dr. Don Graybill, then with the Department of Anthropology, University of Georgia. While Dr. Graybill's detailed comments and suggestions concerning interpretation of the data are greatly appreciated, he should not be held responsible for any misinterpretations of the results of this analysis.

Ms. Sharon Goad, Department of Anthropology, University of Georgia, reordered the data set and rewrote the plotting programs that resulted in Figure 11. Dr. Richard Jefferies provided photographic skills and Mrs. Louise Brice typed the final manuscript. Their efforts and careful attention to detail were invaluable. I would also like to thank my father, Professor Goldwin A. Smith, for taking time from his Christmas holidays to read and correct the page proofs of this book.

Finally, it is a pleasure to acknowledge the debt I owe to James B. Griffin. In addition to providing me with the opportunity and the funding to excavate a small Powers Phase settlement during the summer of 1974, Dr. Griffin was a source of encouragement and advice during the subsequent analysis and writing phase of the project.

Excavations at the Gypsy Joint site represented one aspect of the overall research design of the Powers Phase Project, a long-term archaeological research effort. Funded by the National Science Foundation (Grant GS 3215), the Powers Phase Project was under the direction of Dr. James B. Griffin, with Dr. James E. Price as director of field research activities.

1

The Powers Phase

INTRODUCTION

Before beginning a detailed discussion of the Gypsy Joint site, it is necessary to provide some general background information concerning the larger cultural system within which this single settlement existed and to describe the general environmental setting of the Powers Phase area. Because these topics will be discussed in much greater detail in other publications relating to the Powers Phase, they will be covered in detail here only as they directly relate to interpretation of the Gypsy Joint site.

During 1966 James E. Price, then an undergraduate at the University of Missouri—Columbia, was conducting a site survey in southeast Missouri, near the present-day towns of Naylor and Neelyville. During this survey, Price located a number of late prehistoric (circa A. D. 1300) Middle Mississippi sites that had apparently been burned just prior to being abandoned. Uncontrolled digging by local people at one of these sites (the Turner site) prompted Price to conduct limited excavations in an attempt both to salvage data before it was destroyed and to demonstrate for local people that careful, controlled excavations could yield important information that would otherwise be destroyed. The results of this first summer's work at the Turner site were encouraging. Price and Dr. James B. Griffin, Director of the Museum of Anthropology, University of Michigan, recognized the obvious potential of the area in terms of developing a long-term regional research project directed toward studying Mississippian Period settlement subsistence systems.

The area in question was not only semiisolated geographically, being bounded on the west and northwest by the Ozark Escarpment and on the east and southeast by low-lying swampy areas, but also seemed to encompass an area of cultural uniformity, at least during the Mississippian Period. All of the Mississippian Period sites in the area were, in fact, thought to belong to a single "phase," with the term *phase* indicating the archaeological manifestation of a single prehistoric culture group (most likely a tribe or chiefdom in this case). The largest settlement of this Mississippian phase had been described by Cyrus Thomas in 1894 and named Powers Fort, after the owner of the land at that time. This landowner's name was also adopted by Dr. Griffin to identify the phase as a whole.

Powers Phase sites also showed unusual potential for yielding information concerning the structure of the cultural system of the human populations that occupied them. The settlements seemed to have been occupied for only a short period of time. Midden accumulation was minimal, and little evidence of rebuilding of structures was found. This was in striking contrast to the situation invariably encountered by archaeologists attempting to excavate Mississippian sites located farther to the east in the Mississippi Valley. Such sites were usually occupied over long periods of time; and upon removing the plowzone from these sites, archaeologists were invariably confronted with complex and confusing patterns of superimposed layers of house floors, activity areas, storage and refuse pits, etc., all of which made it very difficult to determine the contemporaneity of utilization of different structures, activity areas, pits, and areas of sites. There were also obvious problems involved in separating undisturbed deposits from those that had been disturbed by subsequent cultural activities. Such obstacles to interpretation were not present in Powers Phase sites. Structures and pits represented a very short time span of cultural activities, and artifact distributions on house floors were often largely undisturbed.

The Powers Phase area was also extremely attractive as a potential research universe in that while a large percentage of the land area was under cultivation, facilitating location of sites through surface survey, agricultural strategies had not at that time resulted in serious damage to sites.

Shortly after Price began graduate studies at the University of Michigan, Professor Griffin applied for and received a grant from the National Science Foundation with whose financial assistance the Powers Phase research project was established in 1968, with Griffin as project director and principal investigator and Price serving as field director. Temporary research laboratory facilities and crew quarters were set up in Neelyville, Missouri, during the first field season in 1968, and a permanent research center was established the next year in Naylor, Missouri. NSF support of the Powers Phase project continued through seven field seasons, ending September 1, 1974.

During the 7-year period of NSF support, research efforts were focused largely on two fortified Powers Phase villages, the Turner site and the Snodgrass site. Limited test excavations were also carried out at two other Powers Phase villages, the Wilborn and Flurry sites, as well as at

Powers Fort, the ceremonial center of the Powers Phase. In addition, limited excavations were conducted at two Mississippian sites in the Ozark uplands, the Gooseneck and Lepold sites. The final Powers Phase site to be investigated under NSF funding was the Gypsy Joint site, excavated during the summer of 1974. Although NSF funding of the Powers Phase project ended in 1974, archaeological research in the area is continuing. Price, now with the University of Missouri—Columbia, has made a long-term commitment to studying the prehistoric and early historic settlements in the Powers Phase area and is maintaining a permanent research facility in Naylor, Missouri.

ENVIRONMENTAL SETTING

The lowland sites of the Powers Phase are located at the extreme western edge of the Mississippi Valley, directly adjacent to the Ozark Escarpment. The section of the Mississippi Valley shown in Figure 1 falls within the northern division of the lower alluvial valley and is composed of an eastern and a western lowlands area, with Crowley's Ridge separating the two.

Even though the Mississippi River has not flowed in the western lowlands for at least 18,000–20,000 years, it is clearly evident that it was a major factor in determining the prehistoric as well as the present-day topography, distribution of soil types, and distribution of vegetational associations in the Powers Phase area and in the western lowlands in general. During the early Wisconsin Glacial Phase (42,000–30,000 B. P.) when the ancestral Mississippi River flowed through the Powers Phase area (Saucier 1974:Figure 3), it was quite different from the meandering, single-main-channel Mississippi River of today. At that time the river was composed of a series of swiftly flowing, intertwined or braided stream channels that carried large volumes of glacial outwash. This braided stream drainage pattern produced a quite distinctive topography in the Powers Phase area, consisting of an intertwined network of sinuous, flat-bottomed relict stream channels that paralleled the Ozark Escarpment in a northeast to southwest direction.

The higher land areas between these relict braided stream channels form a series of isolated sand ridges or interfluves that run in a northeast–southwest direction, are gently rolling in contour, and are usually from 10 to 20 feet higher in elevation than the relict channel beds (Figure 2).

The Little Black River, which flows out of the Ozark uplands in the Powers Phase area, now follows the westernmost of these early Wisconsin relict stream channels. Smaller streams flowed through many of the

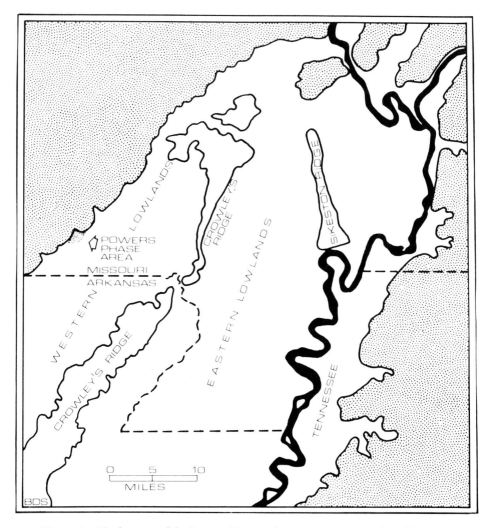

Figure 1. The location of the Powers Phase at the extreme western edge of the Mississippi Valley.

other channel relicts until the Army Corps of Engineers replaced them with a series of drainage ditches. The soil in the relict channels consists of fine-grained silty and clayey sediments, while the interfluve areas consist of sandy, well-drained soils. These sandy, interfluve ridge areas are in many cases locally accentuated by wind-deposited sand dune formations (Saucier 1974:9).

Although there is only 10 to 20 feet of variation in elevation between relict channel beds and sand ridge crests in the Powers Phase area, such apparently minor variations in elevation are especially significant in terms of the occurrence of distinctive vegetation types. Braun has defined four general subdivisions of bottomland forest (1950:291), and although they obviously do not reflect all of the possible variation in community composition and successional stages, they will be adequate for the present discussion.[1] Braun's four bottomland forest subdivisions are (a) stream margin communities; (b) swamp forests; (c) hardwood bottoms; (d) ridge bottoms. The ridge-bottom forest subtype would have covered the higher and subsequently better drained areas of sand ridges in the Powers Phase area. In addition to those hardwood bottom species that would occur on these sand ridges, advanced successional species not usually found at lower elevations such as shagbark hickory, white oak, and cherrybark oak would occur in the sand ridge area overstory. It is possible that a tulip oak climax forest could have existed on these ridge areas, in which case tulip, white basswood, chinkapin oak, shumard oak, cherrybark oak, silver maple, winged elm, pin oak, sugarberry, and elm would have occurred in significant percentages. Dominant understory species would have included sassafras, sugarberry, paw paw, and dogwood.

The ridge-bottom forest subtype would merge with the hardwood-bottom forest subtype on the lower slopes of the sand ridges. The hardwood forest subtype would also occur on the better-drained portions of the lowland areas, with sweetgum, red maple, elm, sugarberry, and numerous species of oaks predominating in the overstory. Undergrowth would have been quite dense, and overstory trees would have been quite large.

In those poorly drained areas between the sand ridges that were inundated throughout the year, mature cypress–tupelo swamps would have existed during the occupation of the Powers Phase sites. Bald cypress and water tupelo would have been the dominant overstory species, with silver maple, red maple, water and pumpkin ash, and box elder occurring in the understory.

Although it is difficult to determine accurately the extent to which cypress swamps filled these low relict stream beds, there are some indications that much of the lowland area may have consisted of mature cypress swamp. A few cypress still exist along drainage ditches south of

[1] The brief and rather general vegetational reconstruction of the Powers Phase area given here assumes that a climax forest community existed in the area during the late prehistoric period. This does not mean, however, that the complex problem of determining the successional stages of vegetation associations that existed in the Powers Phase area during the prehistoric period is being totally ignored, but rather that it will be considered in the detailed environmental reconstructions to be included in later publications concerning the Powers Phase. Those interested in bottomland forest successional stages are referred to Shelford (1954 1963:89–114), Braun (1950), Putnam (1951), Putnam et al. (1960), and Hosner and Minckler (1963).

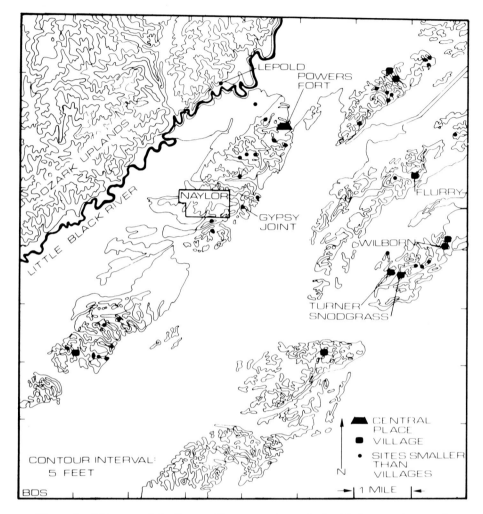

Figure 2. This map of the Powers Phase area shows the braided stream topography, consisting of relict stream beds and interfluve sand ridges running northeast to southwest. Also shown are the locations of many of the Powers Phase sites. Sites that have been excavated are named; sites not named are known only through surface survey. Numerous small sites recently located through surface survey are not shown.

Naylor, and there is quite a sizable cypress swamp area directly adjacent to Powers Fort. During the spring high-water stage of the Little Black River, much of the low area between ridges is flooded, sometimes for weeks at a time. Prior to modern drainage efforts, it is quite possible that many areas were submerged well into the summer months.

The composition of the faunal section of the biotic community of the Powers Phase area will not be discussed here, since it has previously been covered in some detail (Smith 1975).

THE SETTLEMENT PATTERN OF THE POWERS PHASE

The settlements of the Powers Phase consist of a single ceremonial center, a series of smaller fortified villages, and an as yet undetermined number of sites that are smaller in size than the fortified villages. Powers Fort is the ceremonial center of the Powers Phase. A fortification wall and ditch enclose three sides of the 12-acre site; the east side of the site fronts on a cypress swamp area. Within the fortified area there are four mounds: a large, flat-topped pyramidal mound and associated plaza area, as well as three smaller mounds. It is thought that Powers Fort was occupied longer than any other Powers Phase site, probably for approximately 50 to 100 years, circa A. D. 1300. Powers Fort was first described by Cyrus Thomas in 1894. A map made of the site at that time is reproduced in Figure 3. Because of the protective attitude of the present landowner, excavations at Powers Fort have been limited to a single burial excavated during the summer of 1966 and a single structure excavated during the summer of 1969. Measuring approximately 18 by 18 feet, the excavated structure showed evidence of having been rebuilt two times during its occupation. Because access to the site is difficult, no further excavations have been undertaken to date, and relatively little is known about the ceremonial center of the Powers Phase.

A great deal is known, however, about two of the fortified villages of the Powers Phase; the Turner site and the Snodgrass site. These two sites, separated by only one-tenth of a mile, and located on the south end of Sharecropper Ridge (Figure 2), were almost completely excavated during the period 1968–1973.

The Turner site is the smaller of the two sites, having 44 structures with associated refuse pits in a fairly ordered pattern around a central courtyard and burial area, with approximately 1.5 acres enclosed by the fortification ditch and palisade (Figure 4). (A final report on the Turner site is in preparation.) The Snodgrass site is almost twice as large as the Turner site, having a total of 90 structures with associated refuse pits arranged in an ordered streetlike pattern, with approximately 2.5 acres enclosed by the fortification ditch and palisade wall. The internal structure of the Snodgrass site is also more complex than the Turner site, with an internal white clay wall separating a group of 38 structures and a central courtyard area from a group of 52 smaller structures situated outside the white wall (Figure 5). A preliminary analysis and interpretation of the Snodgrass site has been written (Price 1973), and a final report on the site is in preparation. The lack of evidence of rebuilding of structures, and the limited amount of refuse at both the Turner and Snodgrass sites suggests a very short span of occupation for the two sites, perhaps as short as 2 to 3 years (Price 1973:100).

Although the research goals of the Powers Phase Project during the period 1968–1973 centered on extensive excavation of the Turner and

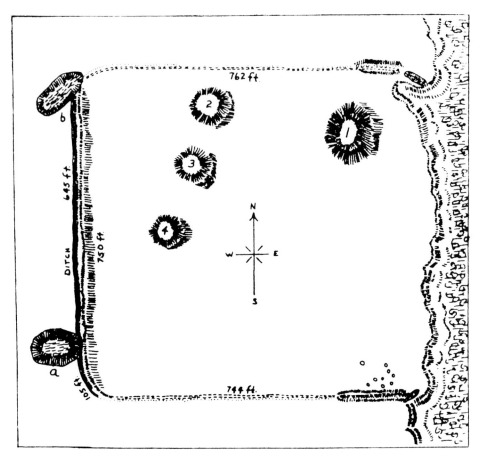

Figure 3. Powers Fort, the ceremonial center of the Powers Phase (after Thomas 1894:195).

Snodgrass sites, limited investigations of two other Powers Phase villages were undertaken during the summer of 1970. The location of burned Powers Phase structures is sometimes indicated by areas of darker surface soil, or "stains," resulting from charcoal having been churned up into the plowzone. Forty-six such surface-stain indications of Powers Phase structures were mapped at the Wilborn site (Figure 6), and 21 were observed at the Flurry site (Figure 7). In addition to mapping the location of surface indications of structures, a single structure was excavated at each of these two sites. (Reports on these sites are in preparation.)

In addition to the four village sites already discussed, six other Powers Phase sites have been identified as fortified villages on the basis of surface collections (Price 1973:Figure 4; Price 1974:Figure 10). The location of these projected villages is shown in Figure 2, but available data concerning these six sites are limited.

The third category of Powers Phase sites shown in Figure 2 is a catch-all category of sites smaller than village size. That this category is deliberately vague reflects the very limited amount of data that is available concerning these smaller sites. Price has divided these smaller Powers Phase sites into two distinct categories: hamlets and extractive sites (Price 1973:Figure 10; Price 1974:10–14, 60–64, Figures 10–14).

Powers Phase hamlets are believed to be approximately .25 acres in size, to contain approximately 12 to 15 structures, and to have had a population of less than 50 people (Price 1974:13, 60). Although a total of six Powers Phase sites have been identified as being hamlets (Price 1974:60, Figure 10), the data available concerning these sites are limited. A single structure was excavated by a local amateur at one of these sites, but no information was obtained concerning overall site size or the total number of structures present. Surface indications of a limited number of structures were observed at two other projected hamlet sites, and this represents the most conclusive evidence available for the existence of hamlet size settlements in the Powers Phase area. Estimating the size of sites on the basis of the number of surface stains observed is not, however, a totally accurate procedure. The Wilborn site, for example, was

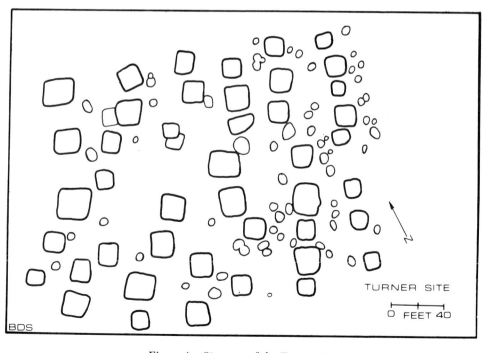

Figure 4.   Site map of the Turner site.

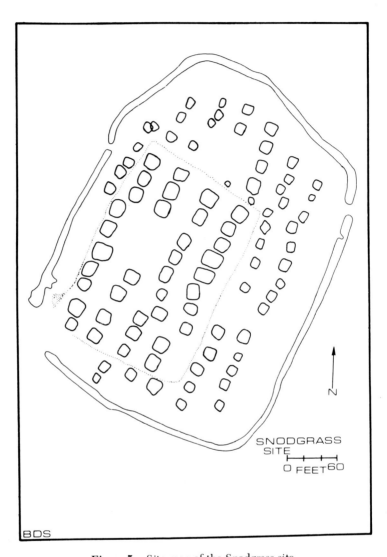

Figure 5. Site map of the Snodgrass site.

identified as a hamlet-sized site prior to 1970. The other three proposed
hamlet sites are known only through surface collections. It is at present
probably better to view the identification of these six sites as hamlets as
tentative.

Powers Phase sites estimated to be smaller than hamlet size (if hamlets do in fact exist) have been placed into an extractive site category
(Price 1973:Figure 4). Such sites (Price 1974) represent "a patterned
locus at which a natural resource was taken from its natural context for

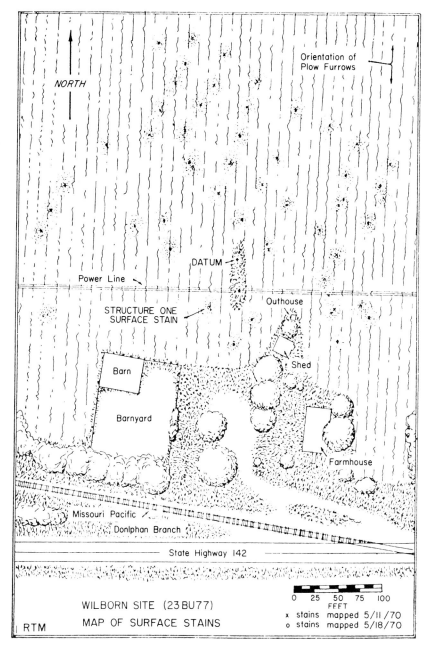

Figure 6. Distribution of surface stains and the location of the excavated structure (Structure 1) at the Wilborn site (drawn by Richard T. Malouf).

11

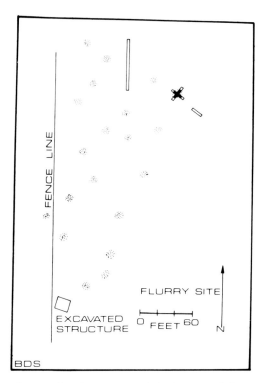

Figure 7. Distribution of surface stains and the location of the excavated structure at the Flurry site.

the purpose of artifact manufacture, nourishment of the society involved, or for the making of nonessential items [p. 10]." Price has further broken down this category into functionally different extractive sites such as hunting camps, extractive sites for the procurement of raw materials and floral products, and agricultural extractive sites, or farmsteads (Price 1974:11–13). Powers Phase crews have excavated two sites in the Ozark uplands that may fall into the hunting camp subcategory, these being the Lepold site (Figure 2) and the Gooseneck site (Smith 1975:Appendix E). Other Powers Phase sites classified as extractive are known only on the basis of surface collections, and in some cases by the presence of surface indications of burned structures.

Possible surface indications of one or two burned structures have been observed at a number of Powers Phase sites, including the Gypsy Joint site. All sites with surface indications of one or two structures have been classified as farmsteads, with farmsteads being seasonally used sites involved in the maintenance of agricultural fields (Price 1974): "Individual structures were probably built in the proximity of the fields and may have been used seasonally during the planting, cultivating, protecting, and harvesting of crops [p. 12]." It is unfortunate that the term *farmstead*, with its inherent connotations of seasonality of occupation and specific function, has been applied to all projected one- or two-structure Powers Phase sites. Such an approach tends to obscure the full range of variation that may quite possibly exist in small single- or double-structure Mississippian sites. This problem of adequately interpreting Mississippian sites below the village level, rather than arbitrarily placing them into preconceived categories, will be discussed in more detail in a later section.

THE SETTLEMENT SYSTEM OF THE POWERS PHASE

Establishing the settlement pattern of a prehistoric human population involves determining the number, size, and spatial distribution of the full range of sites occupied by that population. Establishing the settlement *system* of a prehistoric human population involves the additional, and much more difficult, task of determining the functional role of each site in the overall adaptive strategy of the human population. It involves determining the seasonality of occupation of different sites, as well as the political, kinship, and economic ties existing between groups occupying different sites. It also involves specifying and quantifying the movement of people, energy, and information between sites throughout the annual cycle. Determining the pattern of settlement of a prehistoric human population is possible; determining the structure of the underlying settlement system—the complex web of interaction and interdependence that ties the various sites together in a balanced, functioning, adaptive system—is much more difficult.

A number of problems exist in attempting to develop settlement system models for the Powers Phase. The two most obvious problems are the lack of information concerning sites smaller than village size, and establishing the contemporaneity of occupation of different sites. With the exception of Powers Fort, which may have been occupied for from 50 to 100 years, sites of the Powers Phase show evidence of a very short period of occupation. On the one hand, this apparent short span of occupation of most, if not all, of the Powers Phase sites is an important advantage in terms of analyzing intersite distribution of artifacts and features; on the other, it makes it very difficult to determine if any two sites were occupied at the same point in time. Information from a number of different sources suggests that the Turner and Snodgrass sites were occupied for less than 10 years, perhaps for only 2 to 3 years. It has not, however, been possible to determine to what extent the occupation of these sites overlap in time (Price 1973:48). While radiocarbon-14 dates obtained from Powers Phase sites are not exact enough to allow the pinpointing of actual time spans of occupation of different sites (Price 1973:297–298), it is possible that this crucial question of contemporaneity may be answered either by developing a floating dendrochronology for the Powers Phase or by receiving the results of a large number of archaeomagnetic dating samples taken at Powers Phase sites.

Until this question of contemporaneity of occupation is answered, any one of a number of quite different settlement system models would seem to fit the presently available data equally well. Were, for instance, the Turner, Snodgrass, Wilborn, and Flurry settlements occupied at the same point in time by different segments of the Powers Phase population? Or do they represent sequentially occupied and abandoned settlements of a single Powers Phase population segment over a 40- to 50-year period?

While this complex problem of contemporaneity of occupation of Powers Phase sites has been recognized as a crucial one, it was also clear as the excavations at the Turner and Snodgrass sites neared completion in 1973 that more accurate and solid information was needed concerning Powers Phase sites that were smaller than village size. Excavation of a smaller-than-village-sized Powers Phase site was therefore scheduled for the summer of 1974.

2

The Gypsy Joint Site

I learned another fact: large complicated archaeological sites are very difficult to understand. I generalized this observation into a field strategy which I later implemented, namely, dig the little, simple sites first. What you learn from them might permit you to intelligently dig the big, complicated ones [Binford 1972:130].

RESEARCH GOALS—PROBLEM ORIENTATION

The long-term primary research goal of the Powers Phase Project is to develop an overall predictive model of the cultural system of the prehistoric human population which has been named the Powers Phase. The development of such a complex model of the cultural system of this Middle Mississippi population is contingent on the development of a number of interlocking models of smaller segments, aspects, or subsystems of the total cultural system. The development of such smaller, more specific models has been attempted by James Price in terms of both the sociopolitical implications of the internal organization of Powers Phase villages (Price 1973) and the overall settlement system of the Powers Phase (Price 1974, 1976); I have attempted to develop models describing the subsistence strategy of Powers Phase groups (Smith 1974a, 1974b, 1975). A number of other models pertaining to specific aspects of the Powers Phase cultural system will be forthcoming in the near future.

One segment of the total cultural system of the Powers Phase about which almost nothing was known prior to 1974 was the role or function of smaller-than-village-size sites. The decision to excavate one of these smaller sites involved first establishing, and explicitly stating, the research goals and problem orientation of such an undertaking. The general research goal was to locate and excavate a site smaller then village-size and to determine its functional role within the overall settlement system and cultural system of the Powers Phase. More specifically, the problems to be addressed, and hopefully solved, through excavation were in the following five areas:

1. Seasonality of occupation: Was the site occupied throughout the annual cycle, or during only part of it?
2. Duration of occupation: Was the site occupied for only a few days or weeks at a time, or for longer periods of time, or on a permanent basis over a number of years?
3. Size and composition of occupying group: Was the site occupied by a nuclear or extended family group(s), or by a group of adult men, or by a group of adult and juvenile women, etc?
4. Activities carried out at the site: What was the range and nature of activities carried out at the site? Did the occupants of the site carry out a full range of domestic activities, or was the site task-specific in some sense, centering on such activities as agricultural pursuits or hunting?
5. Relationship of the site to other Powers Phase sites: What were the political, economic, and kinship ties between the occupants of the site and other Powers Phase settlements, and what was the nature of the movement of information, energy, and people between the site and other Powers Phase sites?

These five areas comprised the problem orientation of the planned excavation of a smaller-than-village-size site. The corresponding answers to these five problem areas formed the specific research goals of the Gypsy Joint excavation. If answers to these five problems could be obtained, they in turn would allow us to achieve the general research goal of defining the niche of the site in the overall cultural system of the Powers Phase.

It should, of course, be kept in mind that this problem orientation and corresponding set of research goals was developed and explicitly stated prior to excavation and even prior to the actual selection of the specific site to be excavated. This was necessary to ensure that the research design employed in the actual excavation of the site selected was structured toward recognizing and recovering data relevant to the stated research goals. It should also be kept in mind that while we hoped that data recovered through excavation would result in clear, unequivocal answers to the stated problem areas, we realized that the data needed to provide such clear-cut, conclusive answers might not be obtained from the planned excavations. These five problem areas will be considered in more detail in a later section.

SITE SELECTION

Once the decision had been made to excavate a smaller-than-village-size Powers Phase site and the problem orientation and research goals had been established, the next step in the research procedure was the actual selection of the specific site to be excavated. Quite often the reasons for selecting a specific site are never clearly or explicitly stated. Invariably a variety of factors are taken into consideration, and the selection of the Gypsy Joint site was no exception in this regard.

The first group of factors considered involved purely practical logistical problems. It was hoped that an appropriate site could be located in close geographical proximity to the field research center of the Powers Phase, in the present-day town of Naylor, Missouri, thus keeping travel time to and from the site to a minimum (Figure 2). Minimizing travel time was important for two reasons since, first of all, it would allow the field crew to return to Naylor for the noon meal rather than staying in the field. This would enable students to escape the sun and heat for an hour during the middle of the day, and would hopefully result in an improvement in both the quality and the amount of work accomplished during afternoon sessions. Second, it was estimated that as many as four to five additional round trips would have to be made from the laboratory to the site every day by a single "research vehicle" (a Ford pickup truck suffering from terminal everything). These trips would be necessary, on the one hand, to shuttle fill dirt from the site to the laboratory for water screening and flotation and, on the other, to shuttle water from the laboratory to the site to keep excavation surfaces from drying to a concrete hardness and becoming impossible to work.

Another factor that played an important role in the site-selection process was the attitude of various property owners toward permitting excavation of sites on their land. Not all sites were equally accessible. Due in great measure to the excellent rapport that Price had established with local citizens, many landowners in the Powers Phase area were very cooperative. Some property owners, however, were very strongly opposed to allowing anyone on their land. One site in the Powers Phase area, for instance, has been named The Nasty Man Site, and with good reason.

In addition to the practical considerations involved in selecting a site, there was also an understandable concern with selecting one of appropriate size. It was important, on the one hand, to try to ensure that the site selected was in fact a site—that it was more than a plowzone scatter of artifacts. On many of the crests of the sand ridges in the Powers Phase area, there is an almost continual thin surface scatter of flint chips and occasional Mississippian sherds. Some greater assurance than this was needed that a site actually existed below the plowzone. On the other hand, a site too large to be totally excavated during a single summer excavation season was not wanted. It was hoped that a site consisting of from one to four structures along with associated activity areas and features could be located (if in fact such a site existed in the Powers Phase area).

The procedure followed in identifying a site of the appropriate size involved considering the topographic setting as well as the areal extent, amount, and type of materials recovered from sites through surface collection. The topographic setting of a site was important, for it was hoped that an undesirably large site could be avoided by selecting one in a topographic situation with a limited suitable occupation area. Specifically, we hoped that a site located on the top of one of the small rises on the sand-ridge formations could be found, and that vertical slope characteristics would preclude occupation except on the limited surface area on the crest of the rise. The surface scatter of materials at such a site would be expected to occur only on the crest area of the rise, perhaps covering an area of approximately 1000 m². In addition to topographic setting and areal extent of surface scatter, the type and amount of materials recovered were important in the selection process. It was important, first of all, that surface-collected materials indicate a single-component Powers Phase site; the problems inherent in dealing with a multicomponent site could thereby be avoided. Second, it was hoped that some surface indication of Powers Phase structures would be observable, either in the form of clearly visible "house stains" or perhaps as concentrations of Mississippian ceramics and bits of charcoal. Such surface indications of structures, along with a substantial surface collection of Mississippian ceramics would be, it was hoped, a good indication that the site in fact represented more than a very short-term occupation, and that excavation would yield sufficient data to realize the stated research goals.

To summarize, the process of selecting a smaller-than-village-size Powers Phase site was directed toward locating an accessible, single-component Powers Phase site that was situated on a small hill or rise in close proximity to Naylor, Missouri, and that had significant amounts of Mississippian materials occurring over a surface area of approximately 1000 m² or less, as well as having some surface indications of Powers Phase structures.

The site fitting this profile most closely and hence selected for excavation was the Gypsy Joint site (23 RI 101A),[1] located just east of Naylor, Missouri, less than 1 mile from the field research center of the Powers Phase (Figure 2). Permission to excavate the site was easily obtained, and vehicles could be driven right up to the excavation surface, facilitating loading of fill dirt for flotation. Furthermore, the Gypsy Joint site was situated on the top of a low rise, and surface materials recovered from the site covered the crest of the rise above the 310-foot contour interval over an area of about 1000 m² (Figures 8, 9). These surface materials were predominantly Mississippian, and some possible indications of Powers

[1] The derivation of the name Gypsy Joint is as follows: In the early 1970s a group of nonlocal people moved into a small rundown house or "joint" located about 200 yards south of the site, and proceeded to "decorate" their yard with a large number of items obtained from the local dump. This practice earned them the name "gypsies," and the rundown house and the general area around it became known locally as the "Gypsy Joint."

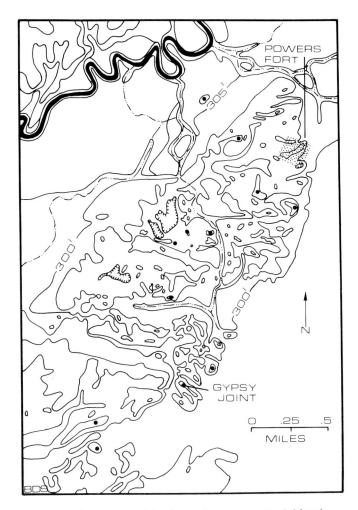

Figure 8. The location of the Gypsy Joint site on Barfield Ridge.

Phase structures in the form of concentrations of ceramics and charcoal fragments were observed. When the Gypsy Joint site was first discovered by Richard Zurel during a site survey in 1970, the following description of the site was given on the survey form: "Two sand hills separated by low sandy area. Mississippian occupations are on the top of the two sand hills, but no definite house stains visible—estimate of approximately three to five structures each [hill] due to sherd concentrations." Subsequent surface collecting on these two adjacent hills and the lower saddle area connecting them indicated that Powers Phase materials were much more abundant on the westernmost hill, where the Gypsy Joint site was situated.

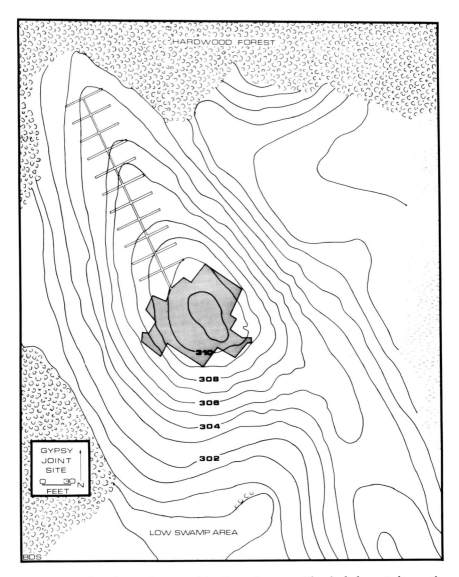

Figure 9. The ridgetop location of the Gypsy Joint site. The shaded area indicates the extent of the block excavation. The slit trench following the crest of the ridge to the north-east is also shown.

EXCAVATIONAL PROCEDURES

Cultural material had been recovered from the surface of the Gypsy Joint site on a number of occasions from its discovery in 1970 to its excavation in 1974. Although these surface collections were not aimed at determining the exact spatial limits and relative density of surface materials, it was observed nonetheless that diagnostic Powers Phase materials occurred almost exclusively above the 310-foot contour interval. It was decided, therefore, to attempt systematically to strip the plowzone from all of the area above the 310-foot contour interval, starting at the crest of the ridge and working outward. It was hoped that this procedure would facilitate the uncovering of the full extent of the Mississippian occupation with a minimum of wasted time and effort.

This general procedure was followed except for a single initial variation. When the winter wheat crop covering the site was harvested and the ground was turned just prior to excavation, two dark soil stains were observed about 40 feet apart on the crest of the ridge. One of these stains was located directly above Structure 1. The second stain was located at the extreme eastern edge of the excavation surface (Figure 9). It was decided to remove the plowzone above the first stain, which turned out to be Structure 1, and to then clear the plowzone from a 15-foot-wide strip connecting Structure 1 with the second soil stain. This was done, but the second soil stain was unfortunately identified as resulting from a burned tree stump of recent origin. This initial trench, which passed between Pits 10 and 1, provided further support for the general law that preliminary trenches invariably turn out to be placed so that a minimum of cultural features will be encountered.

The excavation surface was then gradually extended outward in all directions until the limits shown in Figures 9 and 10 were reached. A total area of 7922 square feet (736 m^2) was uncovered. The plowzone, which consisted of a zone of disturbed soil extending to a depth of from .7 feet to .9 feet below the ground surface, was removed entirely by hand shoveling. The interface between the loosely compacted plowzone soil and the underlying undisturbed soil deposits was easily identified and consisted of an undulating washboard pattern of plow scars running in a north–south direction.

A 5-foot grid system[2] was laid down on the excavation surface as the plowzone was removed, and base of the plowzone elevations were taken at each stake (Figure 10). All features were outlined, recorded, and covered with plastic as they were uncovered. In those 5-foot grid units that did not contain, or border on, features, cultural material at the base of the plowzone and still in situ in undisturbed deposits was bagged according to 5-foot grid unit provenience. Those 5-foot grid units that contained or bordered on features were hand excavated, and the exact vertical and horizontal location of each object uncovered was recorded. As a general

[2] A measurement system employing 5-foot-square grid units and recording vertical and horizontal locations in tenths of feet was employed at the Gypsy Joint site instead of a metric system because of a need for continuity with previous excavation procedures at Powers Phase sites.

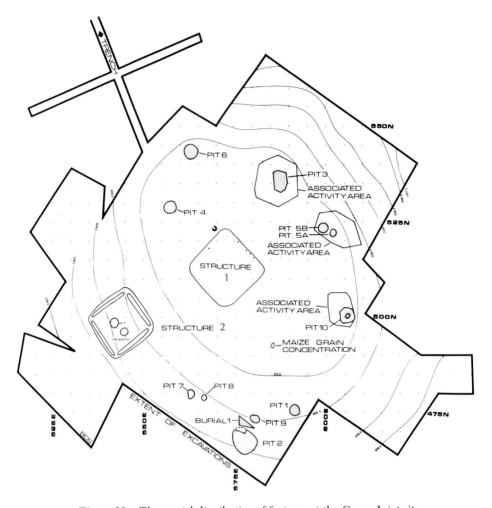

Figure 10. The spatial distribution of features at the Gypsy Joint site.

rule, all soil removed from features was taken back to the research center in Naylor and water screened through window screen. Due to time limitations, however, the soil removed from Structure 2 and Pit 2 was not water screened but dry screened instead through one-quarter-inch mesh screen at the site. All material recovered through water screening was bagged according to 5-foot grid units and feature provenience.

Soil from the plowzone was not screened, but those objects encountered while the plowzone was being removed were bagged according to general site areas, with a total of 10 such plowzone areas established for the site. Material within the plowzone was not in situ, and neither the original location nor the distance and direction of displacement of objects could be accurately determined. We therefore decided that it was not worthwhile to attempt a more careful and complete recovery and a more accurate spatial control of plowzone materials than was employed, especially considering the limited value of such data and the very real time constraints that existed.

In addition to the large block excavation that was opened up, a slit trench 2 feet in width was extended along the ridge crest to the northwest for a distance of approximately 200 feet (Figure 9). Fifty-foot-long side trenches were placed every 15 feet. These slit trenches were designed to determine if there were any Powers Phase structures or other features located along the ridge crest. No features and very little in the way of cultural materials were recovered from these trenches.

DATA PROCESSING

All cultural material recovered from the Gypsy Joint site was subsequently identified according to an artifact-coding system developed for Powers Phase sites. Identifying information, location, and weight were coded on IBM forms for subsequent analysis. The coding format employed and the raw data for each of the items recovered are included in Appendixes A–M. Every item recovered from the Gypsy Joint site (with the exception of small ethnobotanical items, such as hickory nut fragments, which were coded as a group of similar items) was coded on a separate card. Each separate item is therefore represented by a separate line in Appendixes B–M.

While these appendixes represent a total data bank of objects actually recovered in situ from the Gypsy Joint site, it should be stressed that this data bank does not represent the total cultural assemblage of the inhabitants of the site. Some plowzone material, for example, was not recovered, some organic materials were not preserved, and some objects were no doubt carried off by the prehistoric inhabitants of the site. Similarly, while some information concerning each object was coded and is presented in the appendixes, this does not represent all of the possible information that could have been recorded. You can tell, for example, that Field Specimen 40 from Pit 5 had a certain horizontal and vertical location, was an unutilized flake made out of local chert, and weighed 4.3 gm. But you cannot tell from the data coded how thick, how long, or how wide the flake was.

While this data bank only includes objects recovered in situ, and even then does not provide all possible information concerning the objects recovered, I hope that it will allow other interested individuals to analyze the same data base that I had to work with. Others, then, can both determine the accuracy of my analysis and carry it further or along different lines of inquiry. The materials themselves are available for reanalysis, and are stored in the Museum of Anthropology, University of Michigan.

3

Description of Cultural Features and Cultural Materials

INTRODUCTION—GENERAL DESCRIPTION

The block excavation at the Gypsy Joint site uncovered a total area of 7922 square feet (736 m²). During the course of this excavation a total of 15 cultural features were uncovered and excavated. These included two structures, a Woodland burial, a maize grain concentration, and a series of 11 pits: Pits 1–4, 5a, 5b, 6–10 (Figure 10). Four of the pits (3, 5a, 5b, 10) had activity areas associated with them.

If the location of these features is considered in relation to the ridge-top topography, a number of initial observations can be made. The half-foot contour interval lines shown in Figure 10 represent the topography of the ridge top after the plowzone had been removed. Structure 1 is located almost in the center of an elliptically shaped, relatively flat area on the top of the ridge. Reading clockwise, Pits 4, 6, 3, 5b, 5a, 10, the maize concentration, Pit 8, Pit 7, and Structure 2 form a rough circle around Structure 1. The radius of this circle varies from a minimum of 22.5 feet (from the center of Structure 1 to the center of Pit 4) to a maximum of 35 feet (from the center of Structure 1 to the center of Pits 7 and 8). The three remaining pits and the burial are located outside of this circle of features, downslope to the south of Structure 1.

The size of these features and the amount of cultural debris recovered from each is summarized in Table 1. A total of 23,917 objects weighing 40,334 gm were recovered from below the plowzone. A very high percentage of this cultural debris was recovered from within, or in close spatial association with, the cultural features shown in Figure 10. Although these 15 features represent only 10.21% of the total excavated

TABLE 1

Summary Information: Features at the Gypsy Joint Site

Powers Phase features	Area covered by features		Feature configuration		Cultural materials recovered		Percentage of Powers Phase features		
	Square feet	Square meters	Shape	Depth (feet)	Quantity of items	Weight of items	Quantity	Weight	Area
Structure 1	265.9	24.70	Square	.4	588	7,332.1	2.50	31.81	33.48
Structure 2	207.2	19.25	Square	1.2	563	4,931.8	2.40	21.40	26.09
Structure 2—Pit 1	4.9	.46	Circular	.4	13	15.9	.06	.07	
Structure 2—Hearth	4.0	.37	Circular	.1	0	0			
Pit 2	40.6	3.77	Ellipse	.4	36	196.7	.15	.85	5.11
Pit 3	17.6	1.63	Ellipse	.6	229	749.9	.97	3.25	2.21
Pit 3—Activity area	100.0	9.29	Square	.2	309	3,273.9	1.31	14.20	12.59
Pit 4	10.4	.96	Circular	.4	7	122.8	.03	.53	1.30
Pit 5a	4.3	.39	Circular	.8	1,237	639.5	5.27	2.77	.54
Pit 5b	5.8	.53	Circular	.9	5,048	1,453.8	21.53	6.31	.73

				Shape					
Pit 5—Activity area	66.6	6.18	Ellipse	.2	14,379	2,719.2	61.32	11.80	8.39
Pit 6	14.4	1.34	Circular	.4	210	95.3	.89	.41	1.82
Pit 7	3.7	.34	Ovoid	.5	28	30.7	.12	.13	.46
Pit 8	1.7	.16	Ellipse	.5	8	28.1	.03	.12	.21
Pit 10	12.8	1.19	Circular	.6	146	492.5	.62	2.13	1.61
Pit 10—Hearth	1.5	.14	Circular	.1	0	0			
Pit 10—Activity area	42.6	3.95	Ellipse	.2	193	937.5	.82	4.06	5.36
Maize grain concentration	.5	.05	Circular	.2	452	23.1	1.92	.10	.06
Totals—Powers Phase features	794.1	73.73			23,446	23,042.8			
Skim surface (area outside features)	7,109.0	660.6				15,409.4			
Non-Powers Phase features					403				
Burial 1	7.8	.72	Triangular	.2	6	144.9			
Pit 1	6.3	.59	Circular	.3	24	264.9			
Pit 9	4.4	.41	Ellipse	.5	38	1,472.4			

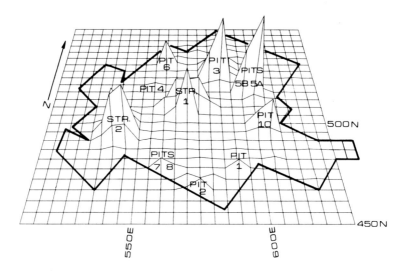

Figure 11. Three-dimensional plot of the Gypsy Joint site, showing the number of items recovered from each 5-foot grid unit. The viewing angle is 45°.

area, they accounted for 98.3% by count and 57.1% by weight of the total recovered cultural assemblage. The high degree to which cultural debris was concentrated within or close to cultural features is shown graphically in Figure 11.

Because cultural debris is clearly clustered spatially in features rather than being uniformly distributed over the site, it is possible to describe and to consider each of these features as a discrete unit of analysis. Before taking a detailed look at these features, however, a number of other topics relating to the spatial extent of the Powers Phase occupation should be considered.

DETERMINATION OF THE SPATIAL EXTENT OF THE POWERS PHASE OCCUPATION

In addition to the Powers Phase (Middle Mississippi) occupation of the Gypsy Joint site, there is evidence of earlier Woodland occupations of the site area. Fortunately, the existence of Woodland components does not present much of a problem in terms of identifying and analyzing the Powers Phase component. The Woodland occupation is very limited in terms of cultural debris, with less than 1% by count of all material recovered from the site being diagnostic Woodland artifacts. The spatial distribution of Powers Phase and Woodland materials is also largely mutually exclusive.

Of the 15 cultural features excavated at the Gypsy Joint site, 12 are clearly associated with the Powers Phase occupation. The three non-Powers Phase features are Pit 1, Pit 9, and the single burial excavated at the site. These three features are grouped in the southern corner of the excavation area at the margin of the Powers Phase occupation. Woodland and Archaic cultural debris also tends to occur around the margin of the Powers Phase area of occupation at the site. Figure 12 illustrates the distribution of diagnostic Woodland cultural material, indicating those grid units that yielded Woodland projectile points and/or Woodland pottery fragments (sand-tempered Barnes Plain, Barnes Cordmarked, and

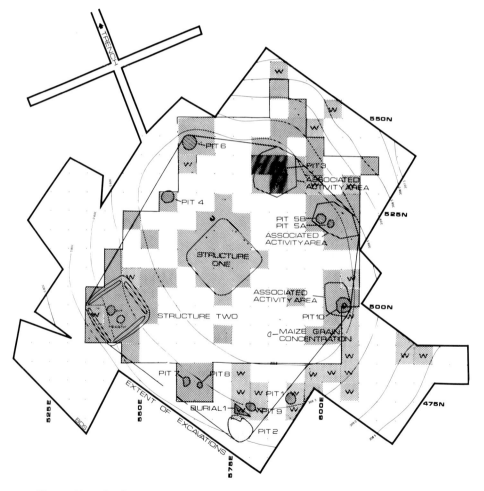

Figure 12.   The distribution of diagnostic Woodland and Mississippian cultural debris. Those 5-foot grid units yielding Powers Phase ceramics are indicated by diagonal lines; those yielding Woodland artifacts are indicated by stippling and the letter W.

Barnes net-impressed and fabric-impressed pottery types). Most of the grid units that contained Woodland cultural debris were located either downslope to the north or downslope to the southeast of the Powers Phase occupation. The southeast concentration of Woodland materials, which also encompasses the three non-Powers Phase features, may represent the western edge of a Woodland site located in the ridge saddle to the east (Figure 9). This spatial distribution of Woodland cultural debris around the edge of the Powers Phase occupation corresponds to a general pattern observed during surface collection at the Gypsy Joint site and other sites in the Powers Phase area. Woodland cultural debris generally tends to occur just below the crests of sand ridges, whereas Powers Phase sites tend to occupy the higher elevations.

Woodland cultural debris was also recovered adjacent to, or from within, three Powers Phase features: Structure 2, Pit 3, and Pit 10. The number of items involved in each case is small, however (two, three, and four items, respectively), and can be viewed as either a result of accidental inclusion or as evidence of the reuse of Woodland tools found by Powers Phase individuals.

The spatial extent of the Powers Phase occupation at the Gypsy Joint site can be estimated by three different methods, each of which yields different results. The method yielding the smallest occupation area involves simply determining the total area covered by Powers Phase features (794 square feet). This would seem to be a fairly reasonable procedure, since judging from the distribution of cultural debris, most of the activities at the site (that resulted in cultural debris) took place within, or directly adjacent, to these features. A much larger estimate of 3739 square feet is obtained by drawing a line around the outside edge of all of the Powers Phase features (Figure 12). Finally, an estimate of 4100 square feet is obtained by drawing a line around the outside edge of all of the 5-foot squares that yielded Powers Phase ceramics (Neelys Ferry Plain) (Figure 12). Since these last two methods of estimating the occupation area of the Gypsy Joint site produce quite similar results, a compromise figure of 4000 square feet can be employed in comparing the Gypsy Joint site with other Powers Phase and Mississippian sites in terms of the size of the occupation area.

NON-POWERS PHASE FEATURES

Of the 15 features uncovered at the Gypsy Joint site, 3 are clearly not associated with the Powers Phase occupation. Artifacts associated with Burial 1 and Pit 1 indicate a Late Archaic–Early Woodland temporal placement for the two features, and a radiocarbon date from Pit 9 shows it to be a Late Woodland feature.

Burial 1

Located at the southern edge of the excavation surface, Burial 1 was uncovered just below the plowzone, and no interment pit was observed. A total of five artifacts were recovered in context with a right occipital skull fragment of an adult individual (Figure 13, Plate II). No indications of further skeletal remains were observed. It was not possible to determine with any certainty if interment activities involved only the recovered skull fragment or if additional skeletal elements were not recovered due to poor preservation or to postdepositional disturbance. The scattered location of grave goods, however, suggests that some disturbance had occurred.

The five artifacts recovered in association with Burial 1 consisted of a broken gray slate two-hole reel gorget, a lithic drill, a large asymmetrical convergent unifacial scraper, a small bifacially flaked piece, and a large projectile point-knife (Plate II). All four of the chipped-stone artifacts were manufactured from local poor-quality white chert, and none of the artifacts showed evidence of any use modification. The general shape of the slate gorget and the limited concavity of its sides suggests a Late Archaic–Early Woodland temporal placement for the burial. Most of the gorgets of similar shape recovered from sites in the eastern United States were found in a Late Archaic–Early Woodland context (Webb 1940:74, 108, Webb 1941:192–218, Smith n. d., Griffin 1952: Figures 22, 97).

Pit 9

Located about 2 feet to the northeast of Burial 1, Pit 9 was a shallow concave pit that contained the almost complete skeleton of an adult male

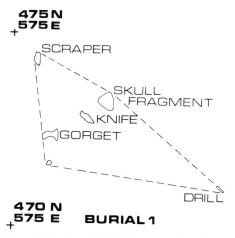

475 N
575 E
+

SCRAPER

SKULL
FRAGMENT

KNIFE

GORGET

DRILL

470 N
575 E   **BURIAL 1**
+

Figure 13.   Burial 1: The location of artifacts.

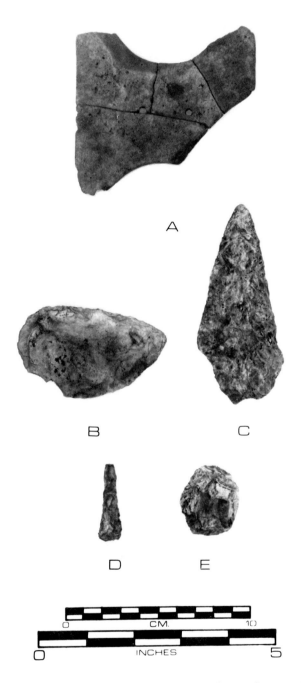

Plate II. Artifacts associated with Burial 1: A. Gray slate reel gorget; B. Scraper; C. Knife; D. Drill; E. Small bifacially flaked piece.

white-tailed deer, with only right front leg elements being absent (Figure 14). A single unmodified chert flake and four carbonized seeds were recovered from the pit (Table 2). The deer's antlers were fully hardened but not yet shed at the time of death, indicating that the animal was killed during the period September to January. Once killed, the deer was first disarticulated, and the skeletal elements (minus perhaps the right front leg) were then shattered into a great number of small fragments. The bone fragments were subsequently tightly packed into the shallow pit, and a fire was then apparently built over the contents of the pit. After the fire had burned out, the contents of the pit were not subsequently disturbed.

No diagnostic cultural debris was recovered from Pit 9, which made it initially impossible to determine its cultural affiliation. Because of the importance of determining if Pit 9 was associated with the Powers Phase occupation at the site, a sample of burned deer bone from the pit was submitted to the Geochron Laboratory at the University of Georgia for radiocarbon analysis. A date of A. D. 780 ± 115 (UGA 1078) was obtained, indicating that Pit 9 clearly predated the Powers Phase occupation at the site.

Pit 1

Located about 10 feet northeast of Pit 9, Pit 1 was a shallow circular pit with a dark soil matrix (Figure 15). A total of 24 items weighing 264.9 gm were recovered from the pit (Table 3). Six of the recovered items represent a flint-knapping tool kit and three finished artifacts (Plate III). A lithic hammerstone, an antler baton, and a beaver incisor (pressure flaker?) were grouped together with three contracting-stem projectile

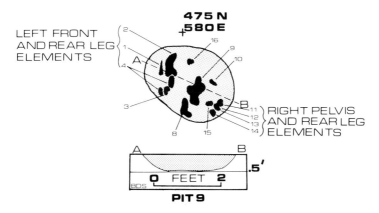

Figure 14. Pit 9, showing the location of skeletal elements of an adult male white-tailed deer. The number sequence corresponds to field specimen numbers in Appendix B.

TABLE 2

Cultural Materials Recovered from Pit 9

Items	Quantity	Weight (gm)	Comments
Lithics			
Chert flakes	1	.3	
Fauna			
White-tailed deer			
Odocoileus virginianus	33	1472.1	Almost a complete skeleton
Plant remains			
Marsh elder			
Iva annua	1	.02	Seed
Knotweed			
Chenopodium sp.	2		Seeds
Grape			
Vitis sp.	1	.01	Seed
Total contents	38	1472.43	

points at the western edge of the pit. Although the grouping of these artifacts would suggest a burial cache, no evidence of a human interment was observed during excavation of the pit. The three projectile points could be taxonomically classified as Gary points, which are usually assigned a Late Archaic temporal placement (Fowler 1957; Bray 1957; Roberts 1965).

POWERS PHASE FEATURES

Introduction—Interrelatedness of Powers Phase Features

The remaining 12 features at the Gypsy Joint site were identified as belonging to the Powers Phase occupation on the basis of recovery of Powers Phase cultural debris from within the fill of each feature. There is the possibility that not all of these features belong to the Powers Phase occupation and that the occurrence of Powers Phase artifacts in them is the result of rodent disturbances, plow action, etc. This possibility of accidental inclusion can be ruled out with 9 of the 12 features, since each of them contained large quantities of Powers Phase materials.

Pit 4, Pit 7, and Pit 8, on the other hand, yielded small amounts of Powers Phase materials (two, three, and three Powers Phase sherds, respectively). Even though these three pits did not contain much Powers Phase cultural debris, I think that they can be assigned to the Powers Phase occupation at the site with a good degree of confidence. There was little evidence of disturbance (rodent or otherwise) observed during ex-

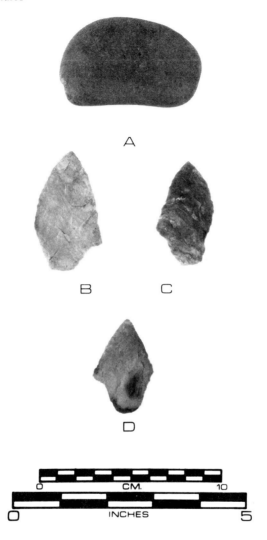

Plate III. Artifacts associated with Pit 1: A. Hammerstone; B. Projectile point; C. Projectile point; D. Projectile point.

cavation of these pits, and in each case the Powers Phase materials were recovered from within the pit fill.

Another and more difficult question involves whether the 12 Powers Phase features are the result of the related activities of the same group of individuals over a fairly short period of time, or whether the features resulted from unrelated activities carried out by a number of different groups or individuals at widely spaced points in time.

A carbonized wall-post section recovered from Structure 1 and iden-

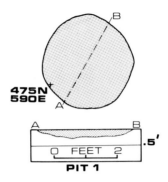

Figure 15. The outline and vertical profile of Pit 1.

tified as *Nyssa aquatica* (Field Specimen 174, Appendix C) was submitted to Radioisotopes Laboratory and yielded a date of A. D. 1330 ± 55 for
the Powers Phase occupation of the Gypsy Joint site. Not surprisingly,
this date falls comfortably within the temporal range determined for the
Powers Phase (Price 1973:297). This single radiocarbon-14 date obtained

TABLE 3

Cultural Materials Recovered from Pit 1

Items	Quantity	Weight (gm)	Comments
Lithics			
Chert flakes	6	3.9	3 heated
Chert angular fragments	5	21.3	3 heated
Quartzite flakes	1	.3	
Quartzite angular fragments	1	10.0	
Sandstone angular fragments	2	28.6	
Woodland projectile points	3	41.0	
Hammerstones	1	117.0	
	19	222.1	
Fauna			
White-tailed deer			
Odocoileus virginianus	3	40.8	Antler base, rib fragment, right scapula fragment
Box turtle			
Terrapene carolina	1	1.0	Carapace fragment
Beaver			
Castor canadensis	1	1.0	Incisor
	5	42.8	
Total contents	24	264.9	

for the Powers Phase occupation of the site does little, however, to answer the question of contemporaneity of use of the different Powers Phase features at the site.

While it is not possible to demonstrate conclusively that the 12 Powers Phase features uncovered at the Gypsy Joint site are the result of the related activities of a group of individuals that were carried out over a fairly short period of time, a number of different types of circumstantial evidence seem to support this hypothesis. The strongest evidence is the spatial distribution of the 12 features. With Structure 1 situated roughly in the center of the hilltop, the other Powers Phase features, with the exception of Pit 2, are arranged in a circular pattern around Structure 1. If the features reflected isolated activities carried out at widely spaced intervals of time, it would seem logical to expect a more random pattern in the spatial distribution of the features. It would also seem logical to expect this more random pattern to encompass the whole crest of the ridge rather than the small hilltop where the features are concentrated. It is interesting to remember that of the four features at the Gypsy Joint site that do not fit into this uniform pattern of feature placement, three are clearly not associated with the Powers Phase occupation at the site.

Further evidence that seems to support the hypothesis involves the activities that were carried out at the Gypsy Joint site. The 12 features reflect a wide variety of activities that, taken together, indicate the organized, interrelated functions of a group of people rather than a random sample of isolated activities that accidentally occurred at this hilltop location.

A third type of evidence involves the short period of occupation of other Powers Phase sites. It has been suggested that the Powers Phase existed at the most for only 50 to 100 years, and with the exception of Powers Fort, it appears that Powers Phase sites may have been occupied for as little as 5 to 10 years.

It was initially hoped that substantial direct archaeological evidence of the interrelated nature of the 12 Powers Phase features would be obtained, but little in the way of convincing evidence was uncovered. Over 200 laboratory hours were devoted to trying to find ceramic, lithic, and faunal fragments from different features that fit together. With a few exceptions, this effort was a total failure. All other possible methods of obtaining direct archaeological evidence were either not applicable or yielded no results.

In summary, while there is some amount of logical circumstantial evidence to support the interrelatedness hypothesis, it is certainly not possible to subject it to any sort of rigorous verification procedure. It is probably better, therefore, to view this "hypothesis" as an initial assumption. The above comments serve both as an explicit statement of this assumption and as a brief discussion of why it did not seem too unreasonable to make it. It is up to the reader, of course, to decide, after reading the following description and analysis, if this initial assumption is in fact justifiable.

Also please note that while it is generally assumed that the 12 features represent the activities carried out by a group of individuals over a fairly short period of time, no more specific assumptions are made concerning the composition of the group, the types of activities carried out at the site, or the duration or seasonality of occupation of the site. These questions will be considered more rigorously in a later section.

Structure 1

Structure 1 was situated almost in the center of the elliptically shaped, relatively flat area above the 310-foot contour interval (Figure 10). The presence and location of Structure 1 was suggested prior to the beginning of excavations at the Gypsy Joint site by a surface "stain," or darker soil area, resulting from some of the architectural charcoal of the structure being churned to the surface by plow action. The plowzone was a few tenths of a foot shallower in the Structure 1 area than in other areas of the site, and some plow disturbance of cultural materials in the upper levels of the house basin may have occurred. There does not, however, appear to have been much cultural material present in this upper portion of the house basin (see east–west profile, Figure 16). The rectangular house basin of Structure 1 was a shallow concave depression reaching a maximum depth of only .4 feet below the base of the plowzone. Once the plowzone had been removed from above Structure 1, the darker fill of the house basin clearly contrasted with the surrounding soil. It was difficult, however, to determine the exact boundary, or shallow outer edge, of the house basin, especially along the southeast and southwest walls; the boundary shown in Figure 16 is therefore only an approximation, but is quite likely accurate to within .5 feet of the actual edge. The floor of the house basin was also easily discernible due to both an abrupt change in soil color and consistency below the house floor and the presence of cultural debris resting on the house floor.

Of the 272 items actually observed and recorded during the excavation of Structure 1, 257 items weighing 5759 gm were lying on the house floor. Fifteen items weighing 681.2 gm were recovered from just below the house floor. None of these items were found to occur more than .1 feet above the house floor. All of the items missed during excavation but recovered through subsequent water screening of fill dirt from the house basin are coded in Appendix C as coming from structure fill. There is no way to determine if such material was close to, or actually on, the house floor. Not surprisingly, large heavy items tended to be observed and recorded during excavation, while smaller items were often overlooked and only later recovered during the water screening of fill dirt. The aver-

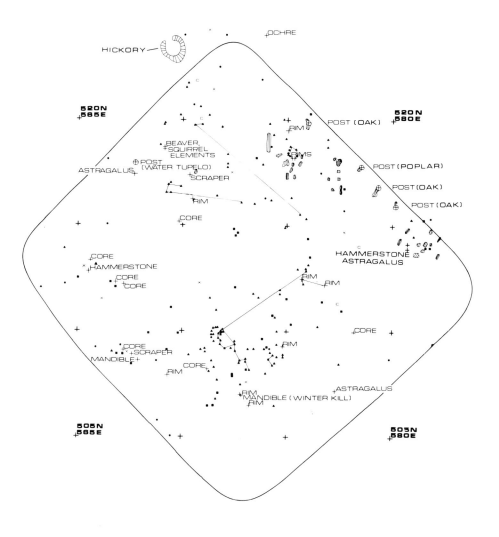

Figure 16. The spatial distribution of cultural materials within Structure 1.

age weight of items recovered through water screening was less than 2 gm, while the average weight of items recovered during excavation was 23.7 gm.

The house basin of Structure 1 measures approximately 17 feet northwest–southeast by 16 feet northeast–southwest, and covers an area of 265.9 square feet (Table 1). The structure is oriented approximately 45 to 50° east of magnetic north, which is fairly comparable to the 25 to 30° east of north orientation of structures at other Powers Phase sites (Price 1973:96).

Structure 1 was apparently a single wall-post structure, judging from the limited architectural evidence that has been recovered. The carbonized bases of four wall-support posts were recovered along the northeast margin of the house basin, along with the carbonized remains of collapsed wall-support posts (Figure 16). A single carbonized wall-support post base of water tupelo *(Nyssa aquatica)* was excavated along the northwest margin of the house basin. Based on the five wall-post bases excavated, trunk sections of young trees approximately .2–.3 feet in diameter were spaced approximately 1.2 to 1.5 feet apart, just inside the margin of the house basin. None of the posts was sharpened at the base, and all appeared to have been set into the ground to a depth of only .2–.3 feet. No indications of wall posts or collapsed architectural elements were observed along the southern margins of the house basin, nor were any indications of internal support posts uncovered. There are at least three possible explanations for this lack of architectural remains along two sides of the structure. It is possible that walls existed only along the two northern sides of the structure. It is also possible that the structure did not completely burn, and that those wall elements that were not carbonized were not preserved. The third possible explanation is a little more involved. Although it is not apparent in either Figure 10 or Figure 16, the ground surface along the northeast wall of Structure 1 is a few tenths of a foot higher in elevation than along the other three sides of the structure. In order to make the house floor level, the northeast edge was dug a little deeper below the ground surface than other areas of the house basin. Since this edge was a little deeper, it may have escaped the destructive force of modern plowing, which may have removed any evidence of architecture that existed along the shallower southern edges of the house basin. Unfortunately there is not sufficient data to justify accepting any one of these three explanations as being most correct. In addition to the wall-support posts observed along the internal margin of the house basin, a large (1.2 feet in diameter) carbonized hickory trunk section was uncovered just to the west of the north corner of the structure. The tree trunk section extended approximately .2 feet into the ground, and was clearly not a modern tree stump or fence post.

A total of 313 lithic items were recovered from Structure 1 (Table 4). Of these, only 5 could be termed tools. Chert flakes and chert angular frag-

TABLE 4

Cultural Materials Recovered from Structure 1

Items	Quantity	Weight (gm)	Comments
Lithics			
Chert flakes	132	78.1	5 heated, 3 retouch modification
Chert cores	5	1143.3	
Chert angular fragments	93	417.5	
Quartzite flakes	18	30.6	
Quartzite cores	3	184.2	
Quartzite angular fragments	36	466.7	
Sandstone angular fragments	21	1669.3	
Hammerstones	2	571.2	
Scrapers	2	25.3	
	313	5330.0	
Ceramics			
Jar rim sherds	21	412.2	
Powers Phase body sherds	166	1375.1	
Clay fragments	19	64.4	
	206	1851.7	
Metallic remains			
Hematite	2	2.8	
Fauna			
White-tailed deer			3 left astragali and
Odocoileus virginianus	5	27.3	left and right mandibles
Beaver			
Castor canadensis	1	.2	Incisor
Fox squirrel			
Sciurus niger	2	1.6	Maxilla, humerus
	8	29.1	
Plant remains			
Hickory			
Carya sp.		115.51	Small carbonized nutshell fragments
Acorn			
Quercus sp.	8	.47	Shell fragments
Black walnut			
Juglans nigra	4	.38	Carbonized nutshell fragments
Maize			
Zea mays	22	2.02	Carbonized kernel and cupule fragments
Marsh elder			
Iva annua	3	.02	Seeds
Knotweed			
Polygonum sp.	6		Seeds

(Continued)

TABLE 4 *(Continued)*

Items	Quantity	Weight (gm)	Comments
Plant remains (cont.)			
Chenopod			
Chenopodium sp.	11		Seeds
Wild bean			
Strophostyles helvola	3	.03	Cotyledons
Grape			
Vitis sp.	2	.02	Seeds
Plum/Cherry			
Prunus sp.		.05	Stone fragments
	59	118.5	
Total Contents	588	7332.1	

ments were the most abundantly represented categories of lithic items recovered from Structure 1, and this abundance of chert debitage represents a pattern that holds for Structure 2 and for Pits 3, 5a, 5b, 10, as well as for their associated activity areas. The size of the items in these two categories is quite small, the average weight of chert flakes being .59 gm, while the average weight of chert angular fragments was 4.49 gm (Figure 17). Five of the chert flakes showed evidence of having been heated, and three showed evidence of retouch modification (four unifacial, one bifacial). Quartzite flakes recovered from Structure 1 also tended to be small in size, whereas quartzite and sandstone angular fragments tended to be both few in number and relatively large in size (Table 4). This pattern also prevails for other features at the site that yielded large lithic assemblages.

Two large river cobbles, one of which had been broken in half, displayed edge battering characteristic of objects employed as hard percussors (hammerstones: Plate IVA, B). The larger of the two hammerstones was recovered in the west corner of the structure, in close association with three cores. The other hammerstone was recovered from the eastern corner of the structure, right next to the wall line.

The large angular sandstone fragment that exhibits some evidence of having been used as a grinding slab (Plate IV) was recovered from the central grid unit of Structure 1 (510N, 570E).[1]

Two scrapers were recovered from Structure 1. A light tan unifacially flaked chert piece with areas of cortex still present (Plate VA) was recovered along the southwest margin of the house basin in association with a core and a deer mandible. The edge angle of this scraper is approxi-

[1] Each 5-foot-square grid unit is identified and designated by the coordinates of its *southwest* corner.

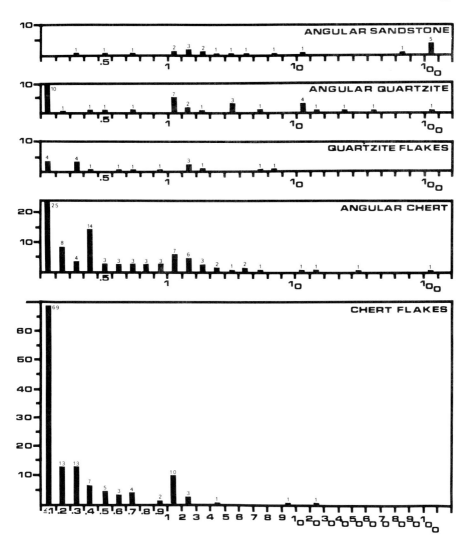

Figure 17. Weight values in grams for lithic materials from Structure 1. Note the changing scale on the horizontal axis.

mately 43°. A second scraper of light gray chert was recovered from the northern area of Structure 1 (Figure 16). The concave working edge, showing evidence of unifacial use and retouch modification, has an edge angle of approximately 50° (Plate VB).

A total of five chert and three quartzite cores was also recovered from Structure 1. Two of the chert cores are large stream cobbles of poor-quality local chert from which only a few flakes were struck prior to the cores being discarded (Plate VIA, B). Two of the remaining chert cores

Plate IV. Hammerstones and grinding implements recovered from the Gypsy Joint site: A. Hammerstone (F.S. 195) from Structure 1; B. Hammerstone (F.S. 254) from Structure 1; C. Grinding slab from Structure 1; D. Anvil–hammerstone (F.S. 37) from Pit 5b; E. Mano (F.S. 25) from the Pit 5 activity area.

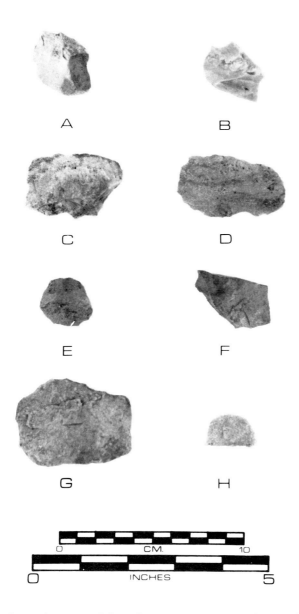

A

B

C

D

E

F

G

H

0   CM.   10

0   INCHES   5

Plate V. Lithic tools recovered from the Gypsy Joint site: A. Scraper (F.S. 169) from Structure 1; B. Scraper (F.S. 95) from Structure 1; C. Biface from Pit 2; D. Biface (F.S. 159) from the Pit 3 activity area; E. Knife fragment (F.S. 259) from Pit 3 activity area; F. Unifacially retouched flake (F.S. 27) from Pit 5a; G. Biface (F.S. 73) from the Pit 5 activity area; H. Scraper from Pit 10 activity area.

Plate VI. Chert and quartzite cores recovered from Structure 1: A. Chert core (F.S. 156); B. Chert core; C. Chert core (F.S. 270); D. Chert core (F.S. 129); E. Chert core (F.S. 131); F. Quartzite core (F.S. 74); G. Quartzite core (F.S. 158); H. Quartzite core (F.S. 124).

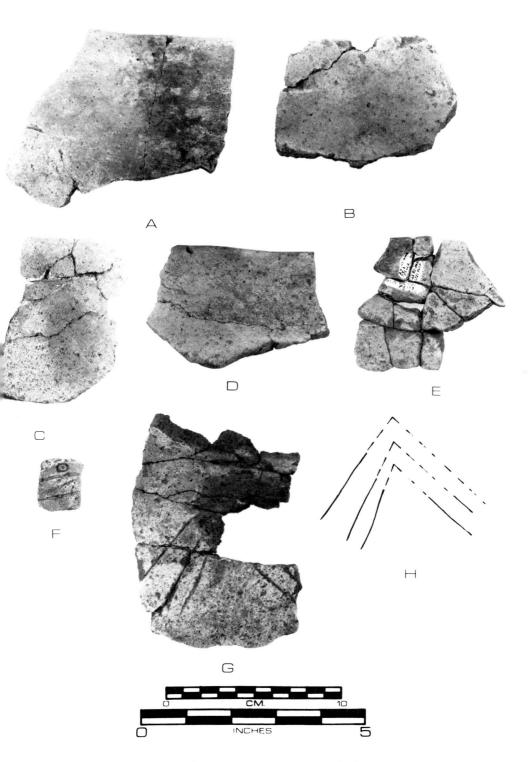

Plate VII. Rim sherds recovered from Structure 1: A. Jar rim sherd (F.S. 18); B. Jar rim sherd (F.S. 104); C. Jar rim sherd (F.S. 223–227); D. Jar rim sherd (F.S. 191, 194); E. Jar rim sherd (F.S. 115, 117, 122, 123); F. Incised jar handle sherd (F.S. 71); G. Incised jar rim sherd (F.S. 25, 43, 44); H. Incised chevron design on G.

are angular fragments of poor-quality local chert from which only a few flakes were struck, without much success (Plate VIC, D). The final chert core is a small stream cobble of light tan good-quality local chert from which a large number of flakes had been struck (Plate VIE). The three quartzite cores are all angular fragments that show evidence of a few flakes having been struck from one or two edges prior to their having been discarded (Plate VIF, G, H). Although numerous hours were spent in the laboratory attempting to reunite Structure 1 flakes with Structure 1 cores, not a single match of flake to core was achieved.

The single small fragment of hematite (ochre) recovered in association with Structure 1 was uncovered just outside of the north corner of the house basin (Figure 16).

In addition to 166 Neelys Ferry Plain body sherds and 19 clay fragments, Structure 1 also yielded a total of 21 rim sherds from a minimum of 3, and perhaps as many as 5, large jar-form vessels. A single large-rim sherd (Field Specimen 18: Plate VIIA) was recovered in the north-central area of Structure 1, just north of a core. The body sherds recovered just to the northwest of this rim may be from the same vessel but did not share any common edges with it. This isolated rim sherd is similar enough in orifice diameter, rim height, rim thickness, and paste and temper characteristics (Table 5) to have come from the same vessel as a concentration of rim sherds located along the northeast wall of the structure (Field Specimens 104, 223–227: Plate VIIB, C). The fact that the isolated rim sherd is 5 feet southwest of this pottery concentration does not rule out its being part of the same vessel since spatial displacement of ceramic materials clearly took place within Structure 1. The lines connecting pottery sherds in Figure 16 indicate sherds that were found to fit together. Unfortunately, it is not possible to determine if this movement of ceramic materials took place before, during, or after the structure was burned and abandoned. The situation in the northern area of the structure is even more complicated. Not only is it not possible to determine conclusively that the isolated rim sherd (Field Specimen 18) is from the same vessel as the rim sherds concentrated along the north wall, it is also not possible to determine if all of the rim sherds in the concentration along the north wall are from the same vessel. Field Specimen 104 in this concentration is very similar to the other rim sherds represented (Field Specimens 223–227: Table 5), but it does not fit any of them. It is possible, then, that there are three different large jar-form vessels represented in the northern half of Structure 1, but it is far more likely that only a single vessel existed.

The situation in the southern half of Structure 1 is much less complex. The partial remains of two large jar-form vessels were recovered from the south central area of the structure. One of these vessels is represented by two rim sherds located to the northeast of this south–central ceramic

TABLE 5

Measurements of Rim Sherds Recovered from the Gypsy Joint Site (in centimeters)[a]

Feature	Field specimen	vessel form	Orifice diameter	Rim height	Rim thickness	Percentage of rim
Structure 1	18	Jar	24	4.0	.8–.9	10
	104	Jar	26	4.0–4.1	.7–.8	10
	223, 224, 225, 226, 227	Jar	26	4.2	.8–.9	12
	191, 194	Jar	28	3.3	.7–.8	12
	115, 117, 122, 123	Jar		3.0	.7–.8	11
	25, 43, 44	Jar	24	3.0	.7–.8	8
Structure 2	29	Jar	24	3.0	.7–.8	11
	55	Jar	24	3.0	.7–.8	13
	122	Jar	26	3.2	.7	10
	138	Jar	20	2.3	.7–.8	10
	36	Jar	7	1.3	.4	22
	40	Bottle	7		.7	50
Pit 3 activity area	307	Jar		1.8	.5–.6	
Pit 5b Pit 10	21	Jar	26	2.3	.6–.7	10
activity area Pit 10	39	Jar	18	3.3	.6–.7	20
activity area	6, 48, 51	Jar	18	3.4	.6–.7	30

[a] Small sherds not included.

concentration (Field Specimens 191–194: Plate VIID), as well as by a number of body and rim sherds located along the western edge of the south central ceramic concentration (Field Specimens 115, 117, 122, 123: Plate VIIE). Lines are drawn connecting these rim and body sherds in Figure 16, indicating that they are from the same vessel. This large jar can be clearly distinguished from the vessel(s) recovered from the northern area of Structure 1 on the basis of having shorter rim-height values (Table 5), as well as having a much sandier paste. The vessel can also be distinguished from the other large jar-form vessel recovered from the south central area of Structure 1 on the basis of its sandy paste and lack of any decoration.

The partial remains of a second jar-form vessel recovered from the eastern edge of the south central ceramic concentration consisted of a rim sherd (Field Specimen 25: Plate VIIG) and a number of shoulder and upper body sherds displaying a rather poorly executed incised nested chevron design (Field Specimens 43, 44: Plate VIIG, H). This chevron

design of three parallel lines is the most commonly observed style element on large Powers Phase jars, and was the only incised decoration
motif present on ceramic vessels recovered at the Snodgrass site (Price
1973:190, Plate 14).

The only other decorated sherd recovered from Structure 1 was a
strap-handle fragment (Field Specimen 71) recovered just north of the
beaver and squirrel skeletal elements (Figure 16). The handle displayed
a poorly executed pattern of three incised lines on its lower part, with a
circular impression (cane impressed) and three more diagonal incised
lines toward the top of the handle (Plate VII F).

In summary, there appear to have been two large jar-form vessels located in the south central area of Structure 1, and a single large jar-form
vessel located along the northeast wall. All of the vessels apparently were
very comparable in size, judging from the projected orifice diameter
values (Table 5). The vessel(s) located in the northern area of Structure 1
appears to have had a slightly higher rim than the other vessels.

There are, however, a number of loose ends that cannot be easily tied
up in reference to the ceramic materials recovered from Structure 1. It
was not possible, for example, to reconstruct more than 15–20% of any
single vessel. Many of the rim and body sherds are missing from the
Gypsy Joint ceramic assemblage. They were either missed in the plowzone, or were disposed of outside of the limits of the site. There are, at the
same time, a few sherds recovered from Structure 1 that clearly do not
belong to any of the large jar forms recognized.

A total of five *Odocoileus virginianus* skeletal elements were recovered from Structure 1. Three left astragali (lower rear-leg elements) were
recovered from along the edge of the house basin (Figure 16). Two deer
mandibles representing two separate animals were also recovered. A
right mandible of an adult deer was recovered along the southwest margin of the house basin, and a left mandible fragment from a 17- to 20-
month-old deer was recovered from the south central area of the structure. The projected season of death for the young deer would be
November 1 through January 30 (Smith 1975:40). In addition to these
skeletal elements, maxilla and humerus fragments of a fox squirrel (*Sciurus niger*), along with a beaver incisor, were recovered from the north
corner of the house basin.

In addition to the 115.5 gm of carbonized hickory nutshell fragments
recovered from Structure 1, small amounts of acorn and black walnut
shell fragments were turned up, as well as carbonized maize kernels,
seeds of marsh elder, knotweed, chenopod, grape, and plum/cherry stone
fragments and wild beans (Table 4).

Once the house basin of Structure 1 was totally excavated, the area
below the house floor was excavated to a depth of 2 feet. Except for the 15
items recovered from just below the house floor, no other cultural mate-

rials were recovered. There were no indications of subfloor burial or storage pits, and no burials or cached artifacts were found beneath the house floor.

Structure 2

Structure 2 at the Gypsy Joint site would never have been observed and excavated were it not for the efforts of James Price. Although the area around Structure 2 was stripped of plowzone overburden early in the excavation of the site, this initial removal of the plowzone failed to uncover the Structure 2 house basin. Apparently because of its location on the side of the hill, Structure 2 was overlaid not only by the plowzone, but also by a layer of sand .1–.2 feet thick deposited just below the plowzone. This was a quite different situation from that encountered over the rest of the site, where features were uncovered at the base of the plowzone, with no intervening layer of sand.

It was not until the end of the field season that the possibility of features existing to the southwest of Structure 1 led Dr. Price to skim a little deeper in this area of the block excavation and to discover Structure 2. Price directed the subsequent excavation of Structure 2, but because the structure was not discovered until the end of the field season, there was neither sufficient personnel nor sufficient time to water screen all of the fill removed from the house basin. All of the dirt removed from Structure 2 was, however, dry screened through one-quarter-inch mesh screen. This means that the cultural assemblage recovered from Structure 2 is not totally comparable to the cultural materials recovered from other Gypsy Joint features. The quantity and variety of types of materials recovered from Structure 2 indicate, however, that recovery was still excellent, even if not totally comparable with the level of recovery obtained through water screening. This discovery of Structure 2 also prompted an expansion of the block excavation in this hill slope area (Figure 10), as well as necessitating a deeper skimming in the southwest corner of the block excavation. No other features or concentrations of cultural material were uncovered.

Structure 2, which was located approximately 15 feet southwest of Structure 1, differed from Structure 1 in a number of respects. While the Structure 2 house basin was deeper than that of Structure 1 (1.2 feet versus .4 feet), it covered a smaller area (207 versus 266 square feet). While Structure 2 yielded both carbonized plant remains and lithic items that showed evidence of having been burned, it did not yield any burned architectural elements. Unlike Structure 1, there is no evidence indicating that it was burned prior to abandonment. Structure 2 was also clearly a wall-trench structure, whereas Structure 1 was a single wall-post structure. Although no wall-support posts were recovered from Structure 2, the four wall trenches showed up clearly once the house basin had been excavated. These wall trenches, which extended almost the full length of each edge of the house basin, contained a grayish black fill, and varied from .75 to 1.25 feet in width and from .5 to .7 feet in depth. In cross section the wall trenches were concave in shape (Figure 18).

Structure 2 is even smaller than Structure 1 if the usable area inside the wall trenches is considered. While the house basin of Structure 2 covers 207 square feet (versus 266 square feet for Structure 1), Structure

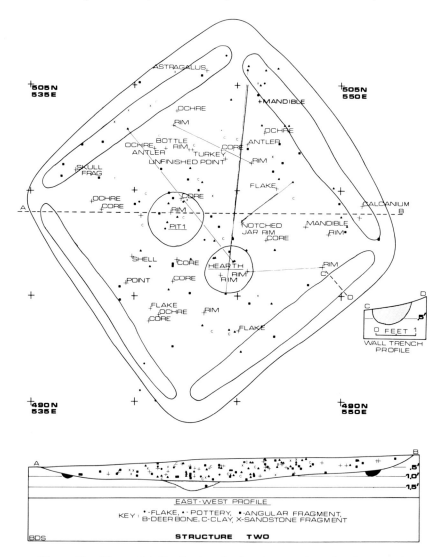

Figure 18. The spatial distribution of cultural materials within Structure 2.

TABLE 6

Cultural Materials Recovered from Pit 1, Structure 2[a]

Items	Quantity	Weight (gm)	Comments
Lithics			
Chert flakes	1	.4	
Chert angular fragments	3	3.3	
	4	3.7	
Ceramics			
Powers Phase			
body sherds	2	4.4	
Clay fragments	2	1.9	
	4	6.3	
Plant remains			
Hickory			
Carya sp.		4.33	Carbonized nut-shell fragments
Maize			
Zea mays		1.49	Carbonized cob and cupule fragments
Chenopod			
Chenopodium sp.	1		Seed
Wild bean			
Strophostyles helvola	2	.01	Cotyledons
Grape			
Vitis sp.	1	.02	Seed
	4	5.85	
Total contents	12	15.85	

[a] Materials listed above are also included in totals for Structure 2 (Table 7).

2 only has 125 square feet of living space occurring inside of the wall trenches. It also contained an internal hearth and a shallow pit, neither of which was observed in Structure 1. The internal pit (Pit 1, Figure 18) was clearly visible after excavation of the house basin due to the dark organic pit fill. Located in the west central area of the structure, Pit 1 was roughly concave in cross section, dipping in the middle to a depth of .4 feet below the house floor. Circular in outline and covering an area of 4.9 square feet, Pit 1 yielded a total of 12 items (Table 6). The internal hearth located just to the southeast of Pit 1 consisted of a shallow, disturbed area of hard, fire-reddened sand that covered an area of 4 square feet and extended only .1 feet below the house floor. No cultural materials were recovered from within the hearth area.

A final comparison that should be made between Structure 2 and Structure 1 before turning to a discussion of the cultural materials recovered from Structure 2 involves the relative location of items within the house basins of the two structures. While most of the items recovered from Structure 1 were found lying on the house floor, most of the items recovered from Structure 2 were located above the house floor in the house basin fill (Figure 18, cross section). Not only does this probably indicate a higher rate of vertical and horizontal disturbance of cultural materials in Structure 2, but it may also indicate that at least some of the materials recovered from Structure 2 represent a secondary rather than a primary deposit. Some of the material recovered from the northeast half of the structure may have been washed down into the house basin after the site was abandoned.

The orientation of Structure 2 is similar to that determined for Structure 1: 45–50° east of north.

A total of 563 items weighing 4931.8 gm was recovered from Structure 2 (Table 7). The 373 lithic items excavated from Structure 2 accounted for two-thirds of the total items recovered by count, and 55% of the total number of items recovered by weight. Chert flakes and chert angular fragments are the most abundantly occurring categories of lithic items recovered from Structure 2, following a pattern that holds for all of the larger Powers Phase features at the Gypsy Joint site. Both the quantity of chert flakes and angular fragments recovered from Structure 2 and their average weight values are quite comparable to the values obtained for the chert flakes and angular fragments recovered from Structure 1 (Figure 19, Figure 17). Six of the chert flakes recovered from Structure 2 showed evidence of having been heated, and nine showed evidence of use modification. Both quartzite and sandstone angular fragments recovered from Structure 2 are relatively few in number, but have high mean-weight values (Figure 19).

Three Powers Phase projectile points in various stages of manufacture were recovered from Structure 2. The single apparently finished point (Plate VIIIB) was recovered along the southwest edge of the house basin (Figure 18). I refer to it as apparently finished because the corner notching and the retouch at the tip do not appear to be fully completed. This projectile point would fall within the category of large points with small corner notches that was established for the Snodgrass site (Price 1973:104, 105, 120). Although this point is somewhat similar to the serrated point fragment recovered from the Pit 5 activity area (Plate VIIIH), the serration flakes are smaller, unifacial, and are not as well executed as those on the Pit 5 activity area specimen. The unfinished red chert point shown in Plate VIIIA was found along the southeast edge of the house basin, and was apparently discarded during the process of manufacture. The unfinished point shown in Plate VIIIC was found just north of Pit 1, and was apparently discarded when attempts at corner notching snapped off the base or stem of the point.

TABLE 7

Cultural Materials Recovered from Structure 2

Items	Quantity	Weight (gm)	Comments
Lithics			
Chert flakes	132	113.7	9 use modifica-tion, 6 heated
Chert cores	6	207.6	
Chert angular fragments	142	743.0	
Quartzite flakes	20	57.8	
Quartzite cores	3	151.0	
Quartzite angular fragments	27	663.1	
Sandstone angular fragments	40	788.3	
Mississippian projectile points	3	4.2	2 rejected
	373	2728.7	1 unbroken
Ceramics			
Jar rim sherds	12	377.1	
Bowl rim sherds	1	4.6	
Bottle rim sherds	1	58.6	
Powers Phase body sherds	94	693.1	
Clay fragments	48	779.1	
Fabric-impressed clay fragments?	2	1.9	
	158	1914.4	
Metallic remains			
Hematite	5	214.3	
Fauna			
White-tailed deer			
Odocoileus virginianus	9	36.2	Left astragalus Left calcanium 2 left mandibles 2 antler fragments 2 long-bone fragments 1 skull fragment
Turkey			
Meleagris gallopavo	1	8.2	Right tibiotarsus
Box turtle			
Terrapene carolina	3	.4	Plastron fragments
Freshwater clam species?	1	1.4	
	14	46.2	
Plant remains			
Hickory			
Carya sp.	5	25.50	Charred nutshell and septum fragments

(Continued)

TABLE 7 *(Continued)*

Items	Quantity	Weight (gm)	Comments
Acorn			
Quercus sp.	2	.26	Carbonized nutshell fragments
Black walnut			
Juglans nigra	4	.94	Shell fragments
Maize			
Zea mays		1.49	Charred cob and cupule fragments
Chenopod			
Chenopodium sp.	1		Seed
Grape			
Vitis sp.	1	.02	Seed
Wild bean			
Strophostyles helvola	1	.01	Cotyledon
	12	28.22	
Total contents	563	4931.82	

Structure 2 also yielded a total of six chert and three quartzite cores. All six chert cores were located in the southern half of Structure 2, with four of the cores recovered from an area just west and southwest of the hearth area. Of the other two chert cores, one was located just northeast of the hearth area (Plate IXB) and one was found just north of Pit 1 (Plate IXC). All of these chert cores were angular fragments or cobble fragments of poor-quality local chert from which only a few flakes had been struck. Although they were much smaller than three of the cores recovered from Structure 1 (Plate VIA, B, C) they were, nonetheless, much larger than the exhausted cores recovered from other features at the Gypsy Joint site (Plate XII). One of the quartzite cores was located just west of the hearth area (Plate IXE), while the other two quartzite cores were recovered from northeast of Pit 1 (Plate IXF) and west of Pit 1 (Plate IXG). All three quartzite cores were angular fragments of local material from which a few flakes had been struck. Although a great amount of lab time was spent attempting to reunite cores and flakes from Structure 2, this effort met with no success.

In addition to the clay fragments and Powers Phase body sherds recovered from Structure 2, a total of 14 rim sherds representing at least six vessels were located in the house basin. Three of the six vessels were large jars. One jar-form vessel with an estimated orifice diameter of 24 to 26 cm and a rim height of 3–3.2 cm was located in the hearth area. Three rim sherds are clearly from this vessel. One of these rims (Plate XA) was located in the eastern corner of the structure, while the other two (Plate XB, C) were located just south of, and within, the hearth area, respectively.

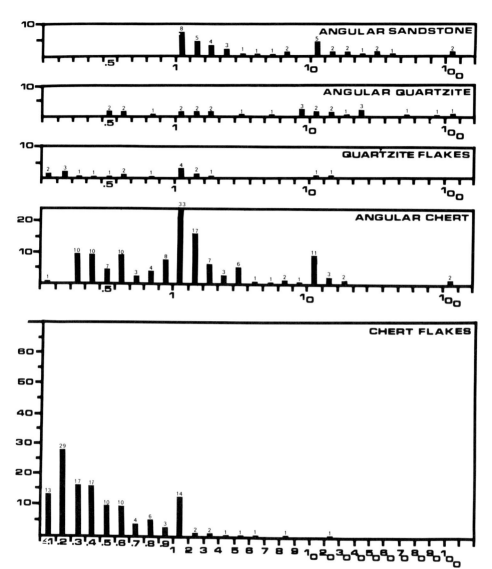

Figure 19.   Weight values in grams for lithic materials recovered from Structure 2. Note the changing scale on the horizontal axis.

A second large jar-form vessel is represented by a notched rim sherd and a shoulder sherd (Plate XE), located northeast of the hearth area. The rim notching consists of a series of shallow concave notches spaced about .5–.7 cm apart and extending vertically about .6 cm down the rounded outside edge of the rim. This notching style is similar to the rectangular side-notching category defined for the Snodgrass site ceramic assemblage, where it was found to occur on three bowl-form vessels (Price

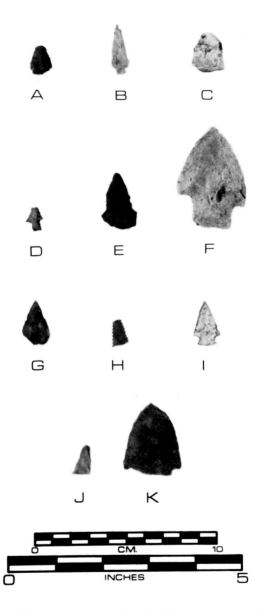

Plate VIII. Projectile points recovered from the Gypsy Joint site: A. Projectile point from Structure 2; B. Projectile point (F.S. 121) from Structure 2; C. Projectile point (F.S. 39) from Structure 2; D. Small incurvate projectile point (F.S. 245) from the Pit 3 activity area; E. Projectile point (F.S. 251) from the Pit 3 activity area; F. Projectile point (F.S. 132) from the Pit 3 activity area; G. Projectile point from Pit 5a; H. Serrated projectile point fragment (F.S. 30) from the Pit 5 activity area; I. Projectile point (F.S. 82) from the Pit 5 activity area; J. Projectile point (F.S. 97) from the Pit 10 activity area; K. Projectile point (F.S. 94) from the Pit 10 activity area.

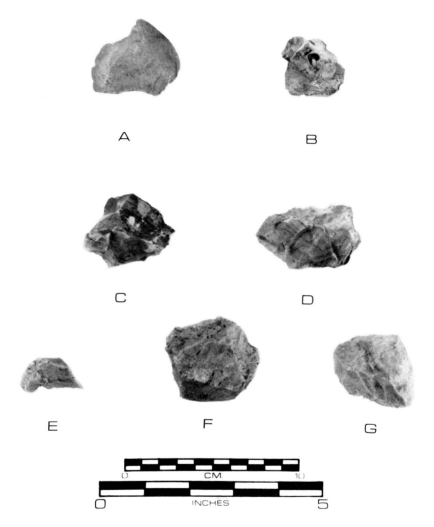

Plate IX. Chert and Quartzite cores recovered from Structure 2: A. Chert core (F.S. 9); B. Chert core (F.S. 23); C. Chert core (F.S. 25); D. Chert core (F.S. 49); E. Quartzite core (F.S. 11); F. Quartzite core (F.S. 42); G. Quartzite core (F.S. 113).

1973:220). No other notched rim sherds or rim sherds with a rounded outside edge were recovered from the Gypsy Joint site.

The third large jar-form vessel with a smaller estimated orifice diameter of 20 cm (Table 5) was represented by a single large-rim sherd located just above Pit 1 within the house basin (Plate XD). A fourth jar-form vessel of a much smaller size (estimated orifice diameter 7 cm) was represented by a large rim sherd in the north corner of the house basin

A

B

D

C

E

F

G

H

0　　　　　CM.　　　　10

0　　　　INCHES　　　　5

Plate XI. Metallic objects recovered from the Gypsy Joint site: A. Hematite (F.S. 34) from Structure 2; B. Hematite (F.S. 50) from Structure 2; C. Hematite (F.S. 98) from Structure 2; D. Hematite (F.S. 114) from Structure 2; E. Hematite (F.S. 124) from Structure 2; F. Galena from Pit 5a

(Plate XH), which fit another rim sherd found about 4 feet to the southeast of it (Figure 18).

While Structure 2, like Structure 1, yielded rim sherds representing three large jar-form vessels, it also yielded rim sherds of a smaller jar-form vessel and of a bowl and a large short-necked bottle. A single rim sherd from a bowl was recovered from the 5-foot-square grid unit located

Plate X. Rim sherds recovered from Structure 2: A. Jar rim sherd (F.S. 29); B. Jar rim sherd (F.S. 55); C. Jar rim sherd (F.S. 122); D. Jar rim sherd (F.S. 138); E. Notched jar rim sherd (F.S. 20, 62); F. Painted bowl rim sherd; G. Short-necked bottle rim sherd (F.S. 40); H. Jar rim sherd (F.S. 36).

just to the east of the hearth area. The rim sherd showed evidence of a red paint (Plate XF). Fifty percent of the rim of a large short-necked bottle (Plate XG) was recovered north of Pit 1 in the structure. No other rim sherds from this vessel were recovered during excavation of the Gypsy Joint site.

As in Structure 1, it was not possible to reconstruct more than 15–20% of any single vessel represented in Structure 2. Many of the rim and body sherds from these vessels are missing from the Gypsy Joint ceramic assemblage. There are at the same time a few sherds recovered from Structure 2 that clearly do not belong to any of the vessels just described.

Structure 2 also differs from Structure 1 in that while only a single small hematite (ochre) fragment was found in Structure 1, Structure 2 yielded five large ochre lumps. Three of the hematite lumps were located along the northwest edge of the house basin, while one fragment was found along the northeast wall and one lump along the southwest edge of the house basin. Only one of the lumps, which was located along the northwest wall trench, showed any signs of having been ground to produce ochre (Plate XIE).

Structure 2 yielded nine skeletal elements of *Odocoileus virginianus*. A left astragalus and left calcanium were recovered from the northern and eastern corners of the structure respectively. A skull fragment was recovered in the western corner of the structure, and antler fragments were found just inside the northeast wall trench. The two left mandible fragments were also recovered along the inside of the northeast wall trench (Figure 18). Skeletal remains of turkey *(Meleagris gallopavo)* and box turtle *(Terrapene carolina)* were also recovered from Structure 2. A tibiotarsus fragment was found north of Pit 1 (Figure 18), and three plastron fragments were found just east of the hearth area.

Because the fill from the Structure 2 house basin was not water screened, only a small sample of plant remains was recovered. The differential recovery bias is evident when the plant remains recovered from the internal pit (the contents of which were flotated) are compared with the plant remains recovered from the house basin (Tables 6 and 7).

Maize Grain Concentration

During the removal of the plowzone from the excavation surface a small compact concentration of maize grains was uncovered about 10 feet southeast of Structure 1. The irregularly shaped area, approximately .8 feet in diameter, contained 441 corn kernels and numerous kernel fragments weighing a total of 22.7 gm, as well as 11 fragments of cane weighing .4 grams. The corn kernels were located at the base of the plowzone and extended about .2 feet into the undisturbed subsoil. No pit outline or evidence of architecture was observed. A light scatter of isolated corn kernels covered an area of about 10 square feet around the corn concentration.

Concerning the maize grains themselves, Dr. Hugh Cutler of the Missouri Botanical Garden provided the following analysis:

> This corn was fully ripe when carbonized. The corn grains are small, probably flint, flattened, and are from 10- and 12-rowed ears. The smallest grains tend to be irregular, suggesting that they are from the tip or base of the ear. The numbers of these tip and base grains, compared with the other flattened grains, suggest that they came from ears that were small, as were those that we saw from the Turner-Snodgrass site (Cutler and Blake 1973:41).
>
> Most of the corn grains were charred on the cob, but we could find no cob fragments. This was presumably because the heat did not last long enough, or was not intense enough to carbonize the cob through the insulation that the corn grains provided.
>
> Most of the corn grains are small, ranging from about 5.5 to 7 mm wide, although there may be a few above or below these limits [personal communication, 1975].

The corn is very similar to other Powers Phase corn that has been recovered, in terms of number of rows per cob and the size of individual grains and whole cobs.

Pit 4

Located about 15 feet northwest of the edge of Structure 1, Pit 4 was a roughly circular, saucer-shaped pit covering an area of 10.4 square feet and reaching a maximum depth of .4 feet (Figure 20). The outline of the pit was clearly visible, with the dark pit fill contrasting sharply with the surrounding lighter colored sterile soil. No internal stratigraphy of the pit fill was observed. The pit was almost devoid of any cultural debris, with only seven items weighing a total of 122.8 gm being recovered (Table 8). On the basis of the two Powers Phase body sherds that were recovered from pit fill, the pit was assigned to the Powers Phase occupation of the site. The chert core recovered from the pit fill is shown in Plate XIIA.

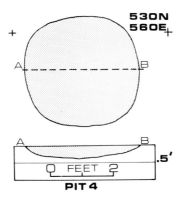

Figure 20.   The outline and vertical profile of Pit 4.

A

B

C

D

E

F

G

H

I

J

K

L

M

N

O

P

Q

R

S

CM.

0   5
INCHES

TABLE 8

Cultural Materials Recovered from Pit 4

Items	Quantity	Weight (gm)	Comments
Lithics			
Chert angular fragments	2	44.2	
Sandstone angular fragments	2	35.0	
Chert core	1	36.9	
Ceramics			
Powers Phase body sherds	2	6.7	
Total contents	7	122.8	

Pit 6

Located about 25 feet northwest of Structure 1, Pit 6 was a roughly circular, saucer-shaped pit covering an area of 14.4 square feet and reaching a maximum depth of .4 square feet (Figure 21). The outline of the pit was clearly visible, with the dark pit fill contrasting sharply with the surrounding lighter-colored soil. There was no observed layering or stratigraphy in the pit fill. A total of 210 items weighing 95.3 gm were recovered from the pit (Table 9). The chert core recovered from the pit is shown in Plate XIIB. Twenty-nine of the 75 items showed evidence of having been burned or heated.

Pit 7

Located about 25 feet south of Structure 1, Pit 7 was a roughly ovoid pit covering an area of 3.7 square feet and having fairly steep concave sides sloping to a flat bottom at a depth of .5 feet (Figure 22). Two distinct strata were observed in the pit fill, with the lower .3 feet of the pit fill consisting of a dark soil that yielded a single Powers Phase body sherd. The upper .2 feet of the pit was filled with a much darker soil–charcoal

Plate XII. Chert and quartzite cores recovered from pits and associated activity areas: A. Chert core from Pit 4; B. Chert core from Pit 6; C. Chert core from Pit 2; D. Chert core (F.S. 30) from the Pit 3 activity area; E. Chert core (F.S. 78) from the Pit 3 activity area; F. Chert core (F.S. 89, 92) from the Pit 3 activity area; G. Chert core (F.S. 94) from the Pit 3 activity area; H. Chert core (F.S. 123) from the Pit 3 activity area; I. Chert core (F.S. 303) from the Pit 3 activity area; J. Chert core (F.S. 11) from the Pit 3 activity area; K. Quartzite core (F.S. 87) from the Pit 3 activity area; L. Quartzite core (F.S. 147) from the Pit 3 activity area; M. Quartzite core (F.S. 150) from the Pit 3 activity area; N. Quartzite core from Pit 5a; O. Quartzite core from Pit 5b; P. Chert core from Pit 5b; Q. Chert core from Pit 5b; R. Quartzite core (F.S. 78) from the Pit 5 activity area; S. Chert core (F.S. 70) from the Pit 5 activity area.

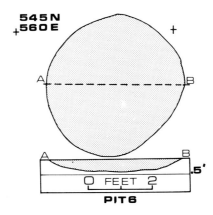

Figure 21. The outline and vertical profile of Pit 6.

admixture. It was from this upper strata that the rest of the cultural debris was recovered. The interface between the two strata was distinct. A total of 28 items weighing 30.7 gm were recovered from the pit fill (Table 10). Thirteen of the items recovered showed evidence of having been burned or heated.

Pit 8

Located about 25 feet south of Structure 1, Pit 8 was a roughly ovoid pit covering an area of 1.7 square feet and having an asymmetrical concave cross section. The maximum depth of the pit was .5 feet. As in Pit 7, two distinct strata were observed in the pit fill. A dark lower strata of about .3 feet in thickness was overlain by a strata of a much darker soil–charcoal admixture. The interface between the two strata was distinct. The lower strata of the pit yielded no cultural materials, while the upper

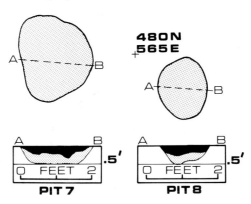

Figure 22. The outline and vertical profiles of Pits 7 and 8.

TABLE 9

Cultural Materials Recovered from Pit 6

Items	Quantity	Weight (gm)	Comments
Lithics			
Chert flakes	20	17.0	9 heated
Chert core	1	14.5	Heated
Chert angular fragments	16	11.6	3 heated
Quartzite flakes	4	2.2	
Quartzite angular fragments	3	13.7	
Sandstone angular fragments	1	8.3	
	45	67.3	
Ceramics			
Clay fragments	2	2.0	
Clay fragments with cane impressions	3	8.2	
Powers Phase body sherds	7	10.8	
	12	21.0	
Fauna			
Box turtle			
Terrapene carolina	2	.2	Carapace fragments
Fox squirrel			
Sciurus niger	2	.2	Left radius and ulna (burned)
Unidentified small mammal	8	.8	Long-bone fragments (burned)
	12	1.2	
Plant remains			
Hickory			
Carya sp.		5.61	Carbonized nutshell fragments
Acorn			
Quercus sp.	2	.01	Carbonized nutshell fragments
Maize			
Zea mays	2	.02	Carbonized kernel fragments
Marsh elder			
Iva annua	1	.01	Carbonized seed
Knotweed			
Polygonum sp.	49	.09	Carbonized seeds
Chenopod			
Chenopodium sp.	86	.02	Carbonized seeds
Wild bean			
Strophostyles helvola	1	.01	Bean
	141	5.82	
Total contents	210	95.32	

TABLE 10

Cultural Materials Recovered from Pit 7

Items	Quantity	Weight (gm)	Comments
Lithics			
Chert flakes	3	3.5	3 heated
Chert angular fragments	2	4.1	2 heated
Quartzite angular fragments	1	3.0	
Sandstone angular fragments	2	.3	
	8	10.9	
Ceramics			
Powers Phase body sherds	3	10.0	
Clay fragments	3	7.6	
	6	17.6	
Fauna			
Box turtle			
Terrapene carolina	5	.5	3 burned carapace fragments
Fox squirrel			
Sciurus niger	2	.2	Left scapula and left calcanium
Unidentified small mammal	5	.6	Long-bone fragments (2 burned)
Plant remains			
Hickory			
Carya sp.		.91	Carbonized nutshell fragments
Black walnut			
Juglans nigra	1	.01	Carbonized nutshell fragment
Maize			
Zea mays	1	.01	Carbonized kernel fragment
Total contents	28	30.73	

strata yielded a total of 8 items weighing 28.1 gm (Table 11). The three Neely's Ferry Plain body sherds recovered from the pit were the only items not showing any clear indications of having been burned or heated.

Pit 2

Located approximately 35 feet south of Structure 1, Pit 2 was a rounded rectangular pit covering an area of 40.6 square feet and having a

TABLE 11

Cultural Materials Recovered from Pit 8

Items	Quantity	Weight (gm)	Comments
Lithics			
Chert flakes	1	2.1	Burned
Ceramics			
Powers Phase body sherds	3	18.4	
Fauna			
Raccoon			
Procyon lotor	2	4.0	Burned left humerus and right mandible
Cottontail rabbit			
Sylvilagus floridanus	2	3.4	Burned left distal humerus and proximal ulna
Plant remains			
Hickory			
Carya sp.		.22	Carbonized nutshell fragments
Total contents	8	28.12	

shallow concave cross section. The pit reached a maximum depth of .4 feet (Figure 23). The pit fill, consisting of a dark, unlayered soil–charcoal admixture, contrasted clearly with the surrounding sterile soil. During the excavation of Burial 1, the shallow northern edge of Pit 2 was accidently skimmed away (Figure 23). No materials were recovered from this area of the pit. A total of 36 items weighing 196.7 gm were recovered from the pit fill (Table 12). Two items showed evidence of having been heated, and one flake showed evidence of use modification. The chert core and biface recovered from the pit are illustrated in Plates XIIC and VC, respectively.

Pit 3 and Associated Activity Area

Located approximately 20 feet northeast of Structure 1, Pit 3 covered an area of approximately 17.6 square feet. The pit was roughly ovoid in shape, with concave sides sloping to a flat pit base at a depth of .8 feet. These measurements for Pit 3 are only approximate, since it was not possible to clearly define the outline of the pit while it was being excavated.

As the plowzone was removed from the Pit 3 area, a concentrated scatter of artifacts was uncovered. There was no observed change in the color or texture of the soil in the area of artifact concentration. During subsequent excavation of the 12 5-foot-square grid units in the Pit 3 area,

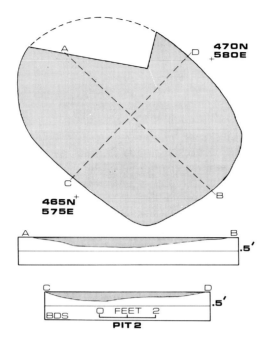

Figure 23. The outline and vertical profile of Pit 2.

it became clear that except for a small area in the center of the artifact scatter, the items were distributed in a shallow lens, extending to a depth of only .2 feet (Figure 24). After this shallow scatter of cultural materials had been excavated, materials were still being recovered from the center of the area. Except for the continuing presence of cultural debris to a depth of .8 feet in this central area, there were no clear indications that a pit actually existed. There was no observable variation in soil texture or color, and there was no layering of soil or cultural debris observable in the pit.

The two excavation grid units in which cultural debris was still being recovered below a depth of .3 feet were excavated to a depth of 1 foot, with sterile soil reached at .8 feet. Subsequent plotting of the horizontal and vertical location of all items observed during excavation allowed the general outline of the pit to be approximated. The dotted lines outlining Pit 3 in Figure 24 were drawn by encompassing almost all items that occurred below a depth of .3 feet. These horizontal and vertical outlines admittedly provide only a rough approximation of the true shape of Pit 3.

A total of 229 items weighing 749.9 gm were recovered from within the estimated boundary of Pit 3 (Table 13). Of the 229 items recovered from the pit, only 70 were actually observed and recorded during excavation. These 70 items weighed a total of 599.6 gm, for an average weight value of 8.56 gm per item. The 159 items that were overlooked during excavation, and were only later recovered during water screening of fill dirt from Pit 3, weighed a total of 150.3 gm, for an average weight value of .94 gm per item. Not surprisingly, it was the smaller but more numerous items that were overlooked during the excavation of the pit.

A total of 170 lithic items, weighing 478.3 gm, were recovered from Pit 3. Chert flakes were the most abundant type of lithic item recovered from the pit fill, followed by chert angular fragments. Since most of the chert flakes and angular fragments recovered from Pit 3 were quite small (Figure 25), they comprised only 20.9% of the total weight of lithic material recovered from the pit. Only two of the flakes showed any evidence of use or retouch modification. Although the 20 quartzite flakes recovered were also quite small (average weight .29 gm), quartzite angular frag-

TABLE 12

Cultural Materials Recovered from Pit 2

Items	Quantity	Weight (gm)	Comments
Lithics			
Chert flakes	4	4.5	1 heated
			1 use modification
Chert cores	1	10.0	
Chert angular fragments	4	5.2	
Quartzite flakes	3	10.0	
Sandstone angular			
fragments	5	48.3	
Bifaces	1	3.0	
	18	81.0	
Ceramics			
Clay fragments	2	2.8	
Powers Phase body sherds	14	74.4	
	16	77.2	
Fauna			
White-tailed deer			
Odocoileus virginianus	2	27.4	Left metacarpal, left mandible
Plant remains			
Hickory			
Carya sp.		9.16	Carbonized small nutshell fragments
Maize			
Zea mays		2.1	Carbonized cupule fragments
	2	11.26	
Total contents	36	196.74	

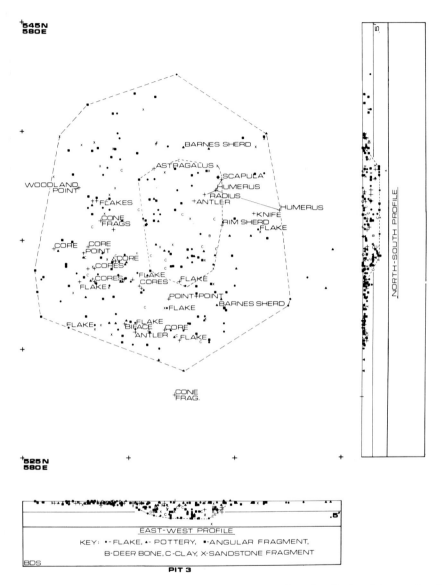

Figure 24. The spatial distribution of cultural materials within Pit 3 and its associated activity area.

ments, along with sandstone angular fragments, had much larger average weight values than other lithic items (Figure 25). None of the chert, quartzite, or sandstone angular fragments showed any evidence of utilization or wear. Only 4 of the 170 lithic items showed any evidence of having been heated.

TABLE 13

Cultural Materials Recovered from Pit 3

Items	Quantity	Weight (gm)	Comments
Lithics			
Chert flakes	73	29.3	2 heated, 1 use modi-fication, 1 retouch modification
Chert angular fragments	43	70.8	2 heated
Quartzite flakes	20	5.9	
Quartzite angular fragments	23	198.4	
Sandstone angular fragments	11	173.9	
	170	478.3	
Ceramics			
Cone fragments	1	22.5	
Clay fragments	16	39.3	
Jar rim sherds	1	31.3	
Powers Phase body sherds	15	70.0	
	33	163.1	
Fauna			
White-tailed deer			
Odocoileus virginianus	6	41.4	Left scapula, left distal humerus, left proximal radius, left astra-galus, 2 long-bone fragments
Plant remains			
Hickory			
Carya sp.		66.40	Carbonized nutshell fragments
Acorn			
Quercus sp.		0.44	Carbonized nutshell and kernel fragments
Maize			
Zea mays		0.18	Carbonized kernel fragments
Knotweed			
Polygonum sp.	12	0.03	Seeds
Chenopod			
Chenopodium sp.	6		Seeds
Plum/cherry			
Prunus sp.	1	0.07	Seed
Morning glory			
Ipomoea lacunosa	1	0.02	Seed
	20	67.14	
Total contents	229	749.94	

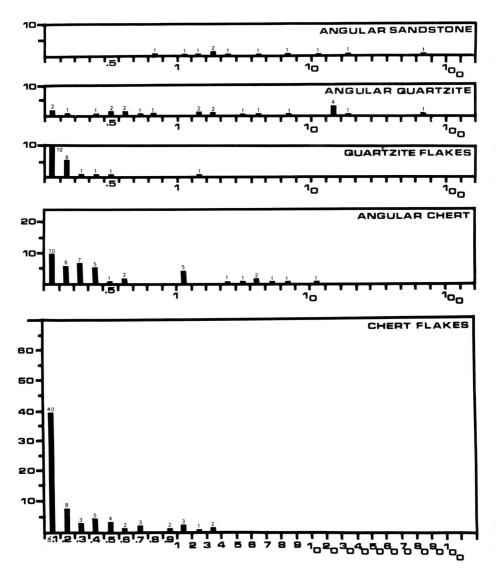

Figure 25. Weight values in grams for lithic materials recovered from Pit 3. Note the changing scale on the horizontal axis.

In addition to 16 clay fragments and 15 Neely's Ferry Plain body sherds, a single rim sherd from a large jar was recovered from the eastern edge of the pit (Plate XIIIA). A fragment of a ceramic cone was also recovered. Such cone-shaped ceramic objects are frequently encountered in Powers Phase sites, and are thought to perhaps have functioned as supports for large cooking vessels (Price 1973).

A   B   C

D

E

Plate XIII. Rim sherds recovered from pits and associated activity areas: A. Jar rim sherd (F.S. 39) from Pit 3; B. Jar rim sherd (F.S. 307) from Pit 3 activity area; C. Jar rim sherd (F.S. 12) from Pit 5b; D. Jar rim sherd (F.S. 39) from the Pit 10 activity area; E. Jar rim sherd (F.S. 6, 48, 51) from the Pit 10 activity area.

Skeletal elements of the upper left front leg of a white-tailed deer and a single left rear leg element were recovered from the north edge of the pit. The distal humerus element was found to fit a left humerus shaft fragment located at the eastern edge of the activity area surrounding Pit 3.

Plant remains recovered from the pit fill are listed in Table 13.

The Activity Area Associated with Pit 3

A shallow scatter of cultural materials extending to a depth of .2 feet was found to surround Pit 3, covering an area of approximately 100 square feet. Although there were no observed indications of any architecture in the vicinity of the Pit 3 activity area, it is interesting to note both the roughly rectangular shape of the artifact scatter and the location of the Pit 3 activity area in relation to Structures 1 and 2 (Figure 10). While it is possible that the Pit 3 activity area may have been enclosed by four walls, or at the least shielded from the elements by a roof of some sort, there is no archaeological evidence to support this possibility.

Two further questions should be considered prior to presenting a description of the cultural materials recovered from the Pit 3 activity area. The first is whether or not the scatter of cultural materials surrounding Pit 3 is simply the result of the contents of the pit being displaced outward, either by erosional processes or as a result of modern plowing. This does not seem likely for several reasons. If the scatter of artifacts was the result of erosional processes, a movement of materials downslope to the north would be expected, rather than to the west and south. Similarly, displacement of the contents of Pit 3 as a result of modern plowing would be expected to produce a scattering of materials along a north–south axis (plow scars were observed to run north–south) rather than to the west and south of the pit. This area of artifact scatter was also encountered below the plowzone, out of reach of the plow.

A related and more difficult question is whether the artifact scatter around the pit is a primary or secondary deposit of cultural materials. Were the activities that resulted in the material remains in this area actually performed in the same vicinity? Or were they performed elsewhere on the site, with the resultant remains subsequently dumped adjacent to Pit 3? While it is not possible to answer this question conclusively, I am of the opinion that the artifact scatter around Pit 3 is a primary deposit, mainly because of the large quantity of very small items that were recovered from the area around Pit 3. Such a large quantity of small items would be expected to occur in a secondary deposit only if the actors involved were very meticulous in picking up and redepositing the material consequences of an activity. Such meticulousness does not seem to be characteristic of Powers Phase populations or individuals, judging from the amount of refuse that occurs in a primary context on house floors, both at the Gypsy Joint site and at the larger Turner and Snodgrass sites. Anyone who has done any thinking on the problem of primary versus secondary deposition of cultural materials is aware, however, of the almost total impossibility of demonstrating that an artifact concentration or scatter is a primary deposit of cultural materials. Viewing the scatter of materials around Pit 3 as a primary deposit or activity area should therefore be recognized as a hypothesis that is supported by little data, rather than as a demonstrated fact.

A total of 220 lithic items, weighing 2778.5 gm, were recovered from the activity area surrounding Pit 3. As in Pit 3, chert flakes and chert angular fragments were the most abundant types of lithic items recovered. Similarly, quartzite flakes tended to be small in size, while quartzite angular fragments and sandstone angular fragments had much larger average weight values than other lithic items (Figure 26). Only 7 of the 66 chert flakes recovered from the Pit 3 activity area showed any evidence of use or retouch modification. None of the chert, quartzite, or sandstone angular fragments showed any evidence of utilization or wear. Only three lithic items (chert angular fragments) showed any evidence of having been heated (Table 14). Average weight values for all of the lithic categories discussed so far (chert and quartzite flakes, chert, quartzite, and sandstone angular fragments) are higher for the Pit 3 activity area than for Pit 3 (Figures 25 and 26).

A single Woodland projectile point of light pink quartzite was recovered from the Pit 3 activity area (Plate VIIIF) along with three Mississippian projectile points. One of the Mississippian projectile points (Field Specimen 228) was lost before the artifacts were photographed and therefore is not illustrated. The tip was missing from the smallest of the three Mississippian projectile points (Plate VIIID). It could not be determined if the tip had been broken off during the process of manufacture or at a later date. This small point is similar to the three incurvate blade points recovered from the Snodgrass site (Price 1973:104–105). The other two Mississippian projectile points were apparently discarded during the manufacturing process. The projectile point not illustrated was broken in half during manufacture and discarded, while the third Mississippian projectile point appears to have been discarded during the manufacture process due to an imperfection in the chert that the flint knapper could not work around (Plate VIIIE). In addition to the projectile points, two other lithic tools were recovered from the Pit 3 activity area. A biface of light gray chert was found on the southern edge of the activity area (Plate VD), and a knife fragment of gray chert was found to the northeast of Pit 3 (Plate VE).

A total of seven chert and three quartzite cores were recovered from within the activity area, to the west and south of Pit 3. Six of the seven chert cores could be characterized as expended or exhausted cores (Plate XIID, E, F, G, H, I). All six are small fragments of river cobbles that still

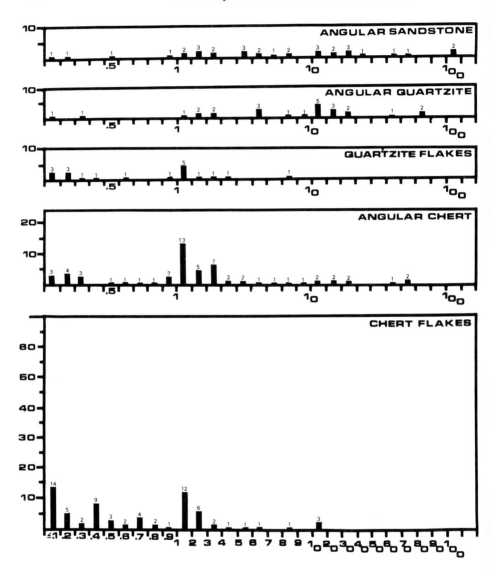

Figure 26. Weight values in grams for lithic materials recovered from the Pit 3 activity area. Note the changing scale on the horizontal axis.

have cortex remaining, and show clear evidence of a number of flakes having been struck from several edges of each core. All six cores are of such a small size that they would be difficult to hold while striking a flake. One of the six was broken in half during an attempt to strike a flake and was discarded, with the two pieces recovered from within a foot of each other. The seventh core (Field Specimen 11) is a larger piece of

TABLE 14

Cultural Materials Recovered from the Pit 3 Activity Area

Items	Quantity	Weight (gm)	Comments
Lithics			
Chert flakes	66	118.0	5 use modification, 2 retouch modification
Chert cores	8	165.4	1 heated
Chert angular fragments	59	489.3	3 heated
Quartzite flakes	19	28.2	
Quartzite cores	3	220.5	
Quartzite angular fragments	25	497.0	
Sandstone angular fragments	32	702.0	
Woodland projectile points	1	18.8	
Mississippian projectile points	3	10.1	1 tip, 2 rejected during manufacture
Knife	1	4.9	Broken
Biface	1	18.5	
Cobble	2	505.8	
	220	2778.5	
Ceramics			
Barnes sherds	2	22.2	
Jar rim sherds	1	5.4	
Powers Phase body sherds	35	256.2	
Cone fragments	6	160.9	
	44	444.7	
Fauna			
White-tailed deer			
Odocoileus virginianus	5	15.9	Left humerus shaft, metatarsal shaft, male skull fragment, antler fragment, long-bone fragment
Plant remains			
Hickory			
Carya sp.		33.68	Small carbonized nutshell and septum fragments
Acorn			
Quercus sp.	8	.02	Small carbonized shell and meat fragments
Black walnut			
Juglans nigra	4	.21	Small carbonized nutshell fragments
Maize			
Zea mays	2	.25	Carbonized cupule and kernel fragments
Wild bean			
Strophostyles helvola	1	.01	
Knotweed			
Polygonum sp.	16	.04	Seed
Chenopod			
Chenopodium sp.	9		Seeds
	40	34.81	
Total contents	309	3273.9	

chert that had been heat treated, and has a glossy light purple surface from which only a few flakes have been struck (Plate XIIJ). The three quartzite cores are also relatively small pieces, each having cortex present, and each showing evidence of only a few flakes having been struck (Plate XIIK, L, M). Although a great amount of laboratory time was spent in attempting to match flakes with cores, only a single flake was successfully reunited with a core. The flake in question (Field Specimen 285), which was recovered from the base of Pit 3, was found to fit a core (Field Specimen 303) located about 5 feet to the southwest. This suggests that the pit was open while flint knapping was being done in the adjacent activity area.

In addition to the two Woodland pottery sherds and 35 Neelys Ferry Plain pottery sherds recovered from the Pit 3 activity area, a single rim sherd from a jar-vessel form was recovered (Plate XIIIB). Judging from the rim height and thickness measurements, the rim sherd was not from the same vessel as the rim sherd recovered from Pit 3 (Plate XIIIA).

The six cone fragments recovered from the Pit 3 activity area are very similar in color and texture to the cone fragment recovered from Pit 3, and may be part of the same cone.

The five skeletal elements of *Odocoileus virginianus* recovered from the Pit 3 activity area included a humerus shaft fragment that was found to fit the distal humerus element in Pit 3 (Figure 24), as well as antler fragments that may have functioned as soft percussors, although the antler was too poorly preserved to exhibit any evidence of utilization. In addition, a skull fragment of an adult male deer was recovered with the antler base attached to the skull. The projected season of death of the animal is therefore September to February (Smith 1975:38).

The carbonized plant remains recovered from the Pit 3 activity area are listed in Table 14.

Pits 5a, 5b, and an Associated Activity Area

Upon removal of the plowzone from the nine 5-foot grid units shown in Figure 27, an oval concentration of a large number of carbonized hickory nut fragments was observed, surrounded by a larger area of a lower-density artifact scatter. This oval concentration of hickory nutshell fragments was initially designated Pit 5. As excavation of Pit 5 was started, it quickly became apparent that there were in fact two adjacent circular pits rather than a single oval pit, which were designated Pits 5a and 5b.

The single overriding impression of these two pits was the great quantity of hickory nutshell fragments that they contained. The 1269.92 gm of hickory nut fragments recovered from Pits 5a, 5b, and the associated activity area represents fully 81% of such fragments recovered from the site as a whole. It was only during subsequent laboratory analysis that the initial impression of two pits full of hickory nut shell fragments was

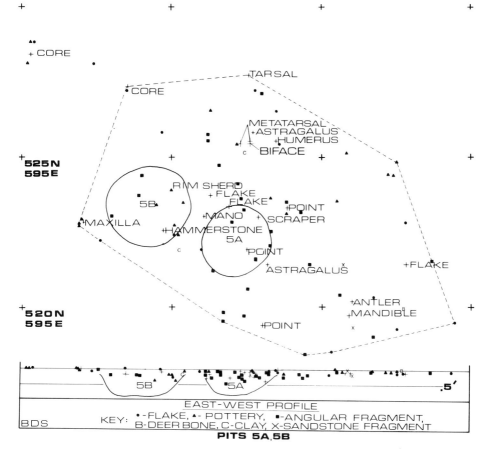

Figure 27. The spatial distribution of cultural materials within Pit 5a, Pit 5b, and the associated activity area.

replaced by a more complex set of impressions concerning these three associated features. It became clear, for example, that rather than being largely restricted to the two adjacent pits, plant remains were very abundant in the surrounding activity area as well. It also became apparent that rather than just containing hickory nutshell fragments, the three associated features had yielded carbonized remains of a wider variety of plant species than any other feature at the site (Table 21). Finally, it became clear that there was both a large quantity and a great variety of cultural materials other than plant remains present in these three associated features.

Pit 5a

Located approximately 20 feet northeast of Structure 1, Pit 5a was a circular pit covering an area of 4.3 square feet, with concave sloping sides, and reaching a depth of .8 feet. The outline of the pit was clearly visible, with the dark organic fill contrasting sharply with the surrounding soil. Although there was no apparent internal stratification or layering observed in the pit, most of the cultural material was recovered from the upper .5 feet of the pit fill (see profile, Figure 27). A total of 1237 items weighing 639.5 gm were recovered from the pit fill (the item count does not include some of the plant remains, for which weight values but not counts were obtained—Table 15).

Eighty-three lithic items weighing 277.5 gm were recovered from Pit 5a. Once again, chert flakes and chert angular fragments were the most abundant lithic items recovered. A single flake out of 25 showed evidence of retouch modification, and 3 of 25 chert flakes showed evidence of having been heated. Eight of 30 chert angular fragments showed evidence of having been heated.

Two Powers Phase projectile points were recovered from Pit 5a. One of the projectile points was unbroken (not illustrated); the second was apparently discarded during manufacture (Plate VIIIG). The unfinished projectile point provides further evidence of the characteristic pattern of arrowhead manufacture employed by Powers Phase flint knappers. The base of the unfinished point retained a small platform and part of a bulb of percussion, indicating that a flake of appropriate dimensions and thickness was first struck from a core. The flake was then retouched into the desired shape, with secondary flaking starting at the dorsal end of the flake (which became the tip of the point), and proceeding back toward the bulb of the percussion and striking platform, which would have formed the base of the finished point.

In addition to the two Mississippian projectile points, a large red chert flake was recovered that had been unifacially retouched along one edge (Plate VF). A single small white quartzite core was also recovered from Pit 5a (Plate XIIN). The core was quite similar in size to the quartzite and chert cores recovered from the Pit 3 activity area, and could be described as an exhausted or expended core. In addition to 5 Neelys Ferry Plain body sherds, 10 clay fragments were recovered from Pit 5a. More clay fragments were recovered from Pits 5a, 5b, and the associated activity area than from any other area of the site except for Structure 2. A single small piece of galena was also recovered from the pit (Plate XIF).

Three hundred and eleven grams of carbonized hickory nutshell fragments, accounting for 48% of the total cultural materials recovered, were found in Pit 5a. Most of the shell fragments were quite small, representing a quarter of a nut or less. A few larger shell fragments, as well as some hickory nutmeat fragments, were recovered. A small number of carbonized shell fragments of acorn were also recovered, along with a few carbonized maize kernels. A large number of knotweed and chenopod seeds were also found in Pit 5a, as well as small amounts of marsh elder seeds and wild bean fragments (Table 15).

TABLE 15

Cultural Materials Recovered from Pit 5a

Items	Quantity	Weight (gm)	Comments
Lithics			
Chert flakes	25	19.2	1 retouch modification, 3 heated
Chert angular fragments	30	141.2	8 heated
Quartzite flakes	10	9.3	
Quartzite cores	1	12.9	
Quartzite angular fragments	13	77.2	
Sandstone angular fragments	1	1.2	
Mississippian projectile points	2	5.1	1 unfinished 1 unbroken
Scrapers	1	11.4	
	83	277.5	
Ceramics			
Powers Phase body sherds	5	17.8	
Clay fragments	10	20.8	
	15	38.6	
Metallic			
Galena	1	1.3	
Fauna			
White-tailed deer			
Odocoileus virginianus	1	8.3	
Plant remains			
Hickory			
Carya sp.		311.48	Carbonized nutshell and nutmeat fragments
Acorn			
Quercus sp.		.16	Carbonized nutshell and nutmeat fragments
Maize			
Zea mays		.57	Carbonized kernels
Marsh elder			
Iva annua	10	.05	Seeds
Knotweed			
Polygonum sp.	712	1.38	Seeds
Chenopod			
Chenopodium sp.	424	.14	Seeds
Wild bean			
Strophostyles helvola	3	.02	Cotyledons
	1150	313.80	
Total contents	1237	639.50	

Pit 5b

Located directly adjacent to Pit 5a, Pit 5b was a circular pit covering an area of 5.8 square feet and having concave sides that sloped to a flat bottom at a depth of .9 feet. The outline of the pit was clearly visible, with the dark organic fill contrasting sharply with the surrounding soil. Although Pit 5b was only slightly larger than Pit 5a and contained a comparable quantity and variety of cultural remains, it yielded almost three times the total weight of cultural materials recovered from Pit 5a. A total of 5048 items weighing 1453.8 gm was recovered from Pit 5b (Table 16).

The 79 lithic items recovered weighed a total of 1110 gm, comprising 78.6% of the total mass of recovered cultural materials. Chert flakes and chert angular fragments were once again the most abundant lithic items present in the pit. Three chert flakes showed indications of use modification, and one chert and one quartzite angular fragment showed evidence of having been heated. Quartzite flake and sandstone angular fragments were recovered in small quantities.

Other than the three utilized flakes, only a single lithic tool, an anvil–hammerstone, was recovered from Pit 5b. The 403.3-gm quartzite cobble shown in Plate IVD has been described as an anvil–hammerstone because in addition to exhibiting two areas of the edge battering, characteristic of hard percussors or hammerstones, it also exhibits areas of battering on one of its flat surfaces. Such wear patterns on a flat surface are characteristic of objects that have been used as anvils.

Two chert cores and a single quartzite core were also recovered from Pit 5b. The chert cores are very similar in size and characteristics to the seven small exhausted chert cores recovered from the Pit 3 activity area. They are both small, angular chert fragments with some cortex remaining, and both have had flakes struck from a number of edges (Plate XIIP, Q). The larger quartzite core showed evidence of only a few flakes having been removed from it (Plate XIIO).

In addition to 12 Neelys Ferry Plain body sherds and 19 clay fragments, a single rim sherd from a large jar-form vessel was recovered from Pit 5b (Plate XIIIC).

Two left rear leg elements and a vertebra fragment of a white-tailed deer were also recovered from Pit 5b, along with two long-bone fragments.

Carbonized hickory nutshell and meat fragments weighing 190.9 gm were recovered from Pit 5b, with most shell fragments representing less than one-quarter of a nut. A few carbonized shell fragments of acorn were also recovered. Pit 5b also yielded very large numbers of knotweed and chenopod seeds, as well as small amounts of marsh elder and morning glory seeds. Two seeds and one-half of a crab apple fruit were also recovered (Table 16).

TABLE 16

Cultural Materials Recovered from Pit 5b

Items	Quantity	Weight (gm)	Comments
Lithics			
Chert flakes	35	34.3	3 use modification 2 heated
Chert cores	2	30.0	
Chert angular fragments	16	263.2	1 heated
Quartzite flakes	4	13.0	
Quartzite cores	1	69.5	
Quartzite angular fragments	14	144.5	1 heated
Sandstone angular fragments	6	152.5	
Anvil hammerstone	1	403.3	
	79	1110.0	
Ceramics			
Jar rim sherds	1	66.7	
Powers Phase body sherds	12	41.8	
Clay, cane impressions	6	8.3	
Clay fragments	13	39.4	
	32	118.5	
Fauna			
White-tailed deer			
Odocoileus virginianus	5	24.8	Right distal femur, right proximal metatarsal, 2 long-bone fragments, 1 vertebrae fragment
Plant remains			
Hickory			
Carya sp.		190.92	Carbonized nutshell and nutmeat fragments
Acorn			
Quercus sp.		1.41	Carbonized nutshell and nutmeat fragments
Maize			
Zea mays		1.6	
Marsh elder			
Iva annua	19	.11	Seeds
Knotweed			
Polygonum sp.	2392	4.04	Seeds
Chenopod			
Chenopodium sp.	2515	1.76	Seeds
Wild bean			
Strophostyles helvola	10	.08	Cotyledon
Crab apple			
Pyrus sp.	3	.37	2 seeds, 1/2 fruit
Morning glory			
Ipomoea lacunosa	2	.02	Seeds
	4943	200.51	
Total Contents	5048	1453.81	

The Activity Area Associated with Pits 5a and 5b

Excavation of the nine grid units centered on Pits 5a and 5b uncovered a shallow scatter of cultural materials over an area of approximately 66.6 square feet, not including the area covered by Pits 5a and 5b (Figure 27). This scatter of cultural materials surrounding Pits 5a and 5b is assumed to be a primary deposit, an activity area, for the same reasons suggested for the Pit 3 activity area. This activity area yielded 14,379 items weighing a total of 2719.2 gm (Table 17). This total weight of cultural materials is greater than the combined mass of cultural debris recovered from Pits 5a and 5b.

Chert flakes and angular fragments were once again the most abundant lithic items recovered. Three chert flakes showed evidence of retouch

TABLE 17

Cultural Materials Recovered from the Activity Area Surrounding Pits 5a and 5b

Items	Quantity	Weight (gm)	Comments
Lithics			
Chert flakes	28	34.9	3 retouch modification, 1 heated
Chert cores	1	6.0	
Chert angular fragments	35	657.4	
Quartzite flakes	20	24.8	
Quartzite cores	1	33.2	
Quartzite angular fragments	15	301.6	
Sandstone angular fragments	3	230.3	
Mississippian projectile points	2	11.0	1 complete 1 midsection
Biface	1	52.6	
Manos	1	118.5	
	107	1,470.3	
Ceramics			
Jar shoulder sherd	1	3.0	
Powers Phase body sherds	18	142.4	
Clay, cane impressions	4	70.0	
Clay fragments	7	147.1	
	30	362.5	
Fauna			
White-tailed deer			
Odocoileus virginianus	10	80.8	Left distal humerus, left astragalus, distal metacarpal, right maxilla fragments, 2 long-bone fragments, antler fragment, left antler pedicle (shed)

(Continued)

TABLE 17 *(Continued)*

Items	Quantity	Weight (gm)	Comments
Plant remains			
Hickory			
Carya sp.		767.52	Carbonized nutshell and kernel fragments
Acorn			
Quercus sp.		6.80	Carbonized nutshell and kernel fragments
Black walnut			
Juglans nigra	7	.54	Carbonized nutshell fragments
Maize			
Zea mays		10.16	Carbonized kernels
Marsh elder			
Iva annua	153	1.13	Seeds
Knotweed			
Polygonum sp.	9,211	15.51	Seeds
Chenopod			
Chenopodium sp.	4,825	3.51	Seeds
Wild bean			
Strophostyles helvola	31	.27	Cotyledons, seeds
Crab apple			
Pyrus sp.	2	.12	1 seed, 1/4 fruit
Morning-glory			
Ipomoea lacunosa	3	.03	Seeds
	14,232	805.59	
Total contents	14,379	2,719.19	

modification, and another chert flake was the single lithic item showing evidence of having been heated. A pattern observed for Pit 3 and its associated activity area was also found to apply to Pits 5a and 5b and their associated area. Although the number of recovered chert flakes, chert angular fragments, quartzite angular fragments, and sandstone angular fragments was roughly comparable for Pit 5a, Pit 5b, and the associated activity area, the average weight value for these four categories of lithic items was larger for the activity area than for either of the pits (Figures 28, 29, 30).

Two Mississippian projectile points were recovered from the activity area. An unbroken point of white mottled chert was uncovered $2\frac{1}{2}$ feet south of Pit 5a (Plate VIIII), and the midsection of a light tan serrated projectile point was recovered approximately 1 foot northeast of Pit 5a (Plate VIIIH, Figure 27). The serrated projectile point fragment displayed a much higher quality of workmanship than any of the other lithic artifacts recovered from the site.

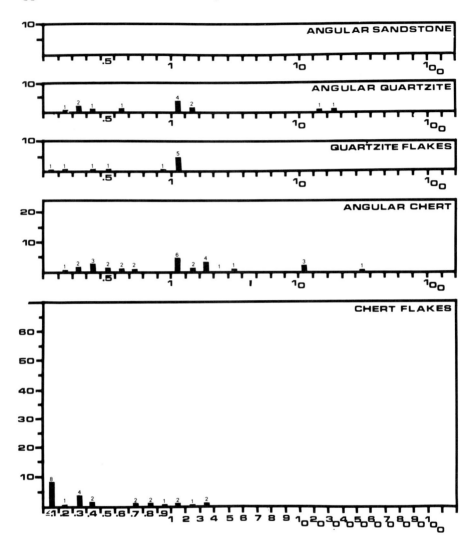

Figure 28. Weight values in grams for lithic materials recovered from Pit 5a. Note the changing scale on the horizontal axis.

The mano recovered from between Pits 5a and 5b was a roughly 2-inch square by 1-inch thick slab of brownish-red sandstone with one surface worn flat (Plate IVE). Microscopic examination of the worked surface failed to turn up any striations or other further indications of use modification.

A single small chert core was recovered at the northwest corner of the activity area. The core is similar to the small expended cores recovered from Pit 5b and the Pit 3 activity area in that it weighed only 6 gm and

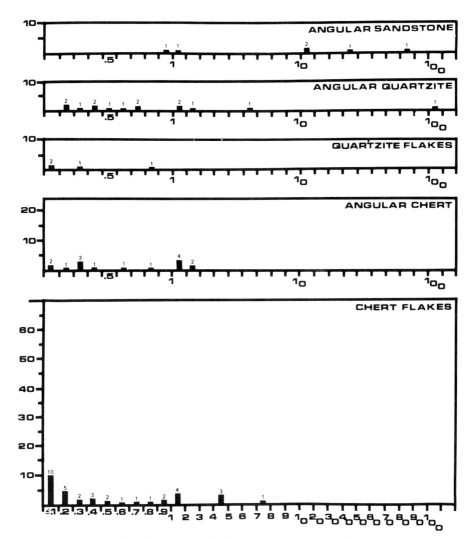

Figure 29. Weight values in grams for lithic materials recovered from Pit 5b. Note the changing scale on the horizontal axis.

showed evidence of flakes having been struck from several edges (Plate XIIS). A large white quartzite core was recovered to the northwest of the activity area outlined in Figure 27, about halfway between the activity area surrounding Pit 3 and the one surrounding Pits 5a and 5b. Numerous flakes had been struck along two edges of the core (Plate XIIR). Many hours were spent in the laboratory trying to reunite chert and quartzite flakes recovered from the two pits and the activity area with cores, but with no success.

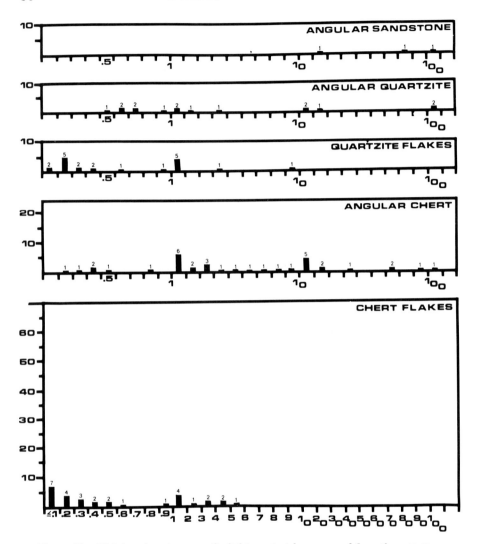

Figure 30.   Weight values in grams for lithic materials recovered from the activity area surrounding Pit 5a and Pit 5b. Note the changing scale on the horizontal axis.

A large (52.6 gm), crudely flaked gray chert biface was uncovered approximately 2 feet north of Pit 5a, in direct association with a concentration of white-tailed deer skeletal elements (Plate VG). The cutting edge of the biface was considerably dulled, with some areas of polish present. Directly north and east of the biface was a left distal humerus, a left astragalus, and a distal metacarpal fragment, all of *Odocoileus virginianus,* and all in a poor state of preservation. Another small concentration of white-tailed deer skeletal elements, consisting of a left antler pedicle and two long-bone fragments, was uncovered approximately 4 feet to the southeast of Pit 5a. The antler pedicle indicated that the adult male deer had shed its antlers at the time of death, suggesting a season of kill covering a 4-month span: January through April (Smith 1975:38). The only other deer skeletal remains recovered from the activity area were a maxilla fragment and upper left first molar, which were located just west of Pit 5b.

Also recovered from the activity area were 767 gm of carbonized hickory nutshell and septum fragments, along with a few shell fragments of acorn and black walnut. Numerous carbonized maize kernels were obtained from the activity area, along with a very large quantity of knotweed and chenopod seeds (Table 17).

Pit 10 and Associated Activity Area

Pit 10, located approximately 25 feet southeast of Structure 1, covered an area of approximately 12.8 square feet. The pit was roughly circular in shape, with a fairly shallow outer margin blending into abruptly concave sides sloping to a flat base at a depth of .6 feet. The outline of the pit was clearly visible, with the darker pit fill contrasting with the surrounding soil. An irregular, circular-shaped area of burned soil was uncovered at the base of the pit. This bright orange burned and hardened soil covered an area of 1.5 square feet and extended to a depth of .1 feet below the base of the pit (Figure 31).

A total of only 146 items weighing 492.5 gm were recovered from Pit 10 (Table 18). Of these, the 64 lithic items, weighing 456.6 gm, comprised 87.6% of the total pit contents by item count, and 92.7% of the total pit contents by weight. Once again, chert flakes and chert angular fragments were the most abundant lithic items and were characteristically small in size. A single large quartzite angular fragment weighing 248.6 gm represented over 50% of the total weight of recovered items (Figure 32).

A single clay fragment, along with five Neelys Ferry Plain body sherds, comprised the ceramic assemblage recovered from Pit 10.

Plant remains included hickory nut and black walnut shell fragments, carbonized maize kernels, and seeds of marsh elder, knotweed, and chenopod (Table 18).

Pit 10 Activity Area

When the outline of Pit 10 was initially defined, a larger scatter of cultural debris was observed to extend to the north and to the west of the pit (Figure 31). Subsequent excavation of the area of scatter showed it to be a thin lens (.1–.2 feet) of cultural materials covering an estimated area of 42.6 square feet. Very little cultural debris was recovered to the east or

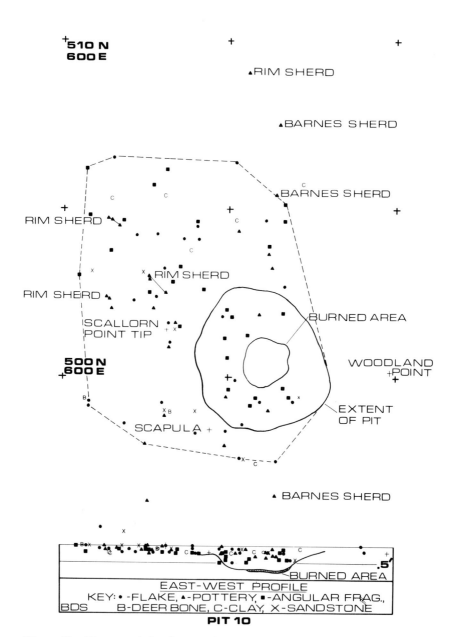

Figure 31. The spatial distribution of cultural materials within Pit 10 and its associated activity area.

TABLE 18

Cultural Materials Recovered from Pit 10

Items	Quantity	Weight (gm)	Comments
Lithics			
Chert flakes	28	7.4	1 heated
Chert angular fragments	16	51.7	
Quartzite flakes	5	1.5	
Quartzite angular fragments	11	358.3	
Sandstone angular fragments	4	37.7	
	64	456.6	
Ceramics			
Powers Phase body sherds	5	28.1	
Clay fragments	1	1.5	
	6	29.6	
Plant remains			
Hickory			
Carya sp.		5.99	Carbonized nutshell fragments
Black walnut			
Juglans nigra		.02	Carbonized nutshell fragments
Maize			
Zea mays		.07	Carbonized kernels
Marsh elder			
Iva annua	1	.03	Seed
Knotweed			
Polygonum sp.	61	.14	Seeds
Chenopod			
Chenopodium sp.	14	.01	Seeds
	76	6.26	
Total contents	146	492.46	

south of the pit. This scatter of cultural materials adjacent to Pit 10 is assumed to be a primary deposit, an activity area, for the same reasons suggested for the Pit 3 activity area.

A total of 193 items weighing 937.5 gm were recovered from the Pit 10 activity area (Table 19). Of the 57 lithic items recovered, chert flakes and chert angular fragments were most abundant (Figure 33). A Woodland projectile point fragment of gray quartzite was recovered approximately 2 feet east of Pit 10 (Plate VIIIK). Three Woodland pottery sherds were also recovered along the eastern edge of the activity area and to the north and south of it. Only two other lithic tools were recovered from the Pit 10 activity area. The tip of a white chert Mississippian (Scallorn) projectile point was recovered a foot west of Pit 10 (Plate VIIIJ), and a unifacially

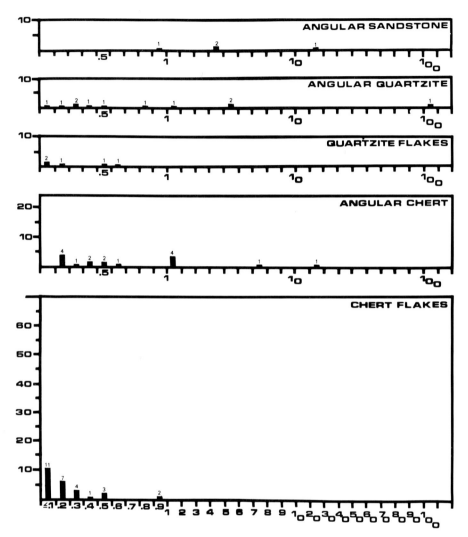

Figure 32. Weight values in grams for lithic materials recovered from Pit 10. Note the changing scale on the horizontal axis.

flaked gray quartzite thumbnail scraper was recovered along the northeast edge of the activity area (Plate VH).

In addition to 13 Neelys Ferry Plain body sherds, five clay fragments, and the three Woodland sherds already mentioned, the Pit 10 activity area yielded five rim sherds from a minimum of two small jar-form vessels. A single large fragmentary rim sherd with a modified strap handle was recovered about 3 feet west of Pit 10. An opening approximately .03 feet in diameter had been molded into the top of the poorly executed

TABLE 19

Cultural Materials Recovered from the Pit 10 Activity Area

Items	Quantity	Weight (gm)	Comments
Lithics			
Chert flakes	23	39.6	2 heated
			1 use modification
Chert angular fragments	9	77.8	1 burned
Quartzite flakes	4	18.6	
Quartzite angular fragments	7	99.1	
Sandstone angular fragments	7	155.4	
Woodland projectile points	1	11.6	Base broken off
Mississippian projectile points	1	.3	Tip only—broken during manufacture
Scrapers	1	3.1	
Unmodified pebbles	5	8.4	
	57	413.9	
Ceramics			
Jar rim sherds	5	217.3	Minimum of 2 jars
Powers Phase body sherds	13	145.3	
Woodland sherds	3	17.3	
Clay fragments	5	94.6	
	26	474.5	
Fauna			
White-tailed deer			
Odocoileus virginianus	3	11.8	1 left scapula
			2 long-bone fragments
Plant remains			
Hickory			
Carya sp.		36.07	Carbonized nutshell fragments
Black walnut			
Juglans nigra	3	.43	Carbonized nutshell fragments
Maize			
Zea mays		.50	Carbonized kernel fragments
Marsh elder			
Iva annua	1	.01	Seed
Sunflower			
Helianthus annuus	1	.01	Seed
Knotweed			
Polygonum sp.	55	.13	Seeds
Chenopod			
Chenopodium sp.	30	.04	Seeds
Wild bean			
Strophostyles helvola	15	.12	12 cotyledon
			3 beans
Grape			
Vitis sp.	2	.03	
	107	37.34	
Total contents	193	937.54	

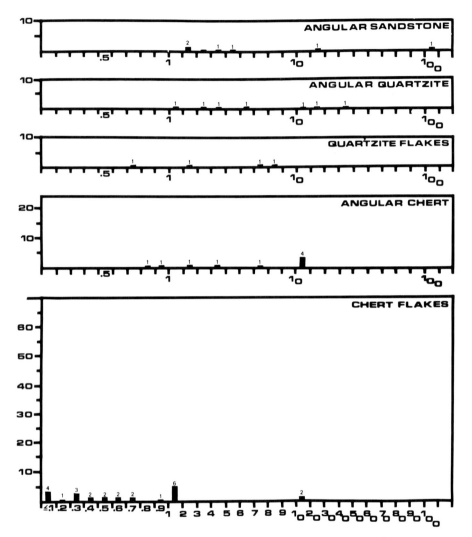

Figure 33. Weight values in grams for lithic materials recovered from the Pit 10 activity area. Note the changing scale on the horizontal axis.

handle, apparently to facilitate suspension of the vessel by cords (Plate XIIID). In viewing this angled strap handle, some observers have termed it a frog effigy, pointing both to its front and rear appendages and its stylized head extending above the rim. The reader is left to his or her own interpretation. A cluster of three rim sherds that were found to fit together occurred about 1 foot northeast of the rim sherd just described (Plate XIIIE). This vessel fragment also exhibits a strap handle, although of a more conventional form.

Even though the two rim fragments are both from small jar-form vessels, it is doubtful that they are from the same vessel. This opinion is based on observed differences in shoulder angle, projected orifice diameter, handle style, and rim height and thickness (Table 5). A third small rim sherd was found approximately 6 feet north of Pit 10 (Figure 31). It is worthwhile to point out at this time, although it will be discussed in more detail later, that all of the plant remains recovered from the Pit 10 activity area came from the area where the vessel fragments were found.

A single sunflower *(Helianthus)* seed was recovered from this area, along with 1 marsh elder seed, 2 grape seeds, 55 knotweed seeds, and 30 chenopod seeds. The Pit 10 activity area also yielded the carbonized remains of hickory, black walnut, and maize (Table 19).

To the south of this area, a left scapula fragment and two long-bone fragments of *Odocoileus virginianus* were recovered.

4

Energy-Capture Analysis[1]

BRUCE D. SMITH   WILMA WETTERSTROM

The excavation of the Gypsy Joint site resulted in the recovery of the remains of a variety of species of plants and animals that had served as energy sources for the occupants of the site. These faunal and ethnobotanical remains, or *ecofacts*, have been identified and quantified for specific features in the preceding chapter, as well as in the Appendixes. Our discussion here is concerned with analysis and interpretation of the total faunal and ethnobotanical assemblages recovered, as well as with a consideration of the subsistence strategy employed by the Gypsy Joint site inhabitants.

FAUNA

A total of 82 skeletal elements, weighing 295.6 gm and representing eight species of animals, were recovered from the Powers Phase component of the Gypsy Joint site (Table 20). All 82 skeletal elements were recovered from within features, with Pit 4 being the only feature not to yield any faunal remains. Although this small sample of recovered animal bones is similar in quantity and variety of species represented to comparable excavated areas at other Powers Phase sites, preservation of faunal materials at the Gypsy Joint site can only be termed poor. Differential preservation of faunal materials has quite likely resulted in certain bones of larger animals being preserved and recovered while both the bones of smaller species and the more delicate bones of larger species

[1] The initial portion of this chapter (Fauna) was written by Bruce Smith, with the subsequent consideration of plant foods written by Wilma Wetterstrom.

TABLE 20

Animal Species Represented at the Gypsy Joint Site

Species	Number of skeletal elements	Weight in grams	Number of features present	Minimum number of individuals	Projected meat yield (pounds)
Box turtle					
Terrapene carolina	10	1.1	3	1	.3
Turkey					
Meleagris gallopavo	1	8.2	1	1	8.5
Cottontail rabbit					
Sylvilagus floridanus	2	3.4	1	1	2.0
Fox squirrel					
Sciurus niger	6	2.0	3	1	1.5
Beaver					
Castor canadensis	1	.2	1	1	20.0
Raccoon					
Procyon lotor	2	4.0	1	1	8.0
White-tailed deer					
Odocoileus virginianus	46	273.9	9	6	450.0
Freshwater clam					
Species?	1	1.4	1	1	
Unidentified small mammal	13	1.4	2		
	82	295.6		13	490.3

have not been preserved. It is quite possible, therefore, that although the faunal sample recovered from the site is a total sample of the faunal materials present in 1974, it may not be a representative sample of the faunal assemblage present at the site during, or just after, occupation. Table 20 may not provide an accurate picture of either the range of species exploited or the relative importance of various species in the diet of the Powers Phase inhabitants of the Gypsy Joint site. The faunal categories most notably absent from Table 20 include species of small mammals, turtles, fish, and birds, especially waterfowl. It is difficult to determine if these faunal categories are not represented because they were not, in fact, exploited or because they were not preserved. The absence of any skeletal elements of fish in the faunal assemblage is especially unfortunate, since they represent a key piece of direct archaeological evidence for seasonality of occupation of the site.

Poor preservation may also account in part for the lack of representation of all body parts of any of the species represented in the faunal assemblage. Very few lower leg bones, vertebrae, or ribs of the white-tailed deer were recovered, for example. While it has sometimes been stated that such missing skeletal elements are a clear indication of primary butchering at another location, it could just as well be a reflection of poor preservation and/or selective destruction of skeletal elements by scavengers, such as dogs.

Even though all of the animal species utilized by the inhabitants of the Gypsy Joint site may not be listed in Table 20, it is quite possible that Table 20 provides a fairly accurate picture of the relative importance of the species that are listed. With the exception of the white-tailed deer, which is probably overrepresented, all of the terrestrial species listed are in the same general size range and would have about the same chance of being preserved.

The total faunal assemblage recovered from the Powers Phase component at the Gypsy Joint site was employed in computing minimum number of individual (MIND) estimates. The white-tailed deer, with six left astragali, was the only species with a MIND value greater than one. It was also the species represented in the greatest number of features (Table 20) and had the highest projected meat-yield value of any species. Projected meat-yield values were determined by multiplying MIND values by average meat-yield values (6 white-tailed deer × 75 pounds average meat yield per individual = 450 pounds).

Even though the faunal assemblage from the Gypsy Joint site is statistically small, making any detailed analysis somewhat questionable, it is nonetheless interesting to note that the species list with respective meat-weight estimates agrees quite well with what would be expected from a Middle Mississippi site (Smith 1975). The white-tailed deer ranked first both in terms of its minimum number of individuals value and its projected meat-yield value, contributing 91.7% of the total meat yield at the site. Similarly, the presence of turkey, raccoon, cottontail rabbit, and fox squirrel is expected. The absence of the opossum and black bear, as well as the high ranking of beaver is likely to be a function of the small sample size.

The spatial distribution of faunal materials across the Gypsy Joint site, as well as the osteological indicators of seasonality of occupation of the site, will be considered in later chapters.

PLANT FOODS FROM THE GYPSY JOINT SITE

Introduction

The large populations and apparently complex, stratified societies of the major Middle Mississippi sites have been attributed in part to the rich agricultural potential of the Mississippi and other large river valleys (e.g., Griffin 1967). According to this model, the more modest communities in the marginal areas of the central Mississippi Valley did not develop into large, complex societies partly because of the limited resources in these regions. Although environmental factors may be responsible for some differences among Mississippian communities, such ecological models are not testable at the present time because there is not enough detailed information about the farming and collecting activities of Middle Mississippi populations to formulate specific hypotheses. For example, it is not known which so-called limited resources were used in the marginal areas, how these resources differed from those in the major river valleys, to what extent they were limited, and how they affected cultural variables such as community size. It is hoped that this analysis of the Gypsy Joint plant materials will provide some of the data which scholars need to study subsistence in marginal areas of the Mississippi Valley.

Although Gypsy Joint is a small site, over 1600 gm of plant material (excluding wood charcoal) were recovered. This includes 1576 gm of nutshells, 40 gm of corn kernels and cob fragments, and about 20,000 seeds. All of these materials are carbonized, and most of them were recovered from the 36 flotation samples analyzed. The flotation samples were visually inspected and all seeds, nuts, nutshells, and other plant structures except wood charcoal were removed. Specimens which were hand-retrieved during excavation were likewise examined and sorted. Material was identified to the genus level where possible and in some cases to the species level. Nutshells, nut kernels, corn kernels, and cob fragments were weighed. The seeds were counted and weighed.

The Gypsy Joint plant food remains, summarized in Table 21, include hickory nuts, acorns, black walnuts, wild beans, the seeds of chenopod, knotweed, grape, morning glory, crab apple, and parts of the crab apple fruit. The cultigens, maize, marsh elder, and sunflower,were also represented. In addition, a plum or cherry pit, a seed belonging to the composite family, and two unidentified species of bean were recovered. Eight different seeds and approximately .1 gm of miscellaneous plant materials could not be identified. The latter consists mainly of seed fragments that are so incomplete the original appearance of the specimens cannot be determined.

The Plants

Nuts

The most abundant and widely distributed plant material at the Gypsy Joint site is the hickory nut (*Carya* sp.) shell. Approximately 1568 gm of shell fragments, most of which were small pieces, were recovered. In addition, there are about .8 gm of kernel fragments that are probably hickory.

The diagnostic traits and original dimensions of the nuts are difficult to determine because only a few large fragments were found. The length of

TABLE 21

Distribution of Plant Remains at the Gypsy Joint Site (weight in grams)[a]

	Structure 1	Structure 2[b]		
	Fill	Fill	Pit 1	Total
Hickory nut shell				
Carya sp.	115.49	21.17	4.33	25.50
Acorn nutshell				
Quercus sp.	.03	.04		.04
Black walnut shell				
Juglans nigra	.38	.94		.94
Hickory kernels				
Carya sp.	.02			
Acorn kernels				
Quercus sp.	.44	.22		.22
Corn kernels, cobs				
Zea mays	2.02		1.49	1.49
Marsh elder seeds	0.02			
Iva annua	(3)			
Sunflower seeds				
Helianthus annuus				
Knotweed seeds	*			
Polygonum	(6)			
Chenopod seeds	*		*	*
Chenopodium sp.	(11)		(1)	(1)
Wild bean				
Strophostyles helvola	.03		.01	.01
(c = cotyledon; b = bean)	(3c)		(1c)	(1c)
Grape seed	.02		.02	.02
Vitis sp.	(2)		(1)	(1)
Crab apple				
Pyrus sp.				
Plum/Cherry	.05			
Prunus sp.	(Endocarp fragments)			
Morning glory seeds				
Ipomoea lacunosa				
Unident. seeds	.01			
	(2)			
Unident. material	*			
Other	Legume seed (1)			
	Composite seed (1)			

[a] Seed counts in parentheses. Asterisk indicates weight less than .01 gm. *(Continued)*
[b] No flotation samples were taken from Structure 2 fill.

the almost complete nut specimens varied from about 2.5 to 3.5 cm. Since most plant material shrinks when it is charred, these dimensions are probably slightly smaller than the original lengths. The variation among these specimens could indicate that more than one species is

TABLE 21 *(Continued)*

Distribution of Plant Remains at the Gypsy Joint Site (weight in grams)

	Maize grain concentration	Pit 2	Pit 3 complex	
			Pit 3	Activity area
Hickory nutshell				
Carya sp.		9.16	66.40	33.68
Acorn nutshell				
Quercus sp.			.04	.02
Black walnut shell				
Juglans nigra				.21
Hickory kernels				
Carya sp.				
Acorn kernels				
Quercus sp.			.40	.09
Corn kernels, cobs				
Zea mays	22.7	2.10	.18	.25
Marsh elder seeds				
Iva annua				
Sunflower seeds				
Helianthus annuus				
Knotweed seeds			.03	.04
Polygonum			(12)	(16)
Chenopod seeds			*	*
Chenopodium sp.			(6)	(9)
Wild bean				
Strophostyles helvola				.01
(c = cotyledon; b = bean)				(1c)
Grape seed				
Vitis sp.				
Crab apple				
Pyrus sp.				
Plum/Cherry				
Prunus sp.				
Morning glory seeds			.02	
Ipomoea lacunosa			(1)	
Unident. seeds			.06	
			(1)	(1)
Unident. material		*	.08	
Other				

(Continued)

included. The larger specimens may be shellbark hickory nuts (*C. laciniosa* Michx.) which are the largest fruits in the genus, ranging from 3–6 cm in length. The smaller specimens could be mockernut (*C. tomentosa* Nutt.) or shagbark (*C. ovata* Mill.) hickory nuts which vary between 3–3.5 cm and 2–3 cm in length, respectively. All three hickory species are common in the oak–hickory forests of southeast Missouri and the

TABLE 21 *(Continued)*

Distribution of Plant Remains at the Gypsy Joint Site (weight in grams)

	Pit 5 complex				Pit 6
	Pit 5a	Pit 5b	Activity area	Total	
Hickory nutshell					
Carya sp.	311.48	190.44	767.25	1,269.17	5.61
Acorn nutshell					
Quercus sp.	.07	.51	4.39	4.97	.01
Black walnut shell					
Juglans nigra			.54	.54	
Hickory kernels					
Carya sp.		.48	.27	.75	
Acorn kernels					
Quercus sp.	.09	.90	2.41	3.40	
Corn kernels, cobs					
Zea mays	.57	1.60	10.16	12.33	.02
Marsh elder seeds	.05	.11	1.13	1.29	.01
Iva annua	(10)	(19)	(153)	(182)	(1)
Sunflower seeds					
Helianthus annuus					
Knotweed seeds	1.38	4.04	15.51	20.93	.09
Polygonum	(712)	(2,392)	(9,211)	(12,313)	(49)
Chenopod seeds	.14	1.76	3.51	5.41	.07
Chenopodium sp.	(424)	(2,515)	(4,825)	(7,764)	(86)
Wild bean					
Strophostyles helvola	.02	.08	.27	.37	.01
(c = cotyledon; b = bean)	(3c)	(10c)	(25c,6b)	(38c,6b)	(1b)
Grape seed					
Vitis sp.					
Crab apple		.37	.12	.49	
Pyrus sp.		(2 seeds, 1/2 fruit)	(1 seed, 1/4 fruit)	(3 seeds, 2 fruit fragments)	
Plum/Cherry					
Prunus sp.					
Morning glory seeds		.02	.03	.05	
Ipomoea lacunosa		(2)	(3)	(5)	
Unident. seeds		.04	.02	.06	
		(1)	(2)	(3)	
Unident. material		.03	.02	.05	
Other			legume seed (1)	legume seed (1)	

(Continued)

shagbark and shellbark nuts are especially tasty (Steyermark 1963:518). Although the pignut hickory (*C. glabra* [Mill.] Sweet) is also abundant in oak–hickory forests, it was probably avoided because of its bitter flavor.

Ethnographic accounts dating from the contact period are useful in determining how the people of Gypsy Joint may have prepared these

TABLE 21 *(Continued)*

Distribution of Plant Remains at the Gypsy Joint Site (weight in grams)

	Pit 7	Pit 8	Pit 9	Pit 10	Activity area	Total	Site total
					Pit 10 complex		
Hickory nutshell							
Carya sp.	.91	.22		5.99	36.07	42.06	1,568.20
Acorn nutshell							
Quercus sp.							5.11
Black walnut shell							
Juglans nigra	.01			.02	.43	.45	2.53
Hickory kernels							
Carya sp.							.77
Acorn kernels							
Quercus sp.							4.55
Corn kernels, cobs							
Zea mays	.01			.07	.50	.57	39.69
Marsh elder seeds			.02	.03	.01	.04	1.38
Iva annua			(1)	(1)	(1)	(2)	(189)
Sunflower seeds					.01	.01	.01
Helianthus annuus					(1)	(1)	(1)
Knotweed seeds			*	.14	.13	.27	21.36
Polygonum			(2)	(61)	(55)	(116)	(12,516)
Chenopod seeds				.01	.04	.05	5.53
Chenopodium sp.				(14)	(30)	(44)	(7,921)
Wild bean							
Strophostyles helvola					.12	.12	.55
(c = cotyledon; b = bean)					(12c,3b)	(12c,3b)	(25c, 6b)
Grape seed			.01		.03	.03	.08
Vitis sp.			(1)		(2)	(2)	(6)
Crab apple							.49
Pyrus sp.							(3 seeds, 2 fruit fragments)
Plum/Cherry							.05
Prunus sp.							(endocarp frags.)
Morning glory seed							.07
Ipomoea lacunosa							(6)
Unident. seeds				.01		.01	.14
				(1)		(1)	(8)
Unident. material					*	*	.13
Other							
							legume seeds (3) composite seed (1)

nuts. According to early travelers, the Indians of the Southeast collected hickory nuts mainly for their oil, although they also ate the nut meats (Swanton 1946:364). An early historian described how the oil was extracted:

> At the fall of the leaf, they gather a number of hiccory-nuts, which they pound with a round stone, upon a stone, thick and hollowed for the purpose. When they are beat fine enough, they mix them with cold water, in a clay bason, where the shells subside. The other part is an oily, tough, thick white substance, called by the traders hiccory milk, and by the Indians the flesh, or fat of hiccory-nuts, with which they eat their bread [Adair 1775:408, quoted in Swanton 1946:365].

The nuts were also pounded into a meal which was prepared as a bread or was used to thicken venison broth. The shell fragments were usually removed by hand except in hickory milk, soups, and stews where they precipitated to the bottom of the pot (Swanton 1946:365).

The hickory nuts found at the Gypsy Joint site may have been pre- pared according to similar recipes which required pounded nuts. Nearly all of the nutshell specimens were small fragments which appear to have been shattered. These specimens are probably stray pieces of nutshell that fell into a fire while the kernels were being extracted. Some may have been intentionally discarded in a fire since nutshells are good fuel. Other specimens may have been dumped from the bottom of a cooking pot after a meal.

Acorns are represented by approximately 5 gm of very small nutshell fragments and about 4.6 gm of kernels. Like the hickory specimens, the acorn shell fragments are too small to possess the diagnostic features necessary for a species identification. However, the variation apparent in the kernels indicates that at least two species could be represented. The kernels range from .9–1.3 cm in length and most of the small specimens are globoid, whereas the larger ones are ellipsoid. White oak (*Quercus alba* L.) is probably represented among these remains. A few fragments of an acorn cup or involucre that were found at the Gypsy Joint site have warty scales similar to those of the white oak involucre. Acorns from other species in the white oak group were probably collected as well, but the members of the red oak subgenus were almost certainly ignored because they have a high concentration of bitter tannic acid.

The acorn is not as oily as the hickory nut, but early travelers in North America reported that it was a very important source of oil for the In- dians, second only to the hickory. The Indians extracted the oil by pounding the acorns on a stone and boiling the meal "till the oil swims on the top [Lawson 1860:80, quoted in Swanton 1946:366]." Boiling also improved the flavor of the oil and the meal by leaching some of the tannic acid which is found in all acorns. The meal was eaten with meat like a bread and the oil was used in cooking. Acorns were also pounded to a fine meal and added to venison broth (Swanton 1946:366–367).

The acorns found at the Gypsy Joint site may have been the product of similar processing techniques. The shells were probably tossed in the fire after the kernels had been extracted. The few charred kernels that were recovered may have been inadvertently dumped with the nutshells or intentionally discarded because they were spoiled.

The third nut recovered from the Gypsy Joint site is the black walnut (*Juglans nigra* L.) which is represented by only 2.5 gm of very small shell fragments. During the historic period, the Indians of the Southeast used this nut in the same manner as hickories: They extracted the oil and ate the ground meal as a nut bread (Swanton 1946:366).

Corn

The 40 gm of corn (*Zea mays* L.) recovered at the Gypsy Joint site include kernels and kernel fragments with a few pieces of cob. Much of this material was sent to Dr. H. Cutler, whose analysis is presented on page 63.

Early travelers in the Southeast reported that the Indians had as many as 42 different corn dishes. Hominy, cornmeal mush, corn bread, and a parched cornmeal were the most important. Hominy was made from corn which was first soaked in water, sometimes with ashes. The kernels were then broken into coarse particles in a mortar, hulled, and cooked for hours. The soaked corn was also pounded fine and cooked in water for corn meal mush. Corn bread was prepared from a fine meal which had been sifted through sieves, blended with water, patted into a flat, broad cake, and covered with ashes until baked. Sunflower seeds and other grains were sometimes added. Parched meal stored well and was often used for travel. The grains were first partially cooked and then placed in a kettle lined with a layer of sand. Hot ashes were added and the corn kernels were stirred. Then they were transferred to a mortar and crushed. Parched corn was said to last for 6 months and could be prepared simply by mixing with water (Swanton 1946:354–359).

The people who occupied the Gypsy Joint farmstead may have used these processing techniques to prepare their corn. Parching could account for some of the charred kernels that were recovered. Since the heat of hot coals is difficult to control, some grain is occasionally burned in the parching process.

Marsh Elder

The marsh elder (*Iva annua* L.) is a weedy annual which occurs in alluvial soils along streams, in moist places, and in disturbed habitats. Although only a wild form of marsh elder is known today, a variety designated *Iva annua* var. *macrocarpa* (Blake) Jackson was cultivated in the eastern woodlands until the historic period. Over a 2000-year time span the achenes of this plant progressively increased in size until they reached a Mississippian maximum of 7–7.5 mm in length, which is more than twice the size of the present wild *Iva* achene (Yarnell 1972). The 189 marsh elder achenes recovered at Gypsy Joint belong to the cultivated variety. Those achenes that could be measured ranged between 4.4–7.1 mm in length with a mean of 5.7 mm. Before charring they were probably 10% larger (Yarnell 1972) or about 4.8–7.8 mm long with a mean of 6.3 mm.

The Indians of the Southeast had apparently abandoned marsh elder seeds before any Europeans started observing Indian life since the seeds are never mentioned in any of the early travelers' accounts. As a result, one can only speculate about how the prehistoric inhabitants may have prepared them. Yarnell (1972) suggested that the Indians used them in the same manner as sunflower seeds, as a source of oil, since *Iva* seeds have a high fat content. Marsh elder seeds also may have been added to breads, soups, and stews. The achenes were probably roasted first before any other processing. (The Indians of North America often parched or roasted seeds in order to increase their storage life.)

Sunflower

The sunflower (*Helianthus annuus* var. *macrocarpus* [D.C.] Cockerell) was also cultivated in the east. The one sunflower achene found at Gypsy Joint may be this domesticated variety although its length, approximately 6 mm, falls within the range of the wild form. The Indians of the Southeast put sunflower seeds in breads and broths and used them as a source of oil (Swanton 1946:260).

Knotweed

Most members of the genus *Polygonum* (knotweed, smartweed) are small herbaceous annuals that grow in disturbed habitats. In mid- to late summer they bear small brown achenes containing an edible seed. Approximately 12,000 knotweed achenes weighing about 20 gm were recovered from the Gypsy Joint site, some of which may have found their way to the site by accident. Knotweed plants almost certainly invaded the gardens, and they probably grew in disturbed areas around the farmstead. The wind could have carried seeds from these plants into the farmstead firehearths, and the inhabitants may have inadvertently collected from these plants when they harvested their crops. However, it seems unlikely that all of the seeds are incidentals. It is hard to imagine that 12,000 seeds were carried to the site, charred, and deposited all by chance alone. The prehistoric inhabitants probably harvested and possibly stored some knotweed seeds. Although knotweed seeds are not represented at many archaeological sites, there is some evidence that Woodland peoples ate them. Yarnell (1974) found knotweed seeds in the intestinal contents of a Salts Cave mummy and in flotation samples from the same cave. The people of the Gypsy Joint farmstead may have prepared knotweed seeds in the same way that North American Indians cooked many wild grains. They may have crushed them in a mortar and added the meal to breads and stews.

Chenopod

This is a familiar garden weed that quickly invades disturbed ground. It is sometimes a welcome intruder because the young shoots are a tasty potherb. The minute black seeds are also edible, and many of North America's indigenous peoples harvested them.

Nearly 8000 chenopod (*Chenopodium* sp.) seeds, weighing about 5.5 gm, were found in the Gypsy Joint flotation samples. While some of these seeds are probably incidental, it is likely that the Gypsy Joint people exploited this potential food source. Indians harvested chenopod seeds very efficiently by pulling up the entire plant and placing it in a sack. After the plant dried,the seeds fell to the bottom of the sack. These were then parched for storage and later crushed in a mortar. The meal was added to breads or cooked in a porridge.

Wild Bean

Like chenopod and knotweed, the wild bean (*Strophostyles helvola* [L.] El.) specimens found at the Gypsy Joint site may be incidental. As an annual that grows on moist alluvial soils, fallow fields, and disturbed ground, the wild bean was probably found near the site and in the gardens. When the plants dispersed their seeds in the summer, the small beans may have been gathered inadvertently with other foods. The 25 cotyledons and 6 complete beans that were recovered do not constitute a large number and could perhaps be accounted for by chance. However, it is unlikely that chance alone was responsible for even these few. Beans preserve poorly and very few common beans are found even at sites where they were raised.

Although the wild beans are small, averaging only one-quarter the size of the common bean, they could have supplemented the Gypsy Joint diet. The plants are abundant, and the bean is said to have a "nutritive and beanlike quality [Steyermark 1963:951]." However, *Strophostyles* beans, like other wild legumes, do not imbibe water readily. The people of Gypsy Joint may have avoided this problem by roasting the beans instead. In Oaxaca, Mexico, for example, the women roast common beans, grind them, and cook the flour as a gruel (Kaplan 1956). The charred beans found at Gypsy Joint may have burned while they were being roasted for a similar dish.

Fruit

The grape (*Vitis* sp.), crab apple (*Pyrus* sp.), and plum or cherry (*Prunus* sp.) were the only forest fruits positively identified among the Gypsy Joint plant remains. The six grape seeds found may belong to one or all of the several species of wild grape vine common in glades, woods, along streams, and in bottom lands of southeast Missouri. Historic Indians collected wild grapes (Swanton 1946:373) and the Gypsy Joint people probably snacked on them and may have dried them for the winter.

Two species of crab apple grow in southeast Missouri and produce small sour apples that are good in jellies and marmalades (Steyermark 1963:799). Mississippian peoples may have dried crab apples and used them in soups, stews, and breads. The crab apple remains found at the site include several seeds and two pieces of charred dried fruit.

The people of Gypsy Joint probably enjoyed the fruits of the wild plum and cherry trees (*Prunus* spp.) which grow along streams and open woods in this area. The flotation samples contained the fragments of one *Prunus* endocarp, the hard covering surrounding the stone.

Incidental Plants

The six seeds of the white morning glory (*Ipomoea lacunosa* L.) found among the Gypsy Joint plant remains were probably deposited by natural forces. The seed has not had any economic uses in North America, to my knowledge. The morning glory vine, a common field weed, probably grew in the gardens and the seeds could have been carried to the farmstead by chance. Any seeds which happened to find their way into a fire and become charred would have been nearly indestructible because the seed is extremely hard.

Discussion

Hickory nuts far outweigh all other plant material and would appear to have constituted a major part of the diet of the Powers Phase inhabitants of the Gypsy Joint site. The other plants, represented by small quantities of remains, would appear to have played a minor role in the diet. However, the relative importance of each of the plant taxa cannot be judged on the basis of quantity. All factors which influence preservation must be considered because archaeological plant remains are neither a large nor representative sample of the diet. At an open site in a temperate environment very little plant material is ever preserved. In order to evade microbial action, the material must become charred, a process that requires special circumstances and rarely happens. The specimen must first find its way into a fire and ignite. Then it must be withdrawn from the flames quickly before it turns to ash, or it must be buried so deep in the coals that it cannot find enough oxygen for complete combustion. Following charring, the specimen must be protected from the elements and disturbance in order to remain intact for succeeding centuries. Finally, it must survive the insults of the excavator's shovel and the flotation tub. Very few materials endure to the end of this process. Clearly, hard dry items such as seeds and nuts are favored, whereas soft, fleshy foods are not likely to be preserved at all. Likewise, foods having an inedible pit, seed, or pericarp are more likely to leave an archaeological record than foods that are completely consumed.

Of all the plant foods that were eaten at the Gypsy Joint site, hickory nuts would have left the most visible archaeological record. Every nut left behind a thick, dense shell that had to be discarded. Any shells tossed into a fire had a good chance of being charred, because the shell burns slowly. Once carbonized, a large proportion of the dense hickory nutshells probably survived burial, excavation, and flotation. By contrast, none of the other plant foods leave behind as much refuse as a hickory nut except the black walnut. Most of them, in fact, are recovered only because a seed or fruit that was intended for a meal was spilled into a fire or accidentally burned. Moreover, many of these seeds, upon charring, became very fragile and probably disintegrated.

Clearly the archaeological plant remains are a biased record of the Gypsy Joint economy. However, they do offer insights into the diet, and the farming and collecting activities of these peoples when they are considered in the light of other information such as plant ecology and ethnohistorical accounts. All of the ethnographic accounts of the historic Indians of the Southeast would suggest that corn was the mainstay of the Gypsy Joint diet, a conclusion which is supported by other data. Corn kernels occurred in more features than any other plant material, except hickory nutshells, and were absent from only two pits, both of which contained almost no plants. Corn also outweighed the other plant foods, including nut kernels, in all features except the Pit 5 complex.

It is unlikely that corn would have been so abundant or widely distributed unless it were a major food. At times, however, corn was probably in short supply. If the ears were small, as Cutler noted they might be, this would suggest that crop yields were low. Droughts could have caused such a reduction in the crop and may have been an occasional threat to Gypsy Joint. Alternatively, if the specimens Cutler examined are characteristic of all the Gypsy Joint corn crops, it could indicate that the soils were poor and the yields were consistently low. Undernourished crops and impoverished soils may have been common in the marginal areas of the Middle Mississippi culture area. In general, the soils in these regions are neither as fertile as the alluvial river deposits nor are they renewed through flooding. In the vicinity of Gypsy Joint, well-drained land of any quality may have been scarce. As a result, the soils may have been even poorer because fallow periods were short.

The other cultigens, marsh elder and possibly the sunflower, were less abundant than corn in the flotation samples and probably less important as well. Although there are no seed-production data for these two plants during the Mississippian period, they probably yielded much less food per unit area than corn since their seeds are so much smaller than a corn kernel. Furthermore, sunflower and marsh elder seeds are not as desirable as corn because the achenes must be threshed to remove the inedible pericarp.

While marsh elder and sunflower seeds probably did not supply a large share of calories, they may have been important for other reasons. They could have provided a hedge against crop failure. Since neither plant is subject to all of the same environmental vagaries that affect corn, they might produce a crop when corn fails. During the years when stored provisions did not last through the summer, marsh elder and sunflower may have been an insurance policy against starvation since they mature before corn. In addition, the oily seeds would have varied a monotonous diet.

No traces were found of two other important North American cultigens, squash (*Cucurbita* sp.) and bean (*Phaseolus vulgaris* L.). Since these plants do not preserve well, their absence is not particularly surprising and does not rule out the possibility that the people of Gypsy Joint raised them.

Hickory nuts were probably one of the most important wild plant foods. Shell fragments were found in all pits except 4 and 9, and were scattered throughout both structures. Hickory trees are abundant in southeast Missouri and their nuts are an excellent food. They are easy to harvest and store, have a good flavor, and are a rich source of oil and concentrated calories.

Acorns were probably important as well, although only 5 gm of acorn shell were recovered. Oak trees are numerous in the forests of southeast Missouri, and they often bear a large crop of acorns which would have been easy to gather and process. Among the plant remains from Gypsy Joint, acorns are almost certainly underrepresented since the carbonized nutshell is very fragile. Indeed, the kernels were almost as numerous as the shell fragments. Although it is not possible to determine the relative importance of acorns and hickories from the plant remains, the acorn probably ranked second since it is inferior to the hickory nut in a number of respects. Acorns do not taste as good as hickories, they do not contain as much oil, and they do not store as well because they are sometimes infested with weevil larvae (Olson 1974:698).

The black walnut was almost certainly less important than the acorn or hickory, as suggested by the small quantity of shell fragments found at the Gypsy Joint site. Although the nut has an excellent flavor and contains much oil, the black walnut tree is greatly outnumbered by oaks and hickories in Missouri forests (Essex and Spencer 1974). Other nut-bearing trees, including the pecan (*Carya illinoensis* [Wang.] K. Koch), hazel (*Corylus americana* Walt.), and butternut (*Juglans cinerea* L.), were scattered through the forests of this area too and may have occasionally provided nuts for the Gypsy Joint population.

Of all the wild plants, nuts as a group were certainly the most important food. They are more abundant than any wild grains or fruits, are easier to harvest, and contain more calories and protein per gram of food. However, nut trees have one major drawback: They do not produce a consistent crop every year. The shellbark hickory, for example, has a large crop only every 2 to 3 years, and the mockernut only every 3 to 4 years (Bonner and Maisenhelder 1974:271). The oaks exhibit similar intervals between good crops (Olson 1974:699). As a result the nut crop is highly variable from year to year. While the people of Gypsy Joint probably ate large quantities of nuts some years, they could not have depended on nuts for a consistent supply of food. They probably compensated for these irregular nut harvests and for poor crops with wild beans, knotweed seeds, and chenopod. Wild grains bear more reliably than nuts and are less sensitive to the floods and droughts that threaten cultivated crops. They require no labor input until the harvest and can be stored afterward. After spring flooding or dry weather, knotweed, chenopod, and wild beans may have been the only plants that came up in the gardens. However, these wild plants were probably no more than a supplement in poor years. The small seeds are more difficult to gather than corn or nuts and they yield much less food per man-hour of effort. Alternatively, the Gypsy Joint people may have collected these plants every year to supplement a consistently poor harvest. The seeds would have been ripe long before corn or nuts and would have offered nourishment after the stored provisions were exhausted. By permitting these weeds to grow in their gardens, the people would have inadvertently improved the soil at the same time because the bacteria in the enlarged root nodules of the wild bean fix nitrogen (Steyermark 1963:951).

The archaeological evidence does not indicate how frequently these wild plants were used. Since the seeds occur throughout the site, the inhabitants may have eaten them regularly. However, the Gypsy Joint site may have been occupied only during poor periods when the larger communities could not support their populations. Alternatively, the people of Gypsy Joint may have inhabited the site continuously through times of abundance and scarcity and reserved the wild grains for lean years. Throughout the site, corn consistently predominates over the other grains except in the Pit 5 complex. Here the concentration of knotweed seeds outweighs corn and may reflect a period when corn was scarce and the people of Gypsy Joint relied more on wild grains. In addition to the grains, the people of Gypsy Joint may have supplemented their diet with other foods that left no archaeological record, such as tubers, buds, and young shoots.

The forest fruits, the crab apple, plum or cherry, and grape, supplemented the Gypsy Joint diet with vitamins and trace elements. Since they are neither very abundant nor rich in calories, they could not have supplied a large portion of the population's energy needs. A variety of other fruits growing in southeast Missouri may have likewise enhanced the diet: persimmons, blackberries, strawberries, raspberries, serviceberries, mulberries, and haws.

While the Gypsy Joint plant remains offer some insight into subsistence, this outline of the plant collecting and farming activities of a marginal Middle Mississippi community is largely conjecture and cannot be refined until further research is conducted. This work must include field studies on the wild grains and nuts, experimental studies on flint corn, detailed environmental reconstructions, and analyses of plant remains from other Middle Mississippi sites.

Acknowledgments

I wish to thank Harold Furchgott for his help in sorting flotation samples. I am especially grateful to Dr. Lawrence Kaplan of the University of Massachusetts, Boston, for generously permitting me to use his laboratory and reference collections and for helping me to identify some of these materials.

5

Spatial Patterning of Cultural Materials

INTRODUCTION

Chapter 3 presented a description of both the features uncovered at the Gypsy Joint site and the material remains recovered from those features. The present chapter will carry this description a step further, concerning itself with describing the spatial distribution of material remains at the site.

Consideration of this spatial distribution will involve, first, defining overall patterns of distribution of cultural materials at Gypsy Joint. Once all of the Powers Phase features have been compared in terms of the quantity and range of cultural materials recovered from each, the internal distribution of cultural materials within the two structures and the three activity areas associated with pits will be analyzed.

Two separate data sets exist for each of these five features. During the excavation of each feature, a certain number of items were observed and assigned a field specimen number. The exact location of each field specimen was recorded, and these items comprise a point data set for each feature. A second data set is composed of the many smaller items that were not observed during excavation and were only later recovered as the fill dirt from each 5-foot-square grid unit was water screened. Since the location of items recovered in this way is known only in terms of a specific grid unit, rather than in terms of exact point location, such a set is usually termed a grid unit data set. The distinction between point data sets and grid unit data sets is an important one, since analysis of the spatial patterning of point data sets requires different statistical techniques than those applicable to grid unit data sets.

It was originally hoped that appropriate statistical techniques could be applied to both the point data set and the grid unit data set for each of the five features mentioned above. The results of spatial analysis of these two different data sets for each feature could then be cross-checked with each other. Once the point data and grid unit data sets for each of the five features had been compiled, however, a number of limitations of the data became apparent.

It was decided that any detailed spatial analysis of the Structure 2 point data and grid unit data sets would be inappropriate since there were clear indications that much of the cultural debris recovered from the house basin may have been spatially disturbed. A second recognized limitation of the data sets for each of the features involved plant and animal remains. The sample of skeletal elements of animal species recovered from within any single feature was so small (the Pit 5 activity area, with 10 skeletal elements recovered, had the highest bone count) that the results of any detailed statistical analysis would have little statistical validity, and would in any case simply quantify the obvious. The pattern of distribution of the small number of animal bones within features was clearly discernible through visual inspection. Plant remains also presented a problem in terms of spatial analysis. Because of their small size, very few ethnobotanical specimens were recorded as field specimens. As a result, point data sets for each of the features contain few if any plant remains. By ruling out ecofacts from any spatial analysis of point data sets from Structure 1 and the activity areas surrounding Pit 3, Pits 5a and 5b, and Pit 10, one is left with lithic and ceramic items to work with.

The problem of small sample size also applied to both lithic and ceramic point data from all of these four features with the exception of Structure 1. The only way that this problem could be resolved was by combining all lithic categories into a single category—lithics—and combining all ceramic categories into a single category—ceramics.

As a result, nearest neighbor analysis of point data sets from within the activity areas of Pit 3, Pits 5a and 5b, and Pit 10 will be limited, first, to determining if general lithic and ceramic categories of items tend to be randomly distributed, uniformly distributed, or clustered, and, second, if lithics and ceramics tend to covary in their pattern of distribution within each of these activity areas. This exercise in spatial analysis will also be found to produce little more insight into the patterning of cultural debris than could be obtained through visual inspection.

Structure 1, then, is the single feature at the Gypsy Joint site that yielded a point data set large enough to warrant nearest neighbor analysis of various categories of lithic and ceramic materials. Even with Structure 1, however, the reader will see that a certain amount of combining of categories of both lithic and ceramic items was necessary.

A number of limitations were also found to exist with the grid unit data sets from the three activity areas. The most obvious problems with attempting spatial analysis of the grid unit data sets involve the small number of grid units or cells per activity area, as well as low item counts for many of the peripheral grid units. The Pit 3 activity area, for example, covers 117.6 square feet (including Pit 3), and extends into at least 12 grid units. Only 2 of the 12 grid units, however, are totally encompassed by the boundary of the Pit 3 activity area. The other 10 grid units are only partially within the activity area. As a result, only 4 of the grid units contain more than 20 items in the grid unit data set. This partial encompassing of grid units within the activity area and the low item counts for peripheral grid units make any detailed spatial analysis rather unnecessary. These problems also apply to the grid unit data sets of the other two activity areas, and even to some extent to the Structure 1 grid unit data set. As a result, spatial analysis of grid unit data sets will be rather conservative.

Some readers, especially those well versed in spatial analysis of archaeological materials, may be disappointed with the hesitancy with which statistical techniques are being employed in spatial analysis of the Gypsy Joint site data sets. This hesitancy reflects a growing recognition that archaeologists should be both more selective and more realistic in their application of complex statistical tests to archaeological data sets. The desire to demonstrate statistical competency should be balanced by both a realistic view of the shortcomings of many archaeological data sets and a willingness to screen out those data sets that do not really need to be subjected to any detailed analysis.

OVERALL DISTRIBUTION PATTERNS OF CULTURAL MATERIALS

Powers Phase cultural materials at the Gypsy Joint site were neither randomly or uniformly distributed, but rather were distributed in a clearly clustered pattern. This trend toward aggregation or clustering of cultural materials is clearly indicated in Figure 11. To quantify this nonrandom distribution pattern more clearly, density values (grams of cultural debris per square foot) were determined for all Powers Phase features, as well as for the excavated areas outside of features.

The average density value for the 794 square feet of excavated area falling within the boundaries of the 14 Powers Phase features was found to be 29 gm of cultural material per square foot (Table 22, bottom of Columns 1, 2). This is over 12 times greater than the average density value of 2.2 grams per square foot determined for the 7109 square feet of excavated area falling outside of the boundaries of features. This is not to say, however, that every square foot of area within features has a higher density of cultural materials than any single square foot of area outside of

TABLE 22

The Degree to Which Powers Phase Features Show Variation from Average Density Values for Different Categories of Cultural Materials[a]

Features	Area (square feet)	Total items	Fauna	Plant remains	Powers Phase pottery	Chert and quartzite	Sandstone
	1	2	3	4	5	6	7
High-density features							
Pit 5b	5.8	+221.5	+3.9	+32.5	+13.6	+150.5	+21.2
Pit 5a	4.3	+119.7	+1.6	+70.9	-1.0	+49.6	-4.7
Pit 3	17.6	+13.6	+2.0	+1.76	+.6	+2.6	+4.9
Average-density features							
Pit 5 activity area	66.6	+11.8	+.8	+10.04	-3.0	4.0	-1.6
Pit 3 activity area	100.0	+3.73	-.2	-1.71	-2.5	+10.0	+2.0
Structure 1	265.9	-1.5	-.3	-1.61	+1.6	-1.7	+1.2
Structure 2	207.2	-5.2	-.2	-1.92	+.4	-5.3	-1.2
Pit 10 activity area	42.6	-7.0	-.1	-1.18	+3.4	-4.8	-4.2
Low-density features							
Pit 10	12.8	-9.5	-.4	-1.57	-3.0	+5.6	+7.1
Pit 8	1.7	-12.5	+3.9	-1.75	+5.7	+63.7	-5.0
Pit 4	10.4	-17.2	-.4	-2.05	-4.5	-6.8	-1.7
Pit 7	3.7	-20.7	-.1	-1.8	-2.4	-11.8	-5.0
Pit 6	14.4	-22.4	-.3	-1.7	-4.4	-10.6	-4.5
Pit 2	40.6	-24.16	+.3	-1.78	-3.3	-13.8	-3.9
Skim surface	7109	-26.8					
Average-density features (grams/square foot)	794	29.0	.37	2.05	5.1	14.6	5.0

[a] Average density values were determined by dividing total weight values for different categories of cultural materials recovered from all fourteen Powers Phase features by the total area covered by Powers Phase features.

120

features. Nor does it mean that the density of materials outside of features is so low that it is not worth discussing. On the contrary, the pattern of distribution and variation in the density of cultural materials in the areas between Powers Phase features will be considered throughout this chapter.

Furthermore, although the average density value within the feature boundaries is much higher than the density value for the nonfeature areas excavated, there is a great amount of variation from this average value within different features at the site. As a result, the 14 Powers Phase features can be separated into three categories based on their density of cultural materials.

High density features: The first category consists of Pit 3, and Pits 5a and 5b. These three features have the highest density of cultural materials of any of the Powers Phase features at the site (Table 22, Column 2). All three are pits, and all three are associated with activity areas.

Average density features: The second category includes Structure 1, Structure 2, and the activity areas surrounding Pit 3, Pits 5a and 5b, and Pit 10. These five features all have density values that are close to the overall average density value of 29 gm of cultural material per square foot. These are also the five largest Powers Phase features at the site (Table 22, Columns 1, 2).

Low density features: The third category includes Pits 10, 8, 4, 7, 6, and 2. All of these features have density values of cultural materials that are far below the overall average density value (Table 22, Column 2).

The features within each of these three categories are not only similar in terms of density of total cultural materials, but also share certain formal and locational attributes. All of the features in the high-density group are pits, all are from .7 to .9 feet in depth, all are associated with activity areas, and all are located to the northeast of Structure 1. There is, however, wide variation in the density of cultural materials values within this group, with Pit 3 having a much lower density value than the Pits 5a and 5b. As already mentioned, the two structures and three activity areas in the average-density category are also the five largest features at the Gypsy Joint site. The six features in the low-density category are all pits, and with the exception of Pit 10, all are located to the south or west of Structure 1. It is also interesting to note that Pit 10 is also at the upper end of the range of density values for low density features. So in both the high- and low-density groups, the two features that are marginal within the group—that are closest to the average-density feature—are single pits associated with activity areas.

A number of other similarities and differences between features placed in these density categories can be observed by considering the distribution and relative density of different categories of cultural debris, rather than by just looking at the density of all cultural materials recovered from each feature.

Distribution of Faunal Remains

The average density value of animal skeletal remains for all Powers Phase features was determined to be .37 gm per square foot. No skeletal remains were recovered from the excavated area outside of features. Because white-tailed deer skeletal elements account for 92.6% (by weight) of the total faunal assemblage, the faunal density values for features given in Table 22, Column 3 do not indicate the distribution of smaller animal species at the Gypsy Joint site. Of the 36 skeletal elements representing seven species of small animals recovered from Powers Phase features, 28 were recovered from three pits in the low density feature category. The 12 bone fragments recovered from Pit 6 represented fox squirrel, box turtle, and unidentified small mammals. Similarly, Pit 7 yielded 12 fragments from fox squirrel, box turtle, and unidentified small mammals. Pit 8 yielded 2 raccoon and 2 cottontail rabbit skeletal elements. Many of these 28 skeletal elements had been burned. The remaining eight small animal skeletal elements were recovered from Structure 1 and Structure 2. Structure 1 yielded a single beaver incisor and two fox squirrel skeletal elements, while Structure 2 yielded a turkey tibiotarsus fragment, a freshwater clam fragment, and three box turtle fragments. No small animal skeletal elements were recovered from the three activity areas at the site or from the pits associated with these activity areas.

The pattern of distribution of white-tailed deer skeletal elements is quite different from the pattern just described for small animal remains. Pit 3 and its activity area yielded 11 deer skeletal elements representing a left front leg and shoulder, a lower left rear leg, and a few skull and antler fragments. Pits 5a, 5b, and the associated activity area yielded 16 skeletal elements representing right and left rear legs, a left front leg, and a few skull and vertebral fragments. A single left scapula fragment and a few long-bone fragments were recovered from the Pit 10 activity area, and Pit 2 yielded a left front leg element and a deer mandible.

Structure 1 and Structure 2 yielded a total of 14 deer skeletal elements, but these elements were quite different from those recovered from the pits and activity areas just discussed. Except for two long-bone fragments, all of the deer skeletal elements recovered from the two structures were either mandibles (four), antler fragments (three), or astragalus–calcanium fragments (five). This is a similar pattern to that observed for structures at other Powers Phase sites. The important common characteristic of mandibles, antler, and astragali is that none of these skeletal elements is associated with cuts of meat. Their presence in the structures probably reflects their role as either tools or gaming items, rather than as the material remains of either butchering or cooking activities. Both the astragalus and calcanium are very dense, compact bones that are from low on the rear leg of a deer, below any muscle mass areas. These bones were often found around the edge of house basins at both the Turner and Snodgrass sites, both singly and in groups. They are usually assumed to have been employed as gaming devices—as dice—and are often recovered from Middle Mississippi sites in a modified smooth cube condition. Antlers may have functioned as either pressure flakers or batons, while mandibles may have functioned as either sickles (Brown 1964) or as plant-processing tools.

With the exception of the two structures, small animal bones were not recovered from any of the features that yielded deer skeletal elements. Similarly, except for the two structures, none of the features that yielded small animal bones yielded deer skeletal elements. Only two features (Pit 4 and Pit 10) failed to yield any faunal materials. Once again, Pit 10 appears to fall between categories, yielding neither deer or small animal skeletal elements.

Distribution of Plant Remains

The average density of plant remains within the 14 Powers Phase features was determined to be 2.05 gm per square foot. Only four features had density values above this average. Three of the four features were earlier classified as high-density features (Pit 3, Pit 5a, Pit 5b); the fourth feature is the activity area surrounding Pits 5a and 5b. While there is not any clear differences between the density values for plant remains among the remaining Power Phase features at the Gypsy Joint site, there is a clear variation in the distribution pattern of different plant species across the site.

Hickory nut fragments were recovered from every Powers Phase feature at the site except for Pit 4, a low-density feature, and the only one not to yield any plant remains. Of the hickory nut fragments, 81% (by weight) were recovered from Pits 5a, 5b and the associated activity area, while Structure 1 yielded 7.3%, Pit 3 and its activity area, 6.4%, Pit 10 and its activity area, 2.7%, and Structure 2, 1.62%. The remaining features combined accounted for only 1.6% of the total hickory nut fragments recovered.

Maize kernels and occasionally cupule fragments were recovered in small amounts from all Powers Phase features except for Pit 4 and Pit 8. Of the maize 54% (by weight) was recovered from the maize grain concentration, while the Pit 5 activity area yielded 29.7% of the total amount of maize, and Structure 1 and Structure 2 followed with 4.8% and 3.5%, respectively. Acorn and black walnut shell fragments were recovered in small amounts from eight and seven features, respectively. Knotweed and chenopod seeds were recovered from eight and nine features, respectively, with the vast majority (92% and 93%) coming from Pit 5b and the associated activity area. Over 18,000 seeds of these two genera were recovered from these two features. The Pit 5a–Pit 5b activity area complex also accounted for 97% of the marsh elder seeds recovered from the Gypsy Joint site.

Distribution of Ceramic Materials

The ceramic materials category includes both clay fragments and pottery fragments. Ninety percent (by weight) of the 133 clay fragments, weighing 1276 gm, were recovered from four average-density Powers Phase features: Structure 2 (61%), Pit 5 activity area (17%), Pit 10 activity area (7%), and Structure 1 (5%). Higher-than-average-density values for clay also existed for the three high-density features (Pit 5b, Pit 5a, Pit 3).

The spatial patterning of pottery across the Gypsy Joint site can be analyzed in terms of the number of vessels represented within different features, as well as the total weight and the density values for pottery recovered from each feature. A minimum of 15 ceramic vessels were represented at the Gypsy Joint site, based on large rim sections. Nine of these 15 vessels were large jars (orifice diameter 24 to 28 cm). Structure 1 and Structure 2 each yielded rim sherds representing 3 large jar form vessels, with Pit 3, the Pit 3 activity area, and Pit 5b each yielding sherds representing a single large jar form vessel. Of the 3 medium-sized jars (orifice diameter 18 to 20 cm) represented at the Gypsy Joint site, 2 were recovered from the Pit 10 activity area, and 1 was recovered from Structure 2.

The 3 remaining vessels—a small jar, a large short-necked water bottle, and a bowl—were all recovered from Structure 2. Thirteen of the 15 vessels represented at the Gypsy Joint site were recovered from the five average-density features. These five features also accounted for over 80% (by weight) of the 4.433.4 gm of Powers Phase pottery sherds recovered from the site: Structure 1 (40.3%), Structure 2 (25.6%), Pit 10 activity area (8.1%), Pit 3 activity area (5.9%) and the Pit 5 activity area (3.2%). Only 8.2% (by weight) of the total Powers Phase ceramic assemblage was recovered from outside of Powers Phase features. In terms of the density of Powers Phase pottery, only three of these five average-density features had higher-than-average density values (Table 22, Column 5). Pits 3, 5b, and 8 also had higher-than-average density values for Powers Phase pottery. The only evidence of the presence of ceramic cones at the Gypsy Joint site was recovered from Pit 3 and the associated activity area.

In summary, it is clear that in terms of both the number of vessels represented and the weight and density values of Powers Phase pottery for different features, a significant percentage of the pottery at the Gypsy

Joint was concentrated within three average-density features: Structure 1, Structure 2, and the Pit 10 activity area.

Distribution of Lithic Materials

The spatial distribution of lithic materials across the Gypsy Joint site can best be analyzed by breaking the general lithics category down into three smaller logical categories: *(a)* finished lithic tools; *(b)* items associated with flint knapping; and *(c)* items associated with grinding activities.

A total of only eight scrapers, bifaces, and knives were recovered from within Powers Phase features. The low occurrence of these types of lithic tools may well be an indication that cane and unmodified flakes were employed to perform cutting and scraping tasks, rather than finished tools. Cane cutting and scraping tools, as well as unmodified flakes used for short periods of time, would not be present or recognizable as tools in the archaeological assemblage recovered from the site. The low frequency of finished tools associated with cutting and scraping activities, therefore, does not necessarily indicate that such activities were rarely carried out at the site.

There is a clear correlation in the spatial distribution of knives, bifaces, and scrapers and the distribution of skeletal elements of the white-tailed deer. The single knife fragment recovered from the Gypsy Joint site was located right next to a concentration of deer skeletal elements within the Pit 3 activity area (Figure 24). The three bifaces were recovered from the Pit 5 activity area (directly adjacent to a deer bone concentration), the Pit 3 activity area, and Pit 2. These three areas also yielded almost all of the deer skeletal elements that represented cuts of meat. The single scraper recovered from the northeast edge of Pit 5a was also within 2 feet of the deer bone concentration just mentioned (Figure 27). Of the two scrapers recovered from Structure 1, one was associated with a deer mandible, and the other with a concentration of small animal skeletal elements (Figure 16). The single scraper recovered from the Pit 10 activity area may be a Woodland artifact since it was recovered from the northeast edge of the feature in association with Woodland pottery. A scraper recovered from the grid unit just northwest of Pit 6 is the only finished tool recovered from outside of Powers Phase features at the site.

The category of items associated with flint knapping includes hammerstones, chert and quartzite cores, chert and quartzite *debitage* (flakes and angular fragments), and projectile points discarded during the manufacturing process. Only three hammerstones were recovered from Powers Phase features. Two were recovered from Structure 1, and a third from the edge of Pit 5b. A fourth hammerstone was recovered just outside of the northeast edge of the Structure 1 house basin (Figure 34).

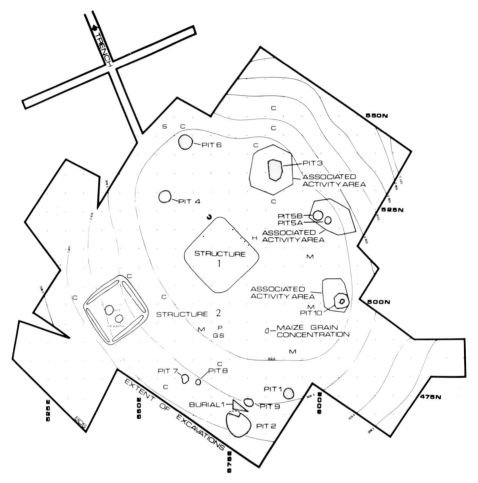

Figure 34. The spatial distribution of lithic artifacts outside of the Powers Phase features at the Gypsy Joint site (C = core; GS = grinding-slab fragment; H = hammerstone; M = mano, P = projectile point; and S = scraper).

In contrast to the small number of hammerstones represented at the Gypsy Joint site, a total of 33 chert and 16 quartzite cores were recovered. Of the 49 cores recovered, 39 were found within the boundaries of Powers Phase features. The Pit 3 activity area yielded 11 cores, Structure 2 yielded 9, Structure 1 yielded 8, and a total of 7 were recovered from Pits 5a, 5b, and their associated activity area. In addition, Pits 2, 4, 6, and 8 each contained a single core. Of the 10 cores recovered from outside of Powers Phase features, 4 were located within 6 feet of the Pit 3 activity area, 3 were located within 5 feet of Structure 2, and the remaining 3 cores were recovered from grid units adjacent to Pits 6, 7, and 8 (Figure 34, Table 23).

The spatial distribution of Powers Phase projectile points across the Gypsy Joint site is very similar to the spatial patterning of cores. Of the 11 projectile points recovered from Powers Phase features, 3 (1 unbroken, 2 rejects) came from Structure 2, 3 (1 broken tip, 2 rejects) were from the Pit 3 activity area, and a total of 4 (2 unbroken, 1 midsection, 1 reject) came from Pit 5a and the associated activity area. A single point (a reject) was recovered from the Pit 10 activity area. The only Powers Phase projectile point located outside of a feature was a rejected point recovered 6 feet south of Structure 1.

TABLE 23

Cultural Materials Recovered from the Excavated Area Outside of Features at the Gypsy Joint Site

Items	Quantity	Weight (gm)	Comments
Lithics			
Chert flakes	104	230.3	9 retouch modification, 1 use modification, 1 heated
Chert cores	7	1,055.9	
Chert angular fragments	106	2,499.0	1 heated
Quartzite flakes	9	32.1	
Quartzite cores	3	483.8	
Quartzite angular fragments	19	1,536.2	
Sandstone angular fragments	60	2,398.9	1 heated
Mississippian projectile points	1	1.5	
Woodland projectile points	7	49.5	
Manos	4	2,976.4	
Grinding slabs	2	1,000.7	
Hammerstones	1	449.5	
Cobbles	5	2,116.3	
Pebbles	1	2.9	
	329	14,833.0	
Ceramics			
Powers Phase body sherds	38	353.5	
Barnes sherds	28	181.5	
Clay fragments	7	28.1	
	74	576.3	
Metallic			
Hematite	1	13.9	
	1	13.9	
Total contents	403	15,409.4	

A consideration of the spatial distribution of chert and quartzite debitage further underscores the apparent pattern of distribution of items associated with flint knapping. Over 90% of the 11,613 gm of chert and quartzite debitage recovered from the Powers Phase features came from the two structures and the Pit 3 and Pit 5 features. Structure 1 yielded the greatest amount of debitage (29.5%), followed by Pit 3 and its activity area (23.8%), Pits 5a, 5b, and the surrounding activity area (21.1%), and Structure 2 (16.7%). The only other Powers Phase features to yield any sizable amount of chert debitage were Pit 10 (2.2%) and its associated activity area (3.6%).

It is clear, from the above, that a significant percentage of the items associated with flint knapping were concentrated with Structure 1, Structure 2, the Pit 3 activity area, and Pits 5a, 5b, along with their surrounding activity area.

The final category, lithic items associated with grinding, includes manos, grinding-slab fragments, and sandstone angular fragments. A single grinding-slab fragment was recovered from Structure 1, and a mano was recovered from the Pit 5 activity area. These were the only two grinding implements found within Powers Phase features. Four mano fragments were, however, found in the area to the east and south of Structure 1 (Figure 34). Two grinding-slab fragments were also recovered from the excavated area outside of the Powers Phase features (Figure 34).

Sandstone angular fragments have a distribution across the Gypsy Joint site that is very similar to the pattern observed for chert and quartzite debitage. Over 90% of the 3988 gm of sandstone fragments recovered from Powers Phase features at the Gypsy Joint site came from the two structures and the Pit 3 and Pit 5 features. Structure 1 yielded the greatest amount of sandstone (41.5%), followed by Pit 3 and its activity area (21.8%), Structure 2 (19.7%), and Pit 5b and its associated activity area (9.5%). The only other Powers Phase feature to yield any sizable amount of sandstone was Pit 10 (3.9%). This suggests that most of the sandstone angular fragments may be associated with flint knapping (platform preperation?) in addition to grinding activities.

SPATIAL PATTERNING OF CULTURAL MATERIALS WITHIN POWERS PHASE FEATURES

Description of the Statistical Methods Employed

Nearest neighbor analysis was employed to analyze the distributional patterning of point data sets from Structure 1 and the three activity areas at the Gypsy Joint site. First developed by plant ecologists in the early

1950s (Clark and Evans 1954) to detect randomness or nonrandomness of the distribution of individual plants over an area, the nearest neighbor method has since been applied to archaeological point data sets (Whallon 1974).

Although the nearest neighbor method is fairly straightforward and uncomplicated in application, the results obtained can be significantly affected by a number of variables. Probably the single most important variable is the initial step of delineating the boundary of each area to be considered. The same point data set, for example, could be found to be randomly distributed when employing one boundary, and nonrandomly distributed if a larger area were employed. Whallon (1974) discusses this potential source of bias, and emphasizes the importance of accurately defining boundaries that encompass total activity areas without also including space outside of activity areas: "If the boundaries of the excavation are made to correspond well to the limits of the site, the existence of the site itself as a spatial phenomenon will play no role in the nearest neighbor statistic; only clusters of items within the site boundaries will be detected [p. 22]." Although this potential problem of boundary definition does not apply to Structure 1 at the Gypsy Joint site, where the edge of the house basin provides a clear boundary for the area to be considered, it does apply to the three activity areas. The boundaries shown in Figures 24, 27, and 31 are the boundaries that were employed in nearest neighbor analysis of point data sets from the Pit 3, Pit 5, and Pit 10 activity areas. Although these boundaries were drawn so as to encompass as much of each point data set as possible without including space outside of activity areas, they would no doubt be drawn somewhat differently by different individuals, and are therefore somewhat arbitrary. It is important to note in this regard, however, that the rather abrupt decrease in items as one moves outside of the boundary of each activity area is a real rather than a cosmetic phenomenon. All of the grid units that activity areas extended into were fully excavated. The blank space outside of activity areas reflects a lack of items observed during excavation, rather than areas that were not excavated or areas for which items were not plotted in an effort to make activity areas stand out. Once the boundaries of Structure 1 and the three activity areas were defined, the size of the area encompassed by these boundaries was determined with the help of a polar planimeter.

With these initial steps completed, the next step in the employment of the nearest neighbor method involves determining what the mean distance would be between each item in the point data set and its nearest neighbor if those items were randomly distributed within the area being considered. This distance value is termed *the expected mean nearest neighbor distance*. The actual mean distance between each item and its nearest neighbor is then determined; this distance is *the observed mean nearest neighbor distance.* The degree to which items in a point data set are randomly or nonrandomly distributed can then be determined by comparing the expected and the observed mean nearest neighbor distance. This comparison is expressed as *the ratio of the observed to the expected mean nearest neighbor distance* [R]. A ratio value close to 1 would indicate that the observed mean nearest neighbor distance is similar to the theoretically expected mean nearest neighbor distance for a random distribution and that the items are probably randomly distributed. Ratio values smaller than 1 indicate that items are closer together than expected for a random distribution (aggregation), whereas ratio values greater than 1 indicate that items are farther apart than expected for a random distribution (tending toward a uniform distribution).

Finally, the statistical level of significance of any ratio value that is either above or below 1 can be measured by employing *the standard normal deviate* statistic whose employment assumes that the statistical distribution of nearest neighbor distances approximates a normal curve. A standard deviation value of 1 would indicate that there is a 33% probability that the observed mean nearest neighbor distance could be obtained from a randomly distributed point data set. Similarly, a standard deviation value of 1.96 would indicate that there is only a 5% probability of the observed mean nearest neighbor distance being obtained from a randomly distributed point data set.

Although the statistical method of nearest neighbor analysis is a fairly straightforward way of determining the randomness or nonrandomness of the spatial distribution of a point data set, the number of distance measurements and mathematical computations involved in the analysis of any sizable point data set demands the use of computer facilities. The author was fortunate enough to have just finished coding the point data sets for Powers Phase features at the Gypsy Joint site at the same time that Dr. Donald Graybill of the Department of Anthropology, University of Georgia, was putting the finishing touches on a new nearest neighbor computer program (MCNNA—Multiple Class Nearest Neighbor Analysis). Dr. Graybill was in need of additional point data sets to test his program, and the author had a number of point data sets to analyze, but lacked the necessary competency in computer programing. Dr. Graybill was generous with his time, and oversaw the computer analysis of the point data sets from the Gypsy Joint site, and also took time to explain a number of nuances of interpretation in the results of the analysis.

One final point about our utilization of the nearest neighbor method: While this statistical method tells one if items in a point data set are spatially clustered, it will not define or locate any such spatial clusters. Although Whallon (1974:23) has tentatively suggested a procedure for defining spatial clusters of items that is based on the results of nearest neighbor analysis, it will not be employed to identify spatial clusters within Powers Phase features for the simple reason that such concentrations of materials, when they occur, can be easily identified through visual inspection of artifact distributions.

Structure 1

The point data set recovered from Structure 1 consisted of 62 lithic and 128 ceramic items. Nearest neighbor analysis of the spatial distribution of all 62 lithic items showed them to be randomly distributed within the structure.

Category of items: All chert and quartzite lithics
Number of items: 62
Expected mean *nn:* 10.33
Observed mean *nn:* 8.90
Ratio *o/e:* .86
Standard deviate: −1.40
Distributional pattern: Random. A tendency toward aggregation, but not significant at the .1 level.

A consideration of the spatial distribution of more specific lithic categories, however, provides quite different results.

Category of items: Chert and quartzite flakes
Number of items: 21
Expected mean *nn:* 17.76
Observed mean *nn:* 19.77
Ratio *o/e:* 1.11
Standard deviate: 1.90
Distributional pattern: Random. A strong tendency toward uniform distribution, but not significant at the .05 level.

Category of items: Chert and quartzite angular fragments
Number of items: 34
Expected mean *nn:* 13.96
Observed mean *nn:* 8.18
Ratio *o/e:* .59
Standard deviate: 3.72
Distributional pattern: Clustered. Significant beyond the .001 level. Visual inspection of Figure 16 indicates that angular fragments form a loose cluster along the southwest edge of the house basin and in the south–central area of the structure.

Category of items: Chert and quartzite cores
Number of items: 7
Expected mean *nn:* 30.76

Observed mean *nn:* 25.95

Ratio *o/e:* .84

Standard deviate: .07

Distributional pattern: Random. Not significant at the .1 level. Visual
   inspection of Figure 16, however, necessitates a rejection of the random distribution of cores indicated by nearest neighbor analysis.
   Three cores are closely associated, along with a hammerstone, in the
   western corner of the structure, and three additional cores are within
   5 feet of the cluster of three. The small sample size and isolated
   occurrence of a single core in the eastern corner of the structure
   combine to make the spatial aggregation of cores statistically
   invisible.

In summary, chert and quartzite flakes are randomly distributed within
Structure 1, angular fragments are spatially clustered over a large area of
the southern half of the structure, and chert and quartzite cores are clustered along the southwest edge of the house basin.

Nearest neighbor analysis of the spatial distribution of all 128 ceramic
items showed them to be nonrandomly distributed within the structure.

Category of items: All Powers Phase body sherds and rim sherds

Number of items: 128

Expected mean *nn:* 7.20

Observed mean *nn:* 4.65

Ratio *o/e:* .64

Standard deviate: −3.52

Distributional pattern: Clustered. Significant beyond the .001 level.
   Visual inspection of Figure 16 indicates a spatial cluster of pottery in
   the south central area of the structure, another along the northeast
   edge of the house basin, and a third small cluster just south of the
   concentration of small-animal skeletal elements.

A consideration of the spatial distribution of more specific ceramic
categories supports the strong tendency toward aggregation that is indicated above.

Category of items: Powers Phase body sherds

Number of items: 113

Expected mean *nn:* 7.65

Observed mean *nn:* 4.84

Ratio *o/e:* .63

Standard deviate: −3.24

Distributional pattern: Clustered. Significant at the .005 level.

Category of items: Powers Phase rim sherds

Number of items: 15

Expected mean *nn:* 21.02
Observed mean *nn:* 11.55
Ratio *o/e:* .55
Standard deviate: −1.77
Distributional pattern: Random. Strong tendency toward aggregation. Significant at the .10 to .05 level. Although the rim sherds from Structure 1 are not clustered according to the nearest neighbor analysis, visual inspection of Figure 16 suggests that the small sample size and isolated occurrence of a few rims combine to make the spatial clusters of rims statistically invisible. Rim sherds within Structure 1 appear to be clustered in the south central area of the structure, and along the northeast edge of the house basin.

In summary, analysis of all three point data sets for Powers Phase pottery from Structure 1 (rim and body sherds, body sherds, rim sherds) indicates nonrandom distribution of pottery, and visual inspection of Figure 16 suggests two and possibly three areas of aggregation.

Analysis of the grid unit data set recovered from Structure 1 not only provides confirmation of the results obtained from nearest neighbor analysis of point data sets, but also allows a more detailed discussion of patterns of distribution of cultural debris within the house basin. It should be pointed out that the grid unit data set for Structure 1 includes the 190 items that made up the point data set recovered from the structure. Almost all of the cultural material recovered from Structure 1 came from the nine central grid units of the structure. The four corners of this block of nine grid units are indicated in Figure 16 by the four sets of grid unit coordinates.

The distribution of chert and quartzite debitage within these nine central grid units corresponds fairly well with the spatial patterns observed in analysis of the lithic point data set. Starting with the upper left grid unit (515N, 565E) and reading left to right, these nine grid units yielded the following chert and quartzite flake counts: 19, 10, 14, 10, 7, 7, 9, 23, 1. This random distribution of flakes corresponds to the random distribution of flakes revealed by the nearest neighbor method. A similar item count of angular fragments recovered from the nine squares also shows a random pattern of distribution: 6, 17, 10, 15, 17, 15, 7, 29, 0, a pattern in contrast to the loose aggregation of angular fragments observed during analysis of the point data set. This contrast can be explained in terms of the larger sample of angular fragments present in the grid unit data set (116 versus 34 in the point data set).

Analysis of chert and quartzite cores in the grid unit data set does not provide any greater insight than was gained from consideration of the point data set, since of the eight cores recovered from Structure 1, seven were included in the point data set.

The distribution pattern of chert and quartzite items within Structure 1 represents a paradox of sorts: On the one hand, there is an obvious aggregation of cores, along with a hammerstone, in the western corner of the structure; on the other hand, chert and quartzite debitage is randomly distributed within the structure rather than being aggregated around the cores, as might be expected. Most of the cores recovered from Structure 1, however, showed little evidence of having been utilized, with only a few flakes having been struck from them. Most of the flakes and angular fragments scattered throughout Structure 1 did not originate from any of these cores.

Although sandstone angular fragments also appear to be randomly distributed in terms of item count within the nine central grid units of Structure 1 (0, 2, 0, 2, 4, 4, 0, 2, 0), there is an interesting aggregation of the larger sandstone angular fragments in three of the grid units. The central grid unit (510N, 570E) along with the adjacent grid units to the north (515N, 570E) and east (510N, 575E), which appear to be largely devoid of cultural debris in Figure 16, yielded a total of 10 large angular fragments that represent over 99% of the total mass of sandstone recovered from Structure 1.

The single grinding-slab fragment (571 gm) recovered from Structure 1 (Plate IVC) was also located in the central grid unit.

A consideration of the spatial distribution of hickory nutshell fragments, which account for 97% of the plant remains recovered from Structure 1, shows them to be clearly concentrated in these same three grid units. Each of these grid units yielded twice the weight of hickory nutshell of any of the other grid units in the structure, and together they accounted for 73% of the total amount of hickory nutshell recovered from the house basin.

The distribution of Powers Phase rim and body sherds in the grid unit data set corresponds very closely to the pattern of distribution observed for the ceramic material in the Structure 1 point data set. Analysis of the spatial distribution of the pottery in the point data set indicated a clustered distribution, and visual inspection of Figure 16 indicated a large concentration of pottery in the grid unit just to the south of the central grid unit and two smaller concentrations within the top row of the nine central grid units. The grid unit to the south of the central grid unit yielded almost half (47% by weight) of the total Structure 1 pottery assemblage, while the three grid units in the top row of the nine central grid units accounted for another 33% of the total Structure 1 pottery assemblage.

Clay fragments were also clearly aggregated within Structure 1, with the northwest grid unit in the block of nine central grid units (515N, 565E) and the grid unit to the northeast of it (520N, 570E) yielding 88% of the total clay recovered from Structure 1.

Summary of the Spatial Distribution of Cultural Debris within Structure 1

Consideration of both the point and grid unit data sets from Structure 1 indicates not only a nonrandom distribution of much of the cultural debris, but also a number of overlapping areas of aggregation of different types of debris existing within the house basin.

The central grid unit, along with the adjacent grid units to the north and to the east, represents an area of aggregation of hickory nut fragments, sandstone angular fragments, and a grinding slab fragment. To the northwest of this central activity area, and overlapping with it to a certain extent, is a concentration of cultural debris that includes the remains of part of a large jar-form vessel, a core, a scraper, small-animal skeletal elements, and most of the clay fragments recovered from the house basin. Another concentration of pottery, representing part of a large jar-form vessel (perhaps the same vessel as the one just mentioned) is situated at the edge of the house basin to the northeast of the central activity area. Directly to the south of this central activity area is a concentration of pottery that represents two large jar-form vessels. This ceramic concentration overlaps both the southern and eastern edge of the central activity area. To the southwest and west of the central activity area is a concentration of six chert and quartzite cores, along with a hammerstone and a core. There was no aggregation of lithic debitage in this area, however, with chert and quartzite flakes and angular fragments distributed randomly throughout the house basin.

Structure 2

The spatial patterning of cultural materials within Structure 2 will not be analyzed in as much detail as the other Powers Phase features discussed in this section because there are clear indications of both vertical and horizontal spatial disturbance of cultural debris within the house basin. Cultural debris is scattered throughout the 1-foot thick deposits that fill the house basin (Figure 18) rather than being concentrated on the floor of the structure. Because of the hillside location of the structure, it is also possible that some of the cultural debris recovered from the house basin represent secondary erosional deposits rather than primary deposits resulting from activities carried out within the structure. For these reasons it is best that the reader keep in mind that the distribution patterns of cultural materials within the house basin described below may not provide an accurate picture of either the location or range of activities carried out within the structure.

Figure 18 suggests a random distribution of the total point data set within the wall trenches, with the exception of two areas largely devoid of cultural debris: one area along the southeast wall just east of the hearth

area, and a second to the southwest and west of Pit 1. The low density of
point data set items within these two areas can also be observed in the
east–west profile of Structure 2 shown in Figure 18. A consideration of
the total grid unit data set also indicates a random distribution of the total
cultural assemblage recovered from the Structure 2 house basin, with a
single exception: the existence of an "empty area" to the southwest and
west of Pit 1. The area east of the hearth area did not show a low density
of items in the grid unit data set.

There were no clear indications of aggregation of lithic debitage within
the house basin, with flakes and angular fragments being randomly distributed except for the low density area to the southwest and west of Pit
1. Of the nine cores recovered from Structure 2, on the other hand, six
were recovered from the grid unit containing Pit 1 and the northern half
of the grid unit adjacent to it on the south. Adjacent grid units to the west,
north, and east of the grid unit containing Pit 1 each yielded a single
core. The nine retouched flakes and three Powers Phase projectile points
recovered from the house basin also appeared to be randomly distributed, as did sandstone angular fragments.

Powers Phase pottery, however, seems to be nonrandomly distributed
within the house basin. A total of two large and one medium jar-form
vessels are represented. Rim sherds representing a large jar-form vessel
with a notched rim were recovered from northeast of the hearth, while
rim sherds representing a second large jar-form vessel were located both
south of the hearth and in the east corner of the house basin. A rim sherd
representing a medium-sized jar-form vessel was found overlying Pit 1.
Powers Phase body sherds in the grid unit data set are distributed in a
pattern similar to the rim sherds of jar-form vessels, with 92% (by weight)
of the Powers Phase pottery coming from grid units including Pit 1 and to
the southeast of it. Three other pottery vessels are represented in Structure 2: a bowl, located east of the hearth; a large short-necked bottle,
located along the northwest wall trench; and a small jar, also located
along the northwest wall trench.

Plant remains recovered from Structure 2 were randomly distributed
in the house basin, except for an almost total lack of any ethnobotanical
remains west of Pit 1.

White-tailed deer skeletal elements were distributed along the edges
of the house basin. Small-animal remains recovered from Structure 2
consisted of box turtle plastron fragments located east of the hearth, a
turkey leg bone (tibiotarsus) recovered north of Pit 1, and a freshwater
clam fragment located along the southwest wall of the structure.

Summary of the Spatial Distribution of Cultural Materials within Structure 2

The centrally located, shallow, saucer-shaped pit, and especially the
hearth located to the southeast of it, appear to have been a focus for

activities carried out within Structure 2. Although there is no associated concentration of lithic debris, an obvious cluster of cores exists just west of the hearth. Two large jar-form vessels were probably located adjacent to the hearth on its southern and northeastern edge, while a medium-sized jar-form vessel was associated with Pit 1.

Two other areas within Structure 2 are worth mentioning. The very low density of cultural materials in the area southwest and west of Pit 1 is interesting in that it may indicate a sleeping area. The area north of Pit 1 and adjacent to the northwest wall trench yielded a turkey tibiotarsus and rim sherds representing a large short-necked bottle and a small jar.

Although Structure 2 differs from Structure 1 in a number of important respects (pp. 51–54), it is also interesting to note similarities between the two structures in terms of internal patterning of cultural materials. Both structures contained a concentration of cores in the southwest quarter of the house basins. Both structures had white-tailed deer skeletal elements scattered around the edges of the house basins. Both structures had small-animal bones occurring in the northwest quarter of the house basins. Both structures had concentrations of pottery representing two large jar-form vessels located in the south–central area of the structure.

Pit 3 and Associated Activity Area

The point data set recovered from Pit 3 and its associated activity area consisted of 158 lithic and 36 ceramic items. Because of the small sample size of items in more specific lithic and ceramic categories, analysis was only carried out on the two basic classes of cultural debris: lithics and ceramics.

Nearest neighbor analysis of the spatial distribution of all 158 lithic items showed them to be randomly distributed.

Category of items: All chert and quartzite lithics
Number of items: 138
Expected mean nn: 4.31
Observed mean nn: 4.09
Ratio o/e: .95
Standard deviate: .56
Distributional pattern: Random. Not significant at the .10 level. Although nearest neighbor analysis of the total lithic point data set from Pit 3 and its associated activity area indicates a random pattern of distribution, visual inspection of Figure 24 indicates a very clear aggregation of chert and quartzite cores just west of Pit 3.

Nearest neighbor analysis of the spatial distribution of the small sample of 36 Powers Phase pottery sherds recovered from Pit 3 and its activity area showed them to be randomly distributed.

Category of items: All Powers Phase body and rim sherds
Number of items: 36
Expected mean *nn:* 9.04
Observed mean *nn:* 9.00
Ratio *o/e:* .99
Standard deviate: .97
Distributional pattern: Random. Not significant at the .1 level.

In summary, both lithic and ceramic point data sets are randomly distributed within Pit 3 and its associated activity area, with visual inspection of Figure 24 indicating a tight cluster of chert and quartzite cores within the activity area.

Analysis of the grid unit data set from the Pit 3 activity area provides a much more detailed, and quite different picture of the distribution of cultural debris than the random pattern of distribution of lithic and ceramic items indicated by analysis of the point data set. The nonrandom distribution of cores in the Pit 3 activity area is clearly shown in analysis of the grid unit data set. The grid unit that includes the south half of Pit 3 (530N, 585E), along with the adjacent grid unit to the west (530N, 580E) yielded all 11 cores recovered from the Pit 3 activity area. Many of these cores differed from those recovered from Structure 1 in that they displayed evidence of having been utilized to a much greater extent, and could be most accurately described as being small exhausted core fragments.

Not surprisingly, analysis of chert and quartzite debitage items included in the grid unit data set indicates a clear aggregation in the same area as the cores. The two grid units just mentioned, along with the grid unit bordering Pit 3 on the west side (535N, 580E), yielded 73.5% (by weight) of the flakes and 70% (by weight) of the angular fragments recovered from the Pit 3 activity area. These three grid units also yielded all but one of the retouched flakes and all of the rejected projectile points that were recovered from the Pit 3 activity area.

This distribution of chert and quartzite debitage (flakes and angular fragments) in the grid unit data set is not, however, in conflict with the random pattern of distribution shown for lithic items in the point data set. These three grid units represent about 70% of the total Pit 3 activity area and contain similar percentages of the lithic debitage recovered. The point, then, is not that lithic debitage is nonrandomly distributed within the Pit 3 activity area, but rather that most of it comes from these three grid units.

Most of the plant remains (80.4% by weight) recovered from the Pit 3 activity area also came from the same three grid units, as did most of the sandstone angular fragments (77% by weight).

While clay and cone fragments in the grid unit data set were randomly distributed throughout the activity area, Powers Phase pottery was concentrated around Pit 3, with the two grid units that contain Pit 3 yielding over 60% (by weight) of the total pottery assemblage recovered from the Pit 3 activity area. This apparent conflict with the random distribution of pottery analyzed in the point data set can be explained by the larger sample size of pottery included in the grid unit data set.

There is also a nonrandom distribution of white-tailed deer skeletal elements within the Pit 3 activity area. All but two of the white-tailed deer bone fragments were recovered from the grid unit that includes the north half of Pit 3 and the grid unit adjacent to it on the east side (535N, 590E). This concentration of deer bone extends into Pit 3 to a certain extent (Figure 24).

Summary of the Spatial Distribution of Cultural Debris within the Pit 3 Activity Area

The activity area surrounds Pit 3, with most of the cultural debris scattered over an area of about 70 square feet along the south, southwest, and western edge of the pit. This area contains cultural debris resulting from a number of different activities, with cores, lithic debitage, utilized flakes, and rejected projectile points represented, along with plant remains, sandstone angular fragments, and clay and cone fragments. Pottery also occurred in this area, but was concentrated along the pit edge.

The area to the north and east of the pit was largely devoid of cultural debris except for the remains of a left front leg and shoulder and lower left rear leg of a white-tailed deer, found in association with a knife.

Although Pit 3 itself provides no clues as to what its initial purpose may have been (no clear outline, no preparation of sides or bottom, no pit lining, no evidence of burning, no layering of contents) it was apparently eventually used as a receptacle for cultural debris resulting from activities carried out adjacent to it. A flake recovered from toward the bottom of the pit was found to fit one of the cores recovered from the activity area, indicating that the pit was probably open while flint knapping was going on. Similarly, white-tailed deer skeletal elements recovered from a higher point in the pit were associated with skeletal elements recovered from the activity area. The distribution of items within the pit fill provides no indication of separate dumping episodes, nor is there any way to determine how long a period of time was involved in filling up the pit with cultural debris and soil.

Pits 5a, 5b, and the Associated Activity Area

The point data set recovered from Pits 5a, 5b, and the associated activity area consisted of 44 lithic and 14 ceramic items. Because of the small sample size of items in more specific lithic and ceramic categories, analysis was only done on the two basic classes of cultural debris: lithic and ceramics.

Nearest neighbor analysis of the spatial distribution of all 44 lithic items showed them to be uniformly distributed within the activity area.

Category of items: All chert and quartzite lithics
Number of items: 44
Expected mean *nn:* 6.59
Observed mean *nn:* 7.82
Ratio *o/e:* 1.19
Standard deviate: 2.05
Distributional pattern: Uniform. Significant at the .05 level. This uniform pattern of distribution of lithics can only be explained in terms of the small (?) sample size. A uniform distribution would certainly not be expected, and has rarely been observed in archaeological data sets.

Nearest neighbor analysis of the spatial distribution of the small sample of 14 Powers Phase pottery sherds showed them to be nonrandomly distributed.

Category of items: Powers Phase body sherds and rim sherds
Number of items: 14
Expected mean *nn:* 11.69
Observed mean *nn:* 5.49
Ratio *o/e:* .47
Standard deviate: −3.21
Distributional pattern: Clustered. Significant beyond the .005 level. Visual inspection of Figure 27 indicates a loose cluster of pottery in the northern half of the Pit 5 activity area.

In summary, lithic items within the Pit 5 activity area are surprisingly uniform in distribution, whereas Powers Phase pottery is loosely aggregated in the northern half of the activity area.

Analysis of the grid unit data set for the activity area surrounding Pits 5a and 5b provides a clearer and somewhat different picture of the distribution of cultural debris than the one obtained through analysis of the point data set. The three cores recovered from the activity area came from the two grid units to the north of Pit 5a and Pit 5b (525N, 595E and 525N, 560E). These two grid units, along with the grid unit that contains Pit 5a, also accounted for over 70% (by weight) of the lithic debitage recovered from the activity area. The grid unit containing Pit 5a, in fact, yielded 34% (by weight) of the flakes and 43% (by weight) of the angular fragments recovered from the activity area, and also contained a rejected point, three retouched flakes, and a mano. Pit 5b also yielded a quartzite core, two projectile points (one rejected) and a scraper, while Pit 5a produced three additional cores, an anvil hammerstone, and three re-touched flakes. The three sandstone angular fragments recovered from the activity area all came from the grid units to the east of Pit 5a.

Analysis of the distribution of the small number of pottery sherds in the grid unit data set ($N = 19$) indicates a loose aggregation in the northern half of the activity area.

The abundant amount of plant remains recovered from the activity area is concentrated around the two pits; the two grid units containing Pits 5a and 5b and the grid unit located to the north of Pit 5a together yield over 90% (by weight) of the plant remains recovered.

White-tailed deer skeletal elements of a left front and a left rear leg were recovered from the grid unit just north of Pit 5a (Figure 24) in association with a biface. It is interesting to note that the deer skeletal elements recovered from Pit 5a and Pit 5b represent a right rear leg. It was not possible to determine if all of these bones were from the same animal. The only other faunal material recovered from the activity area includes several antler fragments located to the southeast of Pit 5a and a maxilla fragment just west of Pit 5b.

Summary of the Spatial Distribution of Cultural Debris within the Activity Area Surrounding Pit 5a and Pit 5b

The activity area surrounding Pits 5a and 5b encompasses an area of 66.6 square feet. With the exception of plant remains, which were con-centrated around the two pits, most of the cultural debris—pottery and lithic and faunal materials—was recovered from an area to the north of both pits. Very few items were recovered to the south or to the east of the two pits, with the exception of sandstone angular fragments, which were recovered to the east of Pit 5a.

Although Pits 5a and 5b are both small saucer-shaped pits that were probably initially constructed for a different purpose, they were appar-ently used finally as receptacles for cultural debris from the surrounding activity area. Each pit was filled with a mixture of plant remains (mostly hickory nutshell fragments), pottery, and lithic materials. There was no apparent layering or lensing of materials within the two pits, and no clear indications of different types of materials being placed in the pit during different dumping episodes. The relative frequency of occurrence of dif-ferent categories of cultural debris within the two pits is also comparable to their relative frequency of occurrence in the surrounding activity area.

Pit 10 and Its Associated Activity Area

The point data set recovered from Pit 10 and the associated activity area consisted of 46 lithic and 19 ceramic items. Because of the small sample of items in more specific lithic and ceramic categories, analysis was only done on the two basic classes of cultural debris: lithics and ceramics.

Nearest neighbor analysis of the spatial distribution of all 46 lithic items showed them to be randomly distributed within the Pit 10 activity area.

Category of items: All chert and quartzite items
Number of items: 46
Expected mean *nn:* 5.49
Observed mean *nn:* 5.55
Ratio *o/e:* 1.01
Standard deviate: 1.70
Distributional pattern: Random. Not significant at the .05 level, but a strong tendency toward a uniform distribution.

Nearest neighbor analysis of the spatial distribution of the small sample of 18 Powers Phase sherds showed them to be randomly distributed.

Category of items: Powers Phase body sherds and rim sherds
Number of items: 18
Expected mean *nn:* 8.54
Observed mean *nn:* 6.45
Ration *o/e:* .76
Standard deviate: −1.54
Distributional pattern: Random. Not significant at the .10 level.

Analysis of the larger grid unit data set from the Pit 10 activity area provided a more detailed picture of the distribution of cultural materials within the activity area. Lithic debitage was randomly distributed within the activity area, with the two grid units to the west and northwest of Pit 10 (500N, 600E, 505N, 600E) accounting for 93% (by weight) of the angular fragments and 77% (by weight) of the flakes recovered from the activity area. Sandstone angular fragments and clay fragments were also randomly distributed within the activity area. In contrast, all of the plant remains, and almost all of the Powers Phase pottery (95% by weight) were concentrated within the grid unit to the west of Pit 10 (500N, 600E). All three white-tailed deer skeletal elements were recovered from the grid unit to the southwest of Pit 10 (495N, 600E).

Summary of the Distribution of Cultural Materials within the Pit 10 Activity Area

The Pit 10 activity area extends away from the pit to the northwest and encompasses an area of 42.6 square feet. Not only is this the smallest activity area excavated at the site, it also has the lowest density and the lowest total mass of cultural debris of any of the high- or average-density features.

The partial remains of two medium sized jar-form vessels were found in association with a concentration of plant remains (mostly hickory nut hulls) to the west of the pit, whereas lithic debitage was randomly scattered over a wider area to the west and northwest of the pit. The Pit 10 activity area is also unique in that neither cores nor artifacts rejected during manufacture were recovered from the feature, or, for that matter, from Pit 10.

Pit 10 fits in the low-density category, but it differs from other low-density features in a number of important respects. It is the only pit within this category that is associated with an activity area. It is also, with the exception of Pit 4, the only feature not to yield either white-tailed deer skeletal elements or small-animal skeletal elements. The burned area at the bottom of Pit 10 is also a unique attribute; the only other hearth area discovered at the Gypsy Joint site was not within a pit (Structure 2). Pit 10 was initially utilized for heating or cooking, judging from the burned soil area at the base of the pit. Unlike Pits 3, 5a, and 5b, it does not appear that Pit 10 was finally employed as a trash pit for cultural debris from the adjacent activity area. Not only did Pit 10 yield a much smaller amount of cultural debris than the pits associated with other activity areas, it also yielded quite different percentages of cultural debris than the adjacent activity area. Lithic angular fragments accounted for 92% (by weight) of the cultural material recovered from Pit 10, but they accounted for only 34% (by weight) of the cultural materials recovered from the activity area. This suggests that perhaps the chert, quartzite, and sandstone angular fragments recovered from Pit 10 played a role in the primary function of the pit, rather than simply representing overflow cultural debris from the adjacent activity area.

6

Five Problem Areas

INTRODUCTION

A series of five interrelated problem areas were stated in Chapter 2 as comprising the overall research goal of the excavation of a smaller-than-village-sized Powers Phase site:

1. The seasonality of occupation of the site
2. The range of activities carried out at the site
3. The size and composition of the occupying group
4. The duration of occupation of the site
5. The relationship of the site to other Powers Phase sites.

As a number of archaeologists, including James Hill (1972), have pointed out, it is necessary for such general problem areas to be identified prior to any actual collection of data. All of the potential information existing in archaeological sites cannot be observed, recorded, and recovered during the process of surface collection or actual excavation. Data recovery is therefore always partial, with some data going unobserved and unrecovered. Excavation always involves destruction and loss of data to some extent. If a general problem area such as seasonality of occupation is recognized prior to data collection, the research design can then be deliberately structured toward maximum recovery of data pertinent to that problem area. In other words, as has often been stated, archaeology must be problem oriented. Collection of data is not a justifiable activity in and of itself.

It is not enough, however, simply to select a general problem area prior to data collection. Such problem areas are quite often not focused enough to guide subsequent collection and analysis of data; they are not stated in terms specific enough to be tested. A more focused, specific statement of general problem area involves formulating or developing hypotheses. A hypothesis can be defined as a precise, explicit, testable statement of a tentative solution to a problem. Such specific statements allow the identification of potentially important data and guide research strategy much more accurately than the simple selection of problem areas. Formulating hypotheses, then, involves making more specific predictions within a general problem area.

Archaeologists should try to formulate and consider not one, but a number of alternative hypotheses. The necessity of working with multiple hypotheses was clearly stated by T. C. Chamberlin over 80 years ago, and recently reprinted (Chamberlin 1965). A scientist working with a single, as yet untested hypothesis is very likely to develop a certain affection for the hypothesis, and along with it an inability to perceive its shortcomings. This in turn increases the probability that the scientist will unconsciously select and magnify the importance of those data that tend to support the hypothesis and will at the same time tend to ignore data that do not tend to support it. How does one avoid this biasing influence of intellectual affection? By giving birth not to a single intellectual offspring but to a heterogenous litter of hypotheses. The scientist then attempts to determine the hypothesis or set of hypotheses that are most supported by the data. This process necessarily involves the rejection of some hypotheses; it also allows a more objective collection and observation of data and a more unbiased consideration of the relative merits of several hypotheses. A number of alternative hypotheses will be presented for most of the general problem areas to be considered in this section.

Once a series of alternative hypotheses are formulated, the next step is to identify a number of specific logical consequences of each of the hypotheses. Such logical consequences are often described as test implications or observational predictions. After the logical consequences for each alternative hypothesis have been developed, and logical bridging arguments have been presented that demonstrate the strength of the cause and effect relationship thought to exist between each hypothesis and its observational predictions (Smith 1977), the next step in the scientific method involves assessing the relative strength of each of the alternative hypotheses. This testing necessitates comparing observational predictions with the available archaeological data base to determine their empirical validity. The hypothesis that has the greatest number and the greatest variety of empirically valid observational predictions can be selected as the best potential solution to the general problem area on the basis of the available data.

The general procedure just described will be followed as closely as possible through the rest of this chapter as each of the five general problem areas is considered in detail.

SEASONALITY OF OCCUPATION

Statement of Hypotheses and Plausibility Considerations

For the general problem area of seasonality of occupation of the Gypsy Joint site, a series of three alternative hypotheses was formulated prior to excavation:

H_1: The Gypsy Joint site was occupied seasonally during the spring and summer (March to September).

H_2: The Gypsy Joint site was occupied seasonally during the fall and winter (September to March).

H_3: The Gypsy Joint site was occupied through the annual cycle.

These three hypotheses were selected for explicit formulation and testing by considering the plausibility, or prior probability, of a wide variety of different hypotheses concerning seasonality of occupation of small Mississippian Period sites. Such plausibility considerations involve consulting a reference class of appropriate ethnohistorical situations to determine what patterns of seasonal occupation are described as being most common. The reference class in this instance consisted of ethnohistorical accounts of the economic cycle and seasonal movements of Amerindian populations in the eastern deciduous woodlands, especially those populations situated either in the lower alluvial valley of the Mississippi River (from Cape Girardeau, Missouri, south) or in the southeast United States. The exhaustive ethnohistorical summary works by Swanton (1911, 1946) were the primary sources consulted.

In both volumes Swanton describes a fairly uniform annual economic cycle for lower valley and southeastern Amerindian populations that consisted of a simple division of the year into a spring–summer period, when horticultural pursuits dominated subsistence activities, and a fall–winter period, when wild species of plants and animals were the focus of energy capture efforts (Swanton 1946:256–257). Patterns of seasonal movements by Indian populations, and their seasonally occupied settlements, paralleled this economic cycle, with three different categories of settlements being described:

1. Villages or towns. The terms *village* and *town* are misleading in that they were used to refer to settlements showing a great variation in relative nucleation. Some villages consisted of strongly nucleated settlements consisting of a hundred houses or more, whereas, more commonly, villages consisted of widely scattered small groups of houses, or even single-family occupations: "Like southeastern towns generally, they [Natchez villages] consisted mainly of neighborhoods scattered through the woods and interspersed with fields [Swanton 1946:638]."

At whatever degree of nucleation, the location of such villages was tied to the location of horticultural fields.

2. Winter camps. Villages were sometimes vacated, at least by part of the population, during the fall and winter of the year, as Indian groups dispersed over the landscape, occupying small winter camps. There are, unfortunately, no detailed ethnohistorical descriptions of such winter camps, nor is it known if fall–winter dispersal of populations was a consistent static adaptational strategy to deal with seasonal changes in the availability of food or if it represented a flexible adaptational response to occasional poor crop years. Similarly, it is not known if fall dispersal from villages occurred at the same time every year or if it was determined by available storable food supplies.

3. Guardian camps. Although there are references to crop guardians structures in the ethnohistorical literature (Swanton 1946:418), there are no detailed descriptions of such camps available. In general, such camps are described as consisting of single structures and associated features located close to horticultural garden plots. Such structures served as temporary shelters for those individuals responsible for guarding fields from destruction by birds and animals. While such structures would only have been occupied during the spring–summer growing season, the frequency and duration of their occupation would have depended on a number of variables, including the distance of the structures from the village, the level of destruction of crops, and the danger of raids from neighboring groups.

Based on the available ethnohistorical descriptions of the seasonal occupation of different settlements by Indian populations in the eastern woodlands, the possible logical alternatives to expect for the seasonality of occupation of the Gypsy Joint were thus determined to be (a) spring–summer occupation, (b) fall–winter occupation, and (c) year-round occupation.

Observational Predictions and Auxiliary Hypotheses

The observational predictions for each of these three alternative hypotheses can be separated into two kinds of direct archaeological evidence of seasonality of occupation: ecofactual seasonality indicators and the artifactual debris of activities that can be projected as being seasonal in nature. Ecofactual observational predictions can be further broken down into faunal and floral seasonality indicators. Faunal indicators consist of a number of different potentially occurring osteological indicators of the season of death of a number of different species.

1. White-tailed deer antlers. The seasonal growth and subsequent dropping of antlers by adult male white-tailed deer is well documented

for present-day white-tailed deer populations in Missouri. Antler growth begins in early May, with the velvet, or growth stage, ending around the beginning of September. The now fully hardened antlers are subsequently dropped during January of each year. Skull fragments showing shed antlers therefore indicate a January to May season of death, while skull fragments having antlers in the growth stage or fully hardened would indicate May to September and September to February seasons of death, respectively. Although I have previously stated (Smith 1975) that it is not possible to distinguish between fully hardened antler and antler in the growth stage, this is not totally correct. It is possible to make such a distinction if the burr, or coronet, at the base of the antler is recovered. Blood vessels that supply antlers with nutrients during the growth stage pass through openings in this burr section. These openings grow shut at the end of the velvet stage, effectively cutting off the blood supply to antlers. Fully closed antler-burr sections therefore indicate a September to February season of death.

2. White-tailed deer mandibles. The rate of growth and eventual replacement of deciduous, or "milk," teeth by white-tailed deer during the first 2 years of life has been well documented for white-tailed deer populations in the eastern deciduous woodlands, allowing the age of mandibles from deer less than 20 months old to be estimated within a 2–3-month span. This predictable growth rate, combined with the short late May–early June birth period for deer in Missouri allows the season of death for subadult deer to be estimated within a 2–3-month period (Smith 1975).

3. Fish scales. Studies of present-day fish populations in temperate zones has demonstrated that the seasonal growth of a variety of species is recorded osteologically as alternating rings or layers of rapid (spring–summer) versus slow or no-growth (fall–winter) deposits on scales. The season of death of fish represented in archaeological sites can therefore be determined within a 3–4-month range by analyzing the outside edge of fish scales (Casteel 1975).

4. Freshwater clams. Annual growth layers similar to those described for fish may also be present in freshwater clams, allowing a determination of season of death (Ray 1976).

5. Migratory waterfowl. Although migratory waterfowl do not produce any direct osteological indicators of season of death, the mere presence of skeletal elements of some species of waterfowl can be employed to determine seasonality of occupation of a site because of the limited seasonal availability of such species (Smith 1975).

Each of these osteological indicators of the season of death–availability of animal species can be employed as observational predictions for the alternative hypotheses presented above. The bridging arguments involved in demonstrating that such osteological indicators do in fact represent evidence concerning the season of occupation of a site involves two auxiliary hypotheses that are rarely explicitly stated by archaeologists. The first of these auxiliary hypotheses involves the concept of uniformitarianism: What is known concerning the growth patterns and seasonal movements of present-day animal populations can be applied to prehistoric animal populations. Most archaeologists would accept this hypothesis as long as reasonable guidelines for employing present-day wildlife studies are followed (Smith 1976:6). The second auxiliary hypothesis involves the assumption that the observed season of death–availability of animal species recovered from an archaeological site corresponds to the actual occupation of the site: that the animals in question were in fact killed during the period of time the site was occupied.

The potential ethnobotanical indicators of seasonal occupation consist primarily of those wild species of plants that are available for collection only during certain restricted seasons of the year. An excellent study of the seasonal availability of different wild plant species in the lower Illinois River valley, which is located approximately 180 miles north of the Gypsy Joint site, is the source for the information given below (Zawacki and Hausfather 1969).

1. Species of plants available only during the spring and summer. Plant utilization during the spring and summer would have been restricted to greens, roots, and berries. While both greens and roots would rarely, if ever, be preserved in an archaeological site, the carbonized seeds of strawberry, raspberry, elderberry, blackberry, and mulberry would represent observational predictions for spring–summer occupation of the site (Asch *et al.* 1972).

2. Species of plants available only during the fall. A wide variety of different species of trees, including black walnut *(Juglans nigra)*, numerous species of hickories *(Cayra* sp.), and oaks *(Quercus* sp.), drop mature nuts only during the 2-month span of September–October. The availability of these nuts would rapidly decline from November on due to consumption by a large number of animal species. Similarly, a number of pioneer species of plants, including, most importantly, chenopod *(Chenopodium* sp.) and knotweed *(Polygonum* sp.) produce mature seeds only during the 3-month span of September–November. Finally, wild plums *(Prunus* sp.) would become available in late August, and wild grapes *(Vitis* sp.) would have been available during September and October.

Although a great number of other wild species of plants are available only during certain seasons of the year, and are therefore potential indicators of seasonality of occupation, a detailed description of these additional indicators will not be included here.

The two auxiliary hypotheses mentioned above as being necessary in employing osteological indicators as observational predictions are also necessary in employing plant remains as evidence of seasonality of occupation. The first hypothesis involves application of the seasonal nut and fruit production characteristics of present-day plant species to prehistoric plant populations; the second hypothesis involves the assumption that the plant foods in question were collected during the period of time the site was occupied. This second auxiliary hypothesis, as will be seen later in this chapter, often plays a central role in deciding between alternative hypotheses concerning seasonality of site occupation.

A final point concerning the employment of plant remains as seasonality indicators is that almost all of the species in question are available during the fall of the year. Few of the spring–summer plant foods would be preserved, and the winter period lacks any seasonally available plant foods (Asch *et al.* 1972).

The presence of the carbonized remains of domestic cultigens such as maize, beans, squash, sunflower, and marsh elder might be employed as indicators of a spring–summer occupation for the site. This would, of course, involve the auxiliary hypothesis that the crops in question were in fact grown during the period of time the site was occupied, rather than carried in from another location to be used as a stored food supply through a fall–winter occupation.

Artifactual indicators of the season of the year during which the site was occupied would consist of those tools or features that might be associated with human activities that were carried out only during certain seasons of the year.

1. House types. Numerous ethnohistorical accounts of Indian populations in the southeastern United States describe two different kinds of domestic habitation structures as being occupied during different seasons of the year (Swanton 1946 provides a good summary of these accounts). A warm weather house, rectangular in shape, was constructed of wall posts, with cane thatch serving as roofing and wall construction material. Some descriptions indicate that such summer houses were sometimes constructed without walls on one or more sides. Winter or "hot" houses were usually circular in shape, although sometimes described as being rectangular; they were smaller in size than summer houses (to retain heat) and were more substantial in construction, with walls often consisting of clay facing over cane thatch (wattle and daub). Such winter houses could also be expected to differ from summer houses in that they would be much more likely to contain internal hearths and food storage facilities. Rather than being continually occupied throughout the fall and winter, such hot houses were apparently used only when cold or otherwise unpleasant weather rendered the warm weather house too uncomfortable.

2. Hoes and hoe flakes. Large chipped and ground stone implements, usually referred to as spades or hoes, were employed by Powers Phase populations for the preparation and maintenance of garden plots. Striation patterns and polish characteristics observed on a number of hoes recovered from the Turner and Snodgrass sites support this functional interpretation. Such hoes have been both recovered from house floors and found buried beneath them at both of these sites.

Because such hoes are usually manufactured from a distinctive non-local chert (Mill Creek chert), and exhibit polish over the working surfaces, the flakes resulting from resharpening the hoes are easily identifiable. The presence of such hoes, and especially the presence of hoe flakes, would be a strong positive observational prediction for spring–summer occupation of a Powers Phase site.

3. Hide smoking and preparation activities. If Binford's (1972) hypothesis is correct, the small pits associated with the smoking of deer hides could be viewed as the material remains of a strictly seasonal activity: "In all the ethnographic cases cited, when temporal data were given, hide smoking was a spring and summer activity [Binford 1972:46]." The presence of such smudge pits might be employed as a positive observational prediction for a spring–summer period of occupation of a Powers Phase site.

The Relative Strength of the Alternative Hypotheses

Having discussed different kinds of potential ecofactual and artifactual seasonality indicators, the relative strength of each of the three alternative hypotheses concerning seasonal occupation of the Gypsy Joint site can now be considered

H_1: The Gypsy Joint site was occupied seasonally during the spring and summer (March to September).

Auxiliary hypotheses (A) for ecofactual observational predictions (P):

A_1: The seasonal growth and availability characteristics of present-day plant and animal populations can be applied to the biotic community that existed within the support area of the Gypsy Joint population.

A_2: The species of plants and animals being employed as seasonality indicators were hunted, collected, or grown during the time the site was occupied.

Ecofactual observational predictions:

P_1: Deer antler–skull fragments showing shed antlers (January to May death) might be recovered (+ = recovered from the Pit 5 activity area).

P_2: Deer antler–skull fragments showing antlers in the growth or velvet stage (May to September) might be recovered (0 = not observed during excavation).

P_3: Deer antler–skull fragments showing full hardened antlers (September to February) should not be recovered (– = recovered from
the Pit 3 activity area).

P_4: Deer mandibles representing a spring–summer season of death
might be recovered (0 = not observed during excavation).

P_5: Deer mandibles representing a season of death other then
spring–summer should not be recovered (– = recovered from
Structure 1).

P_6: Fish scales representing a spring–summer season of death might
be recovered (0 = not observed during excavation).

P_7: Fish scales representing a season of death other than spring–
summer should not be recovered (+ = not observed during
excavation).

P_8: Freshwater clam shells indicating a spring–summer season of
death might be recovered (0 = not observed during excavation).

P_9: Freshwater clam shells indicating a season of death other than
spring–summer should not be recovered (+ = not observed during
excavation).

P_{10}: Those wild plant resources only available during the spring and
summer might be recovered (0 = not observed during excavation).

P_{11}: Those wild plant resources only available during the fall and winter should not be recovered (– = the carbonized remains of large
numbers of hickory nuts, acorns, and walnuts, as well as
thousands of knotweed and chenopod seeds were recovered).

P_{12}: Domestic cultigens might be recovered (+ = carbonized maize
kernel and cob fragments were recovered from all but one Powers
Phase feature; *Iva* and sunflower seeds were recovered from
seven features and one feature, respectively).

Of the 12 ecofactual observational predictions (Ps) listed above for H_1,
7 would have been expected to have been observed if the hypothesis was
true (positive or expected Ps), while 5 would not have been expected to
have been observed if the hypothesis were true (negative or unexpected
Ps).

Five of the seven positive observational predictions were untestable
due to a lack of recovered archaeological data, and two were found to be
empirically valid. The two positive test implications found to be empirically valid actually provide little convincing support for H_1 in and of
themselves, since one (P_1) can also be employed as a positive P for H_2,
while the other (P_{12}) can be employed as a positive P for H_3.

Two of the five negative observational predictions were found to be
empirically valid, and three were found to be empirically invalid. Once

again the observational predictions found to be empirically valid actually provide little support for H_1, since they have to do with not finding any osteological indicators of fall–winter killed fish (P_7) or clams (P_9). Since no fish scales and only a single poorly preserved clam shell were recovered during excavation, such negative evidence can hardly be viewed as strong evidence for a spring–summer occupation.

The three negative observational predictions that were found to be empirically invalid, however, severely undermine the strength of H_1. The presence of fully hardened deer antler (P_3), a mandible from a winter-killed deer (P_5), and plant resources available only during the fall (P_{11}) all strongly suggest that occupation of the Gypsy Joint site was not limited to the spring and summer seasons of the year.

Auxiliary hypotheses (A) for artifactual observational predictions:

A_3: Structure 1 at the Gypsy Joint site is a warm weather structure.
A_4: Structure 2 at the Gypsy Joint site is a cold weather structure.
A_5: Hoes and hoe flakes are the material correlates of a spring–summer activity—preparing and maintaining garden plots.
A_6: Smudge pits are the material correlate of a spring–summer activity—hide smoking (Binford 1972:46).

Before assessing the empirical validity of the artifactual observational predictions of spring–summer occupation of the Gypsy Joing site, the auxiliary hypotheses given above that identify Structures 1 and 2 at the Gypsy Joint site as being warm weather and cold weather structures require further discussion. Although available ethnohistorical descriptions of warm weather and cold weather structures are neither detailed enough nor consistent enough to allow any conclusive identification of such structures in an archaeological context, there is a certain amount of evidence available to support A_3 and A_4 above.

Structure 1 exhibits a number of features characteristic of warm weather structures, including simple single wall-post construction, little indication of substantial walls, and an absence of an internal hearth. Structure 2 differs from Structure 1 in a number of respects (see pp. 51–54), many of which would be expected if it was, in fact, a cold weather structure. Most importantly, Structure 2 is much smaller than Structure 1, and its wall-trench construction suggests a more substantial structure. The small size, more substantial construction (both features making it easier to heat), and the presence of a hearth within Structure 2 all correspond to ethnohistorical descriptions of "hot" houses. Structure 2 differs from such ethnohistorical descriptions in that it is rectangular in shape rather than round (although Creek hot houses are described as rectangular; Swanton 1946:389) and does not appear to have had wattle and daub walls. Structure 2 is also located on the slope of the hill, somewhat shielded from the wind, whereas Structure 1 is located where the full

benefit of breezes can be obtained. The peripheral placement of Structure 2 also corresponds to the role of hot houses as only being occupied
when absolutely necessary, with most activities throughout the year
being centered around the warm weather structure.

Without pursuing the relative strength of A_3 and A_4 any further, it need
only be pointed out that if the reader thinks that Structure 1 might be a
warm weather structure and that Structure 2 might be a cold weather
structure, the observational predictions relating to these structures can
be considered in assessing the strength of the alternative hypotheses
presently being explored. Otherwise such observational predictions can
be ignored.

Artifactual observational predictions:

> P_{13}: A warm weather structure might be observed (+ = Structure 1).
> P_{14}: A cold weather structure should not be observed (− = Structure
> 2).
> P_{15}: Hoes and/or hoe flakes might be recovered (0 = not observed
> during excavation).
> P_{16}: Smudge pits might be observed (0 = not observed during excava-
> tion).

Of the four observational predictions listed above for H_1, two were
found to be untestable due to a lack of recovered archaeological data, one
was found to be empirically valid, and one was found to be empirically
invalid. The single prediction found to be empirically valid (P_{13}) is more
than offset by the empirical invalidity of P_{14}: The presence of a cold
weather structure (if one accepts A_4) strongly suggests that the Gypsy
Joint site was not occupied only during the spring and summer.

Although H_1 has little supporting archaeological evidence, it is necessary to assess the relative strength of alternative hypotheses H_2 and H_3
before any final choice is made as to the most correct hypothesis.

> H_2: The site was occupied seasonally during the fall and winter (Sep-
> tember to March).

Auxiliary hypotheses for ecofactual observational predictions: The two
auxiliary hypotheses listed under H_1 also apply to H_2.

Ecofactual observational predictions:

> P_1: Deer antler–skull fragments showing shed antlers (January to May
> death) might be recovered (+ = recovered from the Pit 5 activity
> area).
> P_2: Deer antler–skull fragments showing antlers in the growth stage
> (May to September) should not be recovered (+ = not observed
> during excavation).

P_3: Deer antler–skull fragments showing fully hardened antlers (September to February) might be recovered (+ = recovered from the Pit 3 activity area).

P_4: Deer mandibles representing a spring–summer season of death should not be recovered (+ = not observed during excavation).

P_5: Deer mandibles representing a fall–winter season of death might be recovered (+ = recovered from Structure 1).

P_6: Fish scales representing a spring–summer season of death should not be recovered (+ = not observed during excavation).

P_7: Fish scales representing a fall–winter season of death might be recovered (0 = not observed during excavation).

P_8: Freshwater clam shells indicating a spring–summer season of death should not be recovered (+ = not observed during excavation).

P_9: Freshwater clam shells indicating a fall–winter season of death might be recovered (0 = not observed during excavation).

P_{10}: Those wild plant resources only available during the spring and summer should not be recovered (+ = not observed during excavation).

P_{11}: Those wild plant resources only available during the fall and winter might be recovered (+ = such plant resources were recovered in large amounts).

P_{12}: Domestic cultigens should not be recovered (− = carbonized maize kernel and cob fragments were recovered from all but one Powers Phase feature while *Iva* and sunflower seeds were recovered from seven features and one feature respectively).

Of the 12 ecofactual observational predictions listed above for H_2, 6 would have been expected to have been observed if the hypothesis was true (positive Ps), and 6 would not have been expected to have been observed if the hypothesis was true (negative Ps).

Two of the six positive Ps were untestable due to a lack of recovered archaeological data, and four were found to be empirically valid.

Five of the six negative observational predictions were found to be empirically valid, while one (P_{12}) was found to be empirically invalid. While this single empirically invalid observational prediction (the presence of domestic cultigens at the site) might be viewed as sufficient cause to reject H_2, it would be more accurate to view it as evidence that either H_2 or A_2 (cultigens recovered from the site were grown while it was occupied) is in fact false. Thus it would be possible to avoid rejecting H_2 by instead rejecting A_2. This choice between H_2 and A_2 will be discussed in more detail later in this chapter.

Auxiliary hypotheses for artifactual observational predictions: The three auxiliary hypotheses listed under H_1 also apply to H_2.

Artifactual observational predictions:

  P_{13}: A warm weather structure might be observed (+ = Structure 1).
  P_{14}: A cold weather structure might be observed (+ = Structure 2).
  P_{15}: Hoes and/or hoe flakes should not be recovered (+ = not observed during excavation).
  P_{16}: Smudge pits should not be observed (+ = not observed during excavation).

Of the four artifactual observational predictions listed above for H_2, all were found to be empirically valid. Thus of a total of 16 observational predictions, 2 were found to be untestable, 13 were found to be empirically valid, and 1 was found to be empirically invalid.

H_3: The Gypsy Joint site was occupied through the annual cycle.

Auxiliary hypotheses for ecofactual and artifactual observational predictions: The five auxiliary hypotheses listed under H_1 and H_2 also apply to H_3.

The ecofactual and artifactual observational predictions for H_3 would consist of all of the positive Ps listed under H_1 and H_2. It is not really necessary to list all of these Ps, since none would be found to be empirically invalid. Of the 16 Ps in question, 9 were found to be untestable due to a lack of recovered data, and 7 were found to be empirically valid.

Having considered the extent to which the observational predictions for each hypothesis agreed with the available relevant archaeological data, it is now possible to assess the relative strength of the hypotheses. In deciding which of a number of alternative hypotheses is best supported by the available data, the following criteria are usually employed:

  1. The greater the number of observational predictions that are shown to be empirically valid, the higher the probability that a hypothesis is true.
  2. The fewer the number of observational predictions that are shown to be empirically invalid, the higher the probability that a hypothesis is true.
  3. The greater the variety of observational predictions that are shown to be empirically valid, the higher the probability that a hypothesis is true.
  4. The relevance of observational predictions. Just as important as the number and the variety of observational predictions that are shown to be empirically valid or invalid is the significance or relevance of various observational predictions. Some Ps are clearly more important than others: They carry more weight.

Although there are additional criteria that can be employed to assess the strength of alternative hypotheses (Smith 1977), these four criteria will be adequate for the present discussion.

In terms of the four criteria, H_1 is the hypothesis that is least supported by the available archaeological data (Table 24). The spring–summer occupation hypothesis has fewer valid Ps and more invalid Ps than either H_2 or H_3. The relative standing of H_1 is even further eroded when the relevance of its valid and invalid Ps are considered. Of the five valid Ps, only three have to do with positive evidence of a spring–summer occupation. The other two have to do with not finding archaeological data (fish scales and clam shells) that would indicate a fall–winter period of occupation. Such negative Ps have low relevance in archaeological reasoning unless they are complemented by parallel positive, empirically valid Ps. The fact that no fish scales or clam shells, indicating a fall–winter period of occupation were recovered, for example, would carry more weight— would be more relevant to the argument—if fish scales and clam shells indicating a spring–summer period of occupation had also been recovered. With the almost total absence of fish scales and clam shells at the Gypsy Joint site, however, the lack of fall–winter ones might well be due to poor preservation rather than a spring–summer occupation.

The four invalid Ps under H_1, on the other hand, all have to do with archaeological data that should not have been observed if H_1 was true (an antler and a mandible from a fall–winter killed deer, fall plant resources, and a cold weather house), and they clearly indicate that H_1 should be rejected in favor of either H_2 or H_3.

Determining which of the two remaining alternative hypotheses is best supported by the available archaeological data is not, however, a simple task. In terms of the number of empirically valid Ps, it might appear at first glance (Table 24) that H_2 (fall–winter occupation) is the best supported of the two remaining hypotheses, since it has almost twice as many valid Ps as H_3. Only 6 of these 13 valid Ps, however, represent positive evidence that the site was occupied during the fall–winter period of the year. The remaining 7 Ps have to do with the lack of

TABLE 24

The Number of Untestable, Empirically Valid, and Empirically Invalid Observational
Predictions for Three Alternative Hypotheses Concerning the Seasonality of
Occupation of the Gypsy Joint Site

Number of Ps	Untestable Ps	Valid Ps (positive)	Invalid Ps
H_1 16	7	5(3)	4
H_2 16	2	13(6)	1
H_3 16	9	7(7)	0

evidence of spring–summer occupation. Three of these 7 negative Ps (no spring–summer deer mandibles, deer antlers, or wild plant resources) are, however, complemented by parallel, positive, empirically valid Ps, making them more relevant to the argument. In terms of the number and the relevance of positive Ps, H_2 has a slight edge over H_3. In terms of empirically invalid Ps, on the other hand, H_2 has one while H_3 has none. This single empirically invalid P for H_2 far outweighs the slight edge given to H_2 in terms of empirically valid Ps. The choice between H_2 and H_3 would thus appear to hinge on this single invalid P under H_2.

The crucial observational prediction here is the presence of the carbonized remains of domestic cultigens at the Gypsy Joint site. This is the only positive archaeological evidence indicating that the Gypsy Joint site was occupied during the spring and summer seasons of the year. The bridging argument that links spring–summer occupation of the site with the occurrence of domestic cultigens includes the auxiliary hypothesis (A_2) that any domestic cultigens recovered from the site were grown during the period of time the site was occupied. If the reader feels that this auxiliary hypothesis is correct, then the year-round occupation hypothesis should be chosen as being best supported by the data. If, on the other hand, the reader feels that A_2 is not correct, the fall–winter occupational hypothesis is best supported by the available data. Thus after full employment of the scientific method, the choice between H_2 and H_3 can be narrowed down to a single question: Does the presence of maize kernels and small amounts of marsh elder and sunflower seeds at the Gypsy Joint site indicate that these crops were being grown during the period of occupation of the site?

In support of A_2, one could argue that the maize kernels and the small amount of cob fragments, along with deer mandibles and a possible wooden mortar, indicate the preliminary processing of corn (shelling, roasting, and grinding). Such preliminary processing is usually described ethnohistorically as being accomplished prior to any movement to fall–winter settlements:

> Then it is gently pounded, which makes the skins of the grains burst and reduces completely to meal. This meal is crushed and dried in the sun. After this last operation this meal may be transported anywhere and kept for six months [Du Pratz, quoted in Swanton 1911:74–75].

In support of a fall–winter occupation, on the other hand, one could argue that the above-mentioned ethnohistorical example may not apply to the Gypsy Joint site, and that corn in kernel form (along with a few incidental cob fragments) was quite likely carried into the site when it was occupied in the fall of the year. This corn could then have served as a stored food supply through the winter months, being further processed as it was needed. This position could be further supported by pointing out the total lack of any other positive evidence of a spring–summer occupation. The lack of hoes or hoe chips at the Gypsy Joint site would be the strongest arguments against a spring–summer occupation.

It is clear, I think, from the preceding discussion, that on the basis of the available archaeological evidence recovered through excavation of the site, it is not possible to determine conclusively whether the site was occupied throughout the annual cycle or only during the fall and winter seasons of the year. When no clear choice between alternative hypotheses seems possible on the basis of available evidence, the researcher must make a selection of the most likely hypothesis on the basis of past experience and any additional available information that was not initially considered (Copi 1972:433). I am of the opinion that the hypothesis that the Gypsy Joint site was occupied on a year-round basis has a closer fit with reality than the fall–winter occupation hypothesis. There are a number of reasons for this opinion. First, the lack of evidence of a spring–summer occupation is not surprising, since ecofactual evidence of spring–summer food sources has a very low probability of being preserved in Powers Phase sites. Some spring–summer plant food resources such as berries and fruits would quite likely have been consumed as they were collected and would not have been brought back to the site, while other spring–summer food resources such as the roots, stems, and leaves of plants would have a very slight possibility of ever being preserved. Similarly, fish scales and clam shells would have a very low probability of ever being preserved in a good enough condition to allow season of death determinations. The extensive excavation of the Turner and Snodgrass sites (over 100 structures excavated), for example, failed to turn up a single fish scale.

The lack of evidence of spring–summer killed white-tailed deer at the Gypsy Joint site, as well as at other Powers Phase sites, is not due to poor preservation, but rather reflects the fact that Powers Phase hunting of deer herds was largely a fall–winter seasonal activity (Smith 1974a, 1974b). Similarly, although hoes or hoe flakes would represent strong artifactual evidence of a spring–summer occupation, they are not recovered with any frequency from Powers Phase sites. Their lack of occurrence at the Gypsy Joint site is therefore not strong evidence against year-round occupation. Thus in terms of ecofactual and artifactual seasonality indicators, spring–summer occupation of Powers Phase sites is to a great extent archaeologically invisible.

Another type of evidence against the Gypsy Joint site being occupied only during the fall and winter is its location less than 1.5 miles south of Powers Fort, the largest of the Powers Phase settlements. If the function of ethnohistorically described fall–winter camps was to distribute human populations more evenly over the landscape so as to utilize efficiently widely scattered wild plant and animal food sources, one would not logically expect such camps to be situated so close to a major settlement. The location of the Gypsy Joint site is, on the other hand, compatible with a role as a year-round habitation site functioning within a dispersed settlement pattern.

PATTERNED HUMAN BEHAVIOR AND THE RESULTANT PATTERNING OF CULTURAL MATERIALS: THE RANGE OF ACTIVITIES AT THE GYPSY JOINT SITE

Statement of Hypotheses and Plausibility Considerations

One of the articles of faith of the "new archaeology" that has been emerging over the last 15 years is that prehistoric archaeologists can, if they are good puzzle solvers, gain an understanding of the total cultural system of the prehistoric human population that they are studying. This article of faith rests upon a number of theoretical assumptions.

The first of these is that the behavior patterns of any human population are organized, predictable, and reflect the structure of the underlying cultural system. Ethnologists study the structure of the cultural system of a present-day human population in part by observing firsthand the degree to which members of that population follow predictable patterns of behavior in their interaction with both the social and natural environment.

The second assumption involves the fact that in the process of acting out such patterns of behavior, human beings often manipulate and modify material objects. These material objects, utilized and perhaps modified during the course of a specific activity, will often be discarded after completion of the task. The cultural debris resulting from any patterned human activity will also be organized or patterned, and will reflect the causative activity. Although prehistoric archaeologists are not able to analyze the structure of the cultural system of a human population through firsthand observation of human behavior patterns, they can analyze the patterns of cultural debris resulting from such patterned human behavior, thereby gaining insight into the associated activity pattern.

This then is the basic puzzle that all archaeologists are confronted with: What do observed patterns of cultural debris mean in terms of human activity patterns? What activity patterns were responsible for the organized assemblage of material objects recovered by the archaeologist? It is often not a simple task, however, to identify with any degree of confidence the specific human activity that resulted in an observed pattern of cultural debris.

An attempt will be made within this section to identify the specific causative human activities reflected in the cultural features and cultural materials described in Chapter 3 of this monograph, as well as to identity the areas within the site where specific activities occurred, based on the analysis of spatial patterning of cultural materials presented in Chapter 5.

A consideration of the specific activities that are hypothesized as causative in producing the patterns of cultural debris observed at the Gypsy Joint site can be facilitated by discussing them in terms of interrelated sets of specific activities. Three such sets of interrelated activities, along with a fourth category of miscellaneous activities, appear to have produced almost all of the cultural debris recovered from the Gypsy Joint site: (a) lithic manufacture; (b) processing of faunal resources; (c) processing of plant resources; and (d) miscellaneous activities.

As each of these sets of interrelated specific activities is discussed, the material consequences of the activities will be explicitly stated, and when necessary, ethnographic analog information will be provided in support of the proposed cause and effect relationship between the activity and the observed pattern of cultural debris. These three sets of interrelated activities were selected as being the most plausible causative behavior patterns for the observed patterns of cultural debris by considering the prior probability of a variety of alternative human activities that might have caused such artifact patterns. Such plausibility considerations involved consulting a reference class of appropriate ethnohistorical situations to determine what kinds of activities were described as resulting in patterns of cultural debris similar to the ones observed at the Gypsy Joint site. The reference class consulted consisted of ethnohistorical accounts of Amerindian populations in the eastern deciduous woodlands, especially those populations situated either in the lower alluvial valley of the Mississippi River or in the southeast United States.

Unfortunately, ethnohistorical accounts of Amerindian populations in this reference class rarely provide accurate accounts of the cultural debris resulting from different human activities. This is especially true for the middle Mississippi Valley area, where few accurate early historical accounts of Indian populations were ever recorded. Because of this lack of specific information within the reference class, it will be necessary in some cases to employ general ethnographic analogs that apply to wide geographical areas. Fortunately, however, the cause and effect relationship between many human activities that are termed technological and the cultural debris is so obvious and so universal that archaeologists need not provide detailed accounts of why they think certain patterns of cultural debris resulted from a certain activity. Most of the activity–debris cause and effect relationships discussed in this chapter fall into this category. An attempt will also be made throughout this discussion to provide, when necessary, a number of alternative explanations of the patterns of cultural debris being discussed.

Lithic Manufacture

The sand ridges in the Powers Phase area, including the one on which the Gypsy Joint site is situated, do not contain any lithic materials larger than pebble size as a result of natural depositional processes. All of the lithic materials recovered from the site were carried in by the prehistoric inhabitants. None of this material recovered from Powers Phase features at the site could be identified as nonlocal material, and almost all of it was very similar in color and physical characteristics to the poor-quality chert that exists just a few miles west of the site in the Ozark uplands. The most likely sources of much, if not all, of the chert and quartzite utilized by the Powers Phase inhabitants of the site are the numerous seasonally active small creeks that flow out of the Ozark uplands into the Little Black River (Figure 2). These creek beds are covered with thousands of water-worn chert and quartzite cobbles that are easily obtained, especially during the dry summer months. Such stream cobbles, which represented an easily accessible, if not high quality, source of raw material for lithic manufacture, have been recovered in unmodified form both from the area outside of features ($N = 5$) and from the Pit 3 activity area ($N = 2$).

A number of the "cores" recovered from the site are best characterized as slightly modified cobbles, since they show evidence of only a few flakes having been struck from them. Such minimally utilized cores, especially those located within the two structures, may represent either cobbles stored for future use or cobbles that were rejected as possible cores due to the poor quality of the raw material.

It is also possible that unmodified cobbles and rejected cores were utilized for other purposes, perhaps as heating stones for boiling or roasting food. It is not possible to confirm this function for cobbles, for although a great number of lithic angular fragments were recovered from the site, most appear to be the by-product of flint knapping rather than the result of heat fracture. And of the angular fragments that show clear evidence of exposure to heat, it is not possible to identify the cause as cooking activities.

The lithic manufacturing activities actually carried out at the Gypsy Joint site were neither very complicated or sophisticated and were not oriented toward the production of specialized lithic tools, except for projectile points. Other than projectile points, a total of only seven finished lithic tools were recovered from the site (Plate V). This low frequency of finished lithic tools can be most easily explained in terms of the possible utilization of cane as the raw material for cutting implements, rather than chert or quartzite. Such a preference for cane is documented ethnohistorically for Indian groups within the Mississippi Valley (Swanton 1911:58). This low frequency of specialized lithic tools could also be viewed as either indicating that few activities requiring such tools were carried out at the site or that such labor-intensive items were not left behind when the site was abandoned.

With the exception of a projectile point midsection recovered from the Pit 5 activity area (Plate VIIIH) the lithic material from the site showed a very low degree of flint-knapping ability. Flint-knapping activities at the Gypsy Joint site could be most accurately described as consisting of a rather haphazard production of primary flakes which in turn were either discarded, utilized without modification, utilized after minimum retouch, or made into projectile points. Evidence for primary-flaking activities at the Gypsy Joint site consists of hard and soft percussors, cores, and lithic debitage. Only three hammerstones (hard percussors) were recovered from the site, with Structure 1 yielding two and the Pit 5 activity area the third. It is quite possible that numerous other cobble or angular fragments classed as debitage may have functioned as hammerstones for brief intervals without producing any clearly observable use modification. Although it is not possible to identify with certainty any soft percussors at the Gypsy Joint site, the antler fragments recovered from Structure 2 and the activity areas associated with Pit 3 and Pits 5a and 5b may have served such a purpose.

Of the 48 chert and quartzite cores recovered from the Gypsy Joint site, 42 were recovered from within or adjacent to four features: Structure 1, Structure 2, and the activity areas associated with Pit 3 and Pits 5a and 5b. It is also from these four features that all of the evidence for known hard and possible soft percussors has been recovered. Structure 1, Structure 2, Pit 3 and its associated activity area, Pit 5a, Pit 5b, and their associated activity area also accounted for 92% of the lithic debitage recovered from Powers Phase features at the Gypsy Joint site.

On the basis of the distribution of cores and percussors, as well as lithic debitage, it would appear that almost all of the primary flint knapping took place within these two structures and two activity areas (Figure 35). This pattern becomes slightly more complicated, however, when we recall that few of the cores recovered from within the structures had more than a few flakes struck from them and that lithic debitage within the structures was randomly distributed rather than aggregated around the cores. Thus while the exhausted cores and aggregated lithic debitage in the Pit 3 and Pit 5 activity areas clearly indicate primary flint-knapping activities, the more random pattern of debitage and the little-used cores in the structures are less easy to explain.

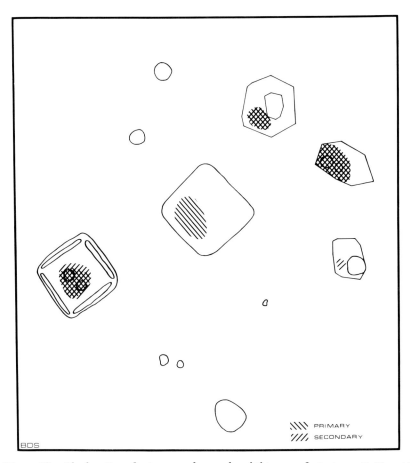

Figure 35. The location of primary and secondary lithic manufacturing activities at the Gypsy Joint site.

Evidence of use modification on primary flakes would include edge polish, striations, or small flakes broken from the cutting edge of the flake. No evidence of edge polish or striations was observed on any of the flakes, and only 11 of over 700 flakes showed any edge battering. It is quite likely, of course, that a much greater number of primary flakes were in fact utilized, but evidence of such use is very difficult to observe on both poor-quality chert and quartzite. Nine of the 11 flakes showing use modification were recovered from the primary flint-knapping areas just discussed, while one of the remaining flakes came from Pit 2 and the other from the Pit 10 activity area.

The material correlates of secondary retouch efforts would include antler tip, bone, or tooth pressure flakers, retouched flakes showing a more uniform spacing of larger flakes being removed along the cutting edge, and projectile points that were discarded during the process of manufacture due to either imperfection in the raw material or to human error. There were no items recovered from the Gypsy Joint site that could be identified as having functioned as pressure flakers. The beaver incisor recovered from Structure 1 and the antler fragments recovered from Structure 2 and the activity areas associated with Pit 3 and Pits 5a and 5b are the only recovered items that may have served such a purpose. The 19 primary flakes that exhibited retouch modification recovered from Powers Phase features came from Structure 2 (9), Structure 1 (3), the Pit 5 activity area (3), the Pit 3 activity area (2), Pit 3 (1), and Pit 5a (1). Of the six Powers Phase projectile points recovered from the Gypsy Joint site that were discarded during secondary retouch, two were recovered from Structure 2, two from the Pit 3 activity area, one from the Pit 10 activity area, and one approximately 10 feet south of Structure 1.

On the basis of the distribution of retouched flakes and rejected projectile points, most of the secondary retouch efforts were carried out in the same areas where production of primary flakes occurred: both structures and the Pit 3 and Pit 5 activity areas (Figure 35). This does not indicate that all of the flint knapping took place within these features, but rather that these were the locations as the Gypsy Joint site where almost all of the primary flaking and secondary retouch activities were carried out. The Pit 10 activity area contained a significant amount of lithic debitage as well as a flake showing use modification and a rejected Powers Phase projectile point.

Similarly, with the exception of Pit 10, one or two cores were recovered either within or closely associated with each of the low-density features. These isolated cores, unaccompanied by either retouched flakes or much lithic debitage, probably represent short-term production of a few primary flakes needed for a specific purpose associated with the function of each of the low-density features.

Two questions concerning the possible function and spatial distribution of lithic material at the Gypsy Joint site remain unresolved. The first involves the extent to which lithic debitage, especially large chert, quartzite, and sandstone angular fragments, may have been employed as heating stones in the roasting or boiling of food. If such lithic items did serve such a purpose, their spatial distribution across the Gypsy Joint site would not be solely a function of primary flaking activities. A second and related question involves the function of the large quantity of sandstone angular fragments recovered from the site. With the exception of Structure 1, where the distribution of sandstone angular fragments paralleled that of plant remains, there was no clear spatial aggregation of sandstone fragments; they have the same spatial distribution as other lithic debris at the site. This co-occurrence with primary flaking debitage could be explained in terms the use of sandstone fragments to prepare the striking platforms on cores, but there is no direct evidence for this functional role, and there are many more sandstone fragments present at the site than would be needed to serve such a purpose. The larger of the sandstone fragments may also have been employed as anvils or grinding stones or as manos, but few show any use modification. This still does not explain the presence of the smaller fragments, unless they represent debitage from battering of anvil stones.

Processing of Faunal Resources

Eighty-two skeletal elements representing a minimum of 12 individual animals provide evidence that the Powers Phase inhabitants of the Gypsy Joint site hunted and killed at least seven different species of animals.

The white-tailed deer was by far the single most important faunal energy source exploited by the Gypsy Joint inhabitants (Table 20). Although a total of 46 white-tailed deer skeletal elements representing a minimum of six individuals were recovered from the site, there was not an equal representation of various body parts. No right front leg elements were recovered from the site, for example. Similarly, no pelvis, rib or tibia fragments, and only a few vertebrae and lower leg elements, were recovered. The absence of certain skeletal remains might be explained by the primary butchering taking place somewhere else, with only certain body parts being brought back to the site. Similarly, the total absence of right front leg elements might be interpreted as evidence of a pattern of distribution—certain cuts of meat might have been given to kinsmen living at another location. While both of these interpretations are interesting, it is much more reasonable to explain the absence of certain skeletal remains as resulting from nonuniform preservation of different bones and perhaps the selective destruction of certain bones by scavengers.

Evidence for the butchering of white-tailed deer would consist primarily of skeletal elements (perhaps showing knife marks or shatter patterns characteristic of butchering activities) along with tools such as knives, bifaces, hammerstones, and anvil stones. No evidence of knife marks or deliberate shattering was observed on any of the poorly preserved deer bones recovered from the Powers Phase features. Skeletal elements indicative of butchering activities were recovered primarily from two areas at the Gypsy Joint site: the Pit 3 activity area and the Pit 5 activity area. While Pit 3 and the surrounding activity area yielded left front and left rear leg elements, Pit 5a, Pit 5b, and the surrounding activity area yielded right rear and left front leg elements. It is interesting to note that in both the Pit 3 activity area and the Pit 5 activity area the deer skeletal elements were tightly clustered and that these bone concentrations were adjacent to, but spatially discrete from, the area of concentration of lithic debris and cores. Possible butchering tools included a knife found in association with the skeletal elements in the Pit 3 activity area and a biface associated with the deer bones in the Pit 5 activity area.

On the basis of the distribution pattern of deer skeletal remains across the Gypsy Joint site it would appear that most of the butchering of white-tailed deer was carried out along the north edge of Pit 3 and Pits 5a and 5b (Figure 36). Possible butchering tools were also recovered in direct association with the deer bones recovered from these two areas. It is also possible that the small number of deer skeletal remains recovered from Pit 2 and the Pit 10 activity area resulted from butchering activities.

Skeletal   elements   of   small   species   were   recovered   from   the

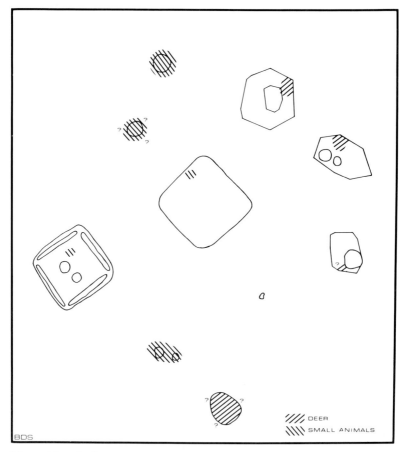

Figure 36.   The location of faunal processing activities at the Gypsy Joint site.

northwest quadrant of both Structure 1 (fox squirrel, beaver) and Structure 2 (turkey) as well as from the following low-density features: Pit 6 (fox squirrel, box turtle, unidentified small mammal), Pit 7 (fox squirrel, box turtle, unidentified small mammal), and Pit 8 (raccoon, cottontail rabbit). None of these skeletal elements exhibited any butchering marks, but 18 of the 28 faunal items recovered from Pits 6, 7, and 8 were partially burned, as was much of the other materials recovered from these pits.

A scraper associated with the small-animal skeletal elements in Structure 1 and the cores associated with Pits 6, 7, 8 are the only potential butchering tools associated with these species. It is, of course, possible that unretouched primary flakes could have functioned in this capacity for short butchering episodes and then have been discarded without any observable use modification. It is not possible to determine if the spatial distribution of small-animal remains within these two structures and three pits was the result of butchering in these areas of the site or if they indicate cooking activities (Figure 36).

Similarly, it is difficult to determine the location(s) of the Gypsy Joint site where venison was cooked. The two hearth areas observed at the site, located in Pit 10 and Structure 2, are not associated with large concentrations of white-tailed deer bone. Pit 3 and Pits 5a and 5b, however, may have originally functioned as cooking pits, but no direct evidence to support this possibility exists. Furthermore, no good ethnographic descriptions of cooking pits could be found.

It is also possible, but difficult to demonstrate conclusively that Pits 6, 7, 8, and perhaps Pit 4 functioned as small-animal cooking pits. All of these pits are similar in size and form, all contained a dark fill, all yielded small amounts of cultural debris, and, with the exception of Pit 4, all yielded burned small-animal bones. The similarity of the features and the presence of burned small-animal remains is, of course, far from convincing evidence concerning the initial purpose of these pits, especially in light of the lack of ethnographic analogs in the eastern deciduous woodlands. But of all of the alternative explanations for the function of these features (trash disposal, storage, mosquito control, smoking of hides or pots, etc.), the small-animal cooking hypothesis is best supported by the available evidence. Choosing one of a number of alternative explanations as best supported by the available evidence does not, however, necessarily mean that the chosen explanation is correct; often it simply indicates that the unknown real function was not considered as a possible explanation. In the present case this may be true because the available ethnographic data base was too limited to present a full range of possible functions of pits of this kind.

A final interesting point concerning the spatial distribution of faunal remains at the Gypsy Joint site is the pattern of mutual exclusion of small-animal and white-tailed deer skeletal elements. The two structures are the only features that contain both white-tailed deer and small-animal bones, and the deer bones found within the structures represent tools and gaming items rather than food remains. This pattern may indicate cultural restrictions concerning either the butchering or the cooking of small animals and white-tailed deer in the same location (Figure 36).

Processing of Plant Resources

Plant remains recovered from the Powers Phase features at the Gypsy Joint site indicate that at least 10 wild species of plants and three domesticated species were utilized as energy sources by the prehistoric inhabitants.

By far the most abundant class of plant remains recovered from the site were carbonized nutshell fragments of hickory, acorn, and black walnut (Table 21). Hickory nuts and acorns would have been both abundant and easily obtained within close proximity of the site, with hickories and oaks being overstory dominants in the ridge bottom hardwood forest areas that would have existed on the crest and upper slopes of sand ridges in the Powers Phase area. Collection of black walnuts, however, would have been less easy because of the low density and widely spaced distribution of trees of this species (Asch et al. 1972:27). The very high representation of hickory nuts at the Gypsy Joint site (comprising 95% by weight of the total ethnobotanical assemblage) is interesting in that hickory nuts have been recognized as an optimum wild plant food source: "In view of their seasonal abundance, storability, caloric value, and complete and high protein content, hickory nuts are an obvious example of a first-line wild plant food [Asch et al.1972:27]." Asch et al. go on to point out that although walnuts are as nutritionally valuable as hickory nuts, they require more complicated processing, and are, as already noted, less easily obtainable.

Further, in comparison to hickory nuts and walnuts, which would be valued because of their high protein and high fat content, acorns are best viewed as being nutritionally inferior in that they are low in protein and fat and high in carbohydrate content (Asch et al. 1972:Table 5). Evidence for primary processing of nuts (breaking of the nutshells for nutmeat extraction) would consist of nutshell fragments, hammerstones, and "nutting" or anvil stones:

> The nuts must be cracked and the kernels or meats must somehow be extracted from the shells. All of this necessarily required laborious work, which fell usually to the women. . . . This was done by means of another stone called a "hammerstone." In many cases the hammerstones are of granular quartz somewhat easily disintegrated, chosen for the reason that the rough surface would not slip from the nut when pounding it [Battle 1922:175–176].

Subsequent separation of the nutmeat from the nutshell fragments would have been very time consuming, and early ethnohistorical accounts indicate that Indian groups in the eastern woodlands often employed a very efficient and much easier method of obtaining the protein and fat contained in hickory and walnuts. This method involved extraction of the nut oil, which comprises from 50% to 67% of the nutmeat (Battle 1922:182), by boiling:

> To separate the oil from the cracked nuts, whether walnuts, hickory nuts, or acorns . . . they boiled the cracked portions in water without separating the meats from the shells, in a suitable pot . . . . This caused the separation of the oil, and owing to its lower specific gravity and insolubility in water it rose rapidly to the top and was skimmed off and stored in pots of suitable size provided with covers [Battle 1922:176].

It is interesting to note that the oil or "nut milk" obtained in this fashion, which was high in both lipids and protein, was often subsequently employed as a food additive in preparing corn dishes (corn being high in carbohydrates) thus resulting in a nutritionally complete dish (see for example, the description of *conutchi* in Wright 1958:163). This is not to say, however, that this was the only method employed in processing nutmeats. Ethnohistorical accounts also describe grinding of nutmeats after separating them from nutshells.

To the hammerstones and anvil stones necessary for primary processing of nuts can be added the material correlates of secondary processing: hearth areas and ceramic vessels for the rendering of oil from the nutmeats, other vessels, small in size, to receive and to store the oil, grinding slabs and manos to grind nutmeats, and, of course, the resultant nutshell debitage.

Although the large number of hickory nuts and smaller amounts of other species of nuts recovered from the Gypsy Joint site indicate that primary and secondary processing of nuts was carried out at the site, and although all of the possible material correlates of nut processing are present at the site, it is still not clear at what location(s) primary and secondary processing of nuts was carried out. Although hickory nut hull fragments are ubiquitous at the site, having been recovered from all but one Powers Phase feature (Pit 4), more than 93% of the total amount of hickory nut fragments were recovered from three areas: Pits 5a, 5b, and their associated activity area (80%), Pit 3 and its activity area (6.4%), and Structure 1 (7.39%). On the basis of the spatial distribution of carbonized hickory nut hulls alone, the Pit 5 activity area is the most likely choice for the location of nut processing, with Structure 1 and the Pit 3 activity area also playing a part in the primary processing of nuts (Figure 37). It should, of course, be kept in mind that the spatial distribution of those shell fragments that were carbonized and thereby assured of being

Figure 37. The location of primary and secondary nut processing activities at the Gypsy Joint site.

preserved may not accurately reflect the spatial distribution of all of the nutshell fragments that existed at the site when it was occupied.

Hammerstones and other large cobbles or angular fragments that may have served to break open nuts were recovered from Structure 1 and the activity areas surrounding Pit 3 and Pits 5a and 5b, as well as from a few other areas of the site, but there is no way conclusively to identify these lithic objects as having served such a specific purpose. Similarly, while no nutting stones were recovered from the Gypsy Joint site, any of the larger sandstone angular fragments may have served such a purpose and yet not exhibit any evidence of use modification.

The distribution of manos and grinding-slab fragments suggests that secondary processing of nutmeats (as well as perhaps seeds, maize, and other materials) took place not only within Structure 1 (grinding slab associated with hickory nut hulls) and the Pit 5 activity area (mano), but also over a wider area to the east and south of Structure 1. Two grinding-slab fragments and four manos were recovered from this general area (Figure 34). Once again, however, it is not possible to state conclusively what materials were ground on these lithic implements. Even the spatial association of a mano with nutshells in the Pit 5 activity area and the association of a grinding-slab fragment with nutshells in Structure 1 do not necessarily allow a clear specific functional identification to be made. Finally, although the ceramic vessels needed for the rendering of oil from nutmeats were represented in all of the areas where carbonized nutshell fragments were concentrated in large amounts, it is not possible to say conclusively that they ever served this specific purpose.

The processing of maize was also carried out at the Gypsy Joint site, judging from the recovery of carbonized corn kernels from all but two of the Powers Phase features (Pits 4 and 8). The largest amounts of maize were recovered from Structure 1 (6%), Structure 2 (4%), the Pit 5 activity area (25%), and the maize grain concentration (58%). Unfortunately, it is impossible to determine if corn was brought to the site prior to being shucked. In fact, the only evidence of maize kernels still on the cob, shucked or unshucked, when brought to the site consists of a few carbonized cob fragments recovered from Structure 2.

Primary processing of corn (removing the kernels from the cob) would have been accomplished by a grater. A number of ethnohistorical accounts identify deer mandibles as functioning in this capacity. Consider the following description of a Choctaw recipe for *paluska mihgofah* (grated bread): "Shuck the ears and grate the corn from the cob on a coarse grater. . . . In tribal days before tin or iron utensils were introduced by foreign traders, the grater used in making fresh meal was the jaw bone with the teeth of a deer [Wright 1958:160–161]." A similar account of the employment of deer-jaw graters by the Seneca is given in Harrington (1908): "Another implement used in the preparation of green corn was the scraper made from one of the rami of a deer's lower jaw by simply removing the projecting processes back of the teeth. . . . This was for scraping the corn from the cob. . . . Corn prepared with its aid is called by a name that signifies 'already chewed' [p. 580]." Of the five deer mandibles that were recovered from Powers Phase features at the Gypsy Joint site, two were recovered from Structure 1, two from Structure 2, and one from Pit 2.

According to many ethnohistorical accounts, secondary processing of maize (breaking the grains) was accomplished with a wooden mortar and pestle. A detailed description of these corn-processing implements is given by Wright: "The mortar and pestle, in fact, were necessary in preparing practically every corn dish [1958:156–157]." Such wooden mortars were manufactured from log sections that ranged from about 1 to

1.5 feet in diameter: "The wooden mortar was made from a log block about two feet long, cut from the trunk of a tree with a diameter of 12 to 16 inches [Wright 1958:156]."

Hickory is often identified in ethnohistorical accounts as being the preferred species for manufacturing such mortars: "A tree which we call red hickory, the heart whereof being very red, firm and durable" was used in making "walking sticks, mortars, pestles [Lawson 1860:165, quoted in Swanton 1946:558]." Similarly: "The Choctaw esteemed most mortars made of hickory as conveying the best taste to the flour. The second choice was usually oak [Swanton 1946:559]."

Such wooden mortars were invariably located close to domestic structures:

> The mortar which is simply a log several feet high with the bark removed having a cavity about eight inches deep, seems, moreover, to be an important domestic fetish. We find that it is connected in some way with the growing up and the future prospects of the children of the family. It occupies a permanent position in the door yard, or the space in front of the house. Only one mortar is owned by the family and there is a strong feeling, even today, against moving it about [Speck 1904:4, quoted in Swanton 1946:561].

(See also Swanton 1946:Plates 72 and 73; Wright 1958: Figure 1, Figure 2, for the location of wooden mortars adjacent to structures.)

A carbonized section of a log recovered directly adjacent to the northeast corner of Structure 1 at the Gypsy Joint site may represent the remains of such a wooden mortar. The carbonized log section is within the size range described for such mortars (1.2 feet), has been identified as hickory, the preferred wood for such mortars, and is situated directly adjacent to a domestic structure, as would be expected.

It is also possible that the grinding slabs and manos already discussed were employed for the grinding of corn. The maize grain concentration located to the southeast of Structure 1 may represent corn kernels accidently discarded during the process of being ground on the grinding-slab fragments located in that general area. It may, on the other hand, represent the only remains of an above-ground corn crib; the carbonized maize grains and cane fragments may have fallen into a rodent hole or post hole and so may have been preserved while the overlying architectural remains of the corn crib were destroyed by plow action. Both of these possible explanations are untestable hypotheses, or speculations, if you wish. It is certainly not reasonable to identify the presence of a corn crib on the basis of only 23 gm of corn kernels and a few cane fragments.

Based on the distribution of corn kernels, deer mandibles, wooden mortars (?), grinding slabs, and manos, it would appear that primary processing of corn took place within Structure 1 and Structure 2, and that secondary processing took place within and directly adjacent to

Structure 1, as well as within the general area to the east and southeast of the Structure 1 house basin (Figure 38).

There are no detailed ethnohistoric descriptions of the methods employed by eastern woodland Amerindian populations in processing the seeds from both domestic and wild species of plants. As a result, it is not possible to identify with any degree of certainty the material consequences of the processing of seeds by the Powers Phase inhabitants of the Gypsy Joint site. The processing of sunflower, marsh elder, chenopod, and knotweed seeds quite likely involved a number of different techniques, including perhaps roasting of seeds prior to either storage or grinding. The 20,000 charred chenopod and knotweed seeds recovered from Pits 5a, 5b, and the associated activity area strongly suggests

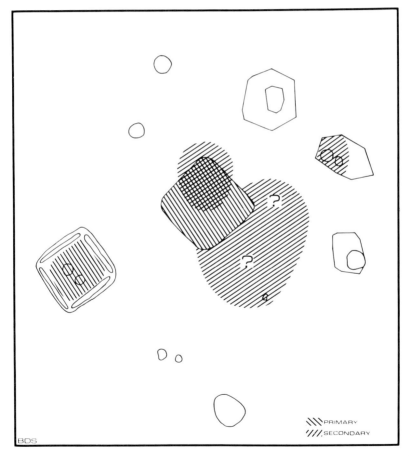

Figure 38. The location of primary and secondary maize processing activities at the Gypsy Joint site.

that roasting of seeds was carried out at this location. Subsequent grinding of seeds could have been accomplished either in the tentatively identified wooden mortar adjacent to Structure 1, or on the sandstone grinding slabs located in the general area bounded by Pits 5a, 5b, Pit 10, and Structure 1.

In conclusion, it should be stressed that the tentative identification of the areas of the site where processing of plant materials was carried out are suggestions—impressions rather than fact. It is difficult to reach firm conclusions primarily because most of the preservable implements associated with plant processing are general purpose items such as grinding slabs, manos, or pots. Second, since those features tentatively identified as plant-processing activity areas (Structures 1 and 2 and the Pits 3 and 5 activity areas) are multiple-activity areas, where a variety of tasks other than plant processing were accomplished, it is impossible to establish a clear association between general purpose items occurring in those areas and the various specific activities. The anvil–hammerstone recovered from Pit 5b, for example, may have been employed in the Pit 5 activity area for any or all of the following specific activities: primary flint knapping, breaking deer bones during butchering, or breaking open a variety of species of nuts and seeds. It is not possible, therefore, to state confidently that its specific function was to crack nuts. Unfortunately, the prehistoric inhabitants of the Gypsy Joint site did not realize that archaeologists prefer that specific activities occur in spatially discrete areas with specific tools so that they can have an easier time in figuring out what was going on.

Miscellaneous Activities

In addition to the above activities, the material evidence of a number of other obvious activities of Powers Phase inhabitants were recovered at the site.

Evidence of house building efforts consists of the house basins of Structure 1 and Structure 2, the wall trenches of Structure 2, and the carbonized architectural remains of Structure 1. A variety of hard and soft wood species were selected for the wall support posts of Structure 1, including water tupelo, poplar, oak, and hickory (Figure 16). Rather than being set into a prepared wall trench, the wall posts of Structure 1 simply were placed, unsharpened, into shallow holes just within the edge of the house basin. Cane was quite likely employed in roof and wall construction, judging from the numerous carbonized cane fragments recovered from the house basin. For a more detailed description of the house building methods of Powers Phase populations, the reader is referred to Price (1969).

The burned soil areas in Structure 2 and at the base of Pit 10 indicate that fires existed at these two locations. These two hearth areas probably served a number of purposes, including providing sources of warmth, and heat for the roasting and boiling of plant and animal foods. Based on the high frequency of burned items, processing and cooking of plant and/or animal foods was quite likely also accomplished within Pits 4, 6, 7, 8, and within the vicinity of Pits 5a and 5b.

Finally, the ochre and galena recovered from within the structures at the Gypsy Joint site can be viewed as the material consequences of pigment production activities. The specific use to which the resultant red and white pigments were put, however, is impossible to determine. Ethnohistorical accounts describe such pigments as being employed for personal adornment, as well as for decorating both clothing and ceramic vessels (Swanton 1911).

THE SIZE AND COMPOSITION OF THE OCCUPYING GROUP

Introduction: The Number of Individuals

The research question of the size of the Powers Phase group occupying the Gypsy Joint site will be considered prior to examining the related issue of the composition of the occupying group. Not surprisingly, this first question clearly fits within the previously discussed general structure of almost all archaeological reasoning (see introduction to this chapter). It pertains to a specific unknown aspect of prehistoric human behavior: How many individuals tend to occupy small, two-structure settlements? Since it is not possible to answer the question through firsthand observation, we must attempt to identify archaeological indicators of the size of the group occupying a settlement. Once such material correlates or observational predictions of relative population size have been identified, the more difficult task still remains of demonstrating the strength of the causal relationship between the hypothesized human behavior pattern (population size) and the proposed archaeological observational predictions.

Total Floor Space and Population Size

The most discussed, and apparently the most accurate, archaeological indicator of the number of individuals occupying a prehistoric site is the total floor space of occupied dwellings. Since the preserved wall posts of Structure 1 at the Gypsy Joint site are located just inside the edge of the house basin (Figure 16), the area covered by the house basin (265 square feet, 24.6 m^2) corresponds closely to the floor area enclosed by the walls of the dwelling. Based on the location of wall trenches within the house basin of Structure 2, however, the floor area enclosed by the walls of this second dwelling (125 square feet, 11.6 m²) was much smaller than the area of the excavated house basin (207 square feet).

Before considering how these floor-area values can be employed in estimating the population of the Gypsy Joint site, the issue of whether both structures were occupied by different groups or by the same group at different seasons of the year should be addressed. Although the author is of the opinion that both structures were occupied by the same group during different seasons of the year, the reader may choose to believe that they were both occupied at the same time by different groups. Population estimates will therefore be presented in the course of the subsequent analysis for both of these interpretations.

Employing information concerning the total floor space of dwellings at the Gypsy Joint site to estimate the population size of the occupying group involves considering the observed relationship between the two variables within an appropriate ethnographic reference class. As already mentioned, the most appropriate ethnographic reference class for the Powers Phase consists of ethnohistorically described Amerindian populations in the lower valley of the Mississippi River, as well as those described in the southeast United States. More specifically, the appropriate reference class would consist of ethnohistorical descriptions of small settlements within a dispersed settlement system that presented detailed information on the size of the occupying group and the number and size of their dwellings. This reference class unfortunately does not exist; the necessary information on population size and dwelling size was never recorded for appropriate settlements in the eastern United States. Since there is a total lack of needed information in the preferred ethnographic reference class, an alternative approach of considering a wide variety of other reference classes (most of questionable applicability) will be employed.

The reference class employed by Naroll (1962: Table 1) consisted of 18 societies: 6 each from North America and Oceania, 3 from South America, 2 from Africa, and 1 from Eurasia. This reference class is less than ideal in terms of estimating the population size of the Gypsy Joint site for a number of reasons. First, all of the 18 cases comprising Naroll's reference class are the largest settlements of the societies being considered. The Gypsy Joint site is clearly at the other end of the hierarchy within a settlement system, being a third- or perhaps fourth-rank settlement (see pp. 7–14). Second, all of the settlements being considered by Naroll are much larger than the Gypsy Joint site in terms of total floor space. The smallest settlement in Naroll's reference class contained 362 m² of floor space, whereas the two structures at the Gypsy Joint site together cover a total of only 36 m². Recognizing the inappropriateness of

Naroll's reference class for this situation, it is still of interest to see what population estimate will be reached by employing the results of his cross-cultural comparison. Although Naroll recognized the logarithmic relationship existing between the two variables of population and estimated floor area, he chose to summarize his results in the form of a simple linear relationship: "Thus, there is a suggestion that the population of a prehistoric settlement can be very roughly estimated by archaeologists as of the order of one-tenth of the floor area in square meters occupied by its dwellings [1962:588]."

If Naroll's ratio of population to floor area is applied to the Gypsy Joint site, a population estimate of 2.5 individuals is reached for Structure 1, while 1.2 individuals are projected for Structure 2. I concur with Binford (1970:85) that Naroll's formula produces population estimates for small settlements that are quite likely too low. This is also suggested by the fact that the four smallest settlements considered by Naroll all fall below the regression line (1962: Figure 1). The mean ratio of floor area to population size for these four settlements (1 individual for each 4.74 m² of floor space) is more than twice as large as Naroll's ratio for the larger sample. Employing this mean ratio of floor area to population size for the four smallest settlements in Naroll's reference class, a population estimate of 5.2 individuals is obtained for Structure 1, and 2.5 individuals for Structure 2.

The reference class employed by Cook and Heizer (1965) in a similar consideration of the relationship between floor space and population is still not ideal, but it is certainly more appropriate than Naroll's. Their reference class, consisting of 30 California tribal or geographical regions (1965, Table 8), exhibited a range of variation of mean total floor space per settlement of 275 to 4360 square feet and a range of variation of total individuals per settlement of 18 to 76. Furthermore, almost all of the settlements within this California reference class contained fewer than 10 structures. This class does, however, have a number of shortcomings. First, few of the groups within the class are horticulturists. Second, the environmental–climatic situation is not very comparable to the Powers Phase area. Third, the small range of variation in settlement size (2.5 to 25 houses per settlement, with the great majority of the settlements having from 4 to 9 houses—1965, Table 8) is very different from the Powers Phase situation.

Even though there are a number of obvious discrepancies between this ethnographic–archaeological reference class and the archaeological situation we are considering, there is no data set available for Amerindian populations that is comparable in terms of the detailed nature of the information relating total floor area and population size of settlements.

Cook and Hiezer present the results of the observed logarithmic relationship between total floor area and population size of the settlements comprising their reference class in Figure 8 (page 86) of their 1965 publication. When the floor area values for Structure 1, Structure 2, and Structures 1 and 2 combined are placed on the regression line of Figure 8, we obtain the following population estimates: (*a*) Structure 2 only, 10.2 individuals; (*b*) Structure 1 only, 13.8 individuals; (*c*) Structures 1 and 2 combined, 15.8 individuals.

The population information for 30 California tribal or geographical regions presented in Table 8 of Cook and Heizer's study also suggests an additional, less complex, procedure that could be employed in estimating the number of Powers Phase individuals occupying the Gypsy Joint site. Regardless of the size of individual structures, Cook and Heizer record the number of persons occupying a single structure as ranging from 5.1 to 7.5 individuals. This range, if applied to the Gypsy Joint site, falls between the lower estimates of Naroll's procedure and the higher estimate resulting from the Cook and Heizer procedure.

In a 1972 publication, which includes an excellent summary of the difficulties involved in population determinations, Cook proposes the following general rule:

> For measured space a fair rule of thumb is to count 25 square feet for each of the first six persons and then 100 square feet for each additional individual [Cook 1972:16].

The reference class employed by Cook in formulating this rule included the California data base of the 1965 study, as well as a number of additional cases from North America (see Cook 1972: 12–18, Table 1). Applying this rule to the Gypsy Joint site results in an estimated population of 5 individuals for Structure 2 and 7.15 individuals for Structure 1.

Finally, two researchers have suggested that Naroll's data set is so generalized as to restrict the applicability of his results, and have proposed variations on the 10 m^2 = 1 individual ratio that would be applicable within specific restricted situations. Clarke (1971) has stated that the population of a southwestern Pueblo can be calculated as one-third the total floor area as measured in square meters, whereas Casselberry (1974) suggests that "the population of a multifamily dwelling can be roughly estimated as one-sixth the floor area of the dwelling as measured in square meters [1974:119]." Although Clarke's reference class of southwestern Pueblos is somewhat inappropriate for the present situation, the results obtained in applying his 3 m^2 = 1 individual rule to the Gypsy Joint site are quite similar to the results obtained by utilizing Cook's 1972 rule (Table 25). Clarke's reference class, which consisted of eight societies occupying large, multifamily structures (minimum size—70 m^2), is also inappropriate to the present situation, but it yields population estimates similar to the ones obtained from the small settlements within Naroll's reference class (Table 25).

TABLE 25

Estimates of the Number of Individuals Occupying the Gypsy Joint Site

	Structure 1 24.6 m^2	Structure 2 11.6 m^2	Average of structures	Both structures 36.2 m^2
Naroll				
10 m^2 = one individual	2.5	1.2	1.9(2)	3.7(4)
Naroll				
4.73 m^2 = one individual	5.2	2.5	3.9(4)	7.7(8)
Cook and Heizer floor area	13.8	10.2	12.0(12)	15.8(16)
Cook and Heizer range of				
occupants	5.1–7.5	5.1–7.5	5.1–7.5	10.2–15.0
Cook rule of thumb	7.2	5.0	6.1(6)	12.2(12)
Clarke				
3 m^2 = one individual	8.2	3.9	6.1(6)	12.1(12)
Casselberry				
6 m^2 = one individual	4.1	1.9	3.0(3)	6.0(6)

A total of seven different procedures were employed in estimating the number of inhabitants of the Gypsy Joint site. The results of each of these procedures are presented in Table 25. The population estimates for Structure 1 ranged from 2.5 to 13.8 individuals, while Structure 2 was projected as housing from 1.2 to 10.2 individuals. The estimates for both structures combined ranged from 3.7 to 15.8 individuals. This wide variation in population estimates is to a great extent a result of both the inappropriateness of most of the reference classes and the fact that the relationship existing between total floor space of dwellings and population size is logarithmic rather than linear. It is possible, however, to narrow the range of variation, thus obtaining a more reasonable population estimate for the Gypsy Joint site, by the simple process of selecting out those reference classes that are clearly the least applicable in terms of the size of dwellings and/or the size of settlements comprising the reference class.

Of all the reference classes considered, the one employed by Naroll is least appropriate for comparison with the Gypsy Joint site for a number of reasons previously stated. Similarly, the population estimates obtained by the Casselberry ratio are clearly inappropriate, since the procedure was developed specifically to deal with large multifamily dwellings. At the upper end of the range, the values obtained for Structure 1 and Structure 2 by employing the Cook and Heizer procedure are also obviously inappropriate. This is indicated by the fact that this procedure yielded a population estimate of 13.8 individuals for Structure 1, even though none of the structures included in Cook and Heizer's reference class had more than 9 occupants. This does not mean that the Cook and

Heizer study is inaccurate or incorrect; it is simply not appropriate for estimating the number of occupants of individual small structures.

The most appropriate procedure presently available for estimating the number of inhabitants of individual small structures, is Cook's 1972 rule of thumb, which appears to have been formulated on the basis of the observed relationship between floor space and population within a restricted reference class: dwellings less than 40 m² in total floor space. This reference class is the most appropriate of those considered for obtaining population estimates for the Gypsy Joint site. The estimates resulting from Cook's rule of thumb for Structure 2 (5 individuals), and Structure 1 (7 individuals) will therefore be employed to define the range estimate of the number of Powers Phase individuals that occupied the Gypsy Joint site (5 to 7 individuals). It is interesting to note that this estimated range corresponds closely to the range for the number of observed inhabitants of dwellings in Cook and Heizer's 1965 study (5.1–7.5 individuals). If the reader is of the opinion that Structure 1 and Structure 2 at the Gypsy Joint site were simultaneously occupied by different groups, a population estimate of 12 to 15 individuals is suggested for the site.

Composition of the Powers Phase Group

The following three hypotheses concerning the composition of the Powers Phase group at the Gypsy Joint site can be seen to represent the complete set of logical possible alternatives:

H_1: The Powers Phase group occupying the site was composed of adult females.

H_2: The Powers Phase group occupying the site was composed of adult males.

H_3: The Powers Phase group occupying the site was composed of both adult males and adult females.

The presence or absence of preadults at the Gypsy Joint site is not considered in the above hypotheses, but will be discussed after determining the relative strength of H_1, H_2, and H_3.

Identifying archaeological observational predictions for each of the three hypotheses and establishing the strength of the bridging arguments involved was not an easy task. The most obvious observational predictions about presence or absence of males and females at the Gypsy Joint site involves burial data. The presence of the skeletal remains of male individuals can be employed as a positive test implication for at least some males being present at the site, while the recovery of skeletal remains of females or infants can be similarly employed as positive test implications for at least some females being present at the site. Employing such burial data as observational predictions for the three hypotheses also involves the following auxiliary hypothesis: Any individual interred at the Gypsy Joint site was a member of the group occupying the site. The other type of recoverable data that can constitute observational predictions for the three alternative hypotheses consists of the material consequences of those specific human activities that are exclusively carried out by males and those activities that are carried out exclusively by females.

The procedure for identifying those specific activities that, because of the sexual division of labor, can be labeled either as exclusively or predominantly masculine or as exclusively or predominantly feminine will differ somewhat from the procedure followed up to this point in Chapter 6. A much larger ethnographic reference class will be consulted initially for descriptions of such sex-linked activities. Those activities identified as being predominantly carried out by males and those predominantly accomplished by females within this initial reference class will then be checked against available information within the smaller ethnographic reference class composed of those Amerindian populations located within the lower Mississippi Valley and the southeast United States.

A large ethnographic reference class is initially consulted because of the exhaustive cross-cultural analysis of the division of labor by sex recently carried out by Murdock and Provost (1973). Their reference class consisted of a representative sample of 185 societies, divided into six major ethnographic regions: Africa, Circum-Mediterranean, East Eurasia, Insular Pacific, North America, and South and Central America. Each of these societies was coded for the presence or absence of 50 technological activities or tasks and their sex assignment, if present. Of the 50 activities surveyed, 14 were identified as being strictly masculine tasks (Murdock and Provost 1973:Table 2):

1. Hunting large aquatic fauna
2. Smelting of ores
3. Metalworking: forging or casting of metal artifacts
4. Lumbering: obtaining wood other than for fuel
5. Hunting large land fauna
6. Work in wood: manufacture of wooden artifacts
7. Fowling: hunting of birds
8. Making musical instruments
9. Trapping or otherwise catching small land fauna
10. Boat building
11. Stoneworking: manufacture of stone artifacts
12. Work in bone, horn, shell
13. Mining and quarrying
14. Bonesetting.

The statistical criteria used in identifying these 14 tasks as being strictly masculine were (a) a worldwide index of sex participation above 92.5; (b) all regional indexes of sex participation falling above 87; and (c) minimal differentiation of indexes from region to region. In addition, "in only seven scattered cases out of the 1215 for which data were available was any of these activities reported as assigned either exclusively or predominantly to females [Murdock and Provost 1973:208]."

Murdock and Provost also identified a cluster of nine activities that were quasi-masculine tasks:

15. Butchering
16. Collection of wild honey
17. Land clearance
18. Fishing
19. Tending large animals
20. Housebuilding
21. Soil preparation
22. Net making
23. Making rope and cordage.

This second cluster of activities was defined in terms of the following statistical criteria: (a) a worldwide index of masculine participation of between approximately 70 and 92; (b) all regional indexes above 50.

Many of the specific activities identified as being strictly masculine or quasi-masculine within the reference class of Murdock and Provost are also recognized as being masculine tasks within the smaller lower Mississippi Valley–southeast United States reference class. In his brief discussion of the division of labor between the sexes in different southeastern Indian groups, Swanton (1946) makes the following references to masculine activities (numbers in brackets indicate the numbers assigned to the masculine activities listed above):

POWHATAN (Virginia)

To male occupations should almost certainly be added the manufacture of all implements of war, the chase [5, 7, 9], fishing [18], . . . and such heavy work as the erection of houses [20], the felling of trees [4], and the hollowing out of canoes [10] [Swanton 1946:710].

SIOUAN

The poorer hunters among them made wooden bowls, dishes, spoons [6] [Swanton 1946:711].

CREEK

Men hunted [5, 7, 9], fished [18], warred, played in the great ball games, led in ceremonies, built houses [20], corncribs, and square ground structures, felled trees [4], hollowed out canoes [10] and mortars [6], made drums [8], pipes, calumets, ball sticks, axes [11], arrows [6, 11], bowls [6] and war clubs [Swanton 1946:715].

CHICKASAW

Labor was divided between the sexes almost exactly as among the Creeks [Swanton 1946:716].

CHOCTAW

The men hunted [5, 7, 9], warred, engaged in official tasks, in games, in races, in jumping and wrestling, built houses [20], made wooden [6] and stone [11] implements, and helped their women in the fields [Swanton 1946:717].

NATCHEZ

The men hunted [5, 7, 9], fished [18], cut down trees [4] and cut them into firewood, cultivated the sacred fields, went to war, played the major part in games, dressed skins, aided one another in building cabins [20], made bows and arrows [6, 11], canoes [10], mattocks, and paddles [6] [Swanton 1946:717].

Of the technological activities mentioned by Swanton as being masculine tasks, 10 were similarly identified in the larger reference class of Murdock and Provost. Eight of these were included in Murdock and Provost's strictly masculine activity cluster, while two were included in their quasi-masculine activity cluster. At the same time it is important to note that none of the strictly masculine activities, and only a few of the quasi-masculine activities, identified by Murdock and Provost are described by Swanton as being possibly carried out by females.

Since 10 technological activities have been identified as strictly masculine or quasi-masculine tasks in a worldwide reference class of 185 societies and are also repeatedly mentioned by Swanton as male tasks within the smaller lower Mississippi Valley–southeast United States reference class, they will be employed in the present study as indicators of at least some males being present at the Gypsy Joint site. More specifically, the ecofactual and artifactual correlates—consequences of the following specific masculine activities—will be employed as observational predictions for H_1, H_2, and H_3:

4. Lumbering: obtaining wood other than for fuel
5. Hunting large land fauna
6. Work in wood: manufacture of wooden artifacts
7. Fowling: hunting of birds
8. Making musical instruments
9. Catching small land fauna
10. Boatbuilding
11. Stoneworking: manufacture of stone artifacts

18. Fishing
20. Housebuilding.

Having identified a total of 10 human activities that can be considered as being primarily masculine, it is now necessary to return to the larger reference class and attempt to identify a parallel set of primarily feminine activities. Although Murdock and Provost did not identify any technological activities that were strictly feminine, they did identify a cluster of nine quasi-feminine activities (Murdock and Provost 1973: Table 5):

40. Fuel gathering
42. Preparation of drinks
43. Pottery making
44. Gathering of wild vegetal foods
45. Dairy production
46. Spinning
47. Laundering
48. Water fetching
49. Cooking
50. Preparation of vegetal food.

The statistical criteria used in identifying these tasks as being quasi-feminine were: (a) They reveal relatively low indexes of masculine participation, in no instance as high as 28; (b) regional indexes are below 50. Although Murdock and Provost list pottery making (43) as a swing activity (neither quasi-masculine nor quasi-feminine), it has been added to the list of nine quasi-feminine activities because of its low index of masculine participation (13.8) within the North American subsample.

Several of the specific activities identified as being quasi-feminine within the reference class of Murdock and Provost are also described as being feminine tasks within the smaller lower Mississippi Valley–southeast United States reference class. In his brief discussion of the division of labor between the sexes in different southeastern Indian groups, Swanton (1946) makes the following references to feminine activities (numbers in brackets indicate the numbers assigned to the feminine activities listed above):

POWHATAN (Virginia)

Women prepared food [50] and cooked [49]; planted and gathered in the corn; dressed skins; made mats, baskets, and pots [43] [Swanton 1946:710].

SIOUAN

Women beat corn in mortars [50], cooked [49], made mats, baskets, girdles of opossum hair, and pots [43] [Swanton 1946:711].

CREEK

> Women made pottery [43] baskets, mats, spun, and wove, . . . dried and cooked food [49], did most of the work of preparing skins and making clothing, pounded corn [50] gathered nuts and acorns [44] and extracted oil from them [50] . . . cut and brought in firewood [40] [Swanton 1946:715].

CHICKASAW

> Labor was divided between the sexes almost exactly as among the creeks [Swanton 1946:716].

CHOCTAW

> Women did most of the farm work and went for water [48] and fire wood [40] [Swanton 1946:717].

NATCHEZ

> The women pounded corn into flour [50] and cooked [49], brought in the firewood [40] and fed the fires, made pottery [43], baskets, mats, and clothes [Swanton 1946:717].

Of the technological activities mentioned by Swanton as being feminine tasks, six were similarly identified in the larger reference class of Murdock and Provost. Furthermore, none of these six activities are described by Swanton as being possibly carried out by males.

Since five of the six technological activities have been identified as quasi-feminine tasks in a worldwide reference class of 185 societies and all six are mentioned by Swanton as male tasks within the smaller lower Mississippi Valley–southeast United States reference class, they will be employed in the present study as indicators of at least some females being present at the Gypsy Joint site. More specifically, the ecofactual and artifactual correlates—consequences of the following specific feminine activities—will be employed as observational predictions for H_1, H_2, and H_3:

40. Fuel gathering
43. Pottery making
44. Gathering of wild vegetal foods
48. Water fetching
49. Cooking
50. Preparation of vegetal food.

Having identified a total of 6 human activities that can be considered primarily feminine and 10 activities that can be considered primarily masculine, the material consequences of these activities, along with burial data, can now be employed to assess the relative strength of the three alternative hypotheses.

H_1: The Powers Phase group occupying the Gypsy Joint site was composed of adult females.

Auxiliary hypotheses:

A_1: Any individual interred at the Gypsy Joint site was a member of the group occupying the site.

A_2: Activities 4, 5, 6, 7, 8, 9, 10, 11, 18, and 20 were carried out only by males.

A_3: Activities 40, 43, 44, 48, 49, and 50 were carried out only by females.

Observational predictions:

P_1: The skeletal remains of females might be present at the Gypsy Joint site (0 = not observed during excavation).

P_2: The skeletal remains of infants might be present at the Gypsy Joint site, especially beneath the floor of Structure 1 or Structure 2 (0 = not observed during excavation).

P_3: The skeletal remains of males should not be present at the Gypsy Joint site (+ = not observed during excavation).

P_4: The material consequences of primarily female activities (40, 43, 44, 48, 49, 50) might be present at the Gypsy Joint site (+): The material consequences of the following activities were observed at the Gypsy Joint site:

44. Gathering of wild vegetal food—see pages 101 and 170
49. Cooking—see pages 101 and 176
50. Preparation of vegetal food—see pages 101 and 170

No clear evidence of (40) fuel gathering, (43) pottery making, or (48) water fetching was recovered from the site.

P_5: The material consequences of primarily male activities (4, 5, 6, 7, 8, 9, 10, 11, 18, 20) should not be present at the Gypsy Joint site (−): The material consequences of the following activities were observed at the Gypsy Joint site:

4. Lumbering—see page 176
5. Hunting large land fauna—see page 167
7. Fowling—see page 167
9. Catching small land fauna—see page 167
11. Stoneworking—see page 163
20. Housebuilding—see page 176

Although only a single observational prediction under H_1 has been shown to be empirically false (P_5), the number and the variety of primarily male activities that were carried out at the Gypsy Joint site serve to question seriously the strength of H_1.

H_2: The Powers Phase group occupying the Gypsy Joint site was composed of adult males.

Since the auxiliary hypotheses under H_2 would be the same as those listed under H_1 and since the observational predictions under H_2 would consist of the exact opposites of P_1 through P_5 under H_1, it is not necessary to present them in any detail. As is the case with H_1, H_2 would have only a single observational prediction shown to be empirically false, but the number and the variety of primarily female activities that were carried out at the Gypsy Joint site serve to question seriously the strength of the adult-males-only hypothesis.

H_3: The Powers Phase group occupying the Gypsy Joint site was composed of both adult males and adult females.

Once again, it is not necessary to list the auxiliary hypotheses and observational predictions under H_3 since they would be the same as those listed under H_1, the single exception being that all of the observational predictions would be positive, taking the "might be present" form. This third alternative hypothesis is clearly the one that is best supported by the relevant data recovered from the site. The abundant material remains of both predominantly male and predominantly female activities carried out at the Gypsy Joint site is, I think, convincing evidence that both adult males and adult females comprised the Powers Phase group of from five to seven individuals.

The question as to whether children or infants were present at the Gypsy Joint site was not considered in the above discussion for the simple reason that children and infants are, to a great extent, archaeologically invisible if burial data are not available. Although observational predictions other than children's skeletal remains could be proposed (i.e., the presence of children's toys, cradle boards, clothing, etc.), such potential material evidence of children has not as yet been recovered from any Powers Phase site. The infant burials frequently found beneath house floors at the Turner and Snodgrass sites, however, provide clear evidence of children being present at the larger fortified Powers Phase settlements.

This is not to say that subadults could not have been present at the Gypsy Joint site, but rather that the argument supporting the hypothesis that subadults were present at the site must be rather tenuous due to the total lack of any direct archaeological evidence. The preceding analysis of the cultural debris recovered from the Gypsy Joint site supports the hypothesis that a group of from five to seven individuals, including both adult males and adult females, occupied this small settlement on a year-round basis. The argument I present now is based on an aspect of the composition of the Powers Phase group occupying the Gypsy Joint site that has not yet been considered: the relative strength of the social ties that existed between the individuals comprising the occupying group.

Judging from the enormous amount of ethnographic information available concerning both historically described and present-day groups of similar size that occupied small settlements on a year-round basis, it would be very surprising if the five to seven individuals occupying the Gypsy Joint site did not share very close ties of kinship. More specifically, if the Gypsy Joint inhabitants were in fact related through kinship, the most likely social grouping would be a nuclear family consisting of an adult male, an adult female (the procreative couple), and their offspring. Discussing the size and composition of such nuclear family groupings, Cook (1972) states the following:

> Family size must conform to certain biological and demographic principles. If a population is to maintain itself, each reproductive pair must produce two offspring who survive to maturity. Hence the absolute minimum family size, if the group is not to head for extinction, is four. Under usual circumstances, in order to allow for death in early years, each pair must produce at least three children. Hence the family size will approach five. If additional members are to be allowed, and these average one per family, the household reaches close to six. Thus it would be expected that, if conditions are normal or nearly so, the number of persons in a nuclear family would range from approximately 4.5 to 6.0 [Cook 1972:13].

It is also possible, however, that the group occupying the Gypsy Joint site was a minimally extended family that included a few secondary relatives. If this was the case, the most likely secondary relatives to be present would have been one or more parents of the procreative couple or the spouse of an older child who married but did not form a separate household. The hypothesis that the Gypsy Joint site was occupied by a nuclear or minimally extended family group may appear to be pure speculation to some readers, especially considering the total lack of burial data for the Gypsy Joint site. I would argue, nevertheless, that it would be difficult to have very much confidence in any alternative hypothesis. The easiest way to demonstrate the strength of the nuclear family hypothesis is by outlining the procedure that could be employed in selecting the largest possible appropriate ethnographic reference class:

1. Begin with all ethnohistorical and ethnographic descriptions of human populations that practice horticulture.
2. Consider all descriptions of settlements of such horticultural populations that consist of not more than two structures, each of which covers less than 30 m^2 in floor space.

3. Consider only those settlements that were occupied for more than 2 months.
4. Determine how many of these settlements were not occupied by nuclear or minimally extended family groups.

Although I have not carried out this procedure, I am willing to predict a very high degree of correlation (>95%) between such settlements and nuclear–minimally extended family occupying groups. If the reader is willing to accept the hypotheses of (a) year-round occupation of the Gypsy Joint site; (b) five to seven individuals comprising the occupying group; and (c) males and females both being present in the occupying group, the strength of the nuclear family hypothesis is increased even more.

Finally, it should be emphasized that it is not possible to determine with absolute certainty that the Gypsy Joint site was occupied by a nuclear family; it is not possible to make a statement of *fact* in this regard. Archaeologists are rarely, if ever, able to make statements of fact concerning human behavior; they are invariably limited to making probability statements concerning the relative strength of alternative hypotheses about such behavior.

DURATION OF OCCUPATION

Statement of Hypotheses and Plausibility Considerations

Under the general problem area of duration of occupation of the Gypsy Joint site, the following pair of alternative hypotheses were formulated:

H_1: The Gypsy Joint site was occupied for a period of time comparable to that of the fortified villages of the Powers Phase.
H_2: The Gypsy Joint site was occupied for a period of time comparable to that of Powers Fort, the ceremonial center of the Powers Phase.

These hypotheses were formulated on the basis of plausibility considerations involving an archaeological rather than an ethnographic reference class. The particular archaeological reference class consists of the Powers Phase sites that had been excavated prior to the Gypsy Joint site. With the exception of Powers Fort, the ceremonial center of the Powers Phase, all of the sites at which excavations were carried out prior to 1974 (Turner, Snodgrass, Wilborn, Flurry) were clearly occupied for only a short period of time, probably for less than 5 years. All four of these sites were fortified villages, and all were located on sand ridges to the east of Powers Fort (Figure 2). Powers Fort, on the other hand, was occupied for a longer period of time, judging from a variety of different kinds of archaeological information, to be discussed below. Powers Fort also differs from the other Powers Phase sites excavated prior to 1974 not only in terms of its larger size and the presence of mounds at the site, but in terms of its location on the same ridge as the Gypsy Joint site.

Prior to the actual excavation of the Gypsy Joint site, and based on the archaeological reference class consisting of previously excavated Powers Phase sites, it was thought, on the one hand, that the Gypsy Joint site may have been occupied for a length of time comparable to that of Powers Fort. Perhaps all of the settlements located on the same ridge as Powers Fort were occupied for fairly long periods of time, whereas settlements located on outlying ridges underwent short-term occupations. On the other hand, it could be argued, that with the exception of Powers Fort, all Powers Phase sites were occupied for only short periods of time. The two alternative hypotheses listed above therefore seemed logical ones to test.

Observational Predictions and Auxiliary Hypotheses

Three different kinds of archaeological data could be employed to formulate observational predictions for each of the alternative hypotheses presented above:

1. The relative degree of midden accumulation at the Gypsy Joint site
2. The number of times structures were rebuilt at the Gypsy Joint site
3. The length of time that the amount of animal meat represented at the Gypsy Joint site would have satisfied the protein requirements of the occupying group.

The relative degree of midden accumulation at the Gypsy Joint site can be employed as a criterion for selecting between H_1 and H_2 in that a fairly thick (1–2 feet) sheet midden of cultural debris has been observed over part of the habitation area within the palisade at Powers Fort. Such a general deposit of accumulated cultural debris has not, however, been observed at any other excavated Powers Phase site. The characteristic pattern of occurrence of cultural debris at the Turner and Snodgrass sites, for example, consisted of fairly high density values of cultural debris within structures and refuse pits, but with very little in the way of cultural debris occurring outside of features. These sites were not occupied for a long enough period of time to allow the accumulation of a general midden deposit comparable to that of Powers Fort.

Similarly, the single structure excavated at Powers Fort contained three separate superimposed house floors and corresponding wall trenches, indicating that the structure had been rebuilt at least twice during its time span of occupation. In contrast, structures at the Turner and Snodgrass sites showed no evidence of having been rebuilt. Clearly, none of these structures were occupied long enough to necessitate rebuilding.

Since only a single structure has been excavated at Powers Fort, it is not possible to estimate accurately either the amount of animal meat represented at the site or the size of the occupying group. It is, however, possible to quantify these variables, at least roughly, for the Turner and Snodgrass sites. The 41 structures and associated refuse pits at the Turner site yielded the skeletal remains of animals representing a minimum of 3582 lb of edible meat (Smith 1975:205–206), or approximately 87 lb of meat per structure. Similarly, the skeletal remains of animals recovered from the Snodgrass site represented a minimum of 13,364 lb of edible meat (Smith 1975:207–209), or approximately 178 lb of edible meat per structure. If the Gypsy Joint site was occupied for approximately the same period of time as the Turner and Snodgrass sites, skeletal remains of animals representing an edible meat yield of from 160 to 360 lb might be expected to be recovered from the two-structure settlement.

The Relative Strength of the Alternative Hypotheses

On the basis of each of the criteria listed above, H_1—the Gypsy Joint site was occupied for a period of time comparable to that of the fortified villages of the Powers Phase—is clearly best supported by the available archaeological information. First, very little in the way of cultural debris was recovered from outside of Powers Phase features at the Gypsy Joint site (Table 1). Second, there was no evidence of structures having been rebuilt at the Gypsy Joint site. Finally, the skeletal elements of six different species of animals, representing an estimated 490 lb of edible meat, were recovered from the Gypsy Joint site (Table 20). While this is a somewhat higher estimated meat yield than was predicted on the basis of the meat-yield estimates obtained for the Turner and Snodgrass sites, it is still much lower than the 672-lb estimate obtained from *a single excavated structure* at Powers Fort (Smith 1975:210–211).

While the preceding discussion has established that the Gypsy Joint site was not occupied for as long a period of time as Powers Fort, and that it appears to have been occupied for approximately the same short period of time as the fortified Powers Phase village sites that have been excavated, the specific length of occupation of the Gypsy Joint site has not yet been considered.

One method of estimating the duration of occupation of the Gypsy Joint site is to compare the estimated total amount of protein consumed by the Powers Phase inhabitants of the site with the estimated daily protein requirements of this occupying group. A necessary first step in arriving at an estimate for the total amount of protein consumed by the inhabitants of the site involves translating the estimated amount of deer meat (venison) represented at the site into a protein estimate. A 100-gm portion of venison (roasted) contains 29.5 gm of protein (Woot-tsuen and

Flores 1961:79), or 134 gm of protein per pound of edible meat. The estimated 450 lb of edible deer meat represented at the site therefore provided approximately 60,300 gm of protein for the inhabitants. Because of the relatively large size of white-tailed deer skeletal elements, and the resultant high probability of their being preserved and recovered during excavation, this value of 60,300 gm probably represents a reasonably accurate estimate of the total amount of protein obtained from deer meat by the inhabitants of the Gypsy Joint site.

A more difficult second step involves estimating to what degree deer meat contributed to the total protein requirements of the Gypsy Joint inhabitants. Although deer meat accounted for between 82 and 91% of the total projected meat yield at each of the excavated Powers Phase sites (Smith 1975:12), these high percentage values may be more a reflection of poor preservation of smaller animals at Powers Phase sites than an indication of the importance of white-tailed deer as a protein source. At the Lilbourn site, for example, which is a Middle Mississippi site with excellent preservation of faunal materials, deer accounted for only 50, 62, and 63%, respectively, of the total meat yield represented in three habitation structures, whereas small animal species, especially fish and migratory waterfowl, played an important role as protein sources (Smith 1975:12).

To complicate this question further, it is obvious that the Powers Phase inhabitants of the Gypsy Joint site were not limited to meat as a source of protein. Much of the plant material recovered from the site, including marsh elder, sunflower, smartweed, and chenopod seeds, as well as walnuts and hickory nuts, would have been excellent sources of protein. Due to poor preservation it is unfortunately not possible to quantify accurately the relative importance of these various plant species as protein sources for the inhabitants of the Gypsy Joint site. Thus while it is possible to arrive at a farily reasonable estimate of the amount of protein the Gypsy Joint inhabitants obtained from a single source (white-tailed deer), it is at the same time not possible to estimate accurately the amount of protein obtained from other potential sources.

It is possible, however, to place arbitrary, but not unreasonable, upper and lower limits on the extent to which deer meat contributed to the total protein capture of the Gypsy Joint occupants. It does not seem unreasonable, for example, to estimate that the 450 lb of deer meat represented at the site accounted for at least 25% of the total protein capture of the inhabitants. Similarly, if the potential protein contribution of small animal and plant species is considered, an upper limit of 75% for the contribution of deer meat to the total protein capture of the Gypsy Joint inhabitants does not seem unreasonable. The range estimate of total protein capture that results from this procedure is 80,400 to 241,200 gm of protein.

Turning to the protein requirements of the five to seven individuals who occupied the Gypsy Joint site, it is necessary to obtain appropriate per capita protein requirement values, with the most appropriate analog situation being a horticulturally based Amerindian population with maize as a primary cultigen. In the absence of any better analog situation, the daily per capita protein requirement values for the 1890 population of San Juan Pueblo, New Mexico, will be applied to the Gypsy Joint population (Ford 1968, Wetterstrom 1970). A value of 26.2 gm of protein will be employed as the minimum daily per capita protein requirement of the Gypsy Joint inhabitants, while a value of 39.5 gm of protein will be employed as the average daily per capita protein requirement of the occupying group.

Using these per capita protein requirement values, it is possible to estimate the duration of occupation of the Gypsy Joint site (Table 26). A minimum duration of occupation estimate of 290 days (9 months) is obtained if it is assumed that the site was occupied by seven individuals, that they had an average daily per capita protein intake of 39.5 gm, and that deer meat accounted for 75% of the total protein intake of the occupying group. A maximum duration of occupation estimate of 1841 days (5 years) is obtained if it is assumed that the site was occupied by five individuals, that they had an average daily per capita protein intake of 26.2 gms, and that deer meat accounted for 25% of the total protein intake of the occupying group. Based on this total protein intake approach it is reasonably safe to conclude that this small settlement was occupied by a nuclear family for less than 5 years, and quite likely for less than 3 years.

TABLE 26

Eight Estimates of the Duration of Occupation of the Gypsy Joint Site

	Seven individuals		Five individuals	
	Average protein requirement (277 gm)	Minimum protein requirement (183 gm)	Average protein requirement (198 gm)	Minimum protein requirement (131 gm)
Deer contribute 75% of the total protein	290 days (9 months)	439 days	406 days	613 days
Deer contribute 25% of the total protein	870 days	1318 days	1218 days	1841 days (5 years)

THE ROLE OF THE GYPSY JOINT SETTLEMENT
WITHIN THE SETTLEMENT SYSTEM

Introduction

The last of the five problem areas established for consideration prior to the excavation of the Gypsy Joint site involved analyzing the niche, or role, of this small settlement within the context of the Powers Phase settlement system. It was hoped that as answers were obtained for each of the four preceding interrelated general research questions, they could be combined to produce an overall understanding of the patterned human behavior of the inhabitants of the Gypsy Joint site. Once a basic understanding of the patterned behavior (and underlying cultural system) of the site inhabitants had been reached, it would then be possible to infer with some degree of confidence the kinds of interrelationships that existed between this small settlement and other component settlements of the Powers Phase.

Unfortunately, this did not turn out to be as straightforward a procedure as was initially thought. Even though basic understanding of the Gypsy Joint site as an isolated entity has been achieved, this helps only to a limited degree in determining its position within the larger Powers Phase settlement system. The Gypsy Joint settlement could, in fact, fit equally well into a variety of different settlement systems (Fish and Fish 1976). This difficulty in fitting the Gypsy Joint site into the larger settlement system of the Powers Phase is due in large measure to a lack of information concerning a number of very elusive aspects of the larger system. Because of this lack of information the following discussion will be limited to first summarizing and providing some elaboration of the patterned human behavior of the Gypsy Joint inhabitants and then presenting an overall hypothetical model of the settlement system of the Powers Phase.

The Gypsy Joint Site: A Nuclear Family Homestead

The following description of the occupation of the Gypsy Joint settlement incorporates all of the hypotheses that appear to provide an accurate fit with reality and have been demonstrated to be best supported by the patterns of cultural debris recovered from the Gypsy Joint site. It should be clearly kept in mind that this account does not consist of conclusions that are known to be factually correct. Rather it represents a set of interrelated conclusions that are supported by explicitly stated inductive arguments within the framework of the full scientific method. It is of course up to the reader to decide whether or not these conclusions are reasonable and, in fact, supported by the arguments presented.

The Gypsy Joint settlement was occupied for a short period of time, quite likely for less than 3 years. Occupation of the settlement was on a permanent year-round basis, although, as will be seen (p. 200) it may have been vacated under certain conditions for short periods of time. The Powers Phase group that occupied the site consisted of from five to seven adult and subadult males and females who were closely related through kinship ties. More specifically, the settlement was quite likely occupied by a nuclear or minimumly extended family group. Judging from lack of human skeletal remains recovered from the Gypsy Joint site, either no individuals died during the occupation of the settlement or they were transported to a different location for interment. Perhaps with the assistance of male kinsmen, adult male members of the occupying group constructed a single wall-post house for warm weather as well as a smaller wall-trench cold-weather house.

A variety of both large and small terrestrial species of animals, including white-tailed deer, raccoon, fox squirrel, beaver, cottontail rabbit, and wild turkey were successfully hunted and brought back to the small settlement by the male inhabitants, with most of this hunting activity probably taking place during the fall and winter seasons of the year. It is also quite probable that a wider variety of smaller species of animals, including such spring- or summer-killed species as fish and waterfowl, were exploited by the inhabitants of the settlement, even though they were not represented in the recovered faunal assemblage.

Butchering and cooking of small species was carried out within and adjacent to a series of small shallow pits along the northwestern and southern edge of the settlement; deer were butchered adjacent to pits along the northeastern and eastern edges of the settlement. Adult males manufactured the lithic tools needed for hunting and butchering activities, as well as for other activities, within both structures and adjacent to the pits along the northeastern and eastern edge of the settlement.

The female inhabitants of the settlement collected a variety of species of wild plants, with the nuts of hickory and oak trees and the seeds of a number of pioneer weeds being the preferred first-line wild plant food sources. Although the carbonized remains of these wild plant food sources were widely scattered over the site, their preparation by females prior to cooking was primarily accomplished within and adjacent to Pits 5a and 5b, Pit 3, and Structure 1.

Males were probably primarily responsible for the initial clearing of horticultural plots, with both males and females quite likely sharing the maintenance and harvesting responsibilities. It should be noted that lithic tools associated with forest clearing (axes) and garden-plot maintenance (hoes) were not represented in the artifact assemblage recovered from the Gypsy Joint site. A tropical flint variety of maize was the primary cultigen grown in these garden plots, with sunflower and marsh elder also being raised. A number of varieties of squash, as well as the common bean, may also have been raised, but evidence in the form of carbonized plant remains is lacking. Once harvested, maize may have been stored in the vicinity of the maize grain concentration at the site, although no conclusive evidence was recovered to indicate the presence of a corn crib. The deer mandible graters within both houses and the wooden mortar located adjacent to the warm-weather house suggests that the processing of maize by females was to a great extent carried out within and adjacent to the two structures, even though carbonized maize kernels were found to be widely scattered across the site.

At the end of the brief 1- to 3-year period of occupation of the Gypsy Joint settlement, the occupying group probably took with them those essential tools, such as adzes and hoes, that could be easily carried, while heavy wooden mortars and broken and discarded artifacts were left behind for archaeologists to recover.

Based upon the variety and the quantity of both wild and domestic food remains recovered from the site, as well as the number of tools associated with processing these energy sources, the nuclear family that occupied the Gypsy Joint settlement was apparently trophically self-sufficient. At the same time, however, the presence of galena and ochre at the settlement provides evidence of the participation of the occupying group in a supralocal exchange network, with these nonlocal raw materials quite likely routed through a larger village on the way to the Gypsy Joint site. Powers Fort, which is located less than 2 miles to the north of the Gypsy Joint site, is the most logical source for these nonlocal raw materials.

Similarly, while the nuclear family occupying the Gypsy Joint settlement was both spatially isolated and trophically independent, they were at the same time quite probably an integral component of a larger sociopolitical group. Because of its spatial proximity, Powers Fort is also the most likely location of the larger sociopolitical group to which the Gypsy Joint inhabitants belonged. Although it is not possible to discuss in any detail, or with any degree of confidence, very many of the aspects of the interrelationships that existed between the nuclear family occupying the Gypsy Joint settlement and the larger lineage–clan social groups to which it belonged, a hypothesized model of the Powers Phase settlement system that considers some of these interrelationships will be presented.

The Powers Phase Settlement System: A Model

The settlement system model of the Powers Phase described here is deliberately brief and general in structure. This is because any detailed locational analysis of Powers Phase sites would have to be based to a great extent on the ongoing research of James Price. It is therefore more appropriate for any detailed analysis of the Powers Phase settlement system to be written by Price himself.

The single most obvious variable influencing the location of lowland Powers Phase settlements is the availability of land suitable for cultivation. Such suitable land areas consist of a series of isolated sand ridge "islands" (Figure 2) separated by low swamp areas containing poorly drained clay soils. Not surprisingly, all of the fortified villages of the Powers Phase are located on these sand ridge islands. It is furthermore not surprising that the largest fortified village of the phase (Powers Fort) is located on the largest of these sand ridges. Each of the other sand ridges in the Powers Phase area has from one to four fortified villages varying from just over an acre to almost 3 acres in size (p. 7). In addition to being composed of clay soils having low potential for cultivation, the low swamp areas between ridges would have effectively hindered movement between ridge islands, especially during the spring and early summer period of high water.

Because of the isolated nature of these ridges, it does not seem unreasonable to postulate that each ridge was occupied by a human population that was economically independent and to a certain extent socially and politically distinct from the Powers Phase populations occupying adjacent ridges. Each ridge would then represent the support area of the resident Powers Phase population in terms of horticultural energy sources. Access to land for horticultural pursuits was probably largely restricted to members of the resident ridge population, with ownership of land probably residing at a subgroup level of the resident ridge population.

The total land area available on each ridge for growing cultigens could be viewed as defining the upper limit of the size of the resident Powers Phase population. While it is, of course, quite possible that the Powers Phase populations occupying each ridge were maintained below this horticultural carrying capacity through internal population control mechanisms, it would, nevertheless, be interesting to determine to what extent there is a correlation between the available land area of each ridge and the size of the resident Powers Phase population (measured in terms of total number of structures, total burial population, etc.).

The Powers Phase populations occupying each sand ridge were distributed in two distinct but functionally overlapping classes of settlements: fortified villages and nuclear family homesteads. Fortified villages were, through most of the seasonal cycle, partially empty. Each such fortified settlement would contain a permanent "core" population consisting of a number of nuclear family households. This core population within each fortified village would carry out the same range of subsistence activities as those nuclear families that were scattered across the sand ridge in isolated homesteads. Nuclear family groups occupying such homesteads would also maintain a structure within a fortified village, and would occupy it for short periods of time under certain circumstances. It is quite likely that a series of ceremonies scheduled throughout the annual cycle required the participation of the total population of a ridge, and functioned to strengthen ties of solidarity and reciprocity between the nuclear family groups and the larger subgroups comprising the population of each ridge.

In addition to occupying structures within the walls of a fortified village during scheduled rituals of group solidarity, homestead nuclear families might also have returned to a fortified village to take part in rituals associated with the burial of a kinsman. Finally, homestead nuclear family groups would retreat to the relative safety of a fortified village when under threat of attack from a hostile group. Judging from ethnohistorical accounts of warfare in the southeast United States, such occasional withdrawal to defensive positions would have taken place primarily during the summer season.

This proposed systemic interaction between fortified villages and nuclear family homesteads such as Gypsy Joint is at the present time only one of a number of alternative settlement system models for the Powers Phase. It can, however, be tested, and it is in fact supported to a certain extent by the extensive excavations carried out at the Turner and Snodgrass sites.

The Snodgrass site (Figure 5) contains 38 structures situated within an internal white wall, with an additional 52 structures situated outside of the wall. The structures located outside of the white wall appear to have been occupied for a much shorter period of time than those inside, and they may represent houses occupied only infrequently by nuclear family homestead groups. Structures outside of the white wall contrast with those within; they are smaller, have shallower house basins, less substantial architecture, and rarely have internal hearths. These structures also differ from those inside the white wall in that they contain significantly less cultural debris and have fewer associated refuse pits. Finally, of the 31 mandibles identified as being from deer killed during the fall and winter seasons of the year, all but 2 were recovered from structures within the white wall.

A similar yet less clear-cut distinction can be made between the two eastern rows of structures at the Turner site, which have a high frequency of refuse pits (core population?) and the structures to the west, which have few refuse pits (infrequent occupation?).

If nuclear family homesteads were in fact extensions of fortified villages, the Powers Phase settlement system on each ridge could be viewed as a dynamic, flexible response to the need for easy access to garden plots on the one hand and for protection from raiding parties on the other. This compromise between total nucleation and a more dispersed settlement pattern may well have shifted toward either greater nucleation or greater dispersion, depending on the year-to-year potential threat of hostilities.

Judging from the short duration of occupation of the Gypsy Joint settlement, the location of nuclear family homesteads may have been shifted fairly frequently as garden plots reached the end of their production cycle. It is also possible that the location of fortified villages was shifted in response to the availability of farmland and that all of the villages so far discovered were not occupied at the same time. Thus the degree of contemporaneity of fortified villages and homesteads within a very short time span continues to be both a very elusive problem to solve and the key to gaining any satisfactory level of understanding of the settlement system of the Powers Phase.

Finally, it is impossible at the present time to assess either the relative strength or the nature of the social, political, and economic ties that existed between the Powers Phase populations occupying different ridges. Did social subgroups such as clans crosscut all of the ridge populations, with each clan being represented within the resident population of each ridge? Or were rules of "ridge" exogamy and the resultant fairly weak agnatic kinship ties all that held the fabric of Powers Phase society together? The answers to these questions, as well as the determination of the relative strength of the settlement system model proposed in the preceding discussion, will hopefully be reached as further excavation and analysis of Powers Phase sites are carried out.

Appendix A

Coding Format: Powers Phase Project

Column Number	Designation
1– 2	Site number
4– 5	Structure number
7– 9	Pit number
11–13	Burial number
15	Type of recovery
17–20	Field specimen number
22	Grid quadrant designator
24–28	North–south axis grid coordinates
29–33	East–west axis grid coordinates
35–38	Datum depth
40	General artifact class
42–43	Species identification
45–47	Plant–animal element identification
49	Animal element side identification
51–53	Artifact identification
55	Broken–unbroken status
57–59	Pattern of breakage
61–62	Alteration–modification
64–65	Raw material identification
67–68	Ceramic rim treatment
70–71	Ceramic appendages
73–80	Artifact weight

SITE NUMBER (COLUMNS 1–2)

01—Powers Fort
02—Snodgrass
03—Turner
04—Flurry
05—Wilborn

06—Gypsy Joint
07—Harris Ridge
08—Hunt
09—Bliss
10—McCarty–Moore

11—Smith   15—Stick Chimney
12—Malcolm Turner   16—Widow Green
13—Steinberg   17—Crazy Brothers
14—Newkirk   18–99—Open

STRUCTURE NUMBER (COLUMNS 4–5)

00—Artifact not from within structure   01—Structure 1, etc.

PIT NUMBER (COLUMNS 7–9)

000—Artifact not from within pit   Intraedifical and extraedifical pits are dif-
001—Pit 1, etc.   ferentiated by the presence or absence of a
                                            structure number.

BURIAL NUMBER (COLUMNS 11–13)

000—Artifact not associated with a burial   Burials located inside and outside struc-
001—Burial 1, etc.   tures are differentiated by the presence or
                                            absence of a structure number.

TYPE OF RECOVERY (COLUMN 15)

1—Provenience unknown   6—Plowzone
2—Surface recovery   7—Back dirt
3—Skim surface recovery   8—Churned floor
4—House floor recovery, basin floor   9—Structure–pit fill
5—Final skim recovery (beneath house
    floor)

FIELD SPECIMEN NUMBER (COLUMNS 17–20)

0000—Artifact not assigned a Field   0001—Field Specimen 1, etc.
    Specimen number

GRID QUADRANT DESIGNATOR (COLUMN 22)

1—North and east   3—South and east
2—North and west   4—South and west

NORTH–SOUTH AXIS GRID COORDINATES (COLUMNS 24–28)

Decimal point placed between columns 27 and 28.

EAST–WEST AXIS GRID COORDINATES (COLUMNS 29–33)

Decimal point placed between columns 32 and 33.

DATUM DEPTH (COLUMNS 35–38)

Decimal point placed between columns 37 and 38.

GENERAL ARTIFACT CLASS (COLUMN 40)

1—Ceramic materials
2—Lithic materials
3—Ethnobotanical materials
4—Faunal materials

5—Metallic materials
6—Human bone
9—Noncultural materials

SPECIES IDENTIFICATION (COLUMNS 42–43)

01—*Odocoileus virginianus* (white-tailed deer)
02—*Procyon lotor* (raccoon)
03—*Terrapene* sp. (box turtle)
04—*Meleagris gallopavo* (wild turkey)
05—*Castor canadensis* (beaver)
06—*Sylvilagus floridanus* (cottontail rabbit)
07—*Sciurus niger* (fox squirrel)
08—Freshwater clam, species unidentified
09–74 reserved for animal species, 75 for *Homo sapiens*, 76–99 for plant species.
76—*Nyssa aquatica* (water tupelo)
77—*Carya* sp. (hickory)
78—*Populus* sp. (poplar)
79—*Fraxinus* sp. (ash)
80—*Quercus* sp. (oak)
81—*Zea mays* (maize)

82—*Iva annua* (marsh elder)
83—*Helianthus annuus* (sunflower)
84—*Polygonum* sp. (knotweed)
85—*Chenopodium* sp. (chenopod)
86—*Strophostyles helvola* (wild bean)
87—*Vitis* sp. (grape)
88—*Pyrus* sp. (crab apple)
89—*Prunus* sp. (plum/cherry)
90—*Ipomoea* sp. (morning glory)
91—*Juglans nigra* (black walnut)
92—*Arundinaria* sp. (cane)
93—Open
94—Open
95—Open
96—Open
97—Open
98—Open
99—Unidentifiable

PLANT–ANIMAL ELEMENT IDENTIFICATION
(COLUMNS 45–47)

000—Unidentifiable fragment
001—Scapula
002—Clavicle
003—Sternum
004—Rib
005—Humerus
006—Ulna
007—Radius
008—Metacarpal
009—Carpal
010—Pelvis
011—Coccyx
012—Femur
013—Tibia–fibula
014—Astragalus
015—Calcanium
016—Naviculo–cuboid
017—Metatarsal
018—Tarsal
019—Phalanges
020—Metatarsal–metacarpal
021—Antler fragment
022—Antler pedicle
023—Antler shaft
024—Antler beam
025—Antler tip
026—Complete antler, except for tips
027—Antler combination
028—Male skull fragment
029—Female skull fragment
030—Skull fragment
031—Maxilla
032—Mandible without teeth
033—Mandible with teeth
034—Open
035—Open
036—Vertebra
037—PM_1

038—PM_2
039—PM_3
040—M_1
041—M_2
042—M_3
043—PM^1
044—PM^2
045—PM^3
046—M^1
047—M^2
048—M^3
049—Inner ear
050—Tooth
051—Atlas
052—Axis
053—Hyoid
054—Thoracic vertebra
055—Lumbar vertebra
056—Cervical vertebra
057—Patella
058—Carapace
059—Plastron
060—Tibiotarsus
501—Trunk section
502—Branch
503—Maize kernels
504—Maize cupules
505—Maize cob
506—Combination of 503/504/505
507—Nutshell
508—Nutmeat
509—Nutmeat and shell
510—Seed
511—Fruit pit
512—Bean
061–500 reserved for other faunal elements
513–999 reserved for other plant elements

ANIMAL ELEMENT SIDE IDENTIFICATION
(COLUMN 49)

0—Not known
1—Left side
2—Right side

3—Not applicable (Vertebra, etc.)
4—Both sides represented

ARTIFACT IDENTIFICATION (COLUMNS 51–53)

Ceramics

000—Item not an artifact
001—Two-handle jar
002—Four-handle jar
003—Jar, number of handles not known
004—Flaring-rim bowl
005—Effigy bowl
006—Incurvate bowl
007—Lensatic bowl
008—Short-neck bottle
009—Medium-neck bottle
010—Long-neck bottle
011—Stirrup bottle
012—Miniature jar
013—Minature bowl
014—Minature vessel other than jar or bowl
015—Undiagnostic sherd, undecorated
016—Undiagnostic sherd, decorated
017—Ear plug
018—Ear spool
019—Ceramic pipe

020—Ceramic bead
021—Ceramic rattle
022—Pottery disc
023—Large pottery disc
024—Pottery sherd arrowshaft abrader
025—Drilled sherd
026—Pottery trowel
027—Wickliffe juice press
028—Kersey clay object
029—Ceramic cone
030—Ceramic cone arrowshaft abrader
031—Ceramic cone awl abrader
032—Smoke-hole daub
033—Fabric-impressed clay
034—Clay coil
035—Open
036—Clay cane cast
037—Barnes pottery
038—Clay
039–047—Open

Lithics

048—Archaic and Woodland artifacts, other
049—Archaic and Woodland drills
050—Archaic and Woodland projectile points
051—Mississippian projectile points
052—Rejected projectile point blank
053—Finished projectile point blank
054—Lithic macro drill
055—Lithic micro drill
056—Knife
057—Biface
058—Graver
059—Scraper
060—Chert flake
061—Chert core
062—Chert angular fragment
063—Quartzite flake
064—Quartzite core
065—Quartzite angular fragment
066—Chipped stone hoe
067—Hoe flake

068—Ground-stone hoe
069—Chipped stone adze
070—Adze flake
071—Ground-stone adze
072—Celt
073—Adze–celt flake
074—Core hammerstone
075—Cobble
076—Cobble–hammerstone
077—Cobble–hammerstone–smoothing stone
078—Anvil stone
079—Anvil–hammerstone
080—Pigment grinder
081—Cup stone
082—Sandstone angular
083—Grinding slab
084—Open
085—Open
086—Open
087—Open
088—Open

089—Open
090—Manos
091—Concave abrader
092—Grooved lithic awl abrader
093—Lithic arrowshaft abrader
094—Lithic awl–arrowshaft abrader

095—Concave abrader–awl abrader
096—Discoidal
097—Pottery smoothing stone
098—Shale–slit stone
099—Pebble

Metallic Materials

100—Galena
101—Copper tool
102—Sheet copper fragments
103—Cylindrical hematite
104—Pure ochre

105—Ochre concretion—full
106—Ochre concretion—empty
107—Open
108—Open
109—Open

Bone Artifacts

110—Awl
111—Flesher
112—Bead
113—Gaming piece
114—Arrow point

115—Flaker
116—Open
117—Open
118—Open
119—Open

Plant Material Artifacts

120—Wall support post
121—Internal post
122—Thatch
123—Cane

124—Wooden artifact
125—Split cane matting
126—Grass matting
127–150—Open

Nonartifacts

151—Mud dauber nests

152–999—Open

BROKEN–UNBROKEN STATUS (COLUMN 55)

0—No data
1—Broken
3—Broken, unfinished
4—Broken, finished

5—Unbroken, unfinished
6—Unbroken, finished
7—Unbroken
8–10—Open

PATTERN OF BREAKAGE (COLUMNS 57–59)

Ceramics

00—No data
01—Body sherd

02—Rim sherd
03—Shoulder sherd

04—Base sherd
05—Complete handle
06—Rim section of handle
07—Midsection of handle

08—Shoulder section of handle
09—Handle, midsection missing
10—Open

Cones

11—Base only
12—Base and side
13—Tip missing

14—Core section
15—Side section
16—Open

Projectile Point

17—Stem only
18—Blade (stem missing)
19—Tip missing
20—Tip only
21—Tip missing, stem missing, notch present

22—Midsection (tip missing, stem missing, notch missing)
23—Longitudinal break
24—Open
25—Open

Projectile point blanks

26—Tip missing
27—Tip only

28—Tip missing, base missing
29—Open

Hoes, Adzes, Celts

30—Bit missing
31—Bit only

32—Open

Faunal elements

33—Shaft fragment
34—Distal end articular fragment
35—Proximal end articular fragment
36—Distal 1/3 of bone
37—Proximal 1/3 of bone

38—Complete
39—Fragmentary
40—Antler intact
41—Antler shed
42–99—Open

ALTERATION–MODIFICATION (COLUMNS 61–62)

00—No alteration–modification
01—White paint
02—Red paint
03—Black paint
04—Red paint and white paint
05—Interior paint deposit—red
06—Interior paint deposit—white
07—Interior paint deposit, alternating white and red
08—Curvilinear incising—indeterminate number of lines
09—Rectilinear incising—indeterminate number of lines

10—Curvilinear incising—one line
11—Curvilinear incising—two lines
12—Curvilinear incising—three lines
13—Open
14—Open
15—Rectilinear incising—one line
16—Rectilinear incising—two lines
17—Rectilinear incising—three lines
18—Open
19—Open
20—Curvilinear zoned punctating
21—Unzoned punctating
22—Fabric impressions

23—Cordmarking
24—Bossed
25—Open
26—Open

27—Open
28—Open
29—Incised, other

Lithics

30—Edge grinding
31—Side grinding
32—Corner grinding
33—Edge and side grinding
34—Polish

35—Use modification
36—Retouch modification
37—Heated
38—Cortex present
39—Open

Pottery discs

40—Unperforated
41—Partially perforated
42—Single hole
43—Two holes
44—Three holes
45—Four holes

46—Five holes
47—Total number of holes unknown, but disc is perforated
48—Not known if disc is perforated or not
49—Open
50—Open

Ceramic cones

51—No hole
52—Hole in top
53—Hole in bottom
54—Hole in side
55—Holes in top and side

56—Open
57—Open
58—Open
59—Open
60—Open

Trowels

61—Plain handle
62—Bifurcated handle

63—Open
64—Open

Bone items

65—Burned
66—Butchering marks
67—Longitudinal split
68—Gnaw marks

69—Epyph. not fused
70—Cut
71–99—Open

RAW MATERIAL (COLUMNS 64–65)

00—No data
01—Nonlocal material
02—Greenstone
03—Fort Payne chert
04—Mill Creek chert
05—White nonlocal sandstone

06—Illinois novaculite
07—Open
08—Open
09—Local material
10—99 Open

CERAMIC RIM TREATMENT (COLUMNS 67–68)

00—No rim treatment
01—Left diagonal incising, rim top
02—Right diagonal incising, rim top
03—Right diagonal side notching
04—Left diagonal side notching
05—Right diagonal corner notching
06—Left diagonal corner notching
07—90° top notching
08—Rectangular side notching
09—Pie crust side notching
10—Closely spaced left diagonal side notching

11—Broadly spaced left diagonal side notching
12—Left diagonal rectangular top notching
13—Scalloping, group of three
14—Scalloping, group of two
15—Scalloping, group of one
16—Noding
17–99—Open

CERAMIC APPENDAGES (COLUMNS 70–71)

00—No appendages present
01—Loop handle
02—Undecorated strap handle
03—Perforated strap handle
04—Bifurcated strap handle
05—Alligator-noded handle
06—Tit-noded handle
07—Bent-noded handle
08—Laterally projecting nodes
09—Flattened laterally projecting nodes
10—Lug handles
11—Effigy, unidentifiable, damaged
12—Effigy, unidentifiable, undamaged

13—Human effigy
14—Frog effigy
15—Deer effigy
16—Crested bird effigy
17—Uncrested bird effigy
18—Owl effigy
19—Conch effigy
20—Tab tail without effigy
21—Ring base
22—Tripod base
23—Annular base, unperforated
24—Annular base, perforated
25—99 Open

ARTIFACT WEIGHT (COLUMNS 73–80)

Weight of item given in grams. Decimal point placed between columns 79 and 80.

Appendix B

```
    BURIAL ONE  DATA BASE
06 00 000 001 3 0001 1 0473305775 3094 6 75 030 4 000 1 039 00 00 00 00 00000284
06 00 000 001 3 0002 1 0474405761 3093 2 00 000 0 048 7 038 36 09 00 00 00000346
06 00 000 001 3 0003 1 0472805770 3093 2 00 000 0 057 7 038 36 09 00 00 00000408
06 00 000 001 3 0004 1 0472405760 3092 2 00 000 0 048 1 039 00 00 00 00 00000329
06 00 000 001 3 0005 1 0471605760 3092 2 00 000 0 048 7 038 36 09 00 00 00000100
06 00 000 001 3 0007 1 0471005805 3094 2 00 000 0 049 7 038 36 09 00 00 00000032
    PIT NINE DATA BASE
06 00 009 000 9 0006 1 0475505744 3091 2 00 000 0 060 1 039 65 09 00 00 00000003
06 00 009 000 9 0001 1 0474105743 3092 4 01 013 1 000 1 034 65 00 00 00 00000409
06 00 009 000 9 0001 1 0474105743 3092 4 01 030 0 000 1 039 65 00 00 00 00000010
06 00 009 000 9 0002 1 0474005740 3092 4 01 033 2 000 1 039 65 00 00 00 00001000
06 00 009 000 9 0002 1 0474005740 3092 4 01 015 1 000 1 039 65 00 00 00 00001000
06 00 009 000 9 0002 1 0474005740 3092 4 01 001 1 000 1 039 65 00 00 00 00001000
06 00 009 000 9 0002 1 0474005740 3092 4 01 029 0 000 1 039 65 00 00 00 00001000
06 00 009 000 9 0002 1 0474005740 3092 4 01 036 0 000 1 039 65 00 00 00 00001000
06 00 009 000 9 0002 1 0474005740 3092 4 01 021 0 000 1 039 65 00 00 00 00001000
06 00 009 000 9 0002 1 0474005740 3092 4 01 013 1 000 1 035 65 00 00 00 00001000
06 00 009 000 9 0002 1 0474005740 3092 4 01 007 1 000 1 037 65 00 00 00 00001000
06 00 009 000 9 0002 1 0474005740 3092 4 01 004 0 000 1 039 65 00 00 00 00001000
06 00 009 000 9 0002 1 0474005740 3092 4 01 004 0 000 1 039 65 00 00 00 00001000
06 00 009 000 9 0003 1 0473405746 3092 4 01 023 0 000 1 039 65 00 00 00 00000429
06 00 009 000 9 0004 1 0473905749 3092 4 01 007 1 000 1 036 65 00 00 00 00001540
06 00 009 000 9 0004 1 0473905749 3092 4 01 004 0 000 1 039 65 00 00 00 00000020
06 00 009 000 9 0004 1 0473905749 3092 4 01 004 0 000 1 039 65 00 00 00 00000009
06 00 009 000 9 0007 1 0473505801 3091 4 01 000 0 000 1 033 65 00 00 00 00000020
06 00 009 000 9 0008 1 0472805802 3092 4 01 030 0 000 1 039 65 00 00 00 00000200
06 00 009 000 9 0008 1 0472805802 3092 4 01 023 0 000 1 039 65 00 00 00 00000200
06 00 009 000 9 0008 1 0472805802 3092 4 01 033 0 000 1 039 65 00 00 00 00000200
06 00 009 000 9 0008 1 0472805802 3092 4 01 050 0 000 1 039 65 00 00 00 00000200
06 00 009 000 9 0009 1 0474605806 3092 4 01 057 1 000 1 039 65 00 00 00 00000250
06 00 009 000 9 0009 1 0474605806 3092 4 01 030 0 000 1 039 65 00 00 00 00000050
06 00 009 000 9 0010 1 0474705800 3091 4 01 000 0 000 1 033 65 00 00 00 00000034
06 00 009 000 9 0011 1 0473205814 3092 4 01 010 2 000 1 039 65 00 00 00 00000342
06 00 009 000 9 0011 1 0473205814 3092 4 01 004 0 000 1 033 65 00 00 00 00000010
06 00 009 000 9 0012 1 0473005811 3092 4 01 013 2 000 1 036 65 00 00 00 00000220
06 00 009 000 9 0012 1 0473005811 3092 4 01 036 0 000 1 039 65 00 00 00 00000010
06 00 009 000 9 0014 1 0473005811 3091 4 01 015 2 000 1 039 65 00 00 00 00000135
06 00 009 000 9 0015 1 0473105809 3092 4 01 022 2 000 1 040 65 00 00 00 00000281
06 00 009 000 9 0016 1 0474205803 3093 4 01 033 2 000 1 039 65 00 00 00 00000132
06 00 009 000 9 0016 1 0474205803 3093 4 01 004 2 000 1 037 65 00 00 00 00000020
06 00 002 000 9 0000 1 0468005770 0000 3 77 507 0 000 1 039 65 00 00 00 00000092
06 00 002 000 9 0000 1 0468005770 0000 3 81 504 0 000 1 039 65 00 00 00 00000001
06 00 009 000 9 0000 1 0000000000 0000 3 82 510 0 000 0 000 65 00 00 00 00000001
06 00 009 000 9 0000 1 0000000000 0000 3 84 510 0 000 0 000 65 00 00 00 00000001
06 00 009 000 9 0000 1 0000000000 0000 3 87 510 0 000 0 000 65 00 00 00 00000001
    PIT ONE DATA BASE
06 00 001 000 9 0000 1 0475805912 0000 2 00 000 0 060 1 039 37 09 00 00 00000010
06 00 001 000 9 0000 1 0475805912 0000 2 00 000 0 060 1 039 37 09 00 00 00000009
06 00 001 000 9 0000 1 0475805912 0000 2 00 000 0 060 1 039 00 09 00 00 00000007
06 00 001 000 9 0000 1 0475805912 0000 2 00 000 0 060 1 039 00 09 00 00 00000006
06 00 001 000 9 0000 1 0475805912 0000 2 00 000 0 060 1 039 00 09 00 00 00000063
06 00 001 000 9 0000 1 0475805912 0000 2 00 000 0 060 1 039 37 09 00 00 00000002
06 00 001 000 9 0000 1 0475805912 0000 2 00 000 0 062 1 039 00 09 00 00 00000200
06 00 001 000 9 0000 1 0475805912 0000 2 00 000 0 062 1 039 00 09 00 00 00000004
06 00 001 000 9 0000 1 0475805912 0000 2 00 000 0 062 1 039 37 09 00 00 00000002
06 00 001 000 9 0000 1 0475805912 0000 2 00 000 0 062 1 039 37 09 00 00 00000003
06 00 001 000 9 0000 1 0475805912 0000 2 00 000 0 062 1 039 37 09 00 00 00000004
06 00 001 000 9 0000 1 0475805912 0000 2 00 000 0 063 1 039 00 09 00 00 00000003
06 00 001 000 9 0000 1 0475805912 0000 2 00 000 0 065 1 039 00 09 00 00 00000010
06 00 001 000 9 0000 1 0475805912 0000 2 00 000 0 082 1 039 00 09 00 00 00000280
06 00 001 000 9 0000 1 0475805912 0000 2 00 000 0 082 1 039 00 09 00 00 00000060
06 00 001 000 9 0000 1 0475805912 0000 2 00 000 0 050 7 000 00 09 00 00 00000140
06 00 001 000 9 0000 1 0475805912 0000 2 00 000 0 050 7 000 00 09 00 00 00000110
06 00 001 000 9 0000 1 0475805912 0000 2 00 000 0 050 7 000 00 09 00 00 00000160
06 00 001 000 9 0000 1 0475805912 0000 2 00 000 0 076 7 000 35 09 00 00 00001170
06 00 001 000 9 0000 1 0475805912 0000 4 03 000 0 000 1 039 00 00 00 00 00000010
06 00 001 000 9 0000 1 0475805912 0000 4 05 050 0 000 1 039 00 00 00 00 00000010
06 00 001 000 9 0000 1 0475805912 0000 4 01 022 1 000 1 041 00 00 00 00 00000380
06 00 001 000 9 0000 1 0475805912 0000 4 01 004 0 000 1 039 00 00 00 00 00000010
06 00 001 000 9 0000 1 0475805912 0000 4 01 001 1 000 1 039 00 00 00 00 00000016
```

STRUCTURE ONE DATA BASE

```
06 01 000 000 9 0000 1 0510005600 0000 2 00 000 0 060 1 000 00 09 00 00 00000014
06 01 000 000 9 0000 1 0510005600 0000 2 00 000 0 060 1 000 00 09 00 00 00000004
06 01 000 000 9 0000 1 0510005600 0000 2 00 000 0 060 1 000 00 09 00 00 00000002
06 01 000 000 9 0000 1 0510005600 0000 2 00 000 0 060 1 000 00 09 00 00 00000001
06 01 000 000 9 0000 1 0510005600 0000 2 00 000 0 060 1 000 00 09 00 00 00000001
06 01 000 000 9 0000 1 0510005600 0000 2 00 000 0 060 1 000 00 09 00 00 00000001
06 01 000 000 9 0000 1 0510005600 0000 2 00 000 0 060 1 000 00 09 00 00 00000001
06 01 000 000 9 0000 1 0510005600 0000 2 00 000 0 060 1 000 00 09 00 00 00000003
06 01 000 000 4 0184 1 0512205644 3100 2 00 000 0 060 1 000 00 09 00 00 0C000013
06 01 000 000 9 0000 1 0505005650 0000 2 00 000 0 060 1 000 36 09 00 00 00000002
06 01 000 000 9 0000 1 0505005650 0000 2 00 000 0 060 1 000 00 09 00 00 00000001
06 01 000 000 9 0000 1 0505005650 0000 2 00 000 0 060 1 000 00 09 00 00 00000001
06 01 000 000 9 0000 1 0505005650 0000 2 00 000 0 060 1 000 00 09 00 00 00000001
06 01 000 000 9 0000 1 0505005650 0000 2 00 000 0 060 1 000 00 09 00 00 00000003
06 01 000 000 4 0161 1 0508605688 3099 2 00 000 0 060 1 000 00 09 00 00 00000011
06 01 000 000 4 0166 1 0505805689 3101 2 00 000 0 060 1 000 00 09 00 00 00000011
06 01 000 000 4 0153 1 0509005659 3102 2 00 000 0 060 1 000 00 09 00 00 00000010
06 01 000 000 9 0000 1 0510005650 0000 2 00 000 0 060 1 000 00 09 00 00 00000004
06 01 000 000 9 0000 1 0515005650 0000 2 00 000 0 060 1 000 00 09 00 00 00000002
06 01 000 000 9 0000 1 0515005650 0000 2 00 000 0 060 1 000 00 09 00 00 00000001
06 01 000 000 9 0000 1 0515005650 0000 2 00 000 0 060 1 000 00 09 00 00 00000001
06 01 000 000 9 0000 1 0515005650 0000 2 00 000 0 060 1 000 00 09 00 00 00000001
06 01 000 000 9 0000 1 0515005650 0000 2 00 000 0 060 1 000 37 09 00 00 00000001
06 01 000 000 9 0000 1 0515005650 0000 2 00 000 0 060 1 000 00 09 00 00 00000001
06 01 000 000 9 0000 1 0515005650 0000 2 00 000 0 060 1 000 00 09 00 00 00000001
06 01 000 000 9 0000 1 0515005650 0000 2 00 000 0 060 1 000 00 09 00 00 00000001
06 01 000 000 9 0000 1 0515005650 0000 2 00 000 0 060 1 000 00 09 00 00 00000001
06 01 000 000 9 0000 1 0515005650 0000 2 00 000 0 060 1 000 00 09 00 00 00000005
06 01 000 000 9 0000 1 0515005650 0000 2 00 000 0 060 1 000 00 09 00 00 00000003
06 01 000 000 9 0000 1 0515005650 0000 2 00 000 0 060 1 000 00 09 00 00 00000005
06 01 000 000 9 0000 1 0515005650 0000 2 00 000 0 060 1 000 00 09 00 00 00000010
06 01 000 000 5 0258 1 0515405658 3102 2 00 000 0 060 1 000 00 09 00 00 00000009
06 01 000 000 4 0172 1 0517005683 3100 2 00 000 0 060 1 000 00 09 00 00 00000007
06 01 000 000 4 0175 1 0516105664 3099 2 00 000 0 060 1 000 00 09 00 00 00000005
06 01 000 000 9 0000 1 0505005700 0000 2 00 000 0 060 1 000 00 09 00 00 00000001
06 01 000 000 9 0000 1 0505005700 0000 2 00 000 0 060 1 000 00 09 00 00 00000002
06 01 000 000 9 0000 1 0505005700 0000 2 00 000 0 060 1 000 00 09 00 00 00000002
06 01 000 000 9 0000 1 0505005700 0000 2 00 000 0 060 1 000 00 09 00 00 00000003
06 01 000 000 9 0000 1 0505005700 0000 2 00 000 0 060 1 000 37 09 00 00 00000003
06 01 000 000 9 0000 1 0505005700 0000 2 00 000 0 060 1 000 00 09 00 00 00000001
06 01 000 000 9 0000 1 0505005700 0000 2 00 000 0 060 1 000 37 09 00 00 00000001
06 01 000 000 9 0000 1 0505005700 0000 2 00 000 0 060 1 000 00 09 00 00 00000001
06 01 000 000 9 0000 1 0505005700 0000 2 00 000 0 060 1 000 00 09 00 00 00000001
06 01 000 000 9 0000 1 0505005700 0000 2 00 000 0 060 1 000 00 09 00 00 00000001
06 01 000 000 9 0000 1 0505005700 0000 2 00 000 0 060 1 000 00 09 00 00 00000001
06 01 000 000 4 0106 1 0509705714 3102 2 00 000 0 060 1 000 00 09 00 00 00000022
06 01 000 000 9 0000 1 0505005700 0000 2 00 000 0 060 1 000 00 09 00 00 00000001
06 01 000 000 9 0000 1 0505005700 0000 2 00 000 0 060 1 000 00 09 00 00 00000001
06 01 000 000 9 0000 1 0505005700 0000 2 00 000 0 060 1 000 00 09 00 00 00000001
06 01 000 000 9 0000 1 0505005700 0000 2 00 000 0 060 1 000 00 09 00 00 00000001
06 01 000 000 9 0000 1 0505005700 0000 2 00 000 0 060 1 000 00 09 00 00 00000001
06 01 000 000 9 0000 1 0510005700 0000 2 00 000 0 060 1 000 00 09 00 00 00000003
06 01 000 000 9 0000 1 0510005700 0000 2 00 000 0 060 1 000 00 09 00 00 00000003
06 01 000 000 9 0000 1 0510005700 0000 2 00 000 0 060 1 000 00 09 00 00 00000003
06 01 000 000 9 0000 1 0510005700 0000 2 00 000 0 060 1 000 00 09 00 00 00000002
06 01 000 000 9 0000 1 0510005700 0000 2 00 000 0 060 1 000 00 09 00 00 00000007
06 01 000 000 9 0000 1 0510005700 0000 2 00 000 0 060 1 000 00 09 00 00 00000001
06 01 000 000 4 0083 1 0518805742 3102 2 00 000 0 060 1 001 00 09 00 00 00000200
06 01 000 000 9 0000 1 0515005700 0000 2 00 000 0 060 1 000 00 09 00 00 00000001
06 01 000 000 9 0000 1 0515005700 0000 2 00 000 0 060 1 000 00 09 00 00 00000001
06 01 000 000 9 0000 1 0515005700 0000 2 00 000 0 060 1 000 00 09 00 00 00000001
```

```
06 01 000 000 9 0000 1 0515005700 0000 2 00 000 0 060 1 000 00 09 00 00 00000001
06 01 000 000 9 0000 1 0515005700 0000 2 00 000 0 060 1 000 00 09 00 00 00000001
06 01 000 000 9 0000 1 0515005700 0000 2 00 000 0 060 1 000 00 09 00 00 00000004
06 01 000 000 9 0000 1 0515005700 0000 2 00 000 0 060 1 000 37 09 00 00 00000007
06 01 000 000 9 0000 1 0515005700 0000 2 00 000 0 060 1 000 00 09 00 00 00000016
06 01 000 000 4 0135 1 0521905737 3101 2 00 000 0 060 1 000 00 09 00 00 00000005
06 01 000 000 4 0148 1 0520705705 3101 2 00 000 0 060 1 000 00 09 00 00 00000016
06 01 000 000 4 0142 1 0524005700 3102 2 00 000 0 060 1 000 00 09 00 00 00000004
06 01 000 000 4 0139 1 0522505717 3100 2 00 000 0 060 1 000 00 09 00 00 00000006
06 01 000 000 4 0138 1 0524005720 3101 2 00 000 0 060 1 000 00 09 00 00 00000009
06 01 000 000 9 0000 1 0520005700 0000 2 00 000 0 060 1 000 00 09 00 00 00000001
06 01 000 000 9 0000 1 0520005700 0000 2 00 000 0 060 1 000 00 09 00 00 00000002
06 01 000 000 9 0000 1 0520005700 0000 2 00 000 0 060 1 000 00 09 00 00 00000002
06 01 000 000 9 0000 1 0520005700 0000 2 00 000 0 060 1 000 00 09 00 00 00000007
06 01 000 000 9 0000 1 0520005700 0000 2 00 000 0 060 1 000 00 09 00 00 00000002
06 01 000 000 9 0000 1 0520005700 0000 2 00 000 0 060 1 000 00 09 00 00 00000003
06 01 000 000 9 0000 1 0520005700 0000 2 00 000 0 060 1 000 00 09 00 00 00000001
06 01 000 000 9 0000 1 0520005700 0000 2 00 000 0 060 1 000 00 09 00 00 00000001
06 01 000 000 9 0000 1 0520005700 0000 2 00 000 0 060 1 000 00 09 00 00 00000001
06 01 000 000 9 0000 1 0520005700 0000 2 00 000 0 060 1 000 00 09 00 00 00000003
06 01 000 000 9 0000 1 0520005700 0000 2 00 000 0 060 1 000 00 09 00 00 00000001
06 01 000 000 9 0000 1 0520005700 0000 2 00 000 0 060 1 000 00 09 00 00 00000001
06 01 000 000 9 0000 1 0520005700 0000 2 00 000 0 060 1 000 00 09 00 00 00000001
06 01 000 000 9 0000 1 0520005700 0000 2 00 000 0 060 1 000 00 09 00 00 00000001
06 01 000 000 9 0000 1 0520005700 0000 2 00 000 0 060 1 000 00 09 00 00 00000001
06 01 000 000 9 0000 1 0520005700 0000 2 00 000 0 060 1 000 00 09 00 00 00000001
06 01 000 000 9 0000 1 0520005700 0000 2 00 000 0 060 1 000 00 09 00 00 00000001
06 01 000 000 9 0000 1 0520005700 0000 2 00 000 0 060 1 000 37 09 00 00 00000001
06 01 000 000 9 0000 1 0520005700 0000 2 00 000 0 060 1 000 36 09 00 00 00000018
06 01 000 000 4 0206 1 0508705799 3102 2 00 000 0 060 1 000 00 09 00 00 00000010
06 01 000 000 9 0000 1 0510005750 0000 2 00 000 0 060 1 000 00 09 00 00 00000001
06 01 000 000 9 0000 1 0510005750 0000 2 00 000 0 060 1 000 00 09 00 00 00000003
06 01 000 000 9 0000 1 0510005750 0000 2 00 000 0 060 1 000 00 09 00 00 00000003
06 01 000 000 9 0000 1 0510005750 0000 2 00 000 0 060 1 000 00 09 00 00 00000001
06 01 000 000 9 0000 1 0510005750 0000 2 00 000 0 060 1 000 00 09 00 00 00000006
06 01 000 000 5 0262 1 0515705777 3101 2 00 000 0 060 1 039 00 09 00 00 00000020
06 01 000 000 4 0230 1 0518405751 3102 2 00 000 0 060 1 000 00 09 00 00 00000042
06 01 000 000 5 0256 1 0515505756 3100 2 00 000 0 060 1 000 36 09 00 00 00000097
06 01 000 000 9 0000 1 0515005750 0000 2 00 000 0 060 1 000 00 09 00 00 00000002
06 01 000 000 9 0000 1 0515005750 0000 2 00 000 0 060 1 000 00 09 00 00 00000004
06 01 000 000 9 0000 1 0515005750 0000 2 00 000 0 060 1 000 00 09 00 00 00000006
06 01 000 000 9 0000 1 0515005750 0000 2 00 000 0 060 1 000 00 09 00 00 00000004
06 01 000 000 9 0000 1 0515005750 0000 2 00 000 0 060 1 000 00 09 00 00 00000001
06 01 000 000 9 0000 1 0515005750 0000 2 00 000 0 060 1 000 00 09 00 00 00000001
06 01 000 000 9 0000 1 0515005750 0000 2 00 000 0 060 1 000 00 09 00 00 00000001
06 01 000 000 9 0000 1 0515005750 0000 2 00 000 0 060 1 000 00 09 00 00 00000001
06 01 000 000 9 0000 1 0510005800 0000 2 00 000 0 060 1 000 00 09 00 00 00000001
06 01 000 000 9 0000 1 0510005800 0000 2 00 000 0 060 1 000 00 09 00 00 00000001
06 01 000 000 4 0129 1 0512305668 3101 2 00 000 0 061 1 000 00 09 00 00 00000348
06 01 000 000 4 0131 1 0513305656 3102 2 00 000 0 061 1 000 00 09 00 00 00001077
06 01 000 000 4 0156 1 0512105672 3102 2 00 000 0 061 1 000 00 09 00 00 00002681
06 01 000 000 5 0270 1 0510005784 3099 2 00 000 0 061 1 000 00 09 00 00 00003579
06 01 000 000 9 0000 1 0510005600 0000 2 00 000 0 061 1 000 00 09 00 00 00003748
06 01 000 000 9 0000 1 0510005600 0000 2 00 000 0 062 1 000 00 09 00 00 00000001
06 01 000 000 9 0000 1 0510005600 0000 2 00 000 0 062 1 000 00 09 00 00 00000004
06 01 000 000 9 0000 1 0510005600 0000 2 00 000 0 062 1 000 00 09 00 00 00000004
06 01 000 000 9 0000 1 0510005600 0000 2 00 000 0 062 1 000 00 09 00 00 00000365
06 01 000 000 4 0155 1 0508905669 3102 2 00 000 0 062 1 000 00 09 00 00 00000017
06 01 000 000 4 0164 1 0509905698 3100 2 00 000 0 062 1 000 00 09 00 00 00000050
06 01 000 000 4 0163 1 0509105693 3099 2 00 000 0 062 1 000 00 09 00 00 00000024
06 01 000 000 5 0268 1 0508405676 3098 2 00 000 0 062 1 000 00 09 00 00 00000009
06 01 000 000 9 0000 1 0510005650 0000 2 00 000 0 062 1 000 00 09 00 00 00000006
06 01 000 000 9 0000 1 0510005650 0000 2 00 000 0 062 1 000 00 09 00 00 00000004
06 01 000 000 9 0000 1 0510005650 0000 2 00 000 0 062 1 000 00 09 00 00 00000020
06 01 000 000 9 0000 1 0510005650 0000 2 00 000 0 062 1 000 00 09 00 00 00000004
06 01 000 000 9 0000 1 0510005650 0000 2 00 000 0 062 1 000 00 09 00 00 00000002
```

```
06 01 000 000 9 0000 1 0510005650 0000 2 00 000 0 062 1 000 00 09 00 00 00000001
06 01 000 000 9 0000 1 0510005650 0000 2 00 000 0 062 1 000 00 09 00 00 00000001
06 01 000 000 9 0000 1 0510005650 0000 2 00 000 0 062 1 000 00 09 00 00 00000003
06 01 000 000 5 0259 1 0511105695 3099 2 00 000 0 062 1 000 00 09 00 00 00000057
06 01 000 000 4 0127 1 0512305666 3100 2 00 000 0 062 1 000 00 09 00 00 00000243
06 01 000 000 9 0000 1 0515005650 0000 2 00 000 0 062 1 000 00 09 00 00 00000001
06 01 000 000 9 0000 1 0515005650 0000 2 00 000 0 062 1 000 00 09 00 00 00000001
06 01 000 000 9 0000 1 0515005650 0000 2 00 000 0 062 1 000 37 09 00 00 00000002
06 01 000 000 9 0000 1 0515005650 0000 2 00 000 0 062 1 000 00 09 00 00 0C000010
06 01 000 000 9 0000 1 0505005700 0000 2 00 000 0 062 1 000 00 09 00 00 00000001
06 01 000 000 9 0000 1 0505005700 0000 2 00 000 0 062 1 000 00 09 00 00 00000008
06 01 000 000 9 0000 1 0505005700 0000 2 00 000 0 062 1 000 00 09 00 00 00000011
06 01 000 000 9 0000 1 0505005700 0000 2 00 000 0 062 1 000 00 09 00 00 00000007
06 01 000 000 9 0000 1 0505005700 0000 2 00 000 0 062 1 000 00 09 00 00 00000004
06 01 000 000 9 0000 1 0505005700 0000 2 00 000 0 062 1 000 00 09 00 00 00000008
06 01 000 000 9 0000 1 0505005700 0000 2 00 000 0 062 1 000 00 09 00 00 00000005
06 01 000 000 9 0000 1 0505005700 0000 2 00 000 0 062 1 000 00 09 00 00 00000002
06 01 000 000 9 0000 1 0505005700 0000 2 00 000 0 062 1 000 00 09 00 00 00000003
06 01 000 000 9 0000 1 0505005700 0000 2 00 000 0 062 1 000 00 09 00 00 00000002
06 01 000 000 9 0000 1 0505005700 0000 2 00 000 0 062 1 000 00 09 00 00 00000001
06 01 000 000 9 0000 1 0505005700 0000 2 00 000 0 062 1 000 00 09 00 00 00000001
06 01 000 000 9 0000 1 0505005700 0000 2 00 000 0 062 1 000 00 09 00 00 00000001
06 01 000 000 9 0000 1 0505005700 0000 2 00 000 0 062 1 000 00 09 00 00 00000001
06 01 000 000 9 0000 1 0505005700 0000 2 00 000 0 062 1 000 00 09 00 00 00000001
06 01 000 000 4 0036 1 0509705738 3102 2 00 000 0 062 1 000 00 09 00 00 00000070
06 01 000 000 4 0021 1 0506505715 3102 2 00 000 0 062 1 000 37 09 00 00 00002283
06 01 000 000 4 0020 1 0506505712 3102 2 00 000 0 062 1 000 00 09 00 00 00000038
06 01 000 000 4 0102 1 0507705717 3102 2 00 000 0 062 1 000 00 09 00 00 00000030
06 01 000 000 4 0012 1 0510805743 3102 2 00 000 0 062 1 000 00 09 00 00 00000043
06 01 000 000 4 0016 1 0514605725 3100 2 00 000 0 062 1 000 00 09 00 00 00000135
06 01 000 000 9 0000 1 0510005700 0000 2 00 000 0 062 1 000 00 09 00 00 00000011
06 01 000 000 9 0000 1 0510005700 0000 2 00 000 0 062 1 000 00 09 00 00 00000010
06 01 000 000 9 0000 1 0510005700 0000 2 00 000 0 062 1 000 00 09 00 00 00000001
06 01 000 000 9 0000 1 0510005700 0000 2 00 000 0 062 1 000 00 09 00 00 00000022
06 01 000 000 9 0000 1 0510005700 0000 2 00 000 0 062 1 000 00 09 00 00 00000004
06 01 000 000 4 0272 1 0518205735 3102 2 00 000 0 062 1 000 00 09 00 00 00000078
06 01 000 000 9 0000 1 0515005700 0000 2 00 000 0 062 1 000 00 09 00 00 00000009
06 01 000 000 9 0000 1 0515005700 0000 2 00 000 0 062 1 000 00 09 00 00 00000006
06 01 000 000 9 0000 1 0515005700 0000 2 00 000 0 062 1 000 00 09 00 00 00000004
06 01 000 000 9 0000 1 0515005700 0000 2 00 000 0 062 1 000 00 09 00 00 00000002
06 01 000 000 9 0000 1 0515005700 0000 2 00 000 0 062 1 000 00 09 00 00 00000001
06 01 000 000 9 0000 1 0515005700 0000 2 00 000 0 062 1 000 00 09 00 00 00000001
06 01 000 000 9 0000 1 0515005700 0000 2 00 000 0 062 1 000 00 09 00 00 00000001
06 01 000 000 9 0000 1 0515005700 0000 2 00 000 0 062 1 000 37 09 00 00 00000001
06 01 000 000 9 0000 1 0515005700 0000 2 00 000 0 062 1 000 00 09 00 00 00000001
06 01 000 000 9 0000 1 0515005700 0000 2 00 000 0 062 1 000 37 09 00 00 00000004
06 01 000 000 9 0000 1 0520005700 0000 2 00 000 0 062 1 000 00 09 00 00 00000001
06 01 000 000 9 0000 1 0520005700 0000 2 00 000 0 062 1 000 00 09 00 00 00000004
06 01 000 000 9 0000 1 0520005700 0000 2 00 000 0 062 1 000 00 09 00 00 00000002
06 01 000 000 9 0000 1 0520005700 0000 2 00 000 0 062 1 000 00 09 00 00 00000009
06 01 000 000 9 0000 1 0510005750 0000 2 00 000 0 062 1 000 00 09 00 00 00000004
06 01 000 000 9 0000 1 0510005750 0000 2 00 000 0 062 1 000 00 09 00 00 00000003
06 01 000 000 9 0000 1 0510005750 0000 2 00 000 0 062 1 000 00 09 00 00 00000005
06 01 000 000 9 0000 1 0510005750 0000 2 00 000 0 062 1 000 00 09 00 00 00000003
06 01 000 000 9 0000 1 0510005750 0000 2 00 000 0 062 1 000 00 09 00 00 00000006
06 01 000 000 9 0000 1 0510005750 0000 2 00 000 0 062 1 000 00 09 00 00 00000013
06 01 000 000 5 0255 1 0511505750 3098 2 00 000 0 062 1 000 00 09 00 00 00000046
06 01 000 000 5 0199 1 0513505761 3102 2 00 000 0 062 1 000 00 09 00 00 00000022
06 01 000 000 4 0200 1 0514405760 3102 2 00 000 0 062 1 000 00 09 00 00 00000002
06 01 000 000 4 0187 1 0510305752 3101 2 00 000 0 062 1 000 00 09 00 00 00000061
06 01 000 000 5 0257 1 0515305765 3100 2 00 000 0 062 1 000 00 09 00 00 00000027
06 01 000 000 9 0000 1 0515005750 0000 2 00 000 0 062 1 000 00 09 00 00 00000001
06 01 000 000 9 0000 1 0515005750 0000 2 00 000 0 062 1 000 00 09 00 00 00000002
06 01 000 000 9 0000 1 0515005750 0000 2 00 000 0 062 1 000 00 09 00 00 00000004
06 01 000 000 4 0251 1 0514005816 3101 2 00 000 0 062 1 000 00 09 00 00 00000513
06 01 000 000 9 0000 1 0510005800 0000 2 00 000 0 062 1 000 00 09 00 00 00000035
06 01 000 000 9 0000 1 0515005750 0000 2 00 000 0 062 1 000 00 09 00 00 00000016
```

```
06 01 000 000 9 0000 1 0515005750 0000 2 00 000 0 062 1 000 00 09 00 00 00000008
06 01 000 000 9 0000 1 0510005766 0000 2 00 000 0 063 1 000 00 09 00 00 00000003
06 01 000 000 4 0167 1 0509305671 3100 2 00 000 0 063 1 000 00 09 00 00 00000028
06 01 000 000 4 0217 1 0505005695 3098 2 00 000 0 063 1 000 00 09 00 00 00000031
06 01 000 000 4 0133 1 0515005664 3101 2 00 000 0 063 1 000 00 09 00 00 00000026
06 01 000 000 9 0000 1 0505005700 0000 2 00 000 0 063 1 000 00 09 00 00 00000001
06 01 000 000 9 0000 1 0505005700 0000 2 00 000 0 063 1 000 00 09 00 00 00000001
06 01 000 000 9 0000 1 0505005700 0000 2 00 000 0 063 1 000 00 09 00 00 00000001
06 01 000 000 9 0000 1 0510005700 0000 2 00 000 0 063 1 000 00 09 00 00 00000020
06 01 000 000 9 0000 1 0510005700 0000 2 00 000 0 063 1 000 00 09 00 00 00000003
06 01 000 000 9 0000 1 0510005700 0000 2 00 000 0 063 1 000 00 09 00 00 00000001
06 01 000 000 9 0000 1 0510005700 0000 2 00 000 0 063 1 000 00 09 00 00 00000004
06 01 000 000 5 0265 1 0516305739 3100 2 00 000 0 063 1 000 00 09 00 00 00000070
06 01 000 000 9 0000 1 0510005750 0000 2 00 000 0 063 1 000 00 09 00 00 00000006
06 01 000 000 9 0000 1 0515005750 0000 2 00 000 0 063 1 000 00 09 00 00 00000007
06 01 000 000 9 0000 1 0515005750 0000 2 00 000 0 063 1 000 00 09 00 00 00000003
06 01 000 000 9 0000 1 0515005750 0000 2 00 000 0 063 1 000 00 09 00 00 00000009
06 01 000 000 5 0264 1 0517505766 3101 2 00 000 0 063 1 000 00 09 00 00 00000089
06 01 000 000 9 0000 1 0510005800 0000 2 00 000 0 063 1 000 00 09 00 00 00000003
06 01 000 000 4 0158 1 0509205676 3102 2 00 000 0 064 1 000 36 09 00 00 00000281
06 01 000 000 4 0074 1 0515205680 3098 2 00 000 0 064 1 000 00 09 00 00 00000381
06 01 000 000 4 0124 1 0508205712 3102 2 00 000 0 064 1 000 00 09 00 00 00001180
06 01 000 000 9 0000 1 0510005600 0000 2 00 000 0 065 1 000 00 09 00 00 00000004
06 01 000 000 9 0000 1 0510005600 0000 2 00 000 0 065 1 000 00 09 00 00 00000001
06 01 000 000 4 0162 1 0509905684 3102 2 00 000 0 065 1 000 00 09 00 00 00000050
06 01 000 000 4 0168 1 0508905672 3101 2 00 000 0 065 1 000 00 09 00 00 00000680
06 01 000 000 9 0000 1 0510005650 0000 2 00 000 0 065 1 000 00 09 00 00 00000001
06 01 000 000 4 0183 1 0512505650 3102 2 00 000 0 065 1 000 00 09 00 00 00000001
06 01 000 000 4 0064 1 0512105668 3101 2 00 000 0 065 1 000 00 09 00 00 00000153
06 01 000 000 9 0000 1 0515005650 0000 2 00 000 0 065 1 000 00 09 00 00 00000001
06 01 000 000 9 0000 1 0515005650 0000 2 00 000 0 065 1 000 00 09 00 00 00000012
06 01 000 000 9 0000 1 0505005700 0000 2 00 000 0 065 1 000 00 09 00 00 00000001
06 01 000 000 9 0000 1 0505005700 0000 2 00 000 0 065 1 000 00 09 00 00 00000001
06 01 000 000 4 0035 1 0509305740 3102 2 00 000 0 065 1 000 00 09 00 00 00000207
06 01 000 000 4 0050 1 0508005724 3102 2 00 000 0 065 1 000 00 09 00 00 00000427
06 01 000 000 4 0051 1 0507905724 3100 2 00 000 0 065 1 000 00 09 00 00 00000026
06 01 000 000 4 0067 1 0507105717 3102 2 00 000 0 065 1 000 00 09 00 00 00000018
06 01 000 000 5 0267 1 0508205731 3100 2 00 000 0 065 1 000 00 09 00 00 00000011
06 01 000 000 9 0000 1 0510005700 0000 2 00 000 0 065 1 000 00 09 00 00 00000001
06 01 000 000 9 0000 1 0510005700 0000 2 00 000 0 065 1 000 00 09 00 00 00000001
06 01 000 000 9 0000 1 0510005700 0000 2 00 000 0 065 1 000 00 09 00 00 00000010
06 01 000 000 9 0000 1 0510005700 0000 2 00 000 0 065 1 000 00 09 00 00 00000039
06 01 000 000 9 0000 1 0510005700 0000 2 00 000 0 065 1 000 00 09 00 00 00000007
06 01 000 000 9 0000 1 0510005700 0000 2 00 000 0 065 1 000 00 09 00 00 00000012
06 01 000 000 4 0007 1 0514905724 3101 2 00 000 0 065 1 000 00 09 00 00 00000104
06 01 000 000 4 0009 1 0512105725 3100 2 00 000 0 065 1 001 00 09 00 00 00000070
06 01 000 000 9 0000 1 0515005700 0000 2 00 000 0 065 1 000 00 09 00 00 00000013
06 01 000 000 9 0000 1 0515005700 0000 2 00 000 0 065 1 000 00 09 00 00 00000005
06 01 000 000 9 0000 1 0515005700 0000 2 00 000 0 065 1 000 00 09 00 00 00000001
06 01 000 000 9 0000 1 0510005750 0000 2 00 000 0 065 1 000 00 09 00 00 00000027
06 01 000 000 9 0000 1 0510005750 0000 2 00 000 0 065 1 000 00 09 00 00 00000001
06 01 000 000 4 0190 1 0511005776 3101 2 00 000 0 065 1 000 00 09 00 00 00000026
06 01 000 000 4 0189 1 0511405767 3101 2 00 000 0 065 1 000 00 09 00 00 00000102
06 01 000 000 9 0000 1 0515005750 0000 2 00 000 0 065 1 000 00 09 00 00 00000010
06 01 000 000 4 0243 1 0516805777 3101 2 00 000 0 065 1 000 00 09 00 00 00002400
06 01 000 000 4 0221 1 0514005818 3103 2 00 000 0 065 1 000 00 09 00 00 00000150
06 01 000 000 9 0000 1 0510005600 0000 2 00 000 0 082 1 000 00 09 00 00 00000003
06 01 000 000 9 0000 1 0510005600 0000 2 00 000 0 082 1 000 00 09 00 00 00000007
06 01 000 000 4 0157 1 0514005724 3102 2 00 000 0 082 1 000 00 09 00 00 00002145
06 01 000 000 9 0000 1 0510005750 0000 2 00 000 0 082 1 000 00 09 00 00 00000005
06 01 000 000 9 0000 1 0510005750 0000 2 00 000 0 082 1 000 00 09 00 00 00000030
06 01 000 000 4 0132 1 0513005753 3100 2 00 000 0 082 1 000 00 09 00 00 00003298
06 01 000 000 4 0107 1 0511505762 3102 2 00 000 0 082 1 000 00 09 00 00 00004332
06 01 000 000 9 0000 1 0500005700 0000 2 00 000 0 082 1 000 00 09 00 00 00000020
06 01 000 000 4 0030 1 0508005734 3103 2 00 000 0 082 1 000 00 09 00 00 00000030
06 01 000 000 4 0048 1 0507605731 3102 2 00 000 0 082 1 000 31 09 00 00 00002740
06 01 000 000 9 0000 1 0510005700 0000 2 00 000 0 082 1 000 00 09 00 00 00000876
06 01 000 000 9 0000 1 0510005700 0000 2 00 000 0 082 1 000 00 09 00 00 00000145
06 01 000 000 5 0266 1 0512305708 3097 2 00 000 0 082 1 000 00 09 00 00 00002741
06 01 000 000 4 0078 1 0507505723 3101 2 00 000 0 082 1 000 00 09 00 00 00000085
06 01 000 000 4 0147 1 0521505714 3100 2 00 000 0 082 1 000 00 09 00 00 00000020
06 01 000 000 4 0141 1 0524205706 3101 2 00 000 0 082 1 000 00 09 00 00 00000068
06 01 000 000 4 0140 1 0524305712 3101 2 00 000 0 082 1 000 00 09 00 00 00000047
```

```
06 01 000 000 9 0000 1 0510005750 0000 2 00 000 0 082 1 000 00 09 00 00 00000017
06 01 000 000 4 0201 1 0514705777 3103 2 00 000 0 082 1 000 00 09 00 00 00000051
06 01 000 000 4 0095 1 0517005703 3102 2 00 000 0 059 7 000 36 09 00 00 00000130
06 01 000 000 4 0169 1 0508905676 3101 2 00 000 0 059 7 000 36 09 00 00 00000123
06 01 000 000 4 0019 1 0519605707 3103 2 00 000 0 075 1 000 00 09 00 00 00001561
06 01 000 000 4 0128 1 0512105667 3102 2 00 000 0 075 1 000 00 09 00 00 00003293
06 01 000 000 4 0195 1 0512805655 3103 2 00 000 0 076 7 000 00 09 00 00 00005076
06 01 000 000 4 0254 1 0513905808 3100 2 00 000 0 076 1 000 00 09 00 00 00002362
06 01 000 000 9 0000 1 0510005700 0000 2 00 000 0 083 1 000 35 09 00 00 00005712
06 01 000 000 9 0000 1 0500005700 0000 2 00 000 0 099 7 038 00 09 00 00 00000002
06 01 000 000 9 0000 1 0505005700 0000 2 00 000 0 099 7 038 00 09 00 00 00000001
06 01 000 000 9 0000 1 0505005700 0000 2 00 000 0 099 7 038 00 09 00 00 00000003
06 01 000 000 9 0000 1 0505005700 0000 2 00 000 0 099 7 038 00 09 00 00 00000001
06 01 000 000 9 0000 1 0515005750 0000 2 00 000 0 106 1 000 00 09 00 00 00000014
06 01 000 000 4 0136 1 0524005739 3101 2 00 000 0 106 1 000 00 09 00 00 00000014
06 01 000 000 4 0044 1 0508905743 3102 1 00 000 0 003 1 001 17 00 00 00 00000284
06 01 000 000 4 0043 1 0508405743 3102 1 00 000 0 003 1 003 17 00 00 00 00000485
06 01 000 000 4 0039 1 0509205739 3101 1 00 000 0 003 1 001 00 00 00 00 00000165
06 01 000 000 4 0037 1 0508005740 3102 1 00 000 0 003 1 001 00 00 00 00 00000250
06 01 000 000 4 0069 1 0509905717 3101 1 00 000 0 003 1 001 00 00 00 00 00000155
06 01 000 000 4 0068 1 0509705717 3101 1 00 000 0 003 1 001 00 00 00 00 00000155
06 01 000 000 4 0066 1 0509605718 3101 1 00 000 0 003 1 001 00 00 00 00 00000155
06 01 000 000 4 0065 1 0509405718 3102 1 00 000 0 003 1 001 00 00 00 00 00000155
06 01 000 000 4 0063 1 0509205720 3102 1 00 000 0 003 1 001 00 00 00 00 00000155
06 01 000 000 4 0062 1 0509605725 3101 1 00 000 0 003 1 001 00 00 00 00 00000165
06 01 000 000 4 0235 1 0515305756 3101 1 00 000 0 003 1 008 00 00 00 00 00000269
06 01 000 000 4 0126 1 0507005728 3102 1 00 000 0 003 1 002 00 00 00 00 00000075
06 01 000 000 4 0100 1 0510005718 3101 1 00 000 0 003 1 001 00 00 00 00 00000155
06 01 000 000 4 0101 1 0510005719 3101 1 00 000 0 003 1 001 00 00 00 00 00000155
06 01 000 000 4 0104 1 0519505750 3102 1 00 000 0 003 1 002 00 00 00 00 00000720
06 01 000 000 4 0115 1 0509505714 3101 1 00 000 0 003 1 002 00 00 00 00 00000059
06 01 000 000 4 0165 1 0507505693 3102 1 00 000 0 003 1 002 00 00 00 00 00000038
06 01 000 000 4 0045 1 0506505732 3099 1 00 000 0 003 1 002 00 00 00 00 00000030
06 01 000 000 4 0018 1 0516305704 3100 1 00 000 0 003 1 002 00 00 00 00 00000890
06 01 000 000 4 0025 1 0509305748 3102 1 00 000 0 003 1 002 00 00 00 00 00000144
06 01 000 000 4 0071 1 0519805709 3101 1 00 000 0 003 1 007 29 00 00 01 00000062
06 01 000 000 5 0271 1 0519505750 3094 1 00 000 0 003 1 002 00 00 00 00 00000017
06 01 000 000 4 0194 1 0512505757 3101 1 00 000 0 003 1 002 00 00 00 00 00000108
06 01 000 000 4 0225 1 0518305754 3102 1 00 000 0 003 1 007 00 00 00 00 00000107
06 01 000 000 4 0191 1 0512205768 3101 1 00 000 0 003 1 002 00 00 00 00 00000549
06 01 000 000 4 0224 1 0518705751 3100 1 00 000 0 003 1 002 00 00 00 00 00000103
06 01 000 000 4 0223 1 0518705754 3102 1 00 000 0 003 1 002 00 00 00 00 00000390
06 01 000 000 4 0087 1 0518405750 3103 1 00 000 0 003 1 003 00 00 00 00 00000120
06 01 000 000 4 0227 1 0518205752 3102 1 00 000 0 003 1 002 00 00 00 00 00000045
06 01 000 000 4 0226 1 0518205753 3102 1 00 000 0 003 1 002 00 00 00 00 00000019
06 01 000 000 9 0000 1 0510005650 0000 1 00 000 0 003 1 002 00 00 00 00 00000066
06 01 000 000 4 0061 1 0509205723 3102 1 00 000 0 003 1 003 00 00 00 00 00000175
06 01 000 000 4 0059 1 0509105725 3101 1 00 000 0 003 1 000 00 00 00 00 00000165
06 01 000 000 4 0056 1 0508705730 3102 1 00 000 0 003 1 001 00 00 00 00 00000165
06 01 000 000 4 0055 1 0508605730 3101 1 00 000 0 003 1 001 00 00 00 00 00000165
06 01 000 000 4 0054 1 0508505727 3102 1 00 000 0 003 1 001 00 00 00 00 00000165
06 01 000 000 4 0052 1 0508205732 3100 1 00 000 0 003 1 001 00 00 00 00 00000165
06 01 000 000 4 0123 1 0509505715 3100 1 00 000 0 003 1 001 00 00 00 00 00000310
06 01 000 000 4 0117 1 0509705714 3101 1 00 000 0 003 1 001 00 00 00 00 00000078
06 01 000 000 9 0000 1 0510005600 0000 1 00 000 0 015 1 001 00 00 00 00 00000002
06 01 000 000 9 0000 1 0510005600 0000 1 00 000 0 015 1 001 00 00 00 00 00000007
06 01 000 000 9 0000 1 0510005600 0000 1 00 000 0 015 1 001 00 00 00 00 00000005
06 01 000 000 9 0000 1 0510005600 0000 1 00 000 0 015 1 001 00 00 00 00 00000006
06 01 000 000 4 0182 1 0513905643 3100 1 00 000 0 015 1 001 00 00 00 00 00000050
06 01 000 000 4 0185 1 0512005632 3102 1 00 000 0 015 1 001 00 00 00 00 00000015
06 01 000 000 9 0000 1 0505005650 0000 1 00 000 0 015 1 001 00 00 00 00 00000002
06 01 000 000 4 0154 1 0509005667 3101 1 00 000 0 015 1 001 00 00 00 00 00000032
06 01 000 000 9 0000 1 0510005650 0000 1 00 000 0 015 1 001 00 00 00 00 00000010
06 01 000 000 9 0000 1 0510005650 0000 1 00 000 0 015 1 001 00 00 00 00 00000003
06 01 000 000 9 0000 1 0510005650 0000 1 00 000 0 015 1 001 00 00 00 00 00000020
06 01 000 000 9 0000 1 0510005650 0000 1 00 000 0 015 1 001 00 00 00 00 00000013
06 01 000 000 4 0130 1 0513205659 3102 1 00 000 0 015 1 001 00 00 00 00 00000114
06 01 000 000 9 0000 1 0515005650 0000 1 00 000 0 015 1 001 00 00 00 00 00000008
06 01 000 000 9 0000 1 0515005650 0000 1 00 000 0 015 1 001 00 00 00 00 00000000
06 01 000 000 9 0000 1 0515005650 0000 1 00 000 0 015 1 001 00 00 00 00 00000002
06 01 000 000 9 0000 1 0515005650 0000 1 00 000 0 015 1 001 00 00 00 00 00000001
06 01 000 000 9 0000 1 0515005650 0000 1 00 000 0 015 1 001 00 00 00 00 00000000
06 01 000 000 9 0000 1 0515005650 0000 1 00 000 0 015 1 001 00 00 00 00 00000000
06 01 000 000 9 0000 1 0515005650 0000 1 00 000 0 015 1 001 00 00 00 00 00000010
06 01 000 000 9 0000 1 0515005650 0000 1 00 000 0 015 1 001 00 00 00 00 00000013
06 01 000 000 9 0000 1 0515005650 0000 1 00 000 0 015 1 001 00 00 00 00 00000025
```

```
06 01 000 000 9 0000 1 0515005650 0000 1 00 000 0 015 1 001 00 00 00 00 00000163
06 01 000 000 4 0177 1 0519705691 3098 1 00 000 0 015 1 001 00 00 00 00 00000203
06 01 000 000 4 0176 1 0518805689 3099 1 00 000 0 015 1 001 00 00 00 00 00001571
06 01 000 000 4 0171 1 0517005694 3100 1 00 000 0 015 1 001 00 00 00 00 00000437
06 01 000 000 4 0090 1 0516805699 3102 1 00 000 0 015 1 001 00 00 00 00 00000307
06 01 000 000 4 0099 1 0516905693 3101 1 00 000 0 015 1 001 00 00 00 00 00000091
06 01 000 000 4 0098 1 0516505692 3101 1 00 000 0 015 1 001 00 00 00 00 00000092
06 01 000 000 4 0097 1 0516505694 3102 1 00 000 0 015 1 001 00 00 00 00 00000059
06 01 000 000 4 0178 1 0520205698 3101 1 00 000 0 015 1 001 00 00 00 00 00000056
06 01 000 000 9 0000 1 0505005700 0000 1 00 000 0 015 1 001 00 00 00 00 00000001
06 01 000 000 9 0000 1 0505005700 0000 1 00 000 0 015 1 001 00 00 00 00 00000000
06 01 000 000 9 0000 1 0505005700 0000 1 00 000 0 015 1 001 00 00 00 00 00000006
06 01 000 000 9 0000 1 0505005700 0000 1 00 000 0 015 1 001 00 00 00 00 00000000
06 01 000 000 9 0000 1 0505005700 0000 1 00 000 0 015 1 001 00 00 00 00 00000004
06 01 000 000 9 0000 1 0505005700 0000 1 00 000 0 015 1 001 00 00 00 00 00000053
06 01 000 000 9 0000 1 0505005700 0000 1 00 000 0 015 1 001 00 00 00 00 00000001
06 01 000 000 9 0000 1 0505005700 0000 1 00 000 0 015 1 001 00 00 00 00 00000000
06 01 000 000 4 0109 1 0508305715 3101 1 00 000 0 015 1 001 00 00 00 00 00000143
06 01 000 000 4 0105 1 0509805717 3102 1 00 000 0 015 1 001 00 00 00 00 00000290
06 01 000 000 4 0103 1 0507705717 3102 1 00 000 0 015 1 001 00 00 00 00 00000015
06 01 000 000 4 0024 1 0508905748 3101 1 00 000 0 015 1 001 00 00 00 00 00000030
06 01 000 000 4 0026 1 0508805745 3102 1 00 000 0 015 1 001 00 00 00 00 00000080
06 01 000 000 4 0027 1 0509405745 3101 1 00 000 0 015 1 001 00 00 00 00 00000230
06 01 000 000 4 0112 1 0509005711 3102 1 00 000 0 015 1 001 00 00 00 00 00000023
06 01 000 000 4 0113 1 0509205711 3102 1 00 000 0 015 1 001 00 00 00 00 00000030
06 01 000 000 4 0114 1 0509105709 3102 1 00 000 0 015 1 001 00 00 00 00 00000059
06 01 000 000 4 0116 1 0509805715 3102 1 00 000 0 015 1 001 00 00 00 00 00000013
06 01 000 000 4 0118 1 0509705714 3100 1 00 000 0 015 1 001 00 00 00 00 00000110
06 01 000 000 4 0119 1 0509805718 3100 1 00 000 0 015 1 001 00 00 00 00 00000225
06 01 000 000 4 0120 1 0509905714 3100 1 00 000 0 015 1 001 00 00 00 00 00000081
06 01 000 000 4 0121 1 0509805714 3101 1 00 000 0 015 1 001 00 00 00 00 00000029
06 01 000 000 4 0122 1 0509805714 3100 1 00 000 0 015 1 002 00 00 00 00 00000069
06 01 000 000 4 0122 1 0507005728 3100 1 00 000 0 015 1 001 00 00 00 00 00000110
06 01 000 000 4 0125 1 0506905703 3102 1 00 000 0 015 1 001 00 00 00 00 00000010
06 01 000 000 4 0029 1 0506505744 3102 1 00 000 0 015 1 001 00 00 00 00 00000040
06 01 000 000 4 0031 1 0508805745 3102 1 00 000 0 015 1 001 00 00 00 00 00000034
06 01 000 000 4 0033 1 0509705744 3102 1 00 000 0 015 1 001 00 00 00 00 00000110
06 01 000 000 4 0034 1 0508505744 3102 1 00 000 0 015 1 001 00 00 00 00 00000076
06 01 000 000 4 0040 1 0509005742 3102 1 00 000 0 015 1 001 00 00 00 00 00000060
06 01 000 000 4 0041 1 0509005742 3102 1 00 000 0 015 1 001 00 00 00 00 00000080
06 01 000 000 4 0042 1 0508705741 3102 1 00 000 0 015 1 001 00 00 00 00 00000086
05 01 000 000 4 0047 1 0507605734 3102 1 00 000 0 015 1 001 00 00 00 00 00000020
06 01 000 000 4 0049 1 0507505728 3100 1 00 000 0 015 1 001 00 00 00 00 00000016
06 01 000 000 4 0053 1 0509205731 3101 1 00 000 0 015 1 001 00 00 00 00 00000260
06 01 000 000 4 0057 1 0509005730 3102 1 00 000 0 015 1 001 00 00 00 00 00000040
06 01 000 000 4 0058 1 0509605727 3100 1 00 000 0 015 1 001 00 00 00 00 00000127
06 01 000 000 4 0060 1 0509405725 3101 1 00 000 0 015 1 001 00 00 00 00 00000047
06 01 000 000 4 0022 1 0506805716 3102 1 00 000 0 015 1 001 00 00 00 00 00000361
06 01 000 000 4 0023 1 0508805748 3103 1 00 000 0 015 1 001 00 00 00 00 00000037
06 01 000 000 5 0110 1 0508605714 3101 1 00 000 0 015 1 001 00 00 00 00 00000027
06 01 000 000 4 0106 1 0508105713 3102 1 00 000 0 015 1 001 00 00 00 00 00000064
06 01 000 000 9 0000 1 0510005700 0000 1 00 000 0 015 1 001 00 00 00 00 00000004
06 01 000 000 9 0000 1 0510005700 0000 1 00 000 0 015 1 001 00 00 00 00 00000004
06 01 000 000 9 0000 1 0510005700 0000 1 00 000 0 015 1 001 00 00 00 00 00000010
06 01 000 000 9 0000 1 0510005700 0000 1 00 000 0 015 1 001 00 00 00 00 00000003
06 01 000 000 9 0000 1 0510005700 0000 1 00 000 0 015 1 001 00 00 00 00 00000053
06 01 000 000 9 0000 1 0510005700 0000 1 00 000 0 015 1 001 00 00 00 00 00000220
06 01 000 000 4 0028 1 0510005745 3101 1 00 000 0 015 1 001 00 00 00 00 00000016
06 01 000 000 4 0001 1 0510005714 3102 1 00 000 0 015 1 001 00 00 00 00 00000023
06 01 000 000 4 0002 1 0511005716 3102 1 00 000 0 015 1 001 00 00 00 00 00000003
06 01 000 000 4 0003 1 0510205715 3102 1 00 000 0 015 1 001 00 00 00 00 00000110
06 01 000 000 4 0004 1 0510205717 3102 1 00 000 0 015 1 001 00 00 00 00 00000028
06 01 000 000 4 0005 1 0510105719 3101 1 00 000 0 015 1 001 00 00 00 00 00000019
06 01 000 000 4 0006 1 0510205716 3101 1 00 000 0 015 1 001 00 00 00 00 00000008
06 01 000 000 4 0008 1 0514705726 3102 1 00 000 0 015 1 001 00 00 00 00 00000040
06 01 000 000 4 0010 1 0511805734 3102 1 00 000 0 015 1 001 00 00 00 00 00000037
06 01 000 000 4 0011 1 0511605736 3101 1 00 000 0 015 1 001 00 00 00 00 00000007
06 01 000 000 4 0013 1 0512005745 3103 1 00 000 0 015 1 001 00 00 00 00 00000000
```

```
06 01 000 000 9 0000 1 0515005700 0000 1 00 000 0 015 1 001 00 00 00 00 00000017
06 01 000 000 9 0000 1 0515005700 0000 1 00 000 0 015 1 001 00 00 00 00 00000003
06 01 000 000 4 0073 1 0519605718 3102 1 00 000 0 015 1 001 00 00 00 00 00000100
06 01 000 000 4 0075 1 0518405721 3101 1 00 000 0 015 1 001 00 00 00 00 00000020
06 01 000 000 4 0076 1 0517905721 3102 1 00 000 0 015 1 001 00 00 00 00 00000045
06 01 000 000 4 0077 1 0517705721 3101 1 00 000 0 015 1 001 00 00 00 00 00000020
06 01 000 000 4 0079 1 0516105728 3101 1 00 000 0 015 1 001 00 00 00 00 00000120
06 01 000 000 4 0080 1 0516005732 3102 1 00 000 0 015 1 001 00 00 00 00 00000026
06 01 000 000 4 0081 1 0517905738 3102 1 00 000 0 015 1 001 00 00 00 00 00000140
06 01 000 000 4 0084 1 0515205742 3102 1 00 000 0 015 1 001 00 00 00 00 00000003
06 01 000 000 4 0085 1 0519305743 3102 1 00 000 0 015 1 001 00 00 00 00 00000060
06 01 000 000 4 0086 1 0519805741 3103 1 00 000 0 015 1 001 00 00 00 00 00000040
06 01 000 000 4 0088 1 0519105749 3103 1 00 000 0 015 1 001 00 00 00 00 00000010
06 01 000 000 4 0072 1 0516405716 3101 1 00 000 0 015 1 001 00 00 00 00 00000020
06 01 000 000 4 0150 1 0519705705 3102 1 00 000 0 015 1 001 00 00 00 00 00000075
06 01 000 000 4 0149 1 0520205712 3100 1 00 000 0 015 1 001 00 00 00 00 00000034
06 01 000 000 4 0148 1 0520605708 3101 1 00 000 0 015 1 001 00 00 00 00 00000040
06 01 000 000 4 0146 1 0521505701 3102 1 00 000 0 015 1 001 00 00 00 00 00000008
06 01 000 000 4 0145 1 0521705702 3102 1 00 000 0 015 1 001 00 00 00 00 00000012
06 01 000 000 4 0134 1 0520005748 3102 1 00 000 0 015 1 001 00 00 00 00 00000015
06 01 000 000 9 0000 1 0520005700 0000 1 00 000 0 015 1 001 00 00 00 00 00000003
06 01 000 000 9 0000 1 0520005700 0000 1 00 000 0 015 1 001 00 00 00 00 00000003
06 01 000 000 9 0000 1 0520005700 0000 1 00 000 0 015 1 001 00 00 00 00 00000006
06 01 000 000 9 0000 1 0520005700 0000 1 00 000 0 015 1 001 00 00 00 00 00000006
06 01 000 000 9 0000 1 0520005700 0000 1 00 000 0 015 1 001 00 00 00 00 00000001
06 01 000 000 9 0000 1 0515005700 0000 1 00 000 0 015 1 001 00 00 00 00 00000010
06 01 000 000 4 0205 1 0508505775 3103 1 00 000 0 015 1 001 00 00 00 00 00000010
06 01 000 000 4 0010 1 0510005750 0000 1 00 000 0 015 1 001 00 00 00 00 00000006
06 01 000 000 4 0193 1 0512205758 3101 1 00 000 0 015 1 001 00 00 00 00 00000082
06 01 000 000 4 0196 1 0512905755 3102 1 00 000 0 015 1 001 00 00 00 00 00000121
06 01 000 000 4 0197 1 0513005759 3102 1 00 000 0 015 1 001 00 00 00 00 00000043
06 01 000 000 4 0198 1 0513205760 3101 1 00 000 0 015 1 001 00 00 00 00 00000009
06 01 000 000 4 0188 1 0510205765 3101 1 00 000 0 015 1 001 00 00 00 00 00000135
06 01 000 000 4 0069 1 0516505760 3103 1 00 000 0 015 1 001 00 00 00 00 00000003
06 01 000 000 4 0229 1 0518305751 3100 1 00 000 0 015 1 001 00 00 00 00 00000002
06 01 000 000 4 0236 1 0518705769 3100 1 00 000 0 015 1 001 00 00 00 00 00000142
06 01 000 000 5 0261 1 0516305752 3098 1 00 000 0 015 1 001 00 00 00 00 00000017
06 01 000 000 5 0261 1 0515305759 3099 1 00 000 0 015 1 001 00 00 00 00 00000033
06 01 000 000 9 0000 1 0515005750 0000 1 00 000 0 015 1 001 00 09 00 00 00000001
06 01 000 000 9 0000 1 0515005750 0000 1 00 000 0 015 1 001 00 09 00 00 00000007
06 01 000 000 9 0000 1 0515005750 0000 1 00 000 0 015 1 001 00 09 00 00 00000005
06 01 000 000 9 0000 1 0515005750 0000 1 00 000 0 015 1 001 00 09 00 00 00000009
06 01 000 000 9 0000 1 0515005750 0000 1 00 000 0 015 1 001 00 09 00 00 00000011
06 01 000 000 9 0000 1 0515005750 0000 1 00 000 0 015 1 001 00 09 00 00 00000022
06 01 000 000 9 0250 1 0514505810 3099 1 00 000 0 015 1 001 00 00 00 00 00000115
06 01 000 000 9 0000 1 0510005650 0000 1 00 000 0 038 1 000 00 00 00 00 00000028
06 01 000 000 9 0000 1 0510005650 0000 1 00 000 0 038 1 000 00 00 00 00 00000027
06 01 000 000 9 0000 1 0515005650 0000 1 00 000 0 038 1 000 00 00 00 00 00000072
06 01 000 000 9 0000 1 0515005650 0000 1 00 000 0 038 1 000 00 00 00 00 00000097
06 01 000 000 9 0000 1 0515005650 0000 1 00 000 0 038 1 000 00 00 00 00 00000069
06 01 000 000 9 0000 1 0515005650 0000 1 00 000 0 038 1 000 00 00 00 00 00000009
06 01 000 000 9 0000 1 0515005650 0000 1 00 000 0 038 1 000 00 00 00 00 00000009
06 01 000 000 9 0000 1 0515005650 0000 1 00 000 0 038 1 000 00 00 00 00 00000007
06 01 000 000 9 0000 1 0515005650 0000 1 00 000 0 038 1 000 00 00 00 00 00000007
06 01 000 000 9 0000 1 0515005700 0000 1 00 000 0 038 1 000 00 00 00 00 00000022
06 01 000 000 4 0144 1 0521805705 3102 1 00 000 0 038 1 000 00 00 00 00 00000106
06 01 000 000 4 0152 1 0520005708 3101 1 00 000 0 038 1 000 37 00 00 00 00000114
06 01 000 000 9 0000 1 0510005750 0000 1 00 000 0 038 1 000 00 00 00 00 00000000
06 01 000 000 4 0202 1 0514005784 3102 1 00 000 0 038 1 000 00 00 00 00 00000007
06 01 000 000 4 0192 1 0513305774 3100 1 00 000 0 038 1 000 00 00 00 00 00000003
06 01 000 000 5 0260 1 0514805630 3102 2 00 000 0 151 1 039 00 00 00 00 00000085
06 01 000 000 4 0160 1 0508605679 3101 4 01 033 2 000 1 036 00 00 00 00 00000037
06 01 000 000 4 0181 1 0518705691 3102 4 07 025 2 000 1 039 00 00 00 00 00000004
06 01 000 000 4 0181 1 0518705691 3099 4 07 031 2 000 1 039 00 00 00 00 00000012
06 01 000 000 4 0173 1 0517405677 3101 4 01 014 1 000 1 039 00 00 00 00 00000016
06 01 000 000 4 0046 1 0507005723 3100 4 01 033 1 000 1 039 00 00 00 00 00000105
06 01 000 000 5 0269 1 0507205773 3099 4 01 014 1 000 7 038 00 00 00 00 00000078
06 01 000 000 4 0186 1 0513805808 3103 4 01 014 1 000 1 120 1 039 37 00 00 00000225
06 01 000 000 4 0038 1 0508805740 3102 3 76 501 0 000 1 039 65 00 00 00000000
```

```
06 01 000 000 4 0082 1 0519005741 3102 3 00 000 0 120 1 000 00 00 00 00 00000000
06 01 000 000 4 0091 1 0519105745 3104 3 00 000 0 000 1 039 65 00 00 00 00000000
06 01 000 000 4 0092 1 0518105749 3103 3 80 501 0 000 1 039 65 00 00 00 00000000
06 01 000 000 4 0093 1 0518005749 3103 3 80 501 0 000 1 039 65 00 00 00 00000000
06 01 000 000 4 0094 1 0517705707 3102 3 00 000 0 120 1 000 00 00 00 00 00000000
06 01 000 000 4 0151 1 0520105706 3101 3 80 501 0 000 1 039 65 00 00 00 00000000
06 01 000 000 4 0174 1 0518005678 3103 3 00 000 0 000 1 039 65 00 00 00 00000000
06 01 000 000 4 0179 1 0524605654 3103 3 78 501 0 000 1 039 65 00 00 00 00000000
06 01 000 000 4 0207 1 0514305803 3103 3 80 501 0 000 1 039 65 00 00 00 00000000
06 01 000 000 4 0208 1 0514905807 3103 3 80 501 0 000 1 039 65 00 00 00 00000000
06 01 000 000 4 0210 1 0513705812 3102 3 80 501 0 000 1 039 65 00 00 00 00000000
06 01 000 000 4 0211 1 0513905814 3103 3 80 501 0 000 1 039 65 00 00 00 00000000
06 01 000 000 4 0212 1 0514805818 3102 3 80 501 0 000 1 039 65 00 00 00 00000000
06 01 000 000 4 0213 1 0513605821 3102 3 80 501 0 000 1 039 65 00 00 00 00000000
06 01 000 000 4 0214 1 0514205815 3102 3 80 501 0 000 1 039 65 00 00 00 00000000
06 01 000 000 4 0215 1 0513405822 3103 3 80 501 0 000 1 039 65 00 00 00 00000000
06 01 000 000 4 0220 1 0504905752 3100 3 91 501 0 000 1 039 65 00 00 00 00000000
06 01 000 000 4 0222 1 0520005760 3100 3 80 501 0 120 1 039 65 00 00 00 00000000
06 01 000 000 4 0228 1 0518505752 3101 0 00 000 0 000 0 000 00 00 00 00 00000000
06 01 000 000 4 0231 1 0518005757 3100 3 77 501 0 000 1 039 65 00 00 00 00000000
06 01 000 000 4 0232 1 0517905752 3100 3 00 000 0 000 1 000 00 00 00 00 00000000
06 01 000 000 4 0233 1 0517605751 3100 3 77 501 0 000 1 039 65 00 00 00 00000000
06 01 000 000 4 0234 1 0517305753 3100 3 77 501 0 000 1 039 65 00 00 00 00000000
06 01 000 000 4 0237 1 0517805769 3102 3 77 501 0 000 1 039 65 00 00 00 00000000
06 01 000 000 4 0238 1 0517805767 3102 3 77 501 0 000 1 039 65 00 00 00 00000000
06 01 000 000 4 0239 1 0517205769 3102 3 77 501 0 000 1 039 65 00 00 00 00000000
06 01 000 000 4 0240 1 0517405772 3101 3 77 501 0 000 1 039 65 00 00 00 00000000
06 01 000 000 4 0241 1 0516705771 3100 3 78 501 0 000 1 039 65 00 00 00 00000000
06 01 000 000 4 0242 1 0516705775 3101 3 78 501 0 000 1 039 65 00 00 00 00000000
06 01 000 000 4 0244 1 0517805786 3101 3 78 501 0 120 1 039 65 00 00 00 00000000
06 01 000 000 4 0245 1 0516805792 3102 3 80 501 0 120 1 039 65 00 00 00 00000000
06 01 000 000 4 0246 1 0515805801 3099 3 80 501 0 120 1 039 65 00 00 00 00000000
06 01 000 000 4 0247 1 0523505695 3103 3 00 000 0 000 0 000 65 00 00 00 00000000
06 01 000 000 5 0249 1 0515305809 3098 1 00 000 0 0/V 1 0TB WV 00 00 00 000000/X
06 01 000 000 4 0252 1 0514205818 3101 3 80 501 0 000 1 039 65 00 00 00 00000000
06 01 000 000 4 0253 1 0514205812 3101 3 80 501 0 000 1 039 65 00 00 00 00000000
06 01 000 000 5 0263 1 0517005770 3101 3 91 511 0 000 1 039 65 00 00 00 00000000
06 01 000 000 9 0000 1 0500005700 0000 3 77 507 0 000 1 039 65 00 00 00 00000001
06 01 000 000 9 0000 1 0505005700 0000 3 77 507 0 000 1 039 65 00 00 00 00000041
06 01 000 000 9 0000 1 0510005800 0000 3 77 507 0 000 1 039 65 00 00 00 00000027
06 01 000 000 9 0000 1 0510005750 0000 3 77 507 0 000 1 039 65 00 00 00 00000293
06 01 000 000 9 0000 1 0510005700 0000 3 77 507 0 000 1 039 65 00 00 00 00000212
06 01 000 000 9 0000 1 0510005650 0000 3 77 507 0 000 1 039 65 00 00 00 00000012
06 01 000 000 9 0000 1 0510005600 0000 3 77 507 0 000 1 039 65 00 00 00 00000004
06 01 000 000 9 0000 1 0515005750 0000 3 77 507 0 000 1 039 65 00 00 00 00000015
06 01 000 000 9 0000 1 0515005700 0000 3 77 507 0 000 1 039 65 00 00 00 00000333
06 01 000 000 9 0000 1 0515005650 0000 3 77 507 0 000 1 039 65 00 00 00 00000085
06 01 000 000 9 0000 1 0520005700 0000 3 77 507 0 000 1 039 65 00 00 00 00000123
06 01 000 000 9 0000 1 0505005700 0000 3 80 507 0 000 1 039 65 00 00 00 00000002
06 01 000 000 9 0000 1 0515005700 0000 3 80 507 0 000 1 039 65 00 00 00 00000002
06 01 000 000 9 0000 1 0510005750 0000 3 80 509 0 000 1 039 65 00 00 00 00000001
06 01 000 000 9 0000 1 0500005700 0000 3 81 503 0 000 1 039 65 00 00 00 00000000
06 01 000 000 9 0000 1 0505005700 0000 3 81 503 0 000 7 000 65 00 00 00 00000026
06 01 000 000 9 0000 1 0510005750 0000 3 81 503 0 000 7 000 65 00 00 00 00000055
06 01 000 000 9 0000 1 0510005700 0000 3 81 503 0 000 7 000 65 00 00 00 00000008
06 01 000 000 9 0000 1 0510005600 0000 3 81 503 0 000 7 000 65 00 00 00 00000002
06 01 000 000 9 0000 1 0515005750 0000 3 81 504 0 000 7 000 65 00 00 00 00000000
06 01 000 000 9 0000 1 0515005650 0000 3 81 503 0 000 7 000 65 00 00 00 00000002
06 01 000 000 9 0000 1 0520005700 0000 3 81 503 0 000 1 039 65 00 00 00 00000000
06 01 000 000 9 0000 1 0510005700 0000 3 82 510 0 000 1 039 65 00 00 00 00000000
06 01 000 000 9 0000 1 0510005750 0000 3 84 510 0 000 1 039 00 00 00 00 00000000
06 01 000 000 9 0000 1 0520005700 0000 3 84 510 0 000 7 000 00 00 00 00 00000000
06 01 000 000 9 0000 1 0510005650 0000 3 85 510 0 000 1 039 00 00 00 00 00000000
06 01 000 000 9 0000 1 0510005600 0000 3 85 510 0 000 1 039 00 00 00 00 00000000
06 01 000 000 9 0000 0 0510005750 0000 3 85 510 0 000 1 039 65 00 00 00 00000000
06 01 000 000 9 0000 1 0520005700 0000 3 85 510 0 000 1 039 65 00 00 00 00000000
06 01 000 000 9 0000 1 0510005700 0000 3 86 512 0 000 1 039 00 00 00 00 00000000
06 01 000 000 9 0000 1 0520005700 0000 3 86 512 0 000 1 039 00 00 00 00 00000000
06 01 000 000 9 0000 1 0510005700 0000 3 87 510 0 000 1 039 00 00 00 00 00000000
06 01 000 000 9 0000 1 0515005650 0000 3 89 511 0 000 1 039 65 00 00 00 00000001
06 01 000 000 9 0000 1 0510005000 0000 3 91 507 0 000 1 039 65 00 00 00 00000000
06 01 000 000 9 0000 1 0510005750 0000 3 91 510 0 000 1 039 65 00 00 00 00000000
06 01 000 000 9 0000 1 0515005700 0000 3 91 510 0 000 1 039 65 00 00 00 00000001
06 01 000 000 9 0000 1 0520005700 0000 3 91 507 0 000 1 039 65 00 00 00 00000000
06 01 000 000 9 0000 1 0510005800 0000 3 91 507 0 000 1 039 65 00 00 00 00000003
06 01 000 000 9 0000 1 0520005700 0000 3 92 000 0 123 1 039 65 00 00 00 00000000
06 01 000 000 9 0000 1 0510005700 0000 3 92 000 0 123 1 039 65 00 00 00 00000000
06 01 000 000 9 0000 1 0510005700 0000 3 92 000 0 123 1 039 65 00 00 00 00000000
06 01 000 000 9 0000 1 0515005750 0000 3 92 000 0 123 1 039 65 00 00 00 00000000
06 01 000 000 9 0000 1 0510005800 0000 3 92 000 0 123 1 039 65 00 00 00 00000000
```

Appendix D

STRUCTURE TWO DATA BASE

```
      STRUCTURE TWO DATA BASE
06 02 000 000 9 0048 1 0494405408 3089 2 00 000 0 060 1 039 35 09 00 00 00000206
06 02 000 000 3 0000 1 0490005400 0000 2 00 000 0 060 1 039 00 09 00 00 00000011
06 02 001 000 9 0000 1 0490005400 0000 2 00 000 0 060 1 039 00 09 00 00 00000004
06 02 000 000 3 0000 1 0490005400 0000 2 00 000 0 060 1 039 00 09 00 00 00000010
06 02 000 000 9 0000 1 0495005350 0000 2 00 000 0 060 1 039 00 09 00 00 00000005
06 02 000 000 9 0000 1 0490005350 0000 2 00 000 0 060 1 039 00 09 00 00 00000006
06 02 000 000 9 0000 1 0490005350 0000 2 00 000 0 060 1 039 00 09 00 00 00000003
06 02 000 000 9 0000 1 0490005350 0000 2 00 000 0 060 1 039 00 09 00 00 00000004
06 02 000 000 9 0000 1 0490005350 0000 2 00 000 0 060 1 039 00 09 00 00 00000007
06 02 000 000 9 0000 1 0490005350 0000 2 00 000 0 060 1 039 00 09 00 00 00000002
06 02 000 000 9 0000 1 0495005350 0000 2 00 000 0 060 1 039 00 09 00 00 00000014
06 02 000 000 9 0000 1 0495005350 0000 2 00 000 0 060 1 039 00 09 00 00 00000000
06 02 000 000 9 0000 1 0495005350 0000 2 00 000 0 060 1 039 00 09 00 00 00000003
06 02 000 000 9 0000 1 0495005350 0000 2 00 000 0 060 1 039 00 09 00 00 00000001
06 02 000 000 9 0000 1 0495005350 0000 2 00 000 0 060 1 039 00 09 00 00 00000002
06 02 000 000 9 0000 1 0495005350 0000 2 00 000 0 060 1 039 00 09 00 00 00000004
06 02 000 000 9 0000 1 0495005350 0000 2 00 000 0 060 1 039 00 09 00 00 00000009
06 02 000 000 9 0000 1 0495005350 0000 2 00 000 0 060 1 039 00 09 00 00 00000006
06 02 000 000 9 0000 1 0495005350 0000 2 00 000 0 060 1 039 00 09 00 00 00000006
06 02 000 000 9 0000 1 0485005400 0000 2 00 000 0 060 1 039 00 09 00 00 00000032
06 02 000 000 9 0000 1 0485005400 0000 2 00 000 0 060 1 039 00 09 00 00 00000005
06 02 000 000 9 0054 1 0490005411 3091 2 00 000 0 060 1 039 00 09 00 00 00000051
06 02 000 000 9 0051 1 0491805405 3090 2 00 000 0 060 1 039 00 09 00 00 00000080
06 02 000 000 9 0000 1 0495005400 0000 2 00 000 0 060 1 039 35 09 00 00 00000006
06 02 000 000 9 0000 1 0495005400 0000 2 00 000 0 060 1 039 35 09 00 00 00000003
06 02 000 000 9 0000 1 0495005400 0000 2 00 000 0 060 1 039 00 09 00 00 00000002
06 02 000 000 9 0000 1 0495005400 0000 2 00 000 0 060 1 039 00 09 00 00 00000002
06 02 000 000 9 0000 1 0495005400 0000 2 00 000 0 060 1 039 00 09 00 00 00000001
06 02 000 000 9 0000 1 0495005400 0000 2 00 000 0 060 1 039 00 09 00 00 00000004
06 02 000 000 9 0000 1 0495005400 0000 2 00 000 0 060 1 039 00 09 00 00 00000000
06 02 000 000 9 0000 1 0495005400 0000 2 00 000 0 060 1 039 00 09 00 00 00000008
06 02 000 000 9 0000 1 0495005400 0000 2 00 000 0 060 1 039 00 09 00 00 00000015
06 02 000 000 9 0000 1 0495005400 0000 2 00 000 0 060 1 039 00 09 00 00 00000003
06 02 000 000 9 0000 1 0495005400 0000 2 00 000 0 060 1 039 00 09 00 00 00000007
06 02 000 000 9 0000 1 0495005400 0000 2 00 000 0 060 1 039 00 09 00 00 00000015
06 02 000 000 9 0150 1 0497705448 3087 2 00 000 0 060 1 039 00 09 00 00 00000001
06 02 000 000 9 0143 1 0496705424 3087 2 00 000 0 060 1 039 37 09 00 00 00000001
06 02 000 000 9 0008 1 0498805403 3090 2 00 000 0 060 1 039 35 06 00 00 00000019
06 02 000 000 9 0000 1 0500005400 0000 2 00 000 0 060 1 039 37 09 00 00 00000002
06 02 000 000 9 0000 1 0500005400 0000 2 00 000 0 060 1 039 37 09 00 00 00000005
06 02 000 000 9 0000 1 0500005400 0000 2 00 000 0 060 1 039 36 09 00 00 00000005
06 02 000 000 9 0000 1 0500005400 0000 2 00 000 0 060 1 039 37 09 00 00 00000005
06 02 000 000 9 0000 1 0500005400 0000 2 00 000 0 060 1 039 00 09 00 00 00000001
06 02 000 000 9 0000 1 0500005400 0000 2 00 000 0 060 1 039 00 09 00 00 00000003
06 02 000 000 9 0000 1 0500005400 0000 2 00 000 0 060 1 039 00 09 00 00 00000004
06 02 000 000 9 0000 1 0500005400 0000 2 00 000 0 060 1 039 00 09 00 00 00000002
06 02 000 000 9 0000 1 0500005400 0000 2 00 000 0 060 1 039 00 09 00 00 00000002
06 02 000 000 9 0000 1 0490005400 0000 2 00 000 0 060 1 039 00 09 00 00 00000005
06 02 000 000 9 0000 1 0490005400 0000 2 00 000 0 060 1 039 00 09 00 00 00000001
06 02 000 000 9 0000 1 0490005400 0000 2 00 000 0 060 1 039 00 09 00 00 00000003
06 02 000 000 9 0000 1 0500005400 0000 2 00 000 0 060 1 039 00 09 00 00 00000015
06 02 000 000 9 0000 1 0500005400 0000 2 00 000 0 060 1 039 00 09 00 00 00000003
06 02 000 000 9 0000 1 0500005400 0000 2 00 000 0 060 1 039 00 09 00 00 00000004
06 02 000 000 9 0000 1 0500005400 0000 2 00 000 0 060 1 039 00 09 00 00 00000003
06 02 000 000 9 0000 1 0500005400 0000 2 00 000 0 060 1 039 00 09 00 00 00000004
06 02 000 000 9 0000 1 0500005400 0000 2 00 000 0 060 1 039 00 09 00 00 00000002
06 02 000 000 9 0000 1 0500005400 0000 2 00 000 0 060 1 039 00 09 00 00 00000004
06 02 000 000 9 0000 1 0500005400 0000 2 00 000 0 060 1 039 00 09 00 00 00000004
06 02 000 000 9 0000 1 0500005400 0000 2 00 000 0 060 1 039 00 09 00 00 00000006
06 02 000 000 9 0000 1 0500005400 0000 2 00 000 0 060 1 039 00 09 00 00 00000007
06 02 000 000 9 0000 1 0500005400 0000 2 00 000 0 060 1 039 00 09 00 00 00000006
06 02 000 000 9 0118 1 0493405451 3092 2 00 000 0 060 1 039 35 09 00 00 00000043
06 02 000 000 9 0000 1 0490005450 0000 2 00 000 0 060 1 039 00 09 00 00 00000002
06 02 000 000 9 0000 1 0490005450 0000 2 00 000 0 060 1 039 00 09 00 00 00000002
06 02 000 000 9 0000 1 0490005450 0000 2 00 000 0 060 1 039 00 09 00 00 00000001
```

221

```
06 02 000 000 9 0000 1 0490005450 0000 2 00 000 0 060 1 039 00 09 00 00 00000001
06 02 000 000 9 0000 1 0490005450 0000 2 00 000 0 060 1 039 00 09 00 00 00000002
06 02 000 000 9 0000 1 0490005450 0000 2 00 000 0 060 1 039 00 09 00 00 00000002
06 02 000 000 9 0000 1 0490005450 0000 2 00 000 0 060 1 039 00 09 00 00 00000006
06 02 000 000 9 0000 1 0490005450 0000 2 00 000 0 060 1 039 00 09 00 00 00000003
06 02 000 000 9 0000 1 0490005450 0000 2 00 000 0 060 1 039 00 09 00 00 00000002
06 02 000 000 9 0000 1 0490005450 0000 2 00 000 0 060 1 039 00 09 00 00 00000005
06 02 000 000 9 0000 1 0490005450 0000 2 00 000 0 060 1 039 00 09 00 00 00000002
06 02 000 000 9 0000 1 0490005450 0000 2 00 000 0 060 1 039 00 09 00 00 00000002
06 02 000 000 9 0000 1 0490005450 0000 2 00 000 0 060 1 039 37 09 00 00 00000006
06 02 000 000 9 0000 1 0490005450 0000 2 00 000 0 060 1 039 00 09 00 00 00000008
06 02 000 000 9 0000 1 0495005450 0000 2 00 000 0 060 1 039 35 09 00 00 00000017
06 02 000 000 9 0000 1 0495005450 0000 2 00 000 0 060 1 039 35 09 00 00 00000008
06 02 000 000 9 0000 1 0495005450 0000 2 00 000 0 060 1 039 35 09 00 00 00000004
06 02 000 000 9 0000 1 0495005450 0000 2 00 000 0 060 1 039 00 09 00 00 00000005
06 02 000 000 9 0000 1 0495005450 0000 2 00 000 0 060 1 039 00 09 00 00 00000001
06 02 000 000 9 0000 1 0495005450 0000 2 00 000 0 060 1 039 00 09 00 00 00000009
06 02 000 000 9 0000 1 0495005450 0000 2 00 000 0 060 1 039 00 09 00 00 00000011
06 02 000 000 9 0000 1 0495005450 0000 2 00 000 0 060 1 039 00 09 00 00 00000002
06 02 000 000 9 0000 1 0495005450 0000 2 00 000 0 060 1 039 00 09 00 00 00000001
06 02 000 000 9 0000 1 0495005450 0000 2 00 000 0 060 1 039 00 09 00 00 00000002
06 02 000 000 9 0000 1 0495005450 0000 2 00 000 0 060 1 039 00 09 00 00 00000003
06 02 000 000 9 0000 1 0495005450 0000 2 00 000 0 060 1 039 00 09 00 00 00000004
06 02 000 000 9 0000 1 0495005450 0000 2 00 000 0 060 1 039 00 09 00 00 00000022
06 02 000 000 9 0000 1 0495005450 0000 2 00 000 0 060 1 039 00 09 00 00 00000004
06 02 000 000 9 0000 1 0495005450 0000 2 00 000 0 060 1 039 00 09 00 00 00000002
06 02 000 000 9 0000 1 0495005450 0000 2 00 000 0 060 1 039 00 09 00 00 00000005
06 02 000 000 9 0000 1 0495005450 0000 2 00 000 0 060 1 039 00 09 00 00 00000005
06 02 000 000 9 0000 1 0495005450 0000 2 00 000 0 060 1 039 00 09 00 00 00000005
06 02 000 000 9 0000 1 0495005450 0000 2 00 000 0 060 1 039 00 09 00 00 00000003
06 02 000 000 9 0000 1 0495005450 0000 2 00 000 0 060 1 039 00 09 00 00 00000008
06 02 000 000 9 0000 1 0495005450 0000 2 00 000 0 060 1 039 00 09 00 00 00000004
06 02 000 000 9 0000 1 0495005450 0000 2 00 000 0 060 1 039 00 09 00 00 00000012
06 02 000 000 9 0000 1 0495005450 0000 2 00 000 0 060 1 039 00 09 00 00 00000011
06 02 000 000 9 0000 1 0495005450 0000 2 00 000 0 060 1 039 00 09 00 00 00000008
06 02 000 000 9 0000 1 0495005450 0000 2 00 000 0 060 1 039 00 09 00 00 00000002
06 02 000 000 9 0000 1 0495005450 0000 2 00 000 0 060 1 039 00 09 00 00 00000035
06 02 000 000 9 0000 1 0495005450 0000 2 00 000 0 060 1 039 00 09 00 00 00000011
06 02 000 000 9 0000 1 0495005450 0000 2 00 000 0 060 1 039 00 09 00 00 00000004
06 02 000 000 9 0000 1 0495005450 0000 2 00 000 0 060 1 039 00 09 00 00 00000007
06 02 000 000 9 0000 1 0495005450 0000 2 00 000 0 060 1 039 00 09 00 00 00000001
06 02 000 000 9 0000 1 0495005450 0000 2 00 000 0 060 1 039 00 09 00 00 00000005
06 02 000 000 9 0000 1 0495005450 0000 2 00 000 0 060 1 039 00 09 00 00 00000003
06 02 000 000 9 0000 1 0495005450 0000 2 00 000 0 060 1 039 00 09 00 00 00000062
06 02 000 000 9 0000 1 0495005450 0000 2 00 000 0 060 1 039 00 09 00 00 00000008
06 02 000 000 9 0130 1 0500005469 3089 2 00 000 0 060 1 039 36 09 00 00 00000020
06 02 000 000 9 0000 1 0500005450 0000 2 00 000 0 060 1 039 00 09 00 00 00000015
06 02 000 000 9 0000 1 0500005450 0000 2 00 000 0 060 1 039 00 09 00 00 00000001
06 02 000 000 9 0000 1 0500005450 0000 2 00 000 0 060 1 039 00 09 00 00 00000001
06 02 000 000 9 0000 1 0500005450 0000 2 00 000 0 060 1 039 00 09 00 00 00000003
06 02 000 000 9 0000 1 0496705421 3086 2 00 000 0 061 1 039 00 09 00 00 00000392
06 02 000 000 9 0023 1 0497705465 3092 2 00 000 0 061 1 039 00 09 00 00 00000205
06 02 000 000 9 0045 1 0499005423 3091 2 00 000 0 061 1 039 00 09 00 00 00000453
06 02 000 000 9 0049 1 0498005407 3068 2 00 000 0 061 1 039 00 09 00 00 00000485
06 02 000 000 3 0000 1 0490005400 0000 2 00 000 0 061 1 039 00 09 00 00 00000449
06 02 000 000 9 0000 1 0490005400 0000 2 00 000 0 061 1 039 00 09 00 00 00000092
06 02 000 000 9 0000 1 0500005350 0000 2 00 000 0 062 1 039 00 09 00 00 00000074
06 02 000 000 9 0000 1 0490005400 0000 2 00 000 0 062 1 039 00 09 00 00 00000394
06 02 000 000 3 0000 1 0490005400 0000 2 00 000 0 062 1 039 00 09 00 00 00000119
06 02 001 000 9 0000 1 0490005400 0000 2 00 000 0 062 1 039 00 09 00 00 00000017
06 02 001 000 9 0000 1 0490005400 0000 2 00 000 0 062 1 039 37 09 00 00 00000006
06 02 001 000 9 0000 1 0490005350 0000 2 00 000 0 062 1 039 37 09 00 00 00000010
06 02 000 000 9 0000 1 0490005350 0000 2 00 000 0 062 1 039 00 09 00 00 00000004
06 02 000 000 9 0000 1 0490005350 0000 2 00 000 0 062 1 039 00 09 00 00 00000016
06 02 000 000 9 0000 1 0490005350 0000 2 00 000 0 062 1 039 00 09 00 00 00000021
06 02 000 000 9 0000 1 0490005350 0000 2 00 000 0 062 1 039 00 09 00 00 00000006
06 02 000 000 9 0000 1 0490005350 0000 2 00 000 0 062 1 039 00 09 00 00 00000006
06 02 000 000 9 0000 1 0495005350 0000 2 00 000 0 062 1 039 00 09 00 00 00000051
06 02 000 000 9 0000 1 0495005350 0000 2 00 000 0 062 1 039 00 09 00 00 00000005
06 02 000 000 9 0000 1 0495005350 0000 2 00 000 0 062 1 039 00 09 00 00 00000006
```

```
06 02 000 000 9 0000 1 0495005350 0000 2 00 000 0 062 1 039 00 09 00 00 00000004
06 02 000 000 9 0000 1 0495005350 0000 2 00 000 0 062 1 039 00 09 00 00 00000006
06 02 000 000 9 0000 1 0495005350 0000 2 00 000 0 062 1 039 00 09 00 00 00000009
06 02 000 000 9 0000 1 0495005350 0000 2 00 000 0 062 1 039 00 09 00 00 00000009
06 02 000 000 9 0000 1 0495005393 3087 2 00 000 0 062 1 039 00 09 00 00 0000011C
06 02 000 000 9 0106 1 0502205375 3089 2 00 000 0 062 1 039 00 09 00 00 00000022
06 02 000 000 9 0107 1 0501205366 3088 2 00 000 0 062 1 039 00 09 00 00 00000034
06 02 000 000 9 0119 1 0500605383 3088 2 00 000 0 062 1 039 00 09 00 00 00000042
06 02 000 000 9 0000 1 0495005400 0000 2 00 000 0 062 1 039 37 09 00 00 00000003
06 02 000 000 9 0000 1 0495005400 0000 2 00 000 0 062 1 039 37 09 00 00 00000008
06 02 000 000 9 0000 1 0495005400 0000 2 00 000 0 062 1 039 00 09 00 00 00000133
06 02 000 000 9 0000 1 0495005400 0000 2 00 000 0 062 1 039 00 09 00 00 00000028
06 02 000 000 9 0000 1 0495005400 0000 2 00 000 0 062 1 039 00 09 00 00 00000104
06 02 000 000 9 0000 1 0495005400 0000 2 00 000 0 062 1 039 00 09 00 00 00000024
06 02 000 000 9 0000 1 0495005400 0000 2 00 000 0 062 1 039 00 09 00 00 00000014
06 02 000 000 9 0000 1 0495005400 0000 2 00 000 0 062 1 039 00 09 00 00 00000012
06 02 000 000 9 0000 1 0495005400 0000 2 00 000 0 062 1 039 00 09 00 00 00000015
06 02 000 000 9 0000 1 0495005400 0000 2 00 000 0 062 1 039 00 09 00 00 00000017
06 02 000 000 9 0000 1 0495005400 0000 2 00 000 0 062 1 039 00 09 00 00 00000013
06 02 000 000 9 0000 1 0495005400 0000 2 00 000 0 062 1 039 00 09 00 00 00000020
06 02 000 000 9 0000 1 0495005400 0000 2 00 000 0 062 1 039 00 09 00 00 00000012
06 02 000 000 9 0000 1 0495005400 0000 2 00 000 0 062 1 039 00 09 00 00 00000012
06 02 000 000 9 0000 1 0495005400 0000 2 00 000 0 062 1 039 00 09 00 00 00000003
06 02 000 000 9 0000 1 0495005400 0000 2 00 000 0 062 1 039 00 09 00 00 00000008
06 02 000 000 9 0000 1 0495005400 0000 2 00 000 0 062 1 039 00 09 00 00 00000013
06 02 000 000 9 0000 1 0495005400 0000 2 00 000 0 062 1 039 00 09 00 00 00000004
06 02 000 000 9 0148 1 0497705448 3087 2 00 000 0 062 1 039 00 09 00 00 00000005
06 02 000 000 9 0147 1 0497705448 3087 2 00 000 0 062 1 039 00 09 00 00 00000023
06 02 000 000 9 0137 1 0498805437 3087 2 00 000 0 062 1 039 00 09 00 00 00000020
06 02 000 000 9 0133 1 0496505419 3086 2 00 000 0 062 1 039 00 09 00 00 00000020
06 02 000 000 9 0134 1 0497105446 3085 2 00 000 0 062 1 039 00 09 00 00 00000022
06 02 000 000 9 0132 1 0495105427 3082 2 00 000 0 062 1 039 00 09 00 00 00000022
06 02 000 000 9 0126 1 0499805417 3087 2 00 000 0 062 1 039 00 09 00 00 00000131
06 02 000 000 9 0014 1 0498305441 3089 2 00 000 0 062 1 039 37 09 00 00 00000088
06 02 000 000 9 0003 1 0499705419 3088 2 00 000 0 062 1 039 37 09 00 00 0000003E
06 02 000 000 9 0000 1 0495005400 0000 2 00 000 0 062 1 039 37 09 00 00 00000003
06 02 000 000 9 0045 1 0500505426 3091 2 00 000 0 062 1 039 37 09 00 00 0000010E
06 02 000 000 9 0127 1 0500005431 3085 2 00 000 0 062 1 039 37 09 00 00 00000017
06 02 000 000 9 0000 1 0500005400 0000 2 00 000 0 062 1 039 00 09 00 00 00000004
06 02 000 000 9 0000 1 0500005400 0000 2 00 000 0 062 1 039 00 09 00 00 00000004
06 02 000 000 9 0000 1 0500005400 0000 2 00 000 0 062 1 039 00 09 00 00 00000006
06 02 000 000 9 0000 1 0500005400 0000 2 00 000 0 062 1 039 00 09 00 00 0000003E
06 02 000 000 9 0000 1 0500005400 0000 2 00 000 0 062 1 039 00 09 00 00 00000017
06 02 000 000 9 0000 1 0500005400 0000 2 00 000 0 062 1 039 00 09 00 00 0000001C
06 02 000 000 9 0000 1 0500005400 0000 2 00 000 0 062 1 039 00 09 00 00 00000006
06 02 000 000 9 0000 1 0500005400 0000 2 00 000 0 062 1 039 00 09 00 00 00000009
06 02 000 000 9 0000 1 0500005400 0000 2 00 000 0 062 1 039 00 09 00 00 00000005
06 02 000 000 9 0000 1 0500005400 0000 2 00 000 0 062 1 039 00 09 00 00 00000003
06 02 000 000 9 0000 1 0500005400 0000 2 00 000 0 062 1 039 00 09 00 00 00000005
06 02 000 000 9 0000 1 0500005400 0000 2 00 000 0 062 1 039 00 09 00 00 00000015
06 02 000 000 9 0000 1 0500005400 0000 2 00 000 0 062 1 039 00 09 00 00 00000004
06 02 000 000 9 0000 1 0500005400 0000 2 00 000 0 062 1 039 00 09 00 00 00000009
06 02 000 000 9 0000 1 0500005400 0000 2 00 000 0 062 1 039 00 09 00 00 00000007
06 02 000 000 9 0000 1 0500005400 0000 2 00 000 0 062 1 039 00 09 00 00 00000016
06 02 000 000 9 0000 1 0500005400 0000 2 00 000 0 062 1 039 00 09 00 00 00000005
06 02 000 000 9 0000 1 0500005400 0000 2 00 000 0 062 1 039 00 09 00 00 00000016
06 02 000 000 9 0000 1 0500005400 0000 2 00 000 0 062 1 039 00 09 00 00 00000012
06 02 000 000 9 0000 1 0500005400 0000 2 00 000 0 062 1 039 00 09 00 00 00000005
06 02 000 000 9 0000 1 0500005400 0000 2 00 000 0 062 1 039 00 09 00 00 00000011
06 02 000 000 9 0000 1 0500005400 0000 2 00 000 0 062 1 039 00 09 00 00 00000022
06 02 000 000 9 0000 1 0500005400 0000 2 00 000 0 062 1 039 00 09 00 00 0000C031
06 02 000 000 9 0000 1 0500005400 0000 2 00 000 0 062 1 039 00 09 00 00 00000046
06 02 000 000 9 0000 1 0500005400 0000 2 00 000 0 062 1 039 00 09 00 00 00000051
06 02 000 000 9 0000 1 0500005400 0000 2 00 000 0 062 1 039 00 09 00 00 00000051
06 02 000 000 9 0080 1 0505505433 3092 2 00 000 0 062 1 039 37 09 00 00 00000159
06 02 000 000 9 0094 1 0498105502 3094 2 00 000 0 062 1 039 00 09 00 00 00000178
06 02 000 000 9 0000 1 0490005450 0000 2 00 000 0 062 1 039 37 09 00 00 00000164
06 02 000 000 9 0000 1 0490005450 0000 2 00 000 0 062 1 039 37 09 00 00 00000029
06 02 000 000 9 0000 1 0490005450 0000 2 00 000 0 062 1 039 00 09 00 00 00000008
```

```
06 02 000 000 9 0000 1 0490005450 0000 2 00 000 0 062 1 039 00 09 00 00 00000020
06 02 000 000 9 0000 1 0490005450 0000 2 00 000 0 062 1 039 00 09 00 00 00000006
06 02 000 000 9 0000 1 0490005450 0000 2 00 000 0 062 1 039 00 09 00 00 00000063
06 02 000 000 9 0000 1 0490005450 0000 2 00 000 0 062 1 039 00 09 00 00 00000009
06 02 000 000 9 0000 1 0490005450 0000 2 00 000 0 062 1 039 00 09 00 00 00000007
06 02 000 000 9 0090 1 0494605456 3092 2 00 000 0 062 1 039 00 09 00 00 00000242
06 02 000 000 9 0031 1 0495505484 3088 2 00 000 0 062 1 039 00 09 00 00 00000019
06 02 000 000 9 0000 1 0495005450 0000 2 00 000 0 062 1 039 00 09 00 00 00000027
06 02 000 000 9 0000 1 0495005450 0000 2 00 000 0 062 1 039 00 09 00 00 00000005
06 02 000 000 9 0000 1 0495005450 0000 2 00 000 0 062 1 039 00 09 00 00 00000019
06 02 000 000 9 0000 1 0495005450 0000 2 00 000 0 062 1 039 00 09 00 00 00000004
06 02 000 000 9 0000 1 0495005450 0000 2 00 000 0 062 1 039 00 09 00 00 00000006
06 02 000 000 9 0000 1 0495005450 0000 2 00 000 0 062 1 039 00 09 00 00 00000003
06 02 000 000 9 0000 1 0495005450 0000 2 00 000 0 062 1 039 00 09 00 00 00000004
06 02 000 000 9 0000 1 0495005450 0000 2 00 000 0 062 1 039 00 09 00 00 00000003
06 02 000 000 9 0000 1 0495005450 0000 2 00 000 0 062 1 039 00 09 00 00 00000010
06 02 000 000 9 0000 1 0495005450 0000 2 00 000 0 062 1 039 00 09 00 00 00000021
06 02 000 000 9 0000 1 0495005450 0000 2 00 000 0 062 1 039 00 09 00 00 00000013
06 02 000 000 9 0000 1 0495005450 0000 2 00 000 0 062 1 039 00 09 00 00 00000009
06 02 000 000 9 0000 1 0495005450 0000 2 00 000 0 062 1 039 00 09 00 00 00000021
06 02 000 000 9 0000 1 0495005450 0000 2 00 000 0 062 1 039 00 09 00 00 00000031
06 02 000 000 9 0000 1 0495005450 0000 2 00 000 0 062 1 039 00 09 00 00 00000007
06 02 000 000 9 0000 1 0495005450 0000 2 00 000 0 062 1 039 00 09 00 00 00000009
06 02 000 000 9 0000 1 0495005450 0000 2 00 000 0 062 1 039 00 09 00 00 00000003
06 02 000 000 9 0000 1 0495005450 0000 2 00 000 0 062 1 039 00 09 00 00 00000003
06 02 000 000 9 0000 1 0495005450 0000 2 00 000 0 062 1 039 00 09 00 00 00000012
06 02 000 000 9 0000 1 0495005450 0000 2 00 000 0 062 1 039 00 09 00 00 00000053
06 02 000 000 9 0000 1 0495005450 0000 2 00 000 0 062 1 039 00 09 00 00 00000015
06 02 000 000 9 0000 1 0495005450 0000 2 00 000 0 062 1 039 00 09 00 00 00000027
06 02 000 000 9 0000 1 0495005450 0000 2 00 000 0 062 1 039 00 09 00 00 00000014
06 02 000 000 9 0000 1 0495005450 0000 2 00 000 0 062 1 039 00 09 00 00 00000085
06 02 000 000 9 0000 1 0495005450 0000 2 00 000 0 062 1 039 00 09 00 00 00000202
06 02 000 000 9 0000 1 0495005450 0000 2 00 000 0 062 1 039 00 09 00 00 00000107
06 02 000 000 9 0000 1 0495005450 0000 2 00 000 0 062 1 039 00 09 00 00 00000068
06 02 000 000 9 0000 1 0495005450 0000 2 00 000 0 062 1 039 00 09 00 00 00000096
06 02 000 000 9 0000 1 0495005450 0000 2 00 000 0 062 1 039 00 09 00 00 00000179
06 02 000 000 9 0000 1 0495005450 0000 2 00 000 0 062 1 039 00 09 00 00 00000058
06 02 000 000 9 0065 1 0501305472 3091 2 00 000 0 062 1 039 00 09 00 00 00000100
06 02 000 000 9 0000 1 0500005450 0000 2 00 000 0 062 1 039 00 09 00 00 00000006
06 02 000 000 9 0000 1 0500005450 0000 2 00 000 0 062 1 039 00 09 00 00 00000019
06 02 000 000 9 0000 1 0500005450 0000 2 00 000 0 062 1 039 00 09 00 00 00000009
06 02 000 000 9 0000 1 0500005450 0000 2 00 000 0 062 1 039 00 09 00 00 00000011
06 02 000 000 9 0000 1 0500005450 0000 2 00 000 0 062 1 039 00 09 00 00 00000012
06 02 000 000 9 0099 1 0502305470 3093 2 00 000 0 062 1 039 00 09 00 00 00001175
06 02 000 000 9 0077 1 0504505460 3095 2 00 000 0 062 1 039 00 09 00 00 00000143
06 02 000 000 9 0070 1 0501905455 3093 2 00 000 0 062 1 039 00 09 00 00 00000342
06 02 000 000 9 0067 1 0501805480 3093 2 00 000 0 062 1 039 37 09 00 00 00000248
06 02 000 000 9 0000 1 0505005450 0000 2 00 000 0 062 1 039 00 09 00 00 00000014
06 02 000 000 9 0000 1 0505005450 0000 2 00 000 0 062 1 039 00 09 00 00 00000024
06 02 000 000 9 0053 1 0490505403 3091 2 00 000 0 063 1 039 00 09 00 00 00000012
06 02 000 000 9 0000 1 0495005350 0000 2 00 000 0 063 1 039 00 09 00 00 00000001
06 02 000 000 9 0000 1 0490005350 0000 2 00 000 0 063 1 039 00 09 00 00 00000006
06 02 000 000 9 0000 1 0485005400 0000 2 00 000 0 063 1 039 00 09 00 00 00000023
06 02 000 000 9 0000 1 0495005400 0000 2 00 000 0 063 1 039 00 09 00 00 00000002
06 02 000 000 9 0000 1 0490005400 0000 2 00 000 0 063 1 039 00 09 00 00 00000003
06 02 000 000 9 0141 1 0498205415 3083 2 00 000 0 063 1 039 00 09 00 00 00000014
06 02 000 000 9 0139 1 0499505424 3087 2 00 000 0 063 1 039 00 09 00 00 00000004
06 02 000 000 9 0136 1 0497705434 3088 2 00 000 0 063 1 039 00 09 00 00 00000001
06 02 000 000 9 0109 1 0499505402 3086 2 00 000 0 063 1 039 00 09 00 00 00000034
06 02 000 000 9 0000 1 0490005400 0000 2 00 000 0 063 1 039 00 09 00 00 00000010
06 02 000 000 9 0000 1 0490005400 0000 2 00 000 0 063 1 039 00 09 00 00 00000002
06 02 000 000 9 0000 1 0500005400 0000 2 00 000 0 063 1 039 00 09 00 00 00000008
06 02 000 000 9 0000 1 0500005400 0000 2 00 000 0 063 1 039 00 09 00 00 00000006
06 02 000 000 9 0000 1 0506005445 3094 2 00 000 0 063 1 039 00 09 00 00 00000120
06 02 000 000 9 0095 1 0498305504 3097 2 00 000 0 063 1 039 00 09 00 00 00000293
06 02 000 000 9 0000 1 0495005450 0000 2 00 000 0 063 1 039 00 09 00 00 00000011
06 02 000 000 9 0000 1 0495005450 0000 2 00 000 0 063 1 039 00 09 00 00 00000002
06 02 000 000 9 0000 1 0495005450 0000 2 00 000 0 063 1 039 00 09 00 00 00000005
05 02 000 000 9 0011 1 0495605419 3094 2 00 000 0 064 1 039 00 09 00 00 00000321
06 02 000 000 9 0042 1 0501905442 3090 2 00 000 0 064 1 039 00 09 00 00 00000109
06 02 000 000 9 0042 1 0501905442 3093 2 00 000 0 064 1 039 00 09 00 00 00000631
06 02 000 000 9 0113 1 0499105384 3089 2 00 000 0 064 1 039 00 09 00 00 00000770
06 02 000 000 3 0000 1 0490005400 0000 2 00 000 0 065 1 039 00 09 00 00 00000037
05 02 000 000 3 0000 1 0490005400 0000 2 00 000 0 065 1 039 00 09 00 00 00000001
06 02 000 000 3 0000 1 0490005400 0000 2 00 000 0 065 1 039 00 09 00 00 00000290
```

```
06 02 000 000 3 0000 1 0490005400 0000 2 00 000 0 065 1 039 00 09 00 00 00000946
06 02 000 000 9 0117 1 0494805393 3089 2 00 000 0 065 1 039 00 09 00 00 00000031
06 02 000 000 9 0108 1 0500705365 3088 2 00 000 0 065 1 039 00 09 00 00 00000211
06 02 000 000 9 0105 1 0502305385 3090 2 00 000 0 065 1 039 00 09 00 00 00000099
06 02 000 000 9 0000 1 0485005400 0000 2 00 000 0 065 1 039 00 09 00 00 00000012
06 02 000 000 9 0052 1 0492605419 3092 2 00 000 0 065 1 039 00 09 00 00 00000093
06 02 000 000 9 0140 1 0498005433 3087 2 00 000 0 065 1 039 00 09 00 00 00000094
06 02 000 000 9 0131 1 0496405419 3087 2 00 000 0 065 1 039 00 09 00 00 00000102
06 02 000 000 9 0110 1 0499405400 3068 2 00 000 0 065 1 039 00 09 00 00 00000076
06 02 000 000 9 0005 1 0498905412 3087 2 00 000 0 065 1 039 00 09 00 00 00000491
06 02 000 000 9 0000 1 0490005400 0000 2 00 000 0 065 1 039 00 09 00 00 00000006
06 02 000 000 9 0000 1 0500005400 0000 2 00 000 0 065 1 039 00 09 00 00 00000008
06 02 000 000 9 0000 1 0505005400 0000 2 00 000 0 065 1 039 00 00 00 00 00000767
06 02 000 000 9 0061 1 0505105403 3093 2 00 000 0 065 1 039 00 09 00 00 00000472
06 02 000 000 9 0093 1 0497705518 3096 2 00 000 0 065 1 039 00 09 00 00 00000170
06 02 000 000 9 0092 1 0493105468 3091 2 00 000 0 065 1 039 00 09 00 00 00001801
06 02 000 000 9 0000 1 0495005450 0000 2 00 000 0 065 1 039 00 09 00 00 00000005
06 02 000 000 9 0000 1 0495005450 0000 2 00 000 0 065 1 039 00 09 00 00 00000005
06 02 000 000 9 0000 1 0495005450 0000 2 00 000 0 065 1 039 00 09 00 00 00000006
06 02 000 000 9 0000 1 0495005450 0000 2 00 000 0 065 1 039 00 09 00 00 00000022
06 02 000 000 9 0000 1 0495005450 0000 2 00 000 0 065 1 039 00 09 00 00 00000028
06 02 000 000 9 0000 1 0495005450 0000 2 00 000 0 065 1 039 00 09 00 00 00000052
06 02 000 000 9 0129 1 0499405499 3092 2 00 000 0 065 1 039 00 09 00 00 00000420
06 02 000 000 9 0064 1 0500905467 3092 2 00 000 0 065 1 039 00 09 00 00 00000373
06 02 000 000 3 0000 1 0490005400 0000 2 00 000 0 082 1 039 00 09 00 00 00000127
06 02 000 000 9 0000 1 0495005350 0000 2 00 000 0 082 1 039 00 09 00 00 00000027
06 02 000 000 9 0000 1 0490005400 0000 2 00 000 0 082 1 039 00 09 00 00 00000029
06 02 000 000 3 0000 1 0505005450 0000 2 00 000 0 082 1 039 00 09 00 00 00001451
06 02 000 000 9 0112 1 0499105391 3090 2 00 000 0 082 1 039 00 09 00 00 00000077
06 02 000 000 9 0111 1 0499805389 3090 2 00 000 0 082 1 039 00 09 00 00 00000147
06 02 000 000 9 0104 1 0503305390 3088 2 00 000 0 082 1 039 00 09 00 00 00000342
06 02 000 000 9 0102 1 0503805397 3090 2 00 000 0 082 1 039 00 09 00 00 00000336
06 02 000 000 9 0013 1 0497705438 3088 2 00 000 0 082 1 039 00 09 00 00 00000086
06 02 000 000 9 0128 1 0499605426 3087 2 00 000 0 082 1 039 37 09 00 00 00000287
06 02 000 000 9 0000 1 0495005400 0000 2 00 000 0 082 1 039 00 09 00 00 00000017
06 02 000 000 9 0000 1 0495005400 0000 2 00 000 0 082 1 039 00 09 00 00 00000012
06 02 000 000 9 0000 1 0495005400 0000 2 00 000 0 082 1 039 00 09 00 00 00000012
06 02 000 000 9 0000 1 0495005400 0000 2 00 000 0 082 1 039 00 09 00 00 00000023
06 02 000 000 9 0000 1 0495005400 0000 2 00 000 0 082 1 039 00 09 00 00 00000019
06 02 000 000 9 0000 1 0490005400 0000 2 00 000 0 082 1 039 00 09 00 00 00000012
06 02 000 000 9 0000 1 0500005400 0000 2 00 000 0 082 1 039 00 09 00 00 00000047
06 02 000 000 9 0000 1 0500005400 0000 2 00 000 0 082 1 039 00 09 00 00 00000038
06 02 000 000 9 0043 1 0501805444 3093 2 00 000 0 082 1 039 00 09 00 00 00000546
06 02 000 000 9 0053 1 0504105408 3091 2 00 000 0 082 1 039 00 00 00 00 00000537
06 02 000 000 9 0100 1 0505105461 3092 2 00 000 0 082 1 039 00 09 00 00 00000484
06 02 000 000 9 0123 1 0505605420 3090 2 00 000 0 082 1 039 00 09 00 00 00000101
06 02 000 000 9 0000 1 0490005450 0000 2 00 000 0 082 1 039 00 09 00 00 00000040
06 02 000 000 9 0000 1 0495005450 0000 2 00 000 0 082 1 039 00 09 00 00 00000035
06 02 000 000 9 0000 1 0490005450 0000 2 00 000 0 082 1 039 00 09 00 00 00000013
06 02 000 000 9 0019 1 0495005460 3088 2 00 000 0 082 1 039 00 09 00 00 00000068
06 02 000 000 9 0000 1 0495005450 0000 2 00 000 0 082 1 039 00 09 00 00 00000026
06 02 000 000 9 0000 1 0495005450 0000 2 00 000 0 082 1 039 00 09 00 00 00000031
06 02 000 000 9 0000 1 0495005450 0000 2 00 000 0 082 1 039 00 09 00 00 00000030
06 02 000 000 9 0000 1 0495005450 0000 2 00 000 0 082 1 039 00 09 00 00 00000053
06 02 000 000 9 0000 1 0495005450 0000 2 00 000 0 082 1 039 00 09 00 00 00000080
06 02 000 000 9 0000 1 0495005450 0000 2 00 000 0 082 1 039 00 09 00 00 00000169
06 02 000 000 9 0000 1 0495005450 0000 2 00 000 0 082 1 039 00 09 00 00 00000195
06 02 000 000 9 0000 1 0495005450 0000 2 00 000 0 082 1 039 00 09 00 00 00000204
06 02 000 000 9 0000 1 0501605467 3095 2 00 000 0 082 1 039 00 09 00 00 00000679
06 02 000 000 9 0068 1 0502305470 3096 2 00 000 0 082 1 039 00 09 00 00 00001412
06 02 000 000 9 0000 1 0505005450 0000 2 00 000 0 082 1 039 00 09 00 00 00000025
06 02 000 000 9 0121 1 0495605396 3098 2 00 000 0 051 7 038 00 09 00 00 00000007
06 02 000 000 9 0039 1 0502605444 3090 2 00 000 0 052 1 018 00 09 00 00 00000028
06 02 000 000 9 0000 1 0495005450 0000 2 00 000 0 052 1 039 00 09 00 00 00000007
06 02 000 000 9 0082 1 0505105454 3095 2 00 000 0 090 1 003 00 00 00 00 00001451
06 02 000 000 9 0062 1 0498005477 3092 1 00 000 0 003 1 003 00 00 00 00 00000110
06 02 000 000 9 0122 1 0498005442 3088 1 00 000 0 003 1 002 00 00 00 00 00000247
06 02 000 000 9 0096 1 0498705509 3095 1 00 000 0 003 1 005 00 00 00 00 00000065
06 02 000 000 9 0055 1 0494205434 3092 1 00 000 0 003 1 002 00 00 00 00 00001023
06 02 000 000 9 0022 1 0496205455 3088 1 00 000 0 003 1 002 00 00 00 00 00000045
06 02 000 000 9 0030 1 0496405491 3093 1 00 000 0 003 1 002 00 00 00 00 00000045
06 02 000 000 9 0012 1 0496705428 3087 1 00 000 0 003 1 003 00 00 00 00 00000135
06 02 000 000 9 0069 1 0501305457 3091 1 00 000 0 003 1 002 00 00 00 00 00000015
06 02 000 000 9 0036 1 0503205419 3092 1 00 000 0 003 1 002 00 00 00 00 00000208
```

```
06 02 000 000 9 0020 1 0498505452 3087 1 00 000 0 003 1 002 00 00 07 00 00000110
06 02 000 000 9 0138 1 0499005418 3086 1 00 000 0 003 1 002 00 00 00 00 00000777
06 02 000 000 9 0029 1 0497905494 3093 1 00 000 0 003 1 002 00 00 00 00 00001001
06 02 000 000 9 0000 1 0495005450 0000 1 00 000 0 007 1 002 02 00 00 00 00000046
06 02 000 000 9 0040 1 0501905428 3091 1 00 000 0 008 1 002 00 00 00 00 00000586
06 02 000 000 9 0004 1 0498705421 3089 1 00 000 0 015 1 001 00 00 00 00 00000056
06 02 000 000 9 0002 1 0499505417 3088 1 00 000 0 015 1 001 00 00 00 00 00000383
05 02 000 000 9 0007 1 0497205403 3087 1 00 000 0 015 1 001 00 00 00 00 00000080
06 02 000 000 9 0008 1 0496405408 3087 1 00 000 0 015 1 001 00 00 00 00 00000438
06 02 000 000 9 0010 1 0495305417 3088 1 00 000 0 015 1 001 00 09 00 00 00000012
06 02 000 000 9 0015 1 0497605439 3090 1 00 000 0 015 1 001 00 00 00 00 00000239
06 02 000 000 9 0016 1 0496805439 3088 1 00 000 0 015 1 001 00 09 00 00 00000081
06 02 000 000 9 018  1 0495105444 3089 1 00 000 0 015 1 001 00 00 00 00 00000050
06 02 000 000 9 0017 1 0496605448 3088 1 00 000 0 015 1 001 00 00 00 00 00000040
06 02 000 000 9 0017 1 0496605448 3088 1 00 000 0 015 1 001 00 00 00 00 00000061
06 02 000 000 9 0016 1 0496805439 3088 1 00 000 0 015 1 001 00 00 00 00 00000024
06 02 000 000 9 0028 1 0496705400 3095 1 00 000 0 015 1 001 00 00 00 00 00000207
06 02 000 000 9 0145 1 0498505416 3084 1 00 000 0 015 1 001 00 00 00 00 00000034
06 02 000 000 9 0146 1 0497705448 3087 1 00 000 0 015 1 001 00 00 00 00 00000022
06 02 000 000 9 0149 1 0497705448 3087 1 00 000 0 015 1 001 00 00 00 00 00000029
06 02 000 000 9 0000 1 0495005400 0000 1 00 000 0 015 1 001 00 00 00 00 00000032
06 02 000 000 9 0000 1 0495005400 0000 1 00 000 0 015 1 001 00 00 00 00 00000025
06 02 000 000 9 0000 1 0495005400 0000 1 00 000 0 015 1 001 00 00 00 00 00000036
06 02 000 000 9 0000 1 0495005400 0000 1 00 000 0 015 1 001 00 00 00 00 00000033
06 02 000 000 9 0000 1 0495005400 0000 1 00 000 0 015 1 001 00 00 00 00 00000036
06 02 000 000 9 0000 1 0495005400 0000 1 00 000 0 015 1 001 00 00 00 00 00000052
06 02 000 000 9 0000 1 0495005400 0000 1 00 000 0 015 1 001 00 00 00 00 00000082
06 02 000 000 9 0000 1 0495005400 0000 1 00 000 0 015 1 001 00 00 00 00 00000090
06 02 000 000 9 0000 1 0495005400 0000 1 00 000 0 015 1 001 00 00 00 00 00000140
06 02 000 000 9 0000 1 0500005350 0000 1 00 000 0 015 1 001 00 00 00 00 00000033
06 02 000 000 3 0000 1 0490005400 0000 1 00 000 0 015 1 001 00 00 00 00 00000046
06 02 000 000 3 0000 1 0490005400 0000 1 00 000 0 015 1 001 00 00 00 00 00000133
06 02 000 000 3 0000 1 0490005400 0000 1 00 000 0 015 1 001 00 00 00 00 00000042
06 02 001 000 9 0000 1 0490005400 0000 1 00 000 0 015 1 001 00 00 00 00 00000024
06 02 001 000 3 0000 1 0490005400 0000 1 00 000 0 015 1 001 00 00 00 00 00000024
06 02 000 000 3 0000 1 0490005400 0000 1 00 000 0 015 1 001 00 00 00 00 00000039
06 02 000 000 9 0000 1 0495005350 0000 1 00 000 0 015 1 001 00 00 00 00 00000029
06 02 000 000 9 0000 1 0495005350 0000 1 00 000 0 015 1 001 00 00 00 00 00000017
06 02 000 000 9 0000 1 0490005350 0000 1 00 000 0 015 1 001 00 00 00 00 00000046
06 02 000 000 9 0103 1 05029C5397 3092 1 00 000 0 015 1 001 00 09 00 00 00000044
06 02 000 000 9 0000 1 0485005400 0000 1 00 000 0 015 1 001 00 00 00 00 00000021
06 02 000 000 9 0000 1 0482005400 0000 1 00 000 0 015 1 001 00 00 00 00 00000042
06 02 000 000 9 0060 1 0493305449 3094 1 00 000 0 015 1 001 00 00 00 00 00000299
06 02 000 000 9 0058 1 0493405446 3094 1 00 000 0 015 1 001 00 00 00 00 00000198
06 02 000 000 9 0056 1 0493605434 3092 1 00 000 0 015 1 001 00 00 00 00 00000125
06 02 000 000 9 0035 1 0504405447 3091 1 00 000 0 015 1 001 00 00 00 00 00000077
06 02 000 000 9 0046 1 0500405433 3091 1 00 000 0 015 1 001 00 09 00 00 00000037
06 02 000 000 9 0044 1 0501105427 3091 1 00 000 0 015 1 001 00 00 00 00 00000025
06 02 000 000 9 0000 1 0500005400 0000 1 00 000 0 015 1 001 00 00 00 00 00000010
06 02 000 000 9 0000 1 0500005400 0000 1 00 000 0 015 1 001 00 00 00 00 00000039
06 02 000 000 9 0000 1 0500005400 0000 1 00 000 0 015 1 001 00 00 00 00 00000011
06 02 000 000 9 0000 1 0500005400 0000 1 00 000 0 015 1 001 00 00 00 00 00000014
06 02 000 000 9 0000 1 0500005400 0000 1 00 000 0 015 1 001 00 00 00 00 00000058
06 02 000 000 9 0000 1 0500005400 0000 1 00 000 0 015 1 001 00 00 00 00 00000022
06 02 000 000 9 0000 1 0500005400 0000 1 00 000 0 015 1 001 00 00 00 00 00000015
06 02 000 000 9 0000 1 0500005400 0000 1 00 000 0 015 1 001 00 00 00 00 00000012
06 02 000 000 9 0000 1 0500005400 0000 1 00 000 0 015 1 001 00 00 00 00 00000005
06 02 000 000 9 0000 1 0505005400 0000 1 00 000 0 015 1 001 00 00 00 00 00000018
06 02 000 000 9 0095 1 0498305504 3097 1 00 000 0 015 1 001 00 00 00 00 00000102
06 02 000 000 9 0047 1 0492305452 3091 1 00 000 0 015 1 001 00 09 00 00 00000046
05 02 000 000 9 0091 1 0494705466 3091 1 00 000 0 015 1 001 00 00 00 00 00000044
06 02 000 000 9 0089 1 0492605452 3091 1 00 000 0 015 1 001 00 00 00 00 00000020
06 02 000 000 9 0000 1 0490005450 0000 1 00 000 0 015 1 001 00 00 00 00 00000026
06 02 000 000 9 0000 1 0490005450 0000 1 00 000 0 015 1 001 00 00 00 00 00000012
06 02 000 000 9 0000 1 0490005450 0000 1 00 000 0 015 1 001 00 00 00 00 00000020
06 02 000 000 9 0000 1 0490005450 0000 1 00 000 0 015 1 001 00 00 00 00 00000020
06 02 000 000 9 0021 1 0497205455 3090 1 00 000 0 015 1 001 00 00 00 00 00000168
06 02 000 000 9 0024 1 0497205468 3088 1 00 000 0 015 1 001 00 00 00 00 00000004
05 02 000 000 9 0000 1 0495005450 0000 1 00 000 0 015 1 001 00 00 00 00 00000030
06 02 000 000 9 0000 1 0495005450 0000 1 00 000 0 015 1 001 00 00 00 00 00000047
06 02 000 000 9 0000 1 0495005450 0000 1 00 000 0 015 1 001 00 00 00 00 00000006
06 02 000 000 9 0000 1 0495005450 0000 1 00 000 0 015 1 001 00 00 00 00 00000036
```

```
06 02 000 000 9 0000 1 0495005450 0000 1 00 000 0 015 1 001 00 00 00 00 00000036
06 02 000 000 9 0000 1 0495005450 0000 1 00 000 0 015 1 001 00 00 00 00 00000022
06 02 000 000 9 0000 1 0495005450 0000 1 00 000 0 015 1 001 00 00 00 00 00000018
06 02 000 000 9 0000 1 0495005450 0000 1 00 000 0 015 1 001 00 00 00 00 00000040
06 02 000 000 9 0000 1 0495005450 0000 1 00 000 0 015 1 001 00 00 00 00 00000093
06 02 000 000 9 0000 1 0495005450 0000 1 00 000 0 015 1 001 00 00 00 00 00000064
06 02 000 000 9 0000 1 0500005450 0000 1 00 000 0 015 1 001 00 00 00 00 00000010
06 02 000 000 9 0000 1 0500005450 0000 1 00 000 0 015 1 001 00 00 00 00 00000009
06 02 000 000 9 0000 1 0500005450 0000 1 00 000 0 015 1 001 00 00 00 00 00000009
06 02 000 000 9 0000 1 0500005450 0000 1 00 000 0 015 1 001 00 00 00 00 00000014
06 02 000 000 9 0000 1 0500005450 0000 1 00 000 0 015 1 001 00 00 00 00 00000006
06 02 000 000 9 0073 1 0503105462 3095 1 00 000 0 015 1 001 00 00 00 00 00000388
06 02 000 000 9 0074 1 0503105475 3095 1 00 000 0 015 1 001 00 00 00 00 00000313
06 02 000 000 9 0075 1 0503105473 3095 1 00 000 0 015 1 001 00 00 00 00 00000056
06 02 000 000 9 0063 1 0500105470 3093 1 00 000 0 015 1 001 00 00 00 00 00000614
06 02 000 000 9 0061 1 0500105496 3093 1 00 000 0 015 1 001 00 00 00 00 00000068
06 02 000 000 9 0000 1 0505005450 0000 1 00 000 0 015 1 001 00 00 00 00 00000007
06 02 000 000 9 0086 1 0505005461 3093 1 00 000 0 015 1 001 00 00 00 00 00000057
06 02 000 000 9 0087 1 0505905455 3094 1 00 000 0 015 1 001 00 00 00 00 00000536
06 02 000 000 9 0086 1 0505805470 3094 1 00 000 0 015 1 001 00 00 00 00 00000117
06 02 000 000 9 0085 1 0505705464 3094 1 00 000 0 015 1 001 00 00 00 00 00000006
06 02 000 000 9 0084 1 0505705465 3096 1 00 000 0 015 1 001 00 00 00 00 00000050
06 02 001 000 9 0000 1 0490005400 0000 1 00 000 0 033 1 039 00 00 00 00 00000009
06 02 001 000 9 0000 1 0490005400 0000 1 00 000 0 033 1 039 00 00 00 00 00000010
06 02 000 000 9 0000 1 0490005350 0000 1 00 000 0 038 1 039 00 00 00 00 00000003
06 02 000 000 9 0059 1 0493205454 3088 1 00 000 0 038 1 039 00 00 00 00 00000100
06 02 000 000 9 0057 1 0493305438 3088 1 00 000 0 038 1 039 00 00 00 00 00000476
06 02 000 000 9 0001 1 0499805405 3085 1 00 000 0 038 1 039 00 00 00 00 00000938
06 02 000 000 9 0101 1 0498305404 3096 1 00 000 0 038 1 039 00 09 00 00 00000061
06 02 000 000 9 0135 1 0497705443 3087 1 00 000 0 038 1 039 00 00 00 00 00000017
06 02 000 000 9 0142 1 0498705424 3087 1 00 000 0 038 1 039 00 00 00 00 00000027
06 02 000 000 9 0000 1 0495005400 0000 1 00 000 0 038 1 039 00 00 00 00 00000002
06 02 000 000 9 0000 1 0495005400 0000 1 00 000 0 038 1 039 00 00 00 00 00000015
06 02 000 000 9 0000 1 0495005400 0000 1 00 000 0 038 1 039 00 00 00 00 00000033
06 02 000 000 9 0000 1 0495005400 0000 1 00 000 0 038 1 039 00 00 00 00 00000046
06 02 000 000 9 0037 1 0502505412 3093 1 00 000 0 038 1 039 00 00 00 00 00000829
06 02 000 000 9 0032 1 0504205411 3093 1 00 000 0 038 1 039 00 00 00 00 00000060
06 02 000 000 9 0041 1 0502105429 3092 1 00 000 0 038 1 039 00 00 00 00 00000586
06 02 000 000 9 0000 1 0500005400 0000 1 00 000 0 038 1 039 00 00 00 00 00000026
06 02 000 000 9 0000 1 0500005400 0000 1 00 000 0 038 1 039 00 00 00 00 00000020
06 02 000 000 9 0000 1 0500005400 0000 1 00 000 0 038 1 039 00 00 00 00 00000011
06 02 000 000 9 0000 1 0500005400 0000 1 00 000 0 038 1 039 00 00 00 00 00000007
06 02 000 000 9 0000 1 0500005400 0000 1 00 000 0 038 1 039 00 00 00 00 00000004
06 02 000 000 9 0000 1 0490005450 0000 1 00 000 0 038 1 039 00 00 00 00 00000012
06 02 000 000 9 0000 1 0490005450 0000 1 00 000 0 038 1 039 00 00 00 00 00000022
06 02 000 000 9 0000 1 0490005450 0000 1 00 000 0 038 1 039 00 00 00 00 00000021
06 02 000 000 9 0000 1 0490005450 0000 1 00 000 0 038 1 039 00 00 00 00 00000032
06 02 000 000 9 0026 1 0499505477 3094 1 00 000 0 038 1 039 00 00 00 00 00000469
06 02 000 000 9 0000 1 0495005450 0000 1 00 000 0 038 1 039 00 00 00 00 00000002
06 02 000 000 9 0000 1 0495005450 0000 1 00 000 0 038 1 039 00 00 00 00 00000047
06 02 000 000 9 0000 1 0495005450 0000 1 00 000 0 038 1 039 00 00 00 00 00000058
06 02 000 000 9 0000 1 0495005450 0000 1 00 000 0 038 1 039 00 00 00 00 00000026
06 02 000 000 9 0000 1 0495005450 0000 1 00 000 0 038 1 039 00 00 00 00 00000050
06 02 000 000 9 0000 1 0495005450 0000 1 00 000 0 038 1 039 00 00 00 00 00000139
06 02 000 000 9 0000 1 0495005450 0000 1 00 000 0 038 1 039 00 00 00 00 00000036
06 02 000 000 9 0000 1 0495005450 0000 1 00 000 0 038 1 039 00 00 00 00 00000002
06 02 000 000 9 0000 1 0495005450 0000 1 00 000 0 038 1 039 00 00 00 00 00000145
06 02 000 000 9 0000 1 0495005450 0000 1 00 000 0 038 1 039 00 00 00 00 00000084
06 02 000 000 9 0000 1 0495005450 0000 1 00 000 0 038 1 039 00 00 00 00 00000085
06 02 000 000 9 0072 1 0502005450 3092 1 00 000 0 038 1 039 00 00 00 00 00002052
06 02 000 000 9 0000 1 0500005450 0000 1 00 000 0 038 1 039 00 00 00 00 00000027
06 02 000 000 9 0000 1 0500005450 0000 1 00 000 0 038 1 039 00 00 00 00 00000028
06 02 000 000 9 0000 1 0500005450 0000 1 00 000 0 038 1 039 00 00 00 00 00000019
06 02 000 000 9 0000 1 0500005450 0000 1 00 000 0 038 1 039 00 00 00 00 00000013
06 02 000 000 9 0000 1 0500005450 0000 1 00 000 0 038 1 039 00 00 00 00 00000014
06 02 000 000 9 0000 1 0500005450 0000 1 00 000 0 038 1 039 00 00 00 00 00000004
06 02 000 000 9 0034 1 0503805450 3090 5 00 000 0 104 1 039 00 00 00 00 00000375
06 02 000 000 9 0050 1 0494105412 3094 5 00 000 0 104 7 038 00 00 00 00 00000824
06 02 000 000 9 0098 1 0502705463 3093 5 00 000 0 104 7 038 00 00 00 00 00000646
06 02 000 000 9 0114 1 0499505379 3069 5 00 000 0 104 1 039 00 00 00 00 00000154
06 02 000 000 9 0124 1 0502005410 3088 5 00 000 0 104 1 039 00 00 00 00 00000144
```

```
06 02 000 000 9 0000 1 0495005450 0000 4 01 000 0 000 1 033 00 00 00 00 00000002
06 02 000 000 9 0000 1 0495005450 0000 4 01 000 0 000 1 033 00 00 00 00 00000018
06 02 000 000 9 0079 1 0505705435 3092 4 01 014 1 000 7 038 00 00 00 00 00000053
06 02 000 000 9 0097 1 0499305512 3095 4 01 015 1 000 1 039 00 00 00 00 00000018
06 02 000 000 9 0071 1 0502205455 3092 4 01 021 0 000 1 039 00 00 00 00 00000012
06 02 000 000 9 0120 1 0510005372 3093 4 01 030 0 000 1 039 00 00 00 00 00000006
06 02 000 000 9 0027 1 0498305483 3094 4 01 032 1 000 1 039 00 00 00 00 00000007
06 02 000 000 9 0076 1 0504005461 3093 4 01 033 1 000 1 039 00 00 00 00 00000014
06 02 000 000 9 0000 1 0495005450 0000 4 03 058 0 000 1 039 00 00 00 00 00000001
06 02 000 000 9 0000 1 0495005450 0000 4 03 059 0 000 1 039 00 00 00 00 00000002
06 02 000 000 9 0000 1 0495005450 0000 4 03 059 0 000 1 039 00 00 00 00 00000001
06 02 000 000 9 0040 1 0501905428 3091 4 04 060 2 000 1 033 00 00 00 00 00000082
06 02 000 000 9 0115 1 0496905399 3089 4 08 000 0 000 1 039 00 00 00 00 00000014
06 02 001 000 9 0000 1 0495005400 0000 3 77 507 0 000 1 039 65 00 00 00 00000053
06 02 000 000 9 0000 1 0485005450 0000 3 77 507 0 000 1 039 65 00 00 00 000000C3
06 02 000 000 9 0000 1 0485005400 0000 3 77 507 0 000 1 039 65 00 00 00 0000002C
06 02 000 000 9 0000 1 0490005450 0000 3 77 507 0 000 1 039 65 00 00 00 00000056
06 02 000 000 9 0000 1 0490005450 0000 3 77 507 0 000 1 039 65 00 00 00 00000040
06 02 000 000 9 0000 1 0490005450 0000 3 77 507 0 000 1 039 65 00 00 00 00000003
06 02 000 000 9 0000 1 0495005450 0000 3 77 507 0 000 1 039 65 00 00 00 00000002
06 02 000 000 9 0000 1 0495005450 0000 3 77 507 0 000 1 039 65 00 00 00 00000077
06 02 000 000 9 0000 1 0500005400 0000 3 77 507 0 000 1 039 65 00 00 00 00000002
06 02 000 000 9 0000 1 0500005400 0000 3 80 507 0 000 1 039 65 00 00 00 00000001
06 02 001 000 9 0000 1 0495005400 0000 3 81 503 0 000 1 039 65 00 00 00 00000015
06 02 001 000 9 0000 1 0495005400 0000 3 85 510 0 000 1 039 65 00 00 00 000000CC
06 02 001 000 9 0000 1 0495005400 0000 3 86 512 0 000 1 039 00 00 00 00 00000000
06 02 000 000 9 0000 1 0500005400 0000 3 87 510 0 000 1 039 65 00 00 00 00000000
06 02 001 000 9 0000 1 0495005400 0000 3 91 507 0 000 1 039 65 00 00 00 00000005
06 02 000 000 9 0000 1 0495005350 0000 3 91 507 0 000 1 039 65 00 00 00 00000002
06 02 000 000 9 0000 1 0500005450 0000 3 91 507 0 000 1 039 65 00 00 00 00000002
06 02 000 000 9 0000 1 0500005400 0000 3 91 507 0 000 1 039 65 00 00 00 00000001
```

Appendix E

```
     PIT FOUR DATA BASE
05 00 004 000 9 0000 1 0527505570 0000 1 00 000 0 015 1 001 00 00 00 00 00000042
06 00 004 000 9 0000 1 0527505570 0000 1 00 000 0 015 1 001 00 00 00 00 00000025
06 00 004 000 9 0000 1 0527505570 0000 2 00 000 0 082 1 039 00 09 00 00 00000296
06 00 004 000 9 0000 1 0527505570 0000 2 00 000 0 082 1 039 00 09 00 00 00000054
06 00 004 000 9 0000 1 0527505570 0000 2 00 000 0 061 1 039 00 09 00 00 00000369
06 00 004 000 9 0000 1 0527505578 0000 0 00 000 0 062 1 039 37 09 00 00 00000195
```

Appendix F

```
     PIT SIX DATA BASE
06 00 006 000 9 0000 1 0543405646 0000 2 00 000 0 060 1 039 00 09 00 00 00000001
06 00 006 000 9 0000 1 0543405646 0000 2 00 000 0 060 1 039 00 09 00 00 00000001
06 00 006 000 9 0000 1 0543405646 0000 2 00 000 0 060 1 039 00 09 00 00 00000001
06 00 006 000 9 0000 1 0543405646 0000 2 00 000 0 060 1 039 37 09 00 00 00000002
06 00 006 000 9 0000 1 0543405646 0000 2 00 000 0 060 1 039 00 09 00 00 00000008
06 00 006 000 9 0000 1 0543405646 0000 2 00 000 0 060 1 039 37 09 00 00 00000008
06 00 006 000 9 0000 1 0543405646 0000 2 00 000 0 060 1 039 37 09 00 00 00000001
06 00 006 000 9 0000 1 0543405646 0000 2 00 000 0 060 1 039 37 09 00 00 00000001
06 00 006 000 9 0000 1 0543405646 0000 2 00 000 0 060 1 039 37 09 00 00 00000001
06 00 006 000 9 0000 1 0543405646 0000 2 00 000 0 060 1 039 37 09 00 00 00000001
06 00 006 000 9 0000 1 0543405646 0000 2 00 000 0 060 1 039 37 09 00 00 00000003
06 00 006 000 9 0000 1 0543405645 0000 2 00 000 0 060 1 039 00 09 00 00 00000009
06 00 006 000 9 0000 1 0543405646 0000 2 00 000 0 060 1 039 00 09 00 00 00000015
06 00 006 000 9 0000 1 0543405646 0000 2 00 000 0 060 1 039 00 09 00 00 00000013
06 00 006 000 9 0000 1 0543405646 0000 2 00 000 0 060 1 039 00 09 00 00 00000013
06 00 006 000 9 0000 1 0543405646 0000 2 00 000 0 060 1 039 00 09 00 00 00000011
06 00 006 000 9 0000 1 0543405646 0000 2 00 000 0 060 1 039 00 09 00 00 00000076
06 00 006 000 9 0000 1 0543405646 0000 2 00 000 0 061 1 039 37 09 00 00 00000145
06 00 006 000 9 0000 1 0543405646 0000 2 00 000 0 062 1 039 00 09 00 00 00000001
06 00 006 000 9 0000 1 0543405646 0000 2 00 000 0 062 1 039 00 09 00 00 00000001
06 00 006 000 9 0000 1 0543405646 0000 2 00 000 0 062 1 039 37 09 00 00 00000002
06 00 006 000 9 0000 1 0543405646 0000 2 00 000 0 062 1 039 00 09 00 00 00000002
06 00 006 000 9 0000 1 0543405646 0000 2 00 000 0 062 1 039 00 09 00 00 00000002
06 00 006 000 9 0000 1 0543405646 0000 2 00 000 0 062 1 039 00 09 00 00 00000004
06 00 006 000 9 0000 1 0543405646 0000 2 00 000 0 062 1 039 37 09 00 00 00000003
06 00 006 000 9 0000 1 0543405646 0000 2 00 000 0 062 1 039 00 09 00 00 00000006
06 00 006 000 9 0000 1 0543405645 0000 2 00 000 0 062 1 039 00 09 00 00 00000003
06 00 006 000 9 0000 1 0543405646 0000 2 00 000 0 062 1 039 37 09 00 00 00000037
06 00 006 000 9 0000 1 0543405645 0000 2 00 000 0 062 1 039 00 09 00 00 00000018
06 00 006 000 9 0000 1 0543405646 0000 2 00 000 0 062 1 039 00 09 00 00 00000007
06 00 006 000 9 0000 1 0543405646 0000 2 00 000 0 063 1 039 00 09 00 00 00000002
06 00 006 000 9 0000 1 0543405646 0000 2 00 000 0 063 1 039 00 09 00 00 00000001
06 00 006 000 9 0000 1 0543405646 0000 2 00 000 0 063 1 039 00 09 00 00 00000018
06 00 006 000 9 0000 1 0543405646 0000 2 00 000 0 063 1 039 00 09 00 00 00000034
06 00 006 000 9 0000 1 0543405646 0000 2 00 000 0 065 1 039 00 09 00 00 00000009
06 00 006 000 9 0000 1 0543405646 0000 2 00 000 0 065 1 039 00 09 00 00 00000094
06 00 006 000 9 0000 1 0543405646 0000 2 00 000 0 082 1 039 00 09 00 00 00000013
06 00 006 000 9 0000 1 0543405645 0000 1 00 000 0 038 1 039 00 00 00 00 00000007
06 00 006 000 9 0000 1 0543405646 0000 1 00 000 0 036 1 039 00 00 00 00 00000023
06 00 006 000 9 0000 1 0543405646 0000 1 00 000 0 036 1 039 00 00 00 00 00000042
06 00 006 000 9 0000 1 0543405646 0000 1 00 000 0 036 1 039 00 00 00 00 00000001
06 00 006 000 9 0000 1 0543405646 0000 1 00 000 0 015 1 001 00 00 00 00 00000025
06 00 006 000 9 0000 1 0543405646 0000 1 00 000 0 015 1 001 00 00 00 00 00000021
06 00 006 000 9 0000 1 0543405646 0000 1 00 000 0 015 1 001 00 00 00 00 00000001
06 00 006 000 9 0000 1 0543405646 0000 1 00 000 0 015 1 001 00 00 00 00 00000018
06 00 006 000 9 0000 1 0543405646 0000 1 00 000 0 015 1 001 00 00 00 00 00000002
06 00 006 000 9 0000 1 0543405646 0000 4 07 007 1 000 1 037 65 00 00 00 00000001
06 00 006 000 9 0000 1 0543405646 0000 4 07 006 1 000 1 037 65 00 00 00 00000001
06 00 006 000 9 0000 1 0543405646 0000 4 74 000 0 000 1 033 65 00 00 00 00000001
06 00 006 000 9 0000 1 0543405646 0000 4 74 000 0 000 1 033 65 00 00 00 00000001
06 00 006 000 9 0000 1 0543405646 0000 4 74 000 0 000 1 033 65 00 00 00 00000001
06 00 006 000 9 0000 1 0543405646 0000 4 74 000 0 000 1 033 65 00 00 00 00000001
06 00 006 000 9 0000 1 0543405646 0000 4 74 000 0 000 1 033 65 00 00 00 00000001
06 00 006 000 9 0000 1 0543405646 0000 4 74 000 0 000 1 033 65 00 00 00 00000001
06 00 006 000 9 0000 1 0543405646 0000 4 03 058 0 000 1 039 00 00 00 00 00000001
06 00 006 000 9 0000 1 0543405646 0000 4 03 058 0 000 1 039 00 00 00 00 00000001
06 00 006 000 9 0000 1 0543405646 0000 3 77 517 0 000 1 039 65 00 00 00 00000056
06 00 006 000 9 0000 1 0543405646 0000 3 80 507 0 000 1 039 65 00 00 00 00000000
06 00 006 000 9 0000 1 0543405645 0000 3 81 503 0 000 7 000 65 00 00 00 00000000
06 00 006 000 9 0000 1 0543405646 0000 3 82 510 0 000 7 000 00 00 00 00 00000001
06 00 006 000 9 0000 1 0543405646 0000 3 84 510 0 000 7 000 65 00 00 00 00000001
06 00 006 000 9 0000 1 0543405646 0000 3 85 510 0 000 7 000 65 00 00 00 00000001
06 00 006 000 9 0000 1 0543405646 0000 3 86 512 0 000 7 000 00 00 00 00 00000000
```

230

Appendix G

```
   PIT SEVEN DATA BASE
06 00 007 000 9 0000 1 0479805629 0000 2 00 000 0 060 1 039 65 09 00 00 00000033
06 00 007 000 9 0000 1 0479805629 0000 2 00 000 0 060 1 039 65 09 00 00 00000001
06 00 007 000 9 0000 1 0479805629 0000 2 00 000 0 060 1 039 65 09 00 00 00000001
06 00 007 000 9 0000 1 0479805629 0000 2 00 000 0 062 1 039 65 09 00 00 00000023
06 00 007 000 9 0000 1 0479805629 0000 2 00 000 0 062 1 039 65 09 00 00 00000018
06 00 007 000 9 0000 1 0479805629 0000 2 00 000 0 065 1 039 00 09 00 00 00000030
06 00 007 000 9 0000 1 0479805629 0000 2 00 000 0 082 1 039 00 09 00 00 00000002
06 00 007 000 9 0000 1 0479805629 0000 1 00 000 0 015 1 001 00 00 00 00 00000032
06 00 007 000 9 0000 1 0479805629 0000 1 00 000 0 015 1 001 00 00 00 00 00000027
06 00 007 000 9 0000 1 0479805629 0000 1 00 000 0 015 1 001 00 00 00 00 00000041
06 00 007 000 9 0000 1 0479805629 0000 1 00 000 0 038 1 039 00 00 00 00 00000050
06 00 007 000 9 0000 1 0479805629 0000 1 00 000 0 038 1 039 00 00 00 00 00000016
06 00 007 000 9 0000 1 0479805629 0000 4 03 058 0 000 1 039 65 00 00 00 00000001
06 00 007 000 9 0000 1 0479805629 0000 4 03 058 0 000 1 039 65 00 00 00 00000001
06 00 007 000 9 0000 1 0479805629 0000 4 03 058 0 000 1 039 65 00 00 00 00000001
06 00 007 000 9 0000 1 0479805629 0000 4 03 058 0 000 1 039 00 00 00 00 00000001
06 00 007 000 9 0000 1 0479805629 0000 4 07 001 1 000 1 035 65 00 00 00 00000001
06 00 007 000 9 0000 1 0479805629 0000 4 07 018 1 000 7 038 00 00 00 00 00000001
06 00 007 000 9 0000 1 0479805629 0000 4 74 000 0 000 1 033 00 00 00 00 00000001
06 00 007 000 9 0000 1 0479805629 0000 4 74 000 0 000 1 033 00 00 00 00 00000001
06 00 007 000 9 0000 1 0479805629 0000 4 74 000 0 000 1 033 65 00 00 00 00000001
06 00 007 000 9 0000 1 0479805629 0000 4 74 000 0 000 1 033 00 00 00 00 00000002
06 00 007 000 9 0000 1 0479805629 0000 3 77 507 0 000 1 039 65 00 00 00 00000009
06 00 007 000 9 0000 1 0479805629 0000 3 81 503 0 000 7 000 65 00 00 00 00000000
06 00 007 000 9 0000 1 0479805629 0000 3 81 507 0 000 1 039 65 00 00 00 00000000
```

Appendix H

```
      PIT EIGHT DATA BASE
05 CC 008 CCC 9 0000 1 0479105663 CCCC 2 00 000 0 060 1 000 37 09 00 00 C0000021
06 0C 008 0C0 9 0000 1 0479105663 CCCC 1 00 000 0 001 1 000 C0 C0 00 00 00000038
06 C0 008 0C0 9 0000 1 0479105663 00C0 1 00 00C 0 001 1 000 00 00 00 00 00000030
06 00 008 000 9 0000 1 0479105663 0C00 1 00 000 0 001 1 000 00 00 C0 0C 0C000116
06 0C C08 0C0 9 0000 1 0479105663 0000 4 02 033 2 000 1 039 65 00 00 00 00000030
06 00 008 0C0 9 0000 1 0479105663 CCC0 4 02 005 1 000 1 036 00 0C 00 00 0000001C
06 00 008 000 9 0000 1 0479105663 0000 4 07 005 1 000 1 036 65 0C 0C 00 00000020
05 00 C08 0C0 9 0000 1 0479105663 CCC0 4 07 006 1 000 1 037 65 0C 0C 00 00000014
06 00 008 0C0 9 0000 1 0479105663 0000 3 77 507 0 000 1 039 65 00 00 00 00000C02
```

Appendix I

PIT TWO DATA BASE

06	00	002	000	9	0000	1	0468005770	0000	4	01	008	1	000	1	037	00	00	00	00	00000054
06	00	002	000	9	0000	1	0468005770	0000	2	00	000	0	057	7	038	35	09	00	00	00000030
06	00	002	000	9	0000	1	0468005770	0000	2	00	000	0	060	1	039	00	09	00	00	00000007
06	00	002	000	9	0000	1	0468005770	0000	2	00	000	0	060	1	039	00	09	00	00	00000005
06	00	002	000	9	0000	1	0468005770	0000	2	00	000	0	060	1	039	37	09	00	00	00000016
06	00	002	000	9	0000	1	0468005770	0000	2	00	000	0	060	1	039	35	09	00	00	00000017
06	00	002	000	9	0000	1	0468005770	0000	2	00	000	0	061	1	039	00	09	00	00	00000100
06	00	002	000	9	0000	1	0468005770	0000	2	00	000	0	062	1	039	00	09	00	00	00000007
06	00	002	000	9	0000	1	0468005770	0000	2	00	000	0	062	1	039	00	09	00	00	00000008
06	00	002	000	9	0000	1	0468005770	0000	2	00	000	0	062	1	039	37	09	00	00	00000010
06	00	002	000	9	0000	1	0468005770	0000	2	00	000	0	062	1	039	37	09	00	00	00000027
06	00	002	000	9	0000	1	0468005770	0000	2	00	000	0	063	1	039	00	09	00	00	00000025
06	00	002	000	9	0000	1	0468005770	0000	2	00	000	0	063	1	039	00	09	00	00	00000035
06	00	002	000	9	0000	1	0468005770	0000	2	00	000	0	063	1	039	00	09	00	00	00000040
06	00	002	000	9	0000	1	0468005770	0000	2	00	000	0	082	1	039	00	09	00	00	00000005
06	00	002	000	9	0000	1	0468005770	0000	2	00	000	0	082	1	039	00	09	00	00	00000006
06	00	002	000	9	0000	1	0468005770	0000	2	00	000	0	082	1	039	00	09	00	00	00000008
06	00	002	000	9	0000	1	0468005770	0000	2	00	000	0	082	1	039	00	09	00	00	00000039
06	00	002	000	9	0000	1	0468005770	0000	2	00	000	0	082	1	039	00	09	00	00	00000425
06	00	002	000	9	0000	1	0468005770	0000	1	00	000	0	038	1	000	00	00	00	00	00000008
06	00	002	000	9	0000	1	0468005770	0000	1	00	000	0	038	1	000	00	00	00	00	00000020
06	00	002	000	9	0000	1	0468005770	0000	1	00	000	0	015	1	001	00	00	00	00	00000264
06	00	002	000	9	0000	1	0468005770	0000	1	00	000	0	015	1	001	00	00	00	00	00000136
06	00	002	000	9	0000	1	0468005770	0000	1	00	000	0	015	1	001	00	00	00	00	00000107
06	00	002	000	9	0000	1	0468005770	0000	1	00	000	0	015	1	001	00	00	00	00	00000035
06	00	002	000	9	0000	1	0468005770	0000	1	00	000	0	015	1	001	00	00	00	00	00000037
06	00	002	000	9	0000	1	0468005770	0000	1	00	000	0	015	1	001	00	00	00	00	00000030
06	00	002	000	9	0000	1	0468005770	0000	1	00	000	0	015	1	001	00	00	00	00	00000027
06	00	002	000	9	0000	1	0468005770	0000	1	00	000	0	015	1	001	00	00	00	00	00000022
06	00	002	000	9	0000	1	0468005770	0000	1	00	000	0	015	1	001	00	00	00	00	00000023
06	00	002	000	9	0000	1	0468005770	0000	1	00	000	0	015	1	001	00	00	00	00	00000017
06	00	002	000	9	0000	1	0468005770	0000	1	00	000	0	015	1	001	00	00	00	00	00000015
06	00	002	000	9	0000	1	0468005770	0000	1	00	000	0	015	1	001	00	00	00	00	00000012
06	00	002	000	9	0000	1	0468005770	0000	1	00	000	0	015	1	001	00	00	00	00	00000010
06	00	002	000	9	0000	1	0468005770	0000	1	00	000	0	015	1	001	00	00	00	00	00000009
06	00	002	000	9	0000	1	0468005770	0000	4	01	033	1	000	1	039	00	00	00	00	00000220

Appendix J

```
    PIT THREE DATA BASE
06 00 003 000 9 0000 1 0530005850 0000 2 00 000 0 060 1 039 00 09 00 00 00000001
06 00 003 000 9 0000 1 0530005850 0000 2 00 000 0 060 1 039 00 09 00 00 00000001
06 00 003 000 9 0000 1 0530005850 0000 2 00 000 0 060 1 039 00 09 00 00 00000001
06 00 003 000 9 0000 1 0530005850 0000 2 00 000 0 060 1 039 00 09 00 00 00000001
06 00 003 000 9 0000 1 0530005850 0000 2 00 000 0 060 1 039 00 09 00 00 00000001
06 00 003 000 9 0000 1 0530005850 0000 2 00 000 0 060 1 039 00 09 00 00 00000001
06 00 003 000 9 0000 1 0530005850 0000 2 00 000 0 060 1 039 00 09 00 00 00000001
06 00 003 000 9 0000 1 0530005850 0000 2 00 000 0 060 1 039 00 09 00 00 00000001
06 00 003 000 9 0000 1 0530005850 0000 2 00 000 0 060 1 039 00 09 00 00 00000001
06 00 003 000 9 0000 1 0530005850 0000 2 00 000 0 060 1 039 00 09 00 00 00000001
06 00 003 000 9 0000 1 0530005850 0000 2 00 000 0 060 1 039 00 09 00 00 00000001
06 00 003 000 9 0000 1 0530005850 0000 2 00 000 0 060 1 039 00 09 00 00 00000001
06 00 003 000 9 0000 1 0530005850 0000 2 00 000 0 060 1 039 00 09 00 00 00000002
06 00 003 000 9 0000 1 0530005850 0000 2 00 000 0 060 1 039 00 09 00 00 00000001
06 00 003 000 9 0000 1 0530005850 0000 2 00 000 0 060 1 039 00 09 00 00 00000001
06 00 003 000 9 0000 1 0530005850 0000 2 00 000 0 060 1 039 00 09 00 00 00000001
06 00 003 000 9 0103 1 0533905890 3097 2 00 000 0 060 1 039 00 09 00 00 00000007
06 00 003 000 9 0112 1 0534005880 3096 2 00 000 0 060 1 039 00 09 00 00 00000005
06 00 003 000 9 0243 1 0532905877 3097 2 00 000 0 060 1 039 00 09 00 00 00000018
06 00 003 000 9 0313 1 0534605880 3094 2 00 000 0 060 1 039 35 09 00 00 00000007
06 00 003 000 9 0000 1 0530005850 0000 2 00 000 0 060 1 039 00 09 00 00 00000009
06 00 003 000 9 0000 1 0530005850 0000 2 00 000 0 060 1 039 00 09 00 00 00000026
06 00 003 000 9 0000 1 0530005850 0000 2 00 000 0 060 1 039 00 09 00 00 00000005
06 00 003 000 9 0000 1 0530005850 0000 2 00 000 0 060 1 039 00 09 00 00 00000006
06 00 003 000 9 0107 1 0534505869 3095 2 00 000 0 060 1 039 00 09 00 00 00000038
06 00 003 000 9 0000 1 0530005850 0000 2 00 000 0 062 1 039 00 09 00 00 00000004
06 00 003 000 9 0000 1 0530005850 0000 2 00 000 0 062 1 039 00 09 00 00 00000003
06 00 003 000 9 0000 1 0530005850 0000 2 00 000 0 062 1 039 00 09 00 00 00000002
06 00 003 000 9 0000 1 0530005850 0000 2 00 000 0 062 1 039 00 09 00 00 00000002
06 00 003 000 9 0000 1 0530005850 0000 2 00 000 0 062 1 039 00 09 00 00 00000003
06 00 003 000 9 0000 1 0530005850 0000 2 00 000 0 062 1 039 00 09 00 00 00000004
06 00 003 000 9 0000 1 0530005850 0000 2 00 000 0 062 1 039 00 09 00 00 00000001
06 00 003 000 9 0000 1 0530005850 0000 2 00 000 0 062 1 039 00 09 00 00 00000004
06 00 003 000 9 0000 1 0530005850 0000 2 00 000 0 062 1 039 00 09 00 00 00000004
06 00 003 000 9 0000 1 0530005850 0000 2 00 000 0 062 1 039 00 09 00 00 00000006
06 00 003 000 9 0000 1 0530005850 0000 2 00 000 0 062 1 039 00 09 00 00 00000005
06 00 003 000 9 0000 1 0530005850 0000 2 00 000 0 062 1 039 00 09 00 00 00000002
06 00 003 000 9 0043 1 0534605878 3095 2 00 000 0 062 1 039 00 09 00 00 00000052
06 00 003 000 9 0105 1 0533805871 3096 2 00 000 0 062 1 039 00 09 00 00 00000177
06 00 003 000 9 0106 1 0533805870 3096 2 00 000 0 062 1 039 00 09 00 00 00000068
06 00 003 000 9 0111 1 0533605880 3097 2 00 000 0 062 1 039 00 09 00 00 00000003
06 00 003 000 9 0250 1 0534305881 3094 2 00 000 0 062 1 039 00 09 00 00 00000017
06 00 003 000 9 0312 1 0534505870 3094 2 00 000 0 062 1 039 00 09 00 00 00000011
06 00 003 000 9 0000 1 0530005850 0000 2 00 000 0 063 1 039 00 09 00 00 00000001
06 00 003 000 9 0000 1 0530005850 0000 2 00 000 0 063 1 039 00 09 00 00 00000001
06 00 003 000 9 0000 1 0530005850 0000 2 00 000 0 063 1 039 00 09 00 00 00000001
06 00 003 000 9 0000 1 0530005850 0000 2 00 000 0 063 1 039 00 09 00 00 00000001
06 00 003 000 9 0000 1 0530005850 0000 2 00 000 0 063 1 039 00 09 00 00 00000001
06 00 003 000 9 0000 1 0530005850 0000 2 00 000 0 063 1 039 00 09 00 00 00000001
06 00 003 000 9 0000 1 0530005850 0000 2 00 000 0 063 1 039 00 09 00 00 00000002
06 00 003 000 9 0000 1 0530005850 0000 2 00 000 0 063 1 039 00 09 00 00 00000002
06 00 003 000 9 0000 1 0530005850 0000 2 00 000 0 063 1 039 00 09 00 00 00000004
06 00 003 000 9 0000 1 0530005850 0000 2 00 000 0 065 1 039 00 09 00 00 00000021
06 00 003 000 9 0000 1 0530005850 0000 2 00 000 0 065 1 039 00 09 00 00 00000041
06 00 003 000 9 0000 1 0530005850 0000 2 00 000 0 065 1 039 00 09 00 00 00000001
06 00 003 000 9 0000 1 0530005850 0000 2 00 000 0 065 1 039 00 09 00 00 00000008
06 00 003 000 9 0000 1 0530005850 0000 2 00 000 0 065 1 039 00 09 00 00 00000006
06 00 003 000 9 0000 1 0530005850 0000 2 00 000 0 065 1 039 00 09 00 00 00000005
06 00 003 000 9 0000 1 0530005850 0000 2 00 000 0 065 1 039 00 09 00 00 00000001
06 00 003 000 9 0000 1 0530005850 0000 2 00 000 0 065 1 039 00 09 00 00 00000001
06 00 003 000 9 0000 1 0530005850 0000 2 00 000 0 065 1 039 00 09 00 00 00000001
06 00 003 000 9 0248 1 0534305880 3095 2 00 000 0 065 1 039 00 09 00 00 00000128
06 00 003 000 9 0246 1 0533705875 3097 2 00 000 0 065 1 039 00 09 00 00 00000007
06 00 003 000 9 0195 1 0534205883 3096 2 00 000 0 065 1 039 00 09 00 00 00000162
06 00 003 000 9 0104 1 0534105884 3096 2 00 000 0 065 1 039 00 09 00 00 00000890
06 00 003 000 9 0042 1 0534805870 3096 2 00 000 0 082 1 039 00 09 00 00 00000890
06 00 003 000 9 0162 1 0534705865 3096 2 00 000 0 082 1 039 00 09 00 00 00000001
06 00 003 000 9 0254 1 0534105886 3095 2 00 000 0 082 1 039 00 09 00 00 00000068
06 00 003 000 9 0000 1 0530005850 0000 2 00 000 0 082 1 039 00 09 00 00 00000025
```

```
6  00  003  000  9  0000  1  0530005850  0000  2  00  000  0  082  1  039  00  09  00  00  00000008
6  00  003  000  9  0000  1  0530005850  0000  2  00  000  0  082  1  039  00  09  00  00  00000048
6  00  003  000  9  0000  1  0530005850  0000  2  00  000  0  082  1  039  00  09  00  00  00000036
6  00  003  000  9  0000  1  0535005850  0000  2  00  000  0  060  1  039  00  09  00  00  00000005
6  00  003  000  9  0000  1  0535005850  0000  2  00  000  0  060  1  039  00  09  00  00  00000009
6  00  003  000  9  0000  1  0535005850  0000  2  00  000  0  060  1  039  00  09  00  00  00000011
6  00  003  000  9  0000  1  0535005850  0000  2  00  000  0  060  1  039  00  09  00  00  00000012
6  00  003  000  9  0000  1  0535005850  0000  2  00  000  0  060  1  039  00  09  00  00  00000004
6  00  003  000  9  0000  1  0535005850  0000  2  00  000  0  060  1  039  36  09  00  00  00000003
6  00  003  000  9  0000  1  0535005850  0000  2  00  000  0  060  1  039  37  09  00  00  00000003
6  00  003  000  9  0000  1  0535005850  0000  2  00  000  0  060  1  039  00  09  00  00  00000002
6  00  003  000  9  0000  1  0535005850  0000  2  00  000  0  060  1  039  00  09  00  00  00000002
6  00  003  000  9  0000  1  0535K05850  0000  2  00  000  0  060  1  039  00  09  00  00  00000003
6  00  003  000  9  0000  1  0535005850  0000  2  00  000  0  060  1  039  00  09  00  00  00000002
6  00  003  000  9  0000  1  0535005850  0000  2  00  000  0  060  1  039  00  09  00  00  00000001
6  00  003  000  9  0000  1  0535005850  0000  2  00  000  0  060  1  039  00  09  00  00  00000002
6  00  003  000  9  0000  1  0535005850  0000  2  00  000  0  060  1  039  00  09  00  00  00000001
6  00  003  000  9  0000  1  0535005850  0000  2  00  000  0  060  1  039  00  09  00  00  00000001
6  00  003  000  9  0000  1  0535005850  0000  2  00  000  0  060  1  039  00  09  00  00  00000001
6  00  003  000  9  0000  1  0535005850  0000  2  00  000  0  060  1  039  00  09  00  00  00000001
6  00  003  000  9  0000  1  0535005850  0000  2  00  000  0  060  1  039  00  09  00  00  00000001
6  00  003  000  9  0000  1  0535005850  0000  2  00  000  0  060  1  039  00  09  00  00  00000001
6  00  003  000  9  0000  1  0535005850  0000  2  00  000  0  060  1  039  00  09  00  00  00000001
6  00  003  000  9  0000  1  0535005850  0000  2  00  000  0  060  1  039  00  09  00  00  00000002
6  00  003  000  9  0000  1  0535005850  0000  2  00  000  0  060  1  039  37  09  00  00  00000001
6  00  003  000  9  0000  1  0535005850  0000  2  00  000  0  060  1  039  00  09  00  00  00000001
6  00  003  000  9  0000  1  0535005850  0000  2  00  000  0  060  1  039  00  09  00  00  00000001
6  00  003  000  9  0000  1  0535005850  0000  2  00  000  0  060  1  039  00  09  00  00  00000001
6  00  003  000  9  0000  1  0535005850  0000  2  00  000  0  060  1  039  00  09  00  00  00000001
6  00  003  000  9  0000  1  0535005850  0000  2  00  000  0  060  1  039  00  09  00  00  00000001
6  00  003  000  9  0000  1  0535005850  0000  2  00  000  0  060  1  039  00  09  00  00  00000001
6  00  003  000  9  0000  1  0535005850  0000  2  00  000  0  060  1  039  00  09  00  00  00000001
6  00  003  000  9  0000  1  0535005850  0000  2  00  000  0  060  1  039  00  09  00  00  00000001
6  00  003  000  9  0027  1  0536005857  3098  2  00  000  0  060  1  039  00  09  00  00  00000004
6  00  003  000  9  0067  1  0537505880  3097  2  00  000  0  060  1  039  00  09  00  00  00000006
6  00  003  000  9  0069  1  0536405864  3097  2  00  000  0  060  1  039  00  09  00  00  00000005
6  00  003  000  9  0270  1  0536205862  3096  2  00  000  0  060  1  039  00  09  00  00  00000004
6  00  003  000  9  0271  1  0537805862  3095  2  00  000  0  060  1  039  00  09  00  00  00000002
6  00  003  000  9  0272  1  0536205865  3094  2  00  000  0  060  1  039  00  09  00  00  00000004
6  00  003  000  9  0276  1  0537305873  3093  2  00  000  0  060  1  039  00  09  00  00  00000002
6  00  003  000  9  0282  1  0538105883  3093  2  00  000  0  060  1  039  00  09  00  00  00000002
6  00  003  000  9  0285  1  0535305884  3093  2  00  000  0  060  1  039  00  09  00  00  00000031
6  00  003  000  9  0000  1  0535005850  0000  2  00  000  0  062  1  039  00  09  00  00  00000002
6  00  003  000  9  0000  1  0535005850  0000  2  00  000  0  062  1  039  37  09  00  00  00000044
6  00  003  000  9  0000  1  0535005850  0000  2  00  000  0  062  1  039  00  09  00  00  00000004
6  00  003  000  9  0000  1  0535005850  0000  2  00  000  0  062  1  039  00  09  00  00  00000003
6  00  003  000  9  0000  1  0535005850  0000  2  00  000  0  062  1  039  00  09  00  00  00000002
6  00  003  000  9  0000  1  0535005850  0000  2  00  000  0  062  1  039  00  09  00  00  00000003
6  00  003  000  9  0000  1  0535005850  0000  2  00  000  0  062  1  039  00  09  00  00  00000002
6  00  003  000  9  0000  1  0535005850  0000  2  00  000  0  062  1  039  00  09  00  00  00000001
6  00  003  000  9  0000  1  0535005850  0000  2  00  000  0  062  1  039  00  09  00  00  00000001
6  00  003  000  9  0000  1  0535005850  0000  2  00  000  0  062  1  039  00  09  00  00  00000001
6  00  003  000  9  0000  1  0535005850  0000  2  00  000  0  062  1  039  00  09  00  00  00000001
6  00  003  000  9  0000  1  0530005850  0000  2  00  000  0  065  1  039  00  09  00  00  00000007
6  00  003  000  9  0000  1  0535005850  0000  2  00  000  0  062  1  039  00  09  00  00  00000001
6  00  003  000  9  0000  1  0535005850  0000  2  00  000  0  062  1  039  00  09  00  00  00000001
6  00  003  000  9  0028  1  0536005858  3097  2  00  000  0  062  1  039  00  09  00  00  00000060
6  00  003  000  9  0060  1  0537905892  3097  2  00  000  0  062  1  039  00  09  00  00  00000013
6  00  003  000  9  0070  1  0536805863  3097  2  00  000  0  062  1  039  00  09  00  00  00000065
6  00  003  000  9  0072  1  0537005858  3096  2  00  000  0  062  1  039  00  09  00  00  00000003
6  00  003  000  9  0273  1  0536405870  3093  2  00  000  0  062  1  039  37  09  00  00  00000003
6  00  003  000  9  0274  1  0537005875  3093  2  00  000  0  062  1  039  00  09  00  00  00000014
6  00  003  000  9  0281  1  0536005880  3093  2  00  000  0  062  1  039  00  09  00  00  00000006
6  00  003  000  9  0284  1  0538205887  3093  2  00  000  0  062  1  039  37  09  00  00  00000011
6  00  003  000  9  0000  1  0535005850  0000  2  00  000  0  063  1  039  00  09  00  00  00000001
6  00  003  000  9  0000  1  0535005850  0000  2  00  000  0  063  1  039  00  09  00  00  00000001
6  00  003  000  9  0000  1  0535005850  0000  2  00  000  0  063  1  039  00  09  00  00  00000001
```

```
06 00 003 000 9 0000 1 0535005850 0000 2 00 000 0 063 1 039 00 09 00 00 C000000C1
06 00 003 000 9 0000 9 0535005850 0U00 2 00 000 0 063 1 039 00 09 00 00 C000000C2
06 00 003 000 9 0000 1 0535005850 00C0 2 00 000 0 063 1 039 00 09 00 00 0000000C2
06 00 003 000 9 0279 1 0537805859 3095 2 00 000 0 063 1 039 00 09 00 00 0000000028
06 00 003 000 9 0000 1 0535005850 00C0 2 00 000 0 065 1 039 00 09 00 00 0C000017
06 00 003 000 9 0000 1 0535005850 0000 2 00 000 0 065 1 039 00 09 00 00 00000004
06 00 003 000 9 0000 1 0535005850 0000 2 00 000 0 065 1 039 00 09 00 00 0000000C5
06 00 003 000 9 0071 1 0535905862 3097 2 00 000 0 065 1 039 00 09 00 00 00000199
06 00 003 000 9 0066 1 0538305872 3097 2 00 000 0 065 1 039 00 09 00 00 00000246
06 00 003 000 9 0064 1 0536005855 3101 2 00 000 0 065 1 039 00 09 00 00 00000109
06 00 003 000 9 0049 1 0539005854 3098 2 00 000 0 065 1 039 00 09 00 00 C000007S
06 00 003 000 9 0048 1 0537805855 3097 2 00 000 0 065 1 039 00 09 00 00 00000051
06 00 003 000 9 0031 1 0538105867 3097 2 00 000 0 082 1 039 00 09 00 00 00000132
06 00 003 000 9 0065 1 0538405892 3096 2 00 000 0 082 1 039 00 09 00 00 00000398
06 00 003 000 9 0286 1 0538205888 3090 2 00 000 0 082 1 039 00 09 00 00 00000036
06 00 003 000 9 0268 1 0536005879 3093 2 00 000 0 082 1 039 00 09 00 00 00000017
06 00 003 000 9 0206 1 0534705891 3095 1 00 000 0 029 1 015 00 00 00 00 00000017
06 00 003 000 9 0184 1 0533605867 3095 1 00 000 0 038 1 039 00 00 00 00 0000012C
06 00 003 000 9 0183 1 0534105867 3097 1 00 000 0 038 1 039 00 00 00 00 00000034
06 00 003 000 9 0180 1 0534305860 3096 1 00 000 0 038 1 039 00 00 00 00 00000029
06 00 003 000 9 0045 1 0534705804 3096 1 00 000 0 038 1 039 00 00 00 00 00000047
06 00 003 000 9 0000 1 0530005850 00C0 1 00 000 0 015 1 001 00 00 00 00 0C00000C0
06 00 003 000 9 0000 1 0530005850 0000 1 00 000 0 015 1 001 00 00 00 00 00000017
06 00 003 000 9 0000 1 0530005850 00C0 1 00 000 0 015 1 001 00 00 00 00 0000004C
06 00 003 000 9 0000 1 0530005850 0000 1 00 000 0 015 1 001 00 00 00 00 000000C5
06 00 003 000 9 0311 1 0534505868 3094 1 00 000 0 015 1 001 00 00 00 00 0000010C
06 00 003 000 9 0253 1 0534305889 3099 1 00 000 0 015 1 001 00 00 00 00 00000000
06 00 003 000 9 0249 1 0534305881 3095 1 00 000 0 015 1 001 00 00 00 00 0000006S
06 00 003 000 9 0247 1 0534205878 3096 1 00 000 0 015 1 001 00 00 00 00 00000043
06 00 003 000 9 0205 1 0534305891 3096 1 00 000 0 015 1 001 00 00 00 00 0000024S
06 00 003 000 9 0201 1 0534605866 3099 1 00 000 0 015 1 001 00 00 00 00 0000000S
06 00 003 000 9 0181 1 0534805863 3096 1 00 000 0 015 1 001 00 00 00 00 00000002
06 00 003 000 9 0000 1 0535005850 0000 1 00 000 0 038 1 039 00 00 00 00 00000000
06 00 003 000 9 0000 1 0535005850 00C0 1 00 000 0 038 1 039 00 00 00 00 00000017
06 00 003 000 9 0000 1 0535005850 00C0 1 00 000 0 038 1 039 00 00 00 00 0000000S
06 00 003 000 9 0000 1 0535005850 0000 1 00 000 0 038 1 039 00 00 00 00 0000000S
06 00 003 000 9 0000 1 0535005850 0000 1 00 000 0 038 1 039 00 00 00 00 0000001S
06 00 003 000 9 0000 1 0535005850 00C0 1 00 000 0 038 1 039 00 00 00 00 0000001S
06 00 003 000 9 0287 1 0535005890 3094 1 00 000 0 038 1 039 00 00 00 00 0000002S
06 00 003 000 9 0055 1 0536205876 3098 1 00 000 0 038 1 039 00 00 00 00 0000003C
06 00 003 000 9 0035 1 0536705873 3098 1 00 000 0 038 1 039 00 00 00 00 0000002S
06 00 003 000 9 0039 1 0535705894 3098 1 00 000 0 003 1 006 00 00 00 02 0000031S
06 00 003 000 9 0000 1 0535005850 00C0 2 00 000 0 015 1 001 00 00 00 00 0000007S
06 00 003 000 9 0000 1 0536905862 3098 1 00 000 0 015 1 001 00 00 00 00 0000003C
06 00 003 000 9 0052 1 0530005850 0000 4 01 000 0 033 1 039 00 00 00 00 00000012
06 00 003 000 9 0061 1 0538805854 3096 4 01 001 1 000 1 039 00 00 00 00 00000021
06 00 003 000 9 0059 1 0537305892 3097 4 01 005 1 000 1 036 00 00 00 00 00000021
06 00 003 000 9 0063 1 0537105886 3097 4 01 007 1 000 1 037 00 00 00 00 00000112
06 00 003 000 9 0029 1 0538305862 3096 4 01 014 1 000 1 039 00 00 00 00 00000012
06 00 003 000 9 0058 1 0535205888 3096 4 01 000 0 000 1 033 00 00 00 00 0000025S
06 00 003 000 9 0000 1 0530005850 0000 3 77 507 0 000 1 039 62 00 00 00 0000025S
06 00 003 000 9 0000 1 0530005850 0000 3 77 527 0 000 1 039 65 00 00 00 0000004C
06 00 003 000 9 0000 1 0530005850 00C0 3 80 509 0 000 1 039 65 00 00 00 0000000C
06 00 003 000 9 0000 1 0530005850 00C0 3 80 509 0 000 1 039 65 00 00 00 00000004
06 00 003 000 9 0000 1 0535005850 0000 3 81 503 0 000 7 000 65 00 00 00 0000001C
06 00 003 000 9 0000 1 0530005850 00C0 3 81 503 0 000 7 000 65 00 00 00 0000000C
06 00 003 000 9 0000 1 0530005850 0000 3 84 510 0 000 7 000 00 00 00 00 0000000C
06 00 003 000 9 0000 1 0530005850 0000 3 85 510 0 000 7 000 65 00 00 00 0000000C
06 00 003 000 9 0000 1 0530005850 0000 3 89 510 0 000 1 039 65 00 00 00 0000000C
06 00 003 000 9 0000 1 0530005850 00C0 3 90 510 0 000 1 039 65 00 00 00 0000000C
          PIT 3 ACTIVITY AREA  DATA BASE
06 00 003 000 3 0000 1 0540005800 0000 2 00 000 0 060 1 039 00 09 00 00 C0000007
06 00 003 000 3 0154 1 0536705846 3099 2 00 000 0 060 1 039 00 09 00 00 0000002C
06 00 003 000 3 0149 1 0535705847 31C0 2 00 000 0 060 1 039 00 09 00 00 00000010
06 00 003 000 3 0130 1 0536805835 31C0 2 00 000 0 060 1 039 36 09 00 00 00000012
06 00 003 000 3 0126 1 0536405841 31C0 2 00 000 0 060 1 039 00 09 00 00 00000002
06 00 003 000 3 0131 1 0536805833 31C0 2 00 000 0 060 1 039 36 09 00 00 0000006S
06 00 003 000 3 0016 1 0539105844 3100 2 00 000 0 060 1 039 00 09 00 00 C000000S
06 00 003 000 3 0006 1 0539105833 31C0 2 00 000 0 060 1 039 00 09 00 00 0000000S
06 00 003 000 3 0000 1 0535005800 00C0 2 00 000 0 060 1 039 00 09 00 00 00000020
06 00 003 000 3 0000 1 0535005800 00C0 2 00 000 0 060 1 039 00 09 00 00 00000001
```

```
06 CC 003 000 3 0082 1 0531605844 31C0 2 00 000 0 060 1 039 00 09 00 00 00000004
06 00 003 000 3 0024 1 0531005822 3101 2 00 000 0 060 1 039 00 09 00 00 00000004
06 00 003 000 3 0020 1 0530905845 3101 2 00 000 0 060 1 039 00 09 00 00 00000007
06 00 003 000 3 0096 1 0532205818 3099 2 00 000 0 060 1 039 00 09 00 00 00000004
06 00 003 000 3 0095 1 0533105826 3100 2 00 000 0 060 1 039 36 09 00 00 00000042
06 00 003 000 3 0174 1 0533205845 3099 2 00 000 0 060 1 039 00 09 00 00 000000C4
06 00 003 000 3 0167 1 0533405836 31C0 2 00 000 0 060 1 039 00 09 00 00 00000005
06 00 003 000 3 0289 1 0531105834 31C0 2 00 000 0 060 1 039 36 09 00 00 00000022
06 00 003 000 3 0300 1 0532905841 3100 2 00 000 0 060 1 039 00 09 00 00 00000057
06 00 003 000 3 0309 1 0534005845 3100 2 00 000 0 060 1 039 00 09 00 00 000000C8
06 00 003 000 3 0310 1 0534405848 3100 2 00 000 0 060 1 039 00 09 00 00 00000006
06 00 003 000 3 0302 1 0535005826 31C0 2 00 000 0 060 1 039 35 09 00 00 00000007
06 00 003 000 3 0000 1 0525005800 0000 2 00 000 0 060 1 039 00 09 00 00 00000001
06 00 003 000 3 0000 1 0525005800 0000 2 00 000 0 060 1 039 00 09 00 00 00000001
06 00 003 000 3 0000 1 0522005800 0000 2 00 000 0 060 1 039 00 09 00 00 00000001
06 00 003 000 3 0000 1 0525005800 0000 2 00 000 0 060 1 039 00 09 00 00 00000001
06 00 003 000 3 0000 1 0540005850 0000 2 00 000 0 060 1 039 00 09 00 00 00000002
06 00 003 000 3 0000 1 0540005850 0000 2 00 000 0 060 1 039 00 09 00 00 00000003
06 00 003 000 3 0056 1 0539305869 3099 2 00 000 0 060 1 039 00 09 00 00 00000004
06 00 003 000 3 0077 1 0532705857 31C0 2 00 000 0 060 1 039 00 09 00 00 00000004
06 00 003 000 3 0054 1 0530905870 3100 2 00 000 0 060 1 039 00 09 00 00 0000001B
06 00 003 000 3 0215 1 0530405874 3099 2 00 000 0 060 1 039 36 09 00 00 00000026
06 00 003 000 3 0214 1 0533105874 3100 2 00 000 0 060 1 039 35 09 00 00 00000024
06 00 003 000 3 0213 1 0530005865 3100 2 00 000 0 060 1 039 00 09 00 00 00000011
06 00 003 000 3 0211 1 0533205852 3100 2 00 000 0 060 1 039 00 09 00 00 00000338
06 00 003 000 3 0200 1 0531505886 3099 2 00 000 0 060 1 039 00 09 00 00 0000001C
06 00 003 000 3 0197 1 0530805885 3100 2 00 000 0 060 1 039 00 09 00 00 00000088
06 00 003 000 3 0186 1 0530905870 3100 2 00 000 0 060 1 039 00 09 00 00 0000002C
06 00 003 000 3 0176 1 0533105851 3100 2 00 000 0 060 1 039 00 09 00 00 00000009
06 00 003 000 3 0121 1 0533505854 31C0 2 00 000 0 060 1 039 35 09 00 00 00000015
06 00 003 000 3 0120 1 0533505854 3099 2 00 000 0 060 1 039 00 09 00 00 00000181
06 00 003 000 3 0117 1 0531305853 3100 2 00 000 0 060 1 039 00 09 00 00 000000C4
06 00 003 000 3 0114 1 0531205878 3100 2 00 000 0 060 1 039 00 09 00 00 00000067
06 00 003 000 3 0110 1 0530705860 31C0 2 00 000 0 060 1 039 35 09 00 00 00000024
06 00 003 000 3 0109 1 0530905853 31C0 2 00 000 0 060 1 039 35 09 00 00 00000013
06 00 003 000 3 0108 1 0531905868 3099 2 00 000 0 060 1 039 36 09 00 00 00000016
06 00 003 000 3 0100 1 0531205895 3101 2 00 000 0 060 1 039 00 09 00 00 000000C3
06 00 003 000 3 0000 1 0525005850 0000 2 00 000 0 060 1 039 00 09 00 00 0000000B
06 00 003 000 3 0000 1 0525005850 0000 2 00 000 0 060 1 039 00 09 00 00 000000C1
05 00 003 000 3 0000 1 0540005900 0000 2 00 000 0 060 1 039 00 09 00 00 00000001
06 00 003 000 3 0000 1 0540005900 0000 2 00 000 0 060 1 039 00 09 00 00 00000001
06 00 003 000 3 0000 1 0540005900 0000 1 00 000 0 060 2 039 00 09 00 00 00000004
06 00 003 000 3 0000 1 0540005900 0000 1 00 000 0 060 2 039 00 09 00 00 00000002
06 00 003 000 3 0000 1 0540005900 0000 1 00 000 0 060 2 039 00 09 00 00 000000C2
05 00 003 000 3 0000 1 0540005900 0000 2 00 000 0 060 1 039 00 09 00 00 000000C1
06 00 003 000 3 0261 1 0538005914 3099 2 00 000 0 060 1 039 00 09 00 00 00000036
06 00 003 000 3 0226 1 0535005900 3099 2 00 000 0 060 1 039 35 09 00 00 0000C012
06 00 003 000 3 0182 1 0532005925 3100 2 00 000 0 060 1 039 00 09 00 00 0000011C
06 00 003 000 3 0116 1 0531C5900 31C0 2 00 000 0 060 1 039 00 09 00 00 00000010
06 00 003 000 3 0000 1 0530005900 0000 2 00 000 0 060 1 039 00 09 00 00 00000005
06 00 003 000 3 0000 1 0530005900 0000 2 00 000 0 060 1 039 00 09 00 00 00000002
06 00 003 000 3 0000 1 0530005900 0000 2 00 000 0 060 1 039 00 09 00 00 00000004
06 00 003 000 3 0000 1 0530005900 0000 2 00 000 0 061 1 039 00 09 00 00 00000001
06 00 003 000 3 0123 1 0533205834 3100 2 00 000 0 061 1 039 00 09 00 00 00000112
06 00 003 000 3 0092 1 0533705831 3099 2 00 000 0 061 1 039 00 09 00 00 00000341
06 00 003 000 3 0030 1 0530905867 3100 2 00 000 0 061 1 039 00 09 00 00 00000110
06 00 003 000 3 0011 1 0533905834 3101 1 00 000 0 061 1 039 00 09 00 00 0000C596
06 00 003 000 3 0094 1 0533105827 3100 2 00 000 0 061 1 039 00 09 00 00 0000015B
06 00 003 000 3 0303 1 0534005842 3100 2 00 000 0 061 1 039 00 09 00 00 00000103
05 00 003 000 3 0078 1 0533205852 31C0 2 00 000 0 061 1 039 00 09 00 00 00000166
06 00 003 000 3 0147 1 0534705831 3099 2 00 000 0 061 1 039 00 09 00 00 00000068
06 00 003 000 3 0124 1 0532905857 3100 2 00 000 0 062 1 039 00 09 00 00 00000690
06 00 003 000 3 0000 1 0533205838 31C0 2 00 000 0 062 1 039 00 09 00 00 00000321
06 00 003 000 3 0000 1 0525005800 0000 2 00 000 0 062 1 039 00 09 00 00 00000003
06 00 003 000 3 0298 1 0533105848 31C0 2 00 000 0 062 1 039 00 09 00 00 0000002C
06 00 003 000 3 0301 1 0533305810 31C0 2 00 000 0 062 1 039 00 09 00 00 00000018
06 00 003 000 3 0239 1 0531505809 31C0 2 00 000 0 062 1 039 00 09 00 00 00000012
06 00 003 000 3 0229 1 0532605807 31C0 2 00 000 0 062 1 039 00 09 00 00 00000045
06 00 003 000 3 0173 1 0533705842 3100 2 00 000 0 062 1 039 00 09 00 00 0000077C
06 00 003 000 3 0161 1 0532905821 31C0 2 00 000 0 062 1 039 00 09 00 00 00000023
06 00 003 000 3 0158 1 0532405843 3100 2 00 000 0 062 1 039 00 09 00 00 0000C394
06 00 003 000 3 0098 1 0533605805 3101 2 00 000 0 062 1 039 00 09 00 00 00000128
05 00 003 000 3 0093 1 0533305829 31C0 2 00 000 0 062 1 039 00 09 00 00 0000C049
06 00 003 000 3 0090 1 0531505830 3100 2 00 000 0 062 1 039 00 09 00 00 0000003C
```

```
06 00 003 000 3 0068 1 0533105834 3100 2 00 000 0 062 1 039 00 09 00 00 00000050
06 00 003 000 3 0086 1 0534205837 3100 2 00 000 0 062 1 039 00 09 00 00 00000740
06 00 003 000 3 0081 1 0530505847 3099 2 00 000 0 062 1 039 00 09 00 00 00000014
06 00 003 000 3 0021 1 0530305847 3100 2 00 000 0 062 1 039 00 09 00 00 00000002
06 00 003 000 3 0000 1 0530005800 0000 2 00 000 0 062 1 039 00 09 00 00 00000019
06 00 003 000 3 0000 1 0530005800 0000 2 00 000 0 062 1 039 00 09 00 00 00000005
06 00 003 000 3 0046 1 0535005819 3099 2 00 000 0 062 1 039 00 09 00 00 00000005
06 00 003 000 3 0010 1 0536205833 3101 2 00 000 0 062 1 039 00 09 00 00 00000230
06 00 003 000 3 0006 1 0539005836 3100 2 00 000 0 062 1 039 00 09 00 00 00000181
06 00 003 000 3 0143 1 0536805835 3099 2 00 000 0 062 1 039 37 09 00 00 00000062
06 00 003 000 3 0133 1 0538005824 3101 2 00 000 0 062 1 039 37 09 00 00 00000032
06 00 003 000 3 0119 1 0532705856 3100 2 00 000 0 062 1 039 00 09 00 00 00000032
06 00 003 000 3 0101 1 0531905895 3100 2 00 000 0 062 1 039 00 09 00 00 00000022
06 00 003 000 3 0241 1 0540805843 3098 2 00 000 0 062 1 039 00 09 00 00 00000096
06 00 003 000 3 0000 1 0540005800 0000 2 00 000 0 062 1 039 00 09 00 00 00000001
06 00 003 000 3 0000 1 0540005800 0000 2 00 000 0 062 1 039 00 09 00 00 00000029
06 00 003 000 3 0188 1 0528705872 3100 2 00 000 0 062 1 039 00 09 00 00 00000058
06 00 003 000 3 0000 1 0525005850 0000 2 00 000 0 062 1 039 00 09 00 00 00000312
06 00 003 000 3 0000 1 0525005850 0000 2 00 000 0 062 1 039 00 09 00 00 00000012
06 00 003 000 3 0000 1 0525005850 0000 2 00 000 0 062 1 039 00 09 00 00 00000008
06 00 003 000 3 0252 1 0532005885 3100 2 00 000 0 062 1 039 00 09 00 00 00000018
06 00 003 000 3 0222 1 0533005889 3100 2 00 000 0 062 1 039 00 09 00 00 00000245
06 00 003 000 3 0212 1 0532305862 3100 2 00 000 0 062 1 039 00 09 00 00 00000036
06 00 003 000 3 0203 1 0530405888 3099 2 00 000 0 062 1 039 00 09 00 00 00000036
06 00 003 000 3 0194 1 0531505883 3099 2 00 000 0 062 1 039 00 09 00 00 00000032
06 00 003 000 3 0192 1 0531805879 3100 2 00 000 0 062 1 039 37 09 00 00 00000036
06 00 003 000 3 0164 1 0531805896 3100 2 00 000 0 062 1 039 00 09 00 00 00000068
06 00 003 000 3 0128 1 0536905841 3100 2 00 000 0 062 1 039 00 09 00 00 00000035
06 00 003 000 3 0000 1 0540005850 0000 2 00 000 0 062 1 039 00 09 00 00 00000001
06 00 003 000 3 0000 1 0540005850 0000 2 00 000 0 062 1 039 00 09 00 00 00000002
06 00 003 000 3 0000 1 0540005850 0000 2 00 000 0 062 1 039 00 09 00 00 00000010
06 00 003 000 3 0000 1 0525005900 0000 2 00 000 0 062 1 039 00 09 00 00 00000014
06 00 003 000 3 0000 1 0530005900 0000 2 00 000 0 062 1 039 00 09 00 00 00000033
06 00 003 000 3 0000 1 0530005900 0000 2 00 000 0 062 1 039 00 09 00 00 00000065
06 00 003 000 3 0000 1 0530005900 0000 2 00 000 0 062 1 039 00 09 00 00 00000007
06 00 003 000 3 0260 1 0538005909 3100 2 00 000 0 062 1 039 00 09 00 00 00000075
06 00 003 000 3 0000 1 0535005900 0000 2 00 000 0 062 1 039 00 09 00 00 00000010
06 00 003 000 3 0000 1 0530005900 0000 2 00 000 0 062 1 039 00 09 00 00 00000003
06 00 003 000 3 0000 1 0540005900 0000 2 00 000 0 062 1 039 00 09 00 00 00000002
06 00 003 000 3 0000 1 0540005900 0000 2 00 000 0 062 1 039 00 09 00 00 00000000
06 00 003 000 3 0148 1 0533205809 3100 2 00 000 0 063 1 039 00 09 00 00 00000006
06 00 003 000 3 0171 1 0534405838 3100 2 00 000 0 063 1 039 00 09 00 00 00000009
06 00 003 000 3 0000 1 0530005800 3100 2 00 000 0 063 1 039 00 09 00 00 00000014
06 00 003 000 3 0012 1 0536505831 3100 2 00 000 0 063 1 039 00 09 00 00 00000003
06 00 003 000 3 0014 1 0538005838 3100 2 00 000 0 063 1 039 00 09 00 00 00000013
06 00 003 000 3 0139 1 0537705846 3099 2 00 000 0 063 1 039 00 09 00 00 00000027
06 00 003 000 3 0240 1 0538305840 3099 2 00 000 0 063 1 039 00 09 00 00 00000031
06 00 003 000 3 0000 1 0540005800 3097 2 00 000 0 063 1 039 00 09 00 00 00000012
06 00 003 000 3 0218 1 0531005875 0000 2 00 000 0 063 1 039 00 09 00 00 00000011
06 00 003 000 3 0000 1 0535005800 3100 2 00 000 0 063 1 039 00 09 00 00 00000004
06 00 003 000 3 0242 1 0542605873 0000 2 00 000 0 063 1 039 00 09 00 00 00000087
06 00 003 000 3 0163 1 0532305926 3100 2 00 000 0 063 1 039 00 09 00 00 00000000
06 00 003 000 3 0268 1 0535505911 3100 2 00 000 0 063 1 039 00 09 00 00 00000002
06 00 003 000 3 0000 1 0540005900 0000 2 00 000 0 063 1 039 36 09 00 00 00000046
06 00 003 000 3 0000 1 0540005900 0000 2 00 000 0 063 1 039 00 09 00 00 00000002
06 00 003 000 3 0000 1 0540005900 0000 2 00 000 0 063 1 039 00 09 00 00 00000002
06 00 003 000 3 0067 1 0534105815 3100 2 00 000 0 064 1 039 00 09 00 00 00000163
06 00 003 000 3 0150 1 0534605815 3100 2 00 000 0 064 1 039 00 09 00 00 00000362
06 00 003 000 3 0026 1 0532805856 3100 2 00 000 0 065 1 039 00 09 00 00 00001680
06 00 003 000 3 0239 1 0541605863 3098 2 00 000 0 065 1 039 00 00 00 00 00000068
06 00 003 000 3 0177 1 0531305852 3100 2 00 000 0 065 1 039 00 09 00 00 00000347
06 00 003 000 3 0193 1 0530705882 3100 2 00 000 0 065 1 039 00 09 00 00 00000146
06 00 003 000 3 0207 1 0532605891 3098 2 00 000 0 065 1 039 00 09 00 00 00000232
06 00 003 000 3 0209 1 0535505896 3100 2 00 000 0 065 1 039 00 09 00 00 00000168
06 00 003 000 3 0075 1 0530205859 3100 2 00 000 0 065 1 039 00 09 00 00 00000112
06 00 003 000 3 0007 1 0537005831 3101 2 00 000 0 065 1 039 00 09 00 00 00000022
06 00 003 000 3 0015 1 0536505838 3100 2 00 000 0 065 1 039 00 09 00 00 00000093
06 00 003 000 3 0237 1 0541705853 3097 2 00 000 0 065 1 039 00 09 00 00 00000864
```

```
06  00  003  000  3  0001  1  0533905821  3101  2  00  000  0  065  1  039  00  09  00  00  00000003
06  00  003  000  3  0002  1  0533805821  3101  2  00  000  0  065  1  039  00  09  00  00  00000123
06  00  003  000  3  0170  1  0534805823  3100  2  00  000  0  065  1  039  00  09  00  00  00000028
06  00  003  000  3  0219  1  0532905882  3098  2  00  000  0  065  1  039  00  09  00  00  00000143
06  00  003  000  3  0292  1  0532305838  3100  2  00  000  0  065  1  039  00  09  00  00  00000250
06  00  003  000  3  0304  1  0534005843  3100  2  00  000  0  065  1  039  00  09  00  00  00000800
06  00  003  000  3  0152  1  0538805842  3099  2  00  000  0  065  1  039  00  09  00  00  00000031
06  00  003  000  3  0153  1  0539205844  3098  2  00  000  0  065  1  039  00  09  00  00  00000038
06  00  003  000  3  0156  1  0539105821  3100  2  00  000  0  065  1  039  00  09  00  00  00000340
06  00  003  000  3  0000  1  0535005800  0000  2  00  000  0  065  1  039  00  09  00  00  00000085
06  00  003  000  3  0000  1  0535005800  0000  2  00  000  0  065  1  039  00  09  00  00  00000012
06  00  003  000  3  0023  1  0541205831  3100  2  00  000  0  065  1  039  00  09  00  00  00000272
06  00  003  000  3  0257  1  0535105916  3100  2  00  000  0  065  1  039  00  09  00  00  00000663
06  00  003  000  3  0265  1  0539705904  3099  2  00  000  0  065  1  039  00  09  00  00  00000065
06  00  003  000  3  0266  1  0538805914  3100  2  00  000  0  065  1  039  00  09  00  00  00000064
06  00  003  000  3  0000  1  0540005900  0000  2  00  000  0  065  1  039  00  09  00  00  00000001
06  00  003  000  3  0000  1  0525005850  0000  2  00  000  0  082  1  039  00  09  00  00  00000021
06  00  003  000  3  0000  1  0525005850  0000  2  00  000  0  082  1  039  00  09  00  00  00000023
06  00  003  000  3  0113  1  0534405853  3099  2  00  000  0  082  1  039  00  09  00  00  00000075
06  00  003  000  3  0185  1  0531905867  3098  2  00  000  0  082  1  039  00  09  00  00  00000113
06  00  003  000  3  0198  1  0531405886  3100  2  00  000  0  082  1  039  00  09  00  00  00000037
06  00  003  000  3  0204  1  0533705890  3097  2  00  000  0  082  1  039  00  09  00  00  00000080
06  00  003  000  3  0223  1  0533005890  3100  2  00  000  0  082  1  039  00  00  00  00  00000231
06  00  003  000  3  0034  1  0539405862  3098  2  00  000  0  082  1  039  00  00  00  00  00001020
06  00  003  000  3  0238  1  0541005857  3098  2  00  000  0  082  1  039  00  09  00  00  00000428
06  00  003  000  3  0000  1  0540005850  0000  2  00  000  0  082  1  039  00  09  00  00  00000005
06  00  003  000  3  0263  1  0539305910  3099  2  00  000  0  082  1  039  00  09  00  00  00000390
06  00  003  000  3  0264  1  0539605913  3099  2  00  000  0  082  1  039  00  09  00  00  00000193
06  00  003  000  3  0000  1  0540005900  0000  2  00  000  0  082  1  039  00  09  00  00  00000001
06  00  003  000  3  0000  1  0540005800  0000  2  00  000  0  082  1  039  00  09  00  00  00000002
06  00  003  000  3  0017  1  0537405843  3101  2  00  000  0  082  1  039  00  09  00  00  00000690
06  00  003  000  3  0125  1  0536205839  3100  2  00  000  0  082  1  039  00  09  00  00  00000015
06  00  003  000  3  0129  1  0537105841  3100  2  00  000  0  082  1  039  00  09  00  00  00000165
06  00  003  000  3  0134  1  0538405836  3100  2  00  000  0  082  1  039  00  09  00  00  00000059
06  00  003  000  3  0136  1  0539505834  3099  2  00  000  0  082  1  039  00  09  00  00  00000080
06  00  003  000  3  0137  1  0539505828  3099  2  00  000  0  082  1  039  00  09  00  00  00000067
06  00  003  000  3  0138  1  0539205844  3099  2  00  000  0  082  1  039  00  09  00  00  00000240
06  00  003  000  3  0151  1  0537905814  3100  2  00  000  0  082  1  039  00  09  00  00  00000323
06  00  003  000  3  0155  1  0539805819  3100  2  00  000  0  082  1  039  00  09  00  00  00000719
06  00  003  000  3  0065  1  0534005842  3100  2  00  000  0  082  1  039  00  09  00  00  00000019
06  00  003  000  3  0099  1  0539005834  3100  2  00  000  0  082  1  039  00  09  00  00  00000300
06  00  003  000  3  0145  1  0534005840  3099  2  00  000  0  082  1  039  00  09  00  00  00000050
06  00  003  000  3  0146  1  0533305837  3099  2  00  000  0  082  1  039  00  09  00  00  00000029
06  00  003  000  3  0232  1  0531105837  3100  2  00  000  0  082  1  039  00  09  00  00  00000034
06  00  003  000  3  0233  1  0530705842  3099  2  00  000  0  082  1  039  00  09  00  00  00000057
06  00  003  000  3  0290  1  0532605824  3100  2  00  000  0  082  1  039  32  09  00  00  00001477
06  00  003  000  3  0293  1  0532805841  3100  2  00  000  0  082  1  039  00  09  00  00  00000068
06  00  003  000  3  0132  1  0537405827  3100  2  00  000  0  050  7  038  00  09  00  00  00000186
06  00  003  000  3  0245  1  0532305869  3100  2  00  000  0  052  1  039  36  09  00  00  00000007
06  00  003  000  3  0251  1  0532405882  3100  2  00  000  0  052  1  039  36  09  00  00  00000060
06  00  003  000  3  0228  1  0532405829  3100  2  00  000  0  052  1  039  36  09  00  00  00000034
06  00  003  000  3  0259  1  0536405909  3100  2  00  000  0  056  1  039  36  09  00  00  00000049
06  00  003  000  3  0159  1  0531205848  3100  2  00  000  0  057  7  038  35  09  00  00  00000185
06  00  003  000  3  0295  1  0533005846  3101  2  00  000  0  075  7  038  00  09  00  00  00004909
06  00  003  000  3  0262  1  0539105910  3100  2  00  000  0  075  7  038  00  09  00  00  00000149
06  00  003  000  3  0217  1  0530105874  3100  2  00  000  0  099  7  038  00  09  00  00  00000052
06  00  003  000  3  0307  1  0533905847  3100  1  00  000  0  003  1  002  00  00  00  00  00000054
06  00  003  000  3  0190  1  0529505864  3100  1  00  000  0  015  1  001  00  00  00  00  00000079
06  00  003  000  3  0191  1  0529005876  3100  1  00  000  0  015  1  001  00  00  00  00  00000052
06  00  003  000  3  0009  1  0536605833  3101  1  00  000  0  015  1  001  00  00  00  00  00000331
06  00  003  000  3  0073  1  0530705858  3098  1  00  000  0  015  1  001  00  00  00  00  00000275
06  00  003  000  3  0179  1  0533305859  3100  1  00  000  0  015  1  001  00  00  00  00  00000018
06  00  003  000  3  0199  1  0531605886  3100  1  00  000  0  015  1  001  00  00  00  00  00000053
06  00  003  000  3  0208  1  0532305894  3099  1  00  000  0  015  1  001  00  00  00  00  00000021
06  00  003  000  3  0234  1  0530605872  3100  1  00  000  0  015  1  001  00  00  00  00  00000039
06  00  003  000  3  0236  1  0530605885  3100  1  00  000  0  015  1  001  00  00  00  00  00000274
06  00  003  000  3  0051  1  0532905864  3099  1  00  000  0  015  1  001  00  00  00  00  00000518
06  00  003  000  3  0057  1  0539005878  3100  1  00  000  0  015  1  001  00  00  00  00  00000025
06  00  003  000  3  0062  1  0535205898  3100  1  00  000  0  015  1  001  00  00  00  00  00000023
06  00  003  000  3  0000  1  0540005850  0000  1  00  000  0  015  1  001  00  00  00  00  00000011
06  00  003  000  3  0000  1  0540005850  0000  1  00  000  0  015  1  001  00  00  00  00  00000016
06  00  003  000  3  0000  1  0540005850  0000  1  00  000  0  015  1  001  00  00  00  00  00000013
06  00  003  000  3  0000  1  0540005800  0000  1  00  000  0  015  1  001  00  00  00  00  00000050
06  00  003  000  3  0000  1  0535005800  0000  1  00  000  0  015  1  001  00  09  00  00  00000006
06  00  003  000  3  0080  1  0531305849  3101  1  00  000  0  015  1  001  00  00  00  00  00000065
06  00  003  000  3  0083  1  0531205844  3100  1  00  000  0  015  1  001  00  00  00  00  00000155
```

```
06  00  003  000  3  0084  1  0531205841  3100  1  00  000  0  015  1  001  00  00  00  00  00000013
06  00  003  000  3  0091  1  0530205830  3100  1  00  000  0  015  1  039  00  00  00  00  00000031
06  00  003  000  3  0160  1  0534505817  3100  1  00  000  0  015  1  039  00  00  00  00  00000015
06  00  003  000  3  0166  1  0533205833  3100  1  00  000  0  015  1  001  00  00  00  00  00000016
06  00  003  000  3  0169  1  0534205829  3099  1  00  000  0  015  1  001  00  00  00  00  00000028
06  00  003  000  3  0291  1  0532405830  3100  1  00  000  0  015  1  001  00  00  00  00  00000046
06  00  003  000  3  0296  1  0533205846  3100  1  00  000  0  015  1  001  00  00  00  00  00000046
06  00  003  000  3  0297  1  0533205847  3100  1  00  000  0  015  1  001  00  00  00  00  00000021
06  00  003  000  3  0308  1  0534105849  3100  1  00  000  0  015  1  001  00  00  00  00  00000053
06  00  003  000  3  0000  1  0540005900  0000  1  00  000  0  015  1  001  00  00  00  00  00000005
06  00  003  000  3  0255  1  0535205908  3100  1  00  000  0  015  1  001  00  00  00  00  00000032
06  00  003  000  3  0267  1  0539905915  3100  1  00  000  0  015  1  001  00  00  00  00  00000022
06  00  003  000  3  0224  1  0533705901  3100  1  00  000  0  015  1  001  00  00  00  00  00000022
06  00  003  000  3  0225  1  0532805943  3100  1  00  000  0  015  1  001  00  00  00  00  00000081
06  00  003  000  3  0227  1  0534605946  3100  1  00  000  0  015  1  001  00  00  00  00  00000100
06  00  003  000  3  0000  1  0530005900  0000  1  00  000  0  015  1  001  00  00  00  00  00000001
06  00  003  000  3  0037  1  0535905837  3099  1  00  000  0  029  1  015  00  00  00  00  00000172
06  00  003  000  3  0050  1  0535005843  3099  1  00  000  0  029  1  015  00  00  00  00  00000038
06  00  003  000  3  0000  1  0535005800  0000  2  00  000  0  029  1  015  00  09  00  00  00000066
06  00  003  000  3  0000  1  0540005900  0000  1  00  000  0  029  1  015  00  00  00  00  00000050
06  00  003  000  3  0256  1  0535405912  3100  1  00  000  0  029  1  015  00  00  00  00  00000005
06  00  003  000  3  0189  1  0528005872  3101  1  00  000  0  029  1  015  00  00  00  00  00000701
06  00  003  000  3  0244  1  0532005892  3100  1  00  000  0  037  1  001  00  00  00  00  00000044
06  00  003  000  3  0036  1  0539305876  3099  1  00  000  0  037  1  001  00  00  00  00  00000178
06  00  003  000  3  0000  1  0525005800  0000  1  00  000  0  038  1  039  00  09  00  00  00000007
06  00  003  000  3  0000  1  0525005800  0000  1  00  000  0  038  1  039  00  09  00  00  00000006
06  00  003  000  3  0000  1  0525005800  0000  1  00  000  0  038  1  039  00  09  00  00  00000004
06  00  003  000  3  0003  1  0534205844  3101  1  00  000  0  038  1  039  00  00  00  00  00000022
06  00  003  000  3  0089  1  0533505831  3101  1  00  000  0  038  1  039  00  00  00  00  00000031
06  00  003  000  3  0168  1  0534205829  3100  1  00  000  0  038  1  039  00  00  00  00  00000025
06  00  003  000  3  0305  1  0534105845  3100  1  00  000  0  038  1  039  00  00  00  00  00000012
06  00  003  000  3  0000  1  0530005800  0000  1  00  000  0  038  1  039  00  00  00  00  00000009
06  00  003  000  3  0004  1  0533205846  3101  1  00  000  0  038  1  039  00  00  00  00  00000090
06  00  003  000  3  0005  1  0535605822  3100  1  00  000  0  038  1  039  00  00  00  00  00000016
06  00  003  000  3  0013  1  0538805872  3101  1  00  000  0  038  1  039  00  00  00  00  00000016
06  00  003  000  3  0000  1  0535005800  0000  1  00  000  0  038  1  039  00  00  00  00  00000013
06  00  003  000  3  0000  1  0530005800  0000  1  00  000  0  038  1  039  00  09  00  00  00000013
06  00  003  000  3  0000  1  0540005800  0000  1  00  000  0  038  1  039  00  09  00  00  00000004
06  00  003  000  3  0000  1  0540005800  0000  1  00  000  0  038  1  039  00  00  00  00  00000006
06  00  003  000  3  0000  1  0540005850  0000  1  00  000  0  038  1  039  00  00  00  00  00000010
06  00  003  000  3  0025  1  0530405855  3100  1  00  000  0  038  1  039  00  00  00  00  00000011
06  00  003  000  3  0074  1  0530705859  3100  1  00  000  0  038  1  039  00  00  00  00  00000022
06  00  003  000  3  0076  1  0531905857  3100  1  00  000  0  038  1  039  00  00  00  00  00000035
06  00  003  000  3  0216  1  0530605874  3099  1  00  000  0  038  1  039  00  00  00  00  00000075
06  00  003  000  3  0221  1  0530405886  3100  1  00  000  0  038  1  039  00  00  00  00  00000168
06  00  003  000  3  0000  1  0525005850  0000  1  00  000  0  038  1  039  00  09  00  00  00000008
06  00  003  000  3  0000  1  0525005850  0000  1  00  000  0  038  1  039  00  00  00  00  00000013
06  00  003  000  3  0000  1  0530005900  0000  1  00  000  0  038  1  039  00  00  00  00  00000002
06  00  003  000  3  0000  1  0530005900  0000  1  00  000  0  038  1  039  00  00  00  00  00000021
06  00  003  000  3  0000  1  0525005900  0000  1  00  000  0  038  1  039  00  00  00  00  00000004
06  00  003  000  3  0000  1  0525005900  0000  1  00  000  0  038  1  039  00  00  00  00  00000011
06  00  003  000  3  0256  1  0525005900  0000  1  00  000  0  038  1  039  00  00  00  00  00000013
06  00  003  00   3  0033  1  0539405862  3098  4  01  000  1  000  1  033  00  00  00  00  00000007
06  00  003  000  9  0068  1  0536805881  3097  4  00  028  0  000  1  033  00  00  00  00  00000003
06  00  003  000  3  0000  1  0530005800  0000  4  01  020  0  000  1  040  00  09  00  00  00000023
06  00  003  000  3  0032  1  0530605853  3100  4  00  021  0  000  1  034  00  09  00  00  00000117
06  00  003  000  3  0000  1  0535005800  0000  3  77  507  0  000  1  039  65  00  00  00  00000269
06  00  003  000  3  0000  1  0530005800  0000  3  77  507  0  000  1  039  65  00  00  00  00000044
06  00  003  000  3  0000  1  0530005800  0000  3  77  507  0  000  1  039  65  00  00  00  00000024
06  00  003  000  3  0000  1  0530005900  0000  3  80  508  0  000  1  039  65  00  00  00  00000000
06  00  003  000  3  0000  1  0535005800  0000  3  81  506  0  000  7  039  65  00  00  00  00000001
06  00  003  000  3  0000  1  0530005900  0000  3  81  506  0  000  7  000  65  00  00  00  00000001
06  00  003  000  3  0000  1  0530005800  0000  3  84  510  0  000  1  039  00  00  00  00  00000000
06  00  003  000  3  0000  1  0530005800  0000  3  85  510  0  000  1  039  65  00  00  00  00000000
06  00  003  000  3  0000  1  0530005800  0000  3  86  512  0  000  7  000  00  00  00  00  00000000
06  00  003  000  3  0000  1  0530005800  0000  3  91  507  0  000  1  039  65  00  00  00  00000002
06  00  003  000  3  0000  1  0535005800  0000  3  91  507  0  000  1  039  65  00  00  00  00000000
```

```
       PIT 5A    DATA BASE
06  00  0A5  000  9  0003 1 0523306019 3095 2 00 000 0 060 7 038 36 09 00 00 00000034
06  00  0A5  000  9  0017 1 0521906010 3099 2 00 000 0 060 1 039 37 09 00 00 00000019
06  00  0A5  000  9  0000 1 0520006000 0000 2 00 000 0 060 1 039 00 09 00 00 00000069
06  00  0A5  000  9  0000 1 0520006000 0000 2 00 000 0 060 1 039 00 09 00 00 00000031
06  00  0A5  000  9  0000 1 0520006000 0000 2 00 000 0 060 1 039 00 09 00 00 00000008
06  00  0A5  000  9  0000 1 0520006000 0000 2 00 000 0 060 1 039 00 09 00 00 00000003
06  00  0A5  000  9  0000 1 0523306023 0000 2 00 000 0 060 1 039 00 09 00 00 00000001
06  00  0A5  000  9  0000 1 0523306023 0000 2 00 000 0 060 1 039 00 09 00 00 00000001
06  00  0A5  000  9  0000 1 0523306023 0000 2 00 000 0 060 1 039 00 09 00 00 00000001
06  00  0A5  000  9  0000 1 0523306023 0000 2 00 000 0 060 1 039 37 09 00 00 00000011
06  00  0A5  000  9  0000 1 0523306023 0000 2 00 000 0 060 1 039 37 09 00 00 00000004
06  00  0A5  000  9  0000 1 0523306023 0000 2 00 000 0 060 1 039 00 09 00 00 00000001
06  00  0A5  000  9  0000 1 0523306023 0000 2 00 000 0 060 1 039 00 09 00 00 00000007
06  00  0A5  000  9  0000 1 0523306023 0000 2 00 000 0 060 1 039 00 09 00 00 00000001
06  00  0A5  000  9  0000 1 0523306023 0000 2 00 000 0 060 1 039 00 09 00 00 00000001
06  00  0A5  000  9  0000 1 0522306023 0000 2 00 000 0 060 1 039 00 09 00 00 00000029
06  00  0A5  000  9  0000 1 0522306023 0000 2 00 000 0 060 1 039 00 09 00 00 00000003
06  00  0A5  000  9  0000 1 0522306023 0000 2 00 000 0 060 1 039 00 09 00 00 00000003
06  00  0A5  000  9  0000 1 0522306023 0000 2 00 000 0 060 1 039 00 09 00 00 00000004
06  00  0A5  000  9  0000 1 0522306023 0000 2 00 000 0 060 1 039 00 09 00 00 00000001
06  00  0A5  000  9  0000 1 0522306023 0000 2 00 000 0 060 1 039 00 09 00 00 00000001
06  00  0A5  000  9  0000 1 0522306023 0000 2 00 000 0 050 1 039 00 09 00 00 00000001
06  00  0A5  000  9  0000 1 0521506029 3099 2 00 000 0 062 1 039 00 09 00 00 00000517
06  00  0A5  000  9  0004 1 0522806020 3097 2 00 000 0 062 1 039 00 09 00 00 00000068
06  00  0A5  000  9  0000 1 0520006000 0000 2 00 000 0 062 1 039 37 09 00 00 00000214
06  00  0A5  000  9  0000 1 0520006000 0000 2 00 000 0 062 1 039 37 09 00 00 00000138
06  00  0A5  000  9  0000 1 0520006000 0000 2 00 000 0 062 1 039 00 09 00 00 00000046
06  00  0A5  000  9  0000 1 0520006000 0000 2 00 000 0 062 1 039 00 09 00 00 00000026
06  00  0A5  000  9  0000 1 0520006000 0000 2 00 000 0 062 1 039 00 09 00 00 00000032
06  00  0A5  000  9  0000 1 0520006000 0000 2 00 000 0 062 1 039 00 09 00 00 00000016
06  00  0A5  000  9  0000 1 0520006000 0000 2 00 000 0 062 1 039 00 09 00 00 00000006
06  00  0A5  000  9  0000 1 0520006000 0000 2 00 000 0 062 1 039 00 09 00 00 00000002
06  00  0A5  000  9  0000 1 0520006000 0000 2 00 000 0 062 1 039 00 09 00 00 00000014
06  00  0A5  000  9  0000 1 0520006000 0000 2 00 000 0 062 1 039 00 09 00 00 00000007
06  00  0A5  000  9  0000 1 0523306023 0000 2 00 000 0 062 1 039 00 09 00 00 00000010
06  00  0A5  000  9  0000 1 0523306023 0000 2 00 000 0 062 1 039 37 09 00 00 00000004
06  00  0A5  000  9  0000 1 0523306023 0000 2 00 000 0 062 1 039 37 09 00 00 00000010
06  00  0A5  000  9  0000 1 0523306023 0000 2 00 000 0 062 1 039 00 09 00 00 00000005
06  00  0A5  000  9  0000 1 0523306023 0000 2 00 000 0 062 1 039 00 09 00 00 00000037
06  00  0A5  000  9  0000 1 0522306023 0000 2 00 000 0 062 1 039 00 09 00 00 00000107
06  00  0A5  000  9  0000 1 0522306023 0000 2 00 000 0 062 1 039 00 09 00 00 00000030
06  00  0A5  000  9  0000 1 0522306023 0000 2 00 000 0 062 1 039 00 09 00 00 00000011
06  00  0A5  000  9  0000 1 0522306023 0000 2 00 000 0 062 1 039 37 09 00 00 00000045
06  00  0A5  000  9  0000 1 0522306023 0000 2 00 000 0 062 1 039 00 09 00 00 00000015
06  00  0A5  000  9  0000 1 0522306023 0000 2 00 000 0 062 1 039 37 09 00 00 00000020
06  00  0A5  000  9  0000 1 0522306023 0000 2 00 000 0 062 1 039 37 09 00 00 00000004
06  00  0A5  000  9  0000 1 0522306023 0000 2 00 000 0 062 1 039 00 09 00 00 00000003
06  00  0A5  000  9  0000 1 0522306023 0000 2 00 000 0 062 1 039 00 09 00 00 00000006
06  00  0A5  000  9  0000 1 0522306023 0000 2 00 000 0 062 1 039 37 09 00 00 00000006
06  00  0A5  000  9  0000 1 0522306023 0000 2 00 000 0 062 1 039 00 09 00 00 00000007
06  00  0A5  000  9  0000 1 0522306023 0000 2 00 000 0 063 1 039 00 09 00 00 00000001
06  00  0A5  000  9  0000 1 0522306023 0000 2 00 000 0 063 1 039 00 09 00 00 00000003
06  00  0A5  000  9  0000 1 0522306023 0000 2 00 000 0 063 1 039 00 09 00 00 00000018
06  00  0A5  000  9  0000 1 0520006000 0000 2 00 000 0 063 1 039 00 09 00 00 00000000
06  00  0A5  000  3  0000 1 0522306023 0000 2 00 000 0 063 1 039 00 09 00 00 00000002
06  00  0A5  000  9  0000 1 0520006000 0000 2 00 000 0 063 1 039 00 09 00 00 00000009
06  00  0A5  000  9  0000 1 0520006000 0000 2 00 000 0 063 1 039 00 09 00 00 00000017
06  00  0A5  000  9  0000 1 0520006000 0000 2 00 000 0 063 1 039 00 09 00 00 00000011
06  00  0A5  000  9  0000 1 0520006000 0000 2 00 000 0 063 1 039 00 09 00 00 00000011
06  00  0A5  000  9  0000 1 0520006000 0000 2 00 000 0 063 1 039 36 09 00 00 00000015
06  00  0A5  000  9  0000 1 0520006000 0000 2 00 000 0 064 1 039 00 09 00 00 00000129
06  00  0A5  000  9  0000 1 0522306023 0000 2 00 000 0 065 1 039 00 09 00 00 00000002
06  00  0A5  000  9  0000 1 0522306023 0000 2 00 000 0 065 1 039 00 09 00 00 00000003
06  00  0A5  000  9  0000 1 0522306023 0000 2 00 000 0 065 1 039 00 09 00 00 00000011
06  00  0A5  000  9  0000 1 0523306023 0000 2 00 000 0 065 1 039 00 09 00 00 00000011
06  00  0A5  000  9  0000 1 0523306023 0000 2 00 000 0 065 1 039 00 09 00 00 00000019
06  00  0A5  000  9  0000 1 0523306023 0000 2 00 000 0 065 1 039 00 09 00 00 00000021
06  00  0A5  000  9  0000 1 0523306023 0000 2 00 000 0 065 1 039 00 09 00 00 00000006
06  00  0A5  000  9  0000 1 0520006000 0000 2 00 000 0 065 1 039 00 09 00 00 00000004
```

```
06 0C 0A5 C0C 9 C0CC 1 0520006000 00C0 2 0C 000 C 065 1 039 00 09 00 00 0000002
06 00 0A5 C0C 9 0002 1 0523206024 3097 2 00 000 0 065 1 039 00 09 0C 00 0C00036
06 00 0A5 C0C 9 0016 1 0521206014 3097 2 00 000 0 065 1 039 C0 09 00 00 00000031
06 CC CA5 C0C 9 0023 1 0522C06C33 31C0 2 00 000 0 065 1 039 00 09 00 00 0000029
06 00 0A5 000 9 000C 1 0520006000 0000 2 0C 000 0 082 1 039 L0 09 0C 0C 0000001
06 00 0A5 C0C 9 0000 1 0520006000 00C0 2 00 000 C 051 5 000 00 09 C0 00 0000001
06 00 0A5 C0C 9 0005 1 0521906025 3096 2 00 000 0 051 7 038 00 09 00 00 0000004
C6 00 0A5 000 9 0027 1 0523006C29 3098 2 00 000 C 059 7 038 35 09 00 00 0000011
06 00 0A5 000 9 000C 1 0520006000 00C0 2 00 000 0 063 1 039 0C 09 0C 00 0000C0C
06 0C 0A5 CCC 9 0000 1 0520006000 0C00 1 00 000 0 015 1 001 00 00 00 00 0000C02
06 CC 0A5 C0C 9 0000 1 0520006000 G0C0 1 00 000 0 015 1 001 CC CC 00 00 0000C01
06 00 0A5 000 9 000C 1 0520006000 00C0 1 00 000 0 015 1 001 00 00 00 0C 0000003
06 00 0A5 000 9 0000 1 0520006000 0000 1 00 000 C 015 1 001 00 00 00 0C 0000001
06 CC CA5 C0C 9 0000 1 0520006000 0000 1 00 000 C 015 1 001 0C 00 00 00 0000010
06 0C 0A5 000 9 0000 1 0520C06C00 C0C0 1 00 000 0 038 1 039 00 00 00 00 0000000
06 0C 0A5 000 9 000C 1 0520006000 00C0 1 00 000 0 038 1 039 CC 00 C0 00 0000000
06 00 0A5 C0C 9 0000 1 0520006000 00C0 1 00 000 0 038 1 039 00 0C CC 00 0000000
06 00 0A5 000 9 000C 1 0520C06C00 00C0 1 00 000 0 038 1 039 00 0C 00 00 0000001
06 0C 0A5 C0C 9 000C 1 0520006000 00C0 1 00 000 0 038 1 039 00 0C 00 00 0000002
06 CC 0A5 C0C 9 000C 1 0520006000 0C00 1 00 000 0 038 1 039 00 0C 00 00 0000004
06 00 0A5 C0C 9 000C 1 0522306023 0000 1 00 000 0 038 1 039 0C 0C 00 00 0000008
06 00 0A5 C0C 9 000C 1 0522306023 0000 1 00 000 0 038 1 039 0C 00 00 00 0000001
06 0C 0A5 000 9 0000 1 0522306023 00C0 5 00 000 0 100 1 039 00 01 00 00 0000001
06 00 0A5 C0C 9 0022 1 0521406C32 3096 4 11 014 2 C00 1 039 00 00 00 00 0000008
06 00 0A5 C0C 9 00C0 1 0523306023 0000 3 77 509 0 000 1 039 65 00 00 00 00003113
06 0C 0A5 000 9 0000 1 0523306023 00C0 3 81 503 0 000 1 039 65 0C CC 00 0000000
06 0C CA5 C0C 9 000C 1 0523306C23 0000 3 82 510 C C00 1 039 65 00 00 00 0000000
06 00 0A5 000 9 0L00 1 0523306023 000C 3 34 510 C C00 7 C0C C0 00 00 00 0000001
06 CC CA5 C0C 9 000C 1 0523306023 00C0 3 85 510 0 000 1 039 65 00 00 00 0000001
06 00 0A5 000 9 000C 1 0523306023 0CC0 3 86 512 0 000 1 039 65 0C CC 00 0000000
   FIT 5B DATA BASE
06 00 0B5 C0C 9 0013 1 0524006005 3099 2 00 000 0 060 1 039 0C 09 00 00 0000004
06 CC CB5 C0C 9 0020 1 0522406001 3098 2 00 000 0 060 1 039 37 09 00 00 0000001
06 00 0B5 000 3 000C 1 0520C05950 0LC0 2 00 000 0 060 1 039 00 09 C0 00 000000-1
06 00 0B5 000 3 00C0 1 0520005950 0000 2 00 000 0 060 1 039 0C 09 00 00 0000000
06 00 0B5 000 3 00C0 1 0520005950 CCC0 2 00 000 0 060 1 039 35 09 CC 00 0000002
06 00 0B5 000 3 0CC0 1 0520005950 0000 2 00 000 0 060 1 039 35 09 00 00 0000004
06 00 0B5 000 3 0LC0 1 0520005950 00C0 2 00 000 0 060 1 039 CC 09 00 00 0000000
C6 0C 0B5 CCC 3 0CC0 1 0520005950 00C0 2 00 000 0 060 1 039 C0 09 00 00 0000041
06 00 0B5 000 3 0CC0 1 0520005950 C0C0 2 00 000 0 060 1 039 C0 09 00 00 0000001
06 00 0B5 000 3 0000 1 0520005950 C0C0 2 00 000 0 060 1 039 C0 09 00 00 0000001
06 CC 0B5 C0C 9 0CC0 1 052C005950 00C0 2 00 000 0 060 1 039 00 09 00 00 0000005
06 CC 0B5 C00 9 0CC0 1 0520005950 CCC0 2 00 000 0 060 1 039 00 09 00 00 0000001
06 00 0B5 CCC 9 0CC0 1 0520005950 CCC0 2 00 000 0 060 1 039 00 09 CC 00 0000001
06 00 0B5 C0C 3 0CC0 1 0520005950 C0C0 2 00 000 0 060 1 039 00 09 00 00 0000002
06 00 0B5 CCC 9 0000 1 0520005950 0000 2 00 000 0 060 1 039 C0 09 00 00 00000C5
06 00 0B5 CCC 9 0000 1 05235C5993 CCC0 2 00 000 0 060 1 039 00 09 00 00 00000070
06 00 0B5 CCC 9 0000 1 0520005950 0000 2 00 000 0 060 1 039 C0 09 00 00 0000001
06 0U 0B5 000 9 0000 1 0520005950 0CC0 2 00 000 0 060 1 039 35 09 00 00 0000005
06 0C 0B5 C0C 9 0000 1 052C005950 000C 2 00 000 0 060 1 039 37 09 00 00 0000003
06 00 0B5 CCC 9 0CCC 1 0520005950 0000 2 00 000 0 060 1 039 C0 09 00 00 0000001
06 00 0B5 C0C 9 00C0 1 0520005950 0000 2 00 000 0 060 1 039 00 09 00 00 0000014
06 00 0B5 000 9 00C0 1 0520005950 0CC0 2 00 000 0 060 1 039 00 09 00 00 0000000
06 00 0B5 000 9 C0C0 1 0520005950 0000 2 00 000 0 060 1 039 00 09 00 00 0000013
06 CC 0B5 CCC 9 00C0 1 052C0C5950 C0C0 2 00 000 0 060 1 039 CC 09 00 00 0000011
06 00 0B5 000 9 00C0 1 0520005950 00C0 2 00 000 0 060 1 039 00 09 00 00 0000001
06 00 0B5 CCC 9 0CC0 1 0520005950 00C0 2 00 000 0 060 1 039 C0 09 CC 00 0000004
06 CC 0B5 C00 9 0CC0 1 0520005950 0000 2 00 000 0 060 1 039 00 09 00 00 0000000
06 C0 0B5 C0C 9 000C 1 0520005950 0000 2 00 000 0 060 1 039 00 09 CC 00 0C00C4
06 00 0B5 CCC 9 000C 1 0523505993 C0C0 2 00 000 0 060 1 039 00 09 00 00 00000139
06 CC 0B5 000 9 00C0 1 05235C5993 CCC0 2 00 000 0 061 1 039 00 09 CC 0C 00000161
06 00 0B5 000 3 CCC0 1 0520005950 00CC 1 00 000 0 052 1 039 00 09 00 00 00000010
C6 0U 0B5 C00 3 0CC0 1 052C005950 0000 2 00 000 0 062 1 039 00 09 00 00 0000012
06 0C 0B5 C00 3 0CC0 1 0520005950 0C00 2 00 000 0 062 1 039 00 09 00 00 0000004
06 0C 0B5 CCC 3 0000 1 0520005950 0C00 2 00 000 0 062 1 039 00 09 00 00 0000006
```

```
6 00 0B5 000 3 0000 1 0520005950 0000 2 00 000 0 062 1 039 00 09 00 00 00000001
6 00 0B5 000 3 0000 1 0520005950 00C0 2 00 000 0 062 1 039 00 09 00 00 0000C0C1
6 00 0B5 000 3 0000 1 0520005950 0000 2 00 000 0 062 1 039 00 09 00 00 00000002
6 00 0B5 000 3 0000 1 0520005950 0000 2 00 000 0 062 1 039 00 09 00 00 00000012
6 00 0B5 000 3 0000 1 0520005950 0000 2 00 000 0 062 1 039 00 09 00 00 00000029
6 00 0B5 000 9 0010 1 0524405990 3098 2 00 000 0 062 1 039 00 09 00 00 00002509
6 00 0B5 000 9 0000 1 0523505993 0000 2 00 000 0 062 1 039 00 09 00 00 00000006
6 00 0B5 000 9 0000 1 0523505993 0000 2 00 000 0 062 1 039 00 09 00 00 00000022
6 00 0B5 000 9 0000 1 0520005950 0000 2 00 000 0 062 1 039 37 09 00 00 00000002
6 00 0B5 000 9 0000 1 0520005950 0000 2 00 000 0 062 1 039 00 09 00 00 00000002
6 00 0B5 000 3 0000 1 0520005950 0000 2 00 000 0 063 1 039 00 09 00 00 00000006
6 00 0B5 000 3 0000 1 0520005950 0000 2 00 000 0 063 1 039 00 09 00 00 00000001
6 00 0B5 000 9 0000 1 0520005950 0000 2 00 000 0 063 1 039 00 09 00 00 00000001
6 00 0B5 000 9 0000 1 0520005950 0000 2 00 000 0 064 1 039 00 09 00 00 00000095
6 00 0B5 000 9 0000 1 0523705989 0000 2 00 000 0 065 1 039 00 09 00 00 00001286
6 00 0B5 000 9 0008 1 0523005980 3098 2 00 000 0 065 1 039 00 09 00 00 00000066
6 00 0B5 000 9 0000 1 0523505993 0000 2 00 000 0 065 1 039 00 09 00 00 00000026
6 00 0B5 000 9 0000 1 0520005950 0000 2 00 000 0 065 1 039 00 09 00 00 00000004
6 00 0B5 000 9 0000 1 0520005950 0000 2 00 000 0 065 1 039 00 09 00 00 00000011
6 00 0B5 000 9 0000 1 0520005950 0000 2 00 000 0 065 1 039 00 09 00 00 00000007
6 00 0B5 000 9 0000 1 0520005950 0000 2 00 000 0 065 1 039 00 09 00 00 00000006
6 00 0B5 000 9 0000 1 0520005950 0000 2 00 000 0 065 1 039 37 09 00 00 00000003
6 00 0B5 000 9 0000 1 0520005950 0000 2 00 000 0 065 1 039 00 09 00 00 00000005
6 00 0B5 000 9 0037 1 0522505957 0000 2 00 000 0 065 1 039 00 09 00 00 00000016
6 00 0B5 000 3 0000 1 0520005950 0000 2 00 000 0 065 1 039 00 09 00 00 00000002
6 00 0B5 000 3 0000 1 0520005950 0000 2 00 000 0 065 1 039 00 09 00 00 00000007
6 00 0B5 000 3 0000 1 0520005950 0000 2 00 000 0 065 1 039 00 09 00 00 00000002
6 00 0B5 000 3 0000 1 0525006000 0000 2 00 000 0 065 1 039 00 09 00 00 00000004
6 00 0B5 000 3 0000 1 0520005950 0000 2 00 000 0 082 1 039 00 09 00 00 00000016
6 00 0B5 000 3 0000 1 0520005950 0000 2 00 000 0 082 1 039 00 09 00 00 00000136
6 00 0B5 000 9 0000 1 0523505993 0000 2 00 000 0 082 1 039 00 09 00 00 00000319
6 00 0B5 000 9 0000 1 0523505993 0000 2 00 000 0 082 1 039 00 09 00 00 00000404
6 00 0B5 000 9 0000 1 0523505993 0000 2 00 000 0 082 1 039 00 09 00 00 00000138
6 00 0B5 000 9 0000 1 0523505993 0000 2 00 000 0 082 1 039 00 09 00 00 00000009
6 00 0B5 000 9 0037 1 0522505957 3100 2 00 000 0 079 7 038 00 09 00 00 00004133
6 00 0B5 000 9 0011 1 0523405995 3096 1 00 000 0 015 1 001 00 00 00 00 00000065
6 00 0B5 000 9 0014 1 0523506004 3098 1 00 000 0 015 1 001 00 00 00 00 00000158
6 00 0B5 000 9 0015 1 0522706001 3097 1 00 000 0 015 1 001 00 00 00 00 00000011
6 00 0B5 000 9 0000 1 0523505993 0000 1 00 000 0 015 1 039 00 00 00 00 00000010
6 00 0B5 000 9 0000 1 0523505993 0000 1 00 000 0 015 1 039 00 00 00 00 00000007
6 00 0B5 000 9 0000 1 0523505993 0000 1 00 000 0 015 1 039 00 00 00 00 00000054
6 00 0B5 000 9 0000 1 0523505993 0000 1 00 000 0 015 1 039 00 00 00 00 00000006
6 00 0B5 000 3 0000 1 0523505993 0000 1 00 000 0 015 1 001 00 00 00 00 00000011
6 00 0B5 000 3 0000 1 0520005950 0000 1 00 000 0 015 1 001 00 00 00 00 00000056
6 00 0B5 000 3 0000 1 0520005950 0000 1 00 000 0 015 1 001 00 00 00 00 00000006
6 00 0B5 000 9 0012 1 0523906000 3098 1 00 000 0 003 1 002 00 00 00 00 00000567
6 00 0B5 000 3 0019 1 0522406002 3096 1 00 000 0 015 1 001 00 00 00 00 00000030
6 00 0B5 000 3 0000 1 0520005950 0000 1 00 000 0 036 1 039 00 00 00 00 00000012
6 00 0B5 000 3 0000 1 0520005950 0000 1 00 000 0 036 1 039 00 00 00 00 00000014
6 00 0B5 000 9 0000 1 0523505993 0000 1 00 000 0 036 1 039 00 00 00 00 00000009
6 00 0B5 000 9 0000 1 0523505993 0000 1 00 000 0 036 1 039 00 00 00 00 00000008
6 00 0B5 000 9 0018 1 0521906002 3096 1 00 000 0 038 1 039 00 00 00 00 00000215
6 00 0B5 000 9 0000 1 0523505993 0000 1 00 000 0 038 1 039 00 00 00 00 00000017
6 00 0B5 000 9 0000 1 0523505993 0000 1 00 000 0 038 1 039 00 00 00 00 00000009
6 00 0B5 000 9 0000 1 0523505993 0000 1 00 000 0 038 1 039 00 00 00 00 00000007
6 00 0B5 000 3 0000 1 0525006000 0000 1 00 000 0 038 1 039 00 00 00 00 00000010
6 00 0B5 000 3 0000 1 0520005950 0000 1 00 000 0 038 1 039 00 00 00 00 00000041
6 00 0B5 000 3 0000 1 0520005950 0000 1 00 000 0 038 1 039 00 00 00 00 00000026
6 00 0B5 000 3 0000 1 0520005950 0000 1 00 000 0 038 1 039 00 00 00 00 00000011
6 00 0B5 000 3 0000 1 0520005950 0000 1 00 000 0 038 1 039 00 00 00 00 00000014
6 00 0B5 000 3 0000 1 0520005950 0000 1 00 000 0 038 1 039 00 00 00 00 00000008
6 00 0B5 000 3 0000 1 0520005950 0000 1 00 000 0 038 1 039 00 00 00 00 00000007
6 00 0B5 000 3 0000 1 0520005950 0000 1 00 000 0 000 1 000 65 00 00 00 00000012
6 00 0B5 000 9 0000 1 0523505993 0000 4 01 000 0 000 1 033 37 00 00 00 00000013
6 00 0B5 000 9 0000 1 0523505993 0000 4 01 000 0 000 1 037 00 00 00 00 00000046
6 00 0B5 000 9 0000 1 0523505993 0000 4 01 012 2 000 1 036 00 00 00 00 00000157
6 00 0B5 000 9 0000 1 0523505993 0000 4 01 035 3 000 1 039 00 00 00 00 00000018
6 00 0B5 000 9 0000 1 0523505993 0000 3 77 503 0 000 1 039 65 00 00 00 00001909
6 00 0B5 000 9 0000 1 0523505993 0000 3 80 503 0 000 1 039 65 00 00 00 00000014
6 00 0B5 000 9 0000 1 0523505993 0000 3 81 503 0 000 7 000 65 00 00 00 00000016
6 00 0B5 000 9 0000 1 0523505993 0000 3 82 510 0 000 7 000 65 00 00 00 00000001
```

06	00	0B5	000	9	0000	1	0523505993	0000	3	34	510	0	000	7	000	00	00	00	00	00000040
06	00	0B5	000	9	0000	1	0523505993	0000	3	85	510	0	000	7	000	65	00	00	00	00000018
06	00	0B5	000	9	0000	1	0523505993	0000	3	86	512	0	000	7	000	00	00	00	00	00000001
06	00	0B5	000	9	0000	1	0523505993	0000	3	88	510	0	000	1	039	65	00	00	00	00000004
06	00	0B5	000	9	0000	1	0523505993	0000	3	90	510	0	000	1	039	65	00	00	00	00000000

PIT 5 ACTIVITY AREA DATA BASE

06	00	005	000	3	0086	1	0518506053	3098	2	00	000	0	060	1	039	00	09	00	00	00000046
06	00	005	000	3	0087	1	0519006067	3099	2	00	000	0	062	1	039	37	09	00	00	00000263
06	00	005	000	3	0090	1	0519306060	3099	2	00	000	0	082	1	039	00	09	00	00	00000263
06	00	005	000	3	0047	1	0520306067	3099	2	00	000	0	060	7	038	00	09	00	00	00000010
06	00	005	000	3	0048	1	0521406078	3099	2	00	000	0	060	7	038	35	09	00	00	00000015
06	00	005	000	3	0049	1	0521506087	3099	2	00	000	0	062	1	039	00	09	00	00	00001872
06	00	005	000	3	0044	1	0520406056	3099	2	00	000	0	062	1	039	00	09	00	00	00000730
06	00	005	000	3	0050	1	0522806078	3099	2	00	000	0	063	1	039	37	09	00	00	00000013
06	00	005	000	3	0046	1	0521406057	3099	2	00	000	0	082	1	039	00	09	00	00	00000807
06	00	005	000	3	0063	1	0525406036	3099	2	00	000	0	060	7	038	00	09	00	00	00000054
06	00	005	000	3	0067	1	0525706012	3099	2	00	000	0	062	1	039	00	09	00	00	00000109
06	00	005	000	3	0060	1	0527106030	3097	2	00	000	0	062	1	039	00	09	00	00	00000074
06	00	005	000	3	0058	1	0525506012	3099	2	00	000	0	065	1	039	00	09	00	00	00000101
06	00	005	000	3	0077	1	0528805954	3100	2	00	000	0	060	1	039	00	09	00	00	00000032
06	00	005	000	3	0075	1	0527505972	3100	2	00	000	0	062	1	039	00	09	00	00	00000735
06	00	005	000	3	0080	1	0528805953	3098	2	00	000	0	062	1	039	00	09	00	00	00000244
06	00	005	000	3	0074	1	0527205972	3100	2	00	000	0	063	7	038	00	09	00	00	00000045
06	00	005	000	3	0072	1	0525805997	3098	2	00	000	0	063	1	039	00	09	00	00	00000094
06	00	005	000	3	0078	1	0528405953	3100	2	00	000	0	064	1	039	00	09	00	00	00000332
06	00	005	000	3	0079	1	0528105952	3100	2	00	000	0	065	1	039	00	09	00	00	00000015
06	00	005	000	3	0076	1	0528105974	3099	2	00	000	0	082	7	038	00	09	00	00	00001233
06	00	005	000	3	0082	1	0519406030	3098	2	00	000	0	051	7	038	00	09	00	00	00000107
06	00	005	000	3	0041	1	0522605967	3100	2	00	000	0	062	1	039	00	09	00	00	00000113
06	00	005	000	3	0000	1	0515006000	0000	2	00	000	0	060	1	039	00	09	00	00	00000002
06	00	005	000	3	0000	1	0515006000	0000	2	00	000	0	060	1	039	00	09	00	00	00000002
06	00	005	000	3	0000	1	0515006000	0000	2	00	000	0	060	1	039	00	09	00	00	00000001
06	00	005	000	3	0000	1	0515006000	0000	2	00	000	0	060	1	039	00	09	00	00	00000001
06	00	005	000	3	0000	1	0515006000	0000	2	00	000	0	060	1	039	00	09	00	00	00000004
06	00	005	000	3	0000	1	0515006000	0000	2	00	000	0	060	1	039	00	09	00	00	00000004
06	00	005	000	3	0092	1	0519506045	3099	2	00	000	0	060	1	039	00	09	00	00	00000009
06	00	005	000	3	0000	1	0515006000	0000	2	00	000	0	062	1	039	00	09	00	00	00000012
06	00	005	000	3	0081	1	0518406044	3099	2	00	000	0	062	1	039	00	09	00	00	00000035
06	00	005	000	3	0083	1	0519706024	3098	2	00	000	0	062	1	039	00	09	00	00	00000027
06	00	005	000	3	0084	1	0519806017	3099	2	00	000	0	062	1	039	00	09	00	00	00000066
06	00	005	000	3	0000	1	0515006000	0000	2	00	000	0	063	1	039	00	09	00	00	00000002
06	00	005	000	3	0000	1	0515006000	0000	2	00	000	0	063	1	039	00	09	00	00	00000013
06	00	005	000	3	0085	1	0519506017	3099	2	00	000	0	065	7	038	00	09	00	00	00001054
06	00	005	000	3	0030	1	0523306038	3097	2	00	000	0	051	1	022	00	09	00	00	00000003
06	00	005	000	3	0025	1	0523006011	3096	2	00	000	0	090	1	039	33	09	00	00	00001185
06	00	005	000	3	0000	1	0520006000	0000	2	00	000	0	060	1	039	36	09	00	00	00000039
06	00	005	000	3	0000	1	0520006000	0000	2	00	000	0	060	1	039	35	09	00	00	00000016
06	00	005	000	3	0034	1	0523706012	3098	2	00	000	0	060	7	038	36	09	00	00	00000025
06	00	005	000	3	0000	1	0520006000	0000	2	00	000	0	060	1	039	00	09	00	00	00000005
06	00	005	000	3	0000	1	0520006000	0000	2	00	000	0	060	1	039	00	09	00	00	00000011
06	00	005	000	3	0000	1	0520006000	0000	2	00	000	0	060	1	039	00	09	00	00	00000003
06	00	005	000	3	0000	1	0520006000	0000	2	00	000	0	060	1	039	00	09	00	00	00000001
06	00	005	000	3	0000	1	0520006000	0000	2	00	000	0	060	1	039	00	09	00	00	00000002
06	00	005	000	3	0000	1	0520006000	0000	2	00	000	0	060	1	039	00	09	00	00	00000005
06	00	005	000	3	0000	1	0520006000	0000	2	00	000	0	060	1	039	00	09	00	00	00000001
06	00	005	000	3	0000	1	0520006000	0000	2	00	000	0	060	1	039	00	09	00	00	00000006
06	00	005	000	3	0000	1	0520006000	0000	2	00	000	0	060	1	039	00	09	00	00	00000004
06	00	005	000	3	0000	1	0520006000	0000	2	00	000	0	060	1	039	00	09	00	00	00000001
06	00	005	000	3	0000	1	0520006000	0000	2	00	000	0	060	1	039	00	09	00	00	00000003
06	00	005	000	3	0000	1	0520006000	0000	2	00	000	0	060	1	039	00	09	00	00	00000001
06	00	005	000	3	0000	1	0520006000	0000	2	00	000	0	060	1	039	00	09	00	00	00000002
06	00	005	000	3	0000	1	0520006000	0000	2	00	000	0	060	1	039	00	09	00	00	00000001
06	00	005	000	3	0070	1	0527305981	3098	2	00	000	0	061	1	039	37	09	00	00	00000060
06	00	005	000	3	0000	1	0520006000	0000	2	00	000	0	062	1	039	37	09	00	00	00000018
06	00	005	000	3	0000	1	0520006000	0000	2	00	000	0	062	1	039	00	09	00	00	00000014
06	00	005	000	3	0000	1	0520006000	0000	2	00	000	0	062	1	039	37	09	00	00	00000014
06	00	005	000	3	0000	1	0520006000	0000	2	00	000	0	062	1	039	00	09	00	00	00000017
06	00	005	000	3	0000	1	0520006000	0000	2	00	000	0	062	1	039	00	09	00	00	00000034
06	00	005	000	3	0000	1	0520006000	0000	2	00	000	0	062	1	039	37	09	00	00	00000110
06	00	005	000	3	0000	1	0520006000	0000	2	00	000	0	062	1	039	37	09	00	00	00000127
06	00	005	000	3	0000	1	0520006000	0000	2	00	000	0	062	1	039	37	09	00	00	00000085
06	00	005	000	3	0000	1	0520006000	0000	2	00	000	0	062	1	039	37	09	00	00	00000053
06	00	005	000	3	0000	1	0520006000	0000	2	00	000	0	062	1	039	37	09	00	00	00000018
06	00	005	000	3	0000	1	0520006000	0000	2	00	000	0	062	1	039	00	09	00	00	00000020
06	00	005	000	3	0000	1	0520006000	0000	2	00	000	0	062	1	039	00	09	00	00	00000040
06	00	005	000	3	0000	1	0520006000	0000	2	00	000	0	062	1	039	00	09	00	00	00000004
06	00	005	000	3	0000	1	0520006000	0000	2	00	000	0	062	1	039	00	09	00	00	00000002

```
 6  00  005  000  3  0000  1  0520006000  0000  2  00  000  0  062  1  039  00  09  00  00  00000004
 6  00  005  000  3  0000  1  0520006000  0000  2  00  000  0  062  1  039  00  09  00  00  00000005
 6  00  005  000  3  0000  1  0520006000  0000  2  00  000  0  062  1  039  00  09  00  00  00000008
 6  00  005  000  3  0000  1  0520006000  0000  2  00  000  0  062  1  039  00  09  00  00  00000003
 6  00  005  000  3  0021  1  0520606025  3099  2  00  000  0  062  1  039  00  09  00  00  00000475
 6  00  005  000  3  0035  1  0524006016  3097  2  00  000  0  062  1  039  00  09  00  00  00000121
 6  00  005  000  3  0032  1  0523206043  3098  2  00  000  0  062  1  039  00  09  00  00  00000091
 6  00  005  000  3  0031  1  0523506038  3098  2  00  000  0  062  1  039  00  09  00  00  00000033
 6  00  005  000  3  0024  1  0521406046  3098  2  00  000  0  062  1  039  00  09  00  00  00000993
 6  00  005  000  3  0000  1  0520006000  0000  2  00  000  0  063  1  039  00  09  00  00  00000002
 6  00  005  000  3  0000  1  0520006000  0000  2  00  000  0  063  1  039  00  09  00  00  00000001
 6  00  005  000  3  0000  1  0520006000  0000  2  00  000  0  063  1  039  00  09  00  00  00000004
 6  00  005  000  3  0000  1  0520006000  0000  2  00  000  0  063  1  039  00  09  00  00  00000002
 6  00  005  000  3  0000  1  0520006000  0000  2  00  000  0  063  1  039  00  09  00  00  00000016
06  00  005  000  3  0000  1  0520006000  0000  2  00  000  0  063  1  039  00  09  00  00  00000014
06  00  005  000  3  0000  1  0520006000  0000  2  00  000  0  063  1  039  00  09  00  00  00000009
06  00  005  000  3  0000  1  0520006000  0000  2  00  000  0  063  1  039  00  09  00  00  00000012
06  00  005  000  3  0000  1  0520006000  0000  2  00  000  0  063  1  039  00  09  00  00  00000001
06  00  005  000  3  0000  1  0520006000  0000  2  00  000  0  063  1  039  00  09  00  00  00000002
06  00  005  000  3  0000  1  0520006000  0000  2  00  000  0  063  1  039  00  09  00  00  00000003
06  00  005  000  3  0000  1  0520006000  0000  2  00  000  0  063  1  039  00  09  00  00  00000004
06  00  005  000  3  0000  1  0520006000  0000  2  00  000  0  063  1  039  00  09  00  00  00000002
06  00  005  000  3  0000  1  0520006000  0000  2  00  000  0  063  1  039  00  09  00  00  00030003
06  00  005  000  3  0000  1  0520006000  0000  2  00  000  0  065  1  039  00  09  00  00  00000007
06  00  005  000  3  0000  1  0520006000  0000  2  00  000  0  065  1  039  00  09  00  00  00000006
06  00  005  000  3  0000  1  0520006000  0000  2  00  000  0  065  1  039  00  09  00  00  00000009
06  00  005  000  3  0000  1  0520006000  0000  2  00  000  0  065  1  039  00  09  00  00  00000007
06  00  005  000  3  0000  1  0520006000  0000  2  00  000  0  065  1  039  00  09  00  00  00000005
06  00  005  000  3  0000  1  0520006000  0000  2  00  000  0  065  1  039  00  09  00  00  00000043
06  00  005  000  3  0000  1  0520006000  0000  2  00  000  0  065  1  039  00  09  00  00  00000017
06  00  005  000  3  0000  1  0520006000  0000  2  00  000  0  065  1  039  00  09  00  00  00000006
06  00  005  000  3  0000  1  0520006000  0000  2  00  000  0  065  1  039  00  09  00  00  00000027
06  00  005  000  3  0036  1  0524706016  3099  2  00  000  0  065  1  039  00  09  00  00  00000279
06  00  005  000  3  0033  1  0524106022  3099  2  00  000  0  065  1  039  00  09  00  00  00001160
06  00  005  000  3  0026  1  0523606023  3097  2  00  000  0  065  1  039  00  09  00  00  00001280
06  00  005  000  3  0073  1  0525506026  3097  2  00  000  0  057  7  038  00  09  00  00  00000526
06  00  005  000  9  0067  1  0000000000  0000  2  00  000  0  082  1  039  00  09  00  00  00000233
06  00  005  000  3  0051  1  0523506055  3100  1  00  000  0  003  1  003  00  00  00  00  00000030
06  00  005  000  3  0052  1  0524006074  3099  1  00  000  0  038  1  039  00  00  00  00  00000405
06  00  005  001  3  0053  1  0524806075  3099  1  00  000  0  038  1  039  00  09  00  00  00000281
06  00  005  000  3  0054  1  0524506072  3099  1  00  000  0  038  1  039  00  09  00  00  00000006
06  00  005  000  3  0055  1  0525106058  3098  1  00  000  0  015  1  001  00  00  00  00  00000582
06  00  005  000  3  0069  1  0524406022  3098  1  00  000  0  015  1  001  00  00  00  00  00000140
06  00  005  000  3  0068  1  0525406023  3097  1  00  000  0  038  1  039  00  00  00  00  00000051
06  00  005  000  3  0057  1  0520506013  3098  1  00  000  0  038  1  039  00  00  00  00  00000137
06  00  005  000  3  0065  1  0525106024  3098  1  00  000  0  015  1  001  00  00  00  00  00000041
06  00  005  000  3  0093  1  0526106952  3100  1  00  000  0  015  1  001  00  00  00  00  00000111
06  00  005  000  3  0040  1  0528805953  3100  1  00  000  0  060  1  039  37  09  00  00  00000043
06  00  005  000  3  0042  1  0522205976  3100  2  00  000  0  015  1  001  00  00  00  00  00000047
06  00  005  000  3  0039  1  0522905970  3099  1  00  000  0  015  1  001  00  00  00  00  00000563
06  00  005  000  3  0038  1  0522705969  3100  1  00  000  0  038  1  039  00  00  00  00  00000176
06  00  005  000  3  0000  1  0515006000  0000  1  00  000  0  015  1  001  00  00  00  00  00000018
06  00  005  000  3  0000  1  0520006000  0000  1  00  000  0  015  1  001  00  00  00  00  00000007
06  00  005  000  3  0000  1  0520006000  0000  1  00  000  0  015  1  001  00  00  00  00  00000025
06  00  005  000  3  0000  1  0520006000  0000  1  00  000  0  015  1  001  00  00  00  00  00000011
06  00  005  000  3  0000  1  0520006000  0000  1  00  000  0  015  1  001  00  00  00  00  00000019
06  00  005  000  3  0000  1  0520006000  0000  1  00  000  0  015  1  001  00  00  00  00  00000013
06  00  005  000  3  0000  1  0520006000  0000  1  00  000  0  015  1  001  00  00  00  00  00000007
06  00  005  000  3  0000  1  0520006000  0000  1  00  000  0  015  1  001  00  00  00  00  00000009
06  00  005  000  3  0029  1  0523106038  3097  1  00  000  0  015  1  001  00  00  00  00  00000070
06  00  005  000  3  0028  1  0523606033  3098  1  00  000  0  015  1  001  00  00  00  00  00000025
06  00  005  000  3  0000  1  0520006000  0000  1  00  000  0  036  1  039  00  00  00  00  00000015
06  00  005  000  3  0000  1  0520006000  0000  1  00  000  0  036  1  039  00  00  00  00  00000013
06  00  005  000  3  0000  1  0520006000  0000  1  00  000  0  036  1  039  00  00  00  00  00000017
06  00  005  000  3  0000  1  0520006000  0000  1  00  000  0  038  1  033  00  00  00  00  00000045
06  00  005  000  3  0043  1  0522805970  3099  4  01  046  2  000  1  039  00  00  00  00  00000018
06  00  005  000  3  0056  1  0527606026  3099  4  01  018  0  000  1  039  00  00  00  00  00000013
06  00  005  000  3  0064  1  0525506025  3098  4  01  017  0  000  1  036  00  00  00  00  00000006
06  00  005  000  3  0071  1  0525406023  3100  4  01  017  0  000  1  039  00  00  00  00  00000037
06  00  005  000  3  0062  1  0525806027  3098  4  01  014  1  000  1  034  00  00  00  00  00000092
06  00  005  000  3  0045  1  0520206060  3098  4  01  023  0  000  1  039  00  00  00  00  00000029
```

```
06 00 005 000 3 0091 1 0519706059 3098 4 01 022 1 000 1 041 00 00 00 00 00000628
06 00 005 000 3 0089 1 0519906076 3098 4 01 000 0 000 1 039 00 00 00 00 00000017
06 00 005 000 3 0000 1 0515006000 0000 3 77 507 0 000 1 039 65 00 00 00 00000308
06 00 005 000 3 0000 1 0520006050 0000 3 77 517 0 000 1 039 00 00 00 00 00000382
06 00 005 000 3 0000 1 0520006000 0000 3 77 507 0 000 1 039 65 00 00 00 00004387
06 00 005 000 3 0000 1 0520005950 0000 3 77 507 0 000 1 039 65 00 00 00 00000669
06 00 005 000 3 0000 1 0515006050 0000 3 77 507 0 000 1 039 65 00 00 00 0000004C
06 00 005 000 3 0000 1 0525006000 0000 3 77 507 0 000 1 039 65 00 00 00 0000071C
06 00 005 000 3 0000 1 0520006000 0000 3 77 507 0 000 1 039 65 00 00 00 00000694
06 00 005 000 3 0000 1 0530006000 0000 3 77 507 0 000 1 039 65 00 00 00 00000028
06 00 005 000 3 0000 1 0525006000 0000 3 80 507 0 000 1 039 65 00 00 00 00000014
06 00 005 000 3 0000 1 0520005950 0000 3 80 507 0 000 1 039 65 00 00 00 00000008
06 00 005 000 3 0000 1 0520006000 0000 3 80 507 0 000 1 039 65 00 00 00 00000033
06 00 005 000 3 0000 1 0520006050 0000 3 80 509 0 000 1 039 00 00 00 00 0000000C
06 00 005 000 3 0000 1 0515006000 0000 3 80 507 0 000 1 039 65 00 00 00 00000001
06 00 005 000 3 0000 1 0520006000 0000 3 80 509 0 000 1 039 65 00 00 00 00000008
06 00 005 000 3 0000 1 0515006000 0000 3 81 506 0 000 1 039 65 00 00 00 00000008
06 00 005 000 3 0000 1 0515006000 0000 3 81 506 0 000 1 039 65 00 00 00 0000000C
06 00 005 000 3 0000 1 0520005950 0000 3 81 503 0 000 7 009 65 00 00 00 00000023
06 00 005 000 3 0000 1 0520006050 0000 3 81 503 0 000 7 000 00 00 00 00 0000003C
06 00 005 000 3 0000 1 0525006000 0000 3 81 503 0 000 1 039 65 00 00 00 0000003C
06 00 005 000 3 0000 1 0520006000 0000 3 81 503 0 000 1 039 65 00 00 00 00000016
06 00 005 000 3 0000 1 0530006000 0000 3 81 503 0 000 1 039 65 00 00 00 0000000A
06 00 005 000 3 0000 1 0520006000 0000 3 82 503 0 000 1 039 65 00 00 00 00000000
06 00 005 000 3 0000 1 0525006000 0000 3 82 510 0 000 1 039 65 00 00 00 00000000
06 00 005 000 3 0000 1 0515006000 0000 3 82 510 0 000 1 039 65 00 00 00 0000000A
06 00 005 000 3 0000 1 0520005950 0000 3 82 510 0 000 1 039 65 00 00 00 00000002
06 00 005 000 3 0000 1 0520006000 0000 3 82 510 0 000 1 039 65 00 00 00 00000002
06 00 005 000 3 0000 1 0520006000 0000 3 82 510 0 000 1 039 65 00 00 00 0000000C
06 00 005 000 3 0000 1 0520005950 0000 3 84 510 0 000 7 000 65 00 00 00 00000092
06 00 005 000 3 0000 1 0525006000 0000 3 84 510 0 000 7 000 65 00 00 00 0000002C
06 00 005 000 3 0000 1 0520006000 0000 3 84 510 0 000 7 000 00 00 00 00 0000000C
06 00 005 000 3 0088 1 0519306075 3097 3 84 510 0 000 7 000 65 00 00 00 0000000C
06 00 005 000 3 0000 1 0520006050 0000 3 84 510 0 000 7 000 00 00 00 00 00000002
06 00 005 000 3 0000 1 0515006000 0000 3 84 510 0 000 7 000 00 00 00 00 0000000A
06 00 005 000 3 0000 1 0515006050 0000 3 84 510 0 000 7 000 00 00 00 00 0000000C
06 00 005 000 3 0000 1 0530006000 0000 3 84 510 0 000 1 039 65 00 00 00 0000000C
06 00 005 000 3 0000 1 0520006000 0000 3 84 510 0 000 1 039 65 00 00 00 00000026
06 00 005 000 3 0000 1 0520006000 0000 3 85 510 0 000 7 000 65 00 00 00 0000000C
06 00 005 000 3 0000 1 0520005950 0000 3 85 510 0 000 7 000 65 00 00 00 00000015
06 00 005 000 3 0000 1 0525006000 0000 3 85 510 0 000 7 000 65 00 00 00 0000000C
06 00 005 000 3 0000 1 0520006000 0000 3 85 510 0 000 1 039 65 00 00 00 00000051
06 00 005 000 3 0000 1 0520006050 0000 3 85 510 0 000 1 039 65 00 00 00 0000000C
06 00 005 000 3 0000 1 0515006000 0000 3 85 510 0 000 1 039 65 00 00 00 0000000C
06 00 005 000 3 0000 1 0530006000 0000 3 85 510 0 000 1 039 65 00 00 00 0000000C
06 00 005 000 3 0000 1 0525006000 0000 3 86 512 0 000 1 039 65 00 00 00 0000000C
06 00 005 000 3 0000 1 0520006000 0000 3 86 512 0 000 7 000 00 00 00 00 0000000C
06 00 005 000 3 0000 1 0520006050 0000 3 86 512 0 000 7 000 00 00 00 00 0000000C
06 00 005 000 3 0000 1 0515006000 0000 3 86 512 0 000 7 000 65 00 00 00 00000001
06 00 005 000 3 0000 1 0520005950 0000 3 86 512 0 000 1 039 65 00 00 00 0000000C
06 00 005 000 3 0000 1 0515006050 0000 3 86 512 0 000 1 039 65 00 00 00 0000000C
06 00 005 000 3 0000 1 0520006000 0000 3 88 510 0 000 1 039 65 00 00 00 0000000C
06 00 005 000 3 0000 1 0515006000 0000 3 90 510 0 000 1 039 65 00 00 00 0000000C
06 00 005 000 3 0000 1 0520006000 0000 3 91 507 0 000 1 039 65 00 00 00 0000000C
06 00 005 000 3 0000 1 0520006000 0000 3 91 507 0 000 1 039 65 00 00 00 0000000C
06 00 005 000 3 0000 1 0515006000 0000 3 91 507 0 000 1 039 65 00 00 00 0000000C
06 00 005 000 3 0000 1 0515006050 0000 3 91 507 0 000 1 039 65 00 00 00 0000000C
06 00 005 000 3 0000 1 0520006000 0000 3 91 507 0 000 1 039 65 00 00 00 00000002
```

Appendix L

PIT TEN DATA BASE

06	00	010	000	9	0093	1	0499906052	3095	2	00	000	0	060	1	039	00	09	00	00	00000002
06	00	010	000	9	0000	1	0500006050	0000	2	00	000	0	060	1	039	00	09	00	00	00000005
06	00	010	000	9	0000	1	0500006050	0000	2	00	000	0	060	1	039	00	09	00	00	00000001
06	00	010	000	9	0000	1	0500006050	0000	2	00	000	0	060	1	039	00	09	00	00	00000001
06	00	010	000	9	0000	1	0500006050	0000	2	00	000	0	060	1	039	37	09	00	00	00000003
06	00	010	000	9	0000	1	0500006050	0000	2	00	000	0	060	1	039	00	09	00	00	00000005
06	00	010	000	9	0000	1	0500006050	0000	2	00	000	0	060	1	039	00	09	00	00	00000005
06	00	010	000	9	0000	1	0500006050	0000	2	00	000	0	060	1	039	00	09	00	00	00000009
06	00	010	000	9	0000	1	0500006050	0000	2	00	000	0	060	1	039	00	09	00	00	00000009
06	00	010	000	9	0000	1	0500006050	0000	2	00	000	0	060	1	037	00	09	00	00	00000002
06	00	010	000	9	0000	1	0500006050	0000	2	00	000	0	060	1	037	00	09	00	00	00000001
06	00	010	000	9	0000	1	0500006050	0000	2	00	000	0	060	1	037	00	09	00	00	00000001
06	00	010	000	9	0000	1	0500006050	0000	2	00	000	0	060	1	000	00	09	00	00	00000002
06	00	010	000	9	0000	1	0500006050	0000	2	00	000	0	060	1	000	00	09	00	00	00000001
06	00	010	000	9	0000	1	0500006050	0000	2	00	000	0	060	1	000	00	09	00	00	00000003
06	00	010	000	9	0000	1	0500006050	0000	2	00	000	0	060	1	000	00	09	00	00	00000002
06	00	010	000	9	0000	1	0500006050	0000	2	00	000	0	060	1	000	00	09	00	00	00000002
06	00	010	000	9	0000	1	0500006050	0000	2	00	000	0	060	1	000	00	09	00	00	00000004
06	00	010	000	9	0000	1	0500006050	0000	2	00	000	0	060	1	000	00	09	00	00	00000002
06	00	010	000	9	0000	1	0500006050	0000	2	00	000	0	060	1	000	00	09	00	00	00000001
06	00	010	000	9	0000	1	0500006050	0000	2	00	000	0	060	1	000	00	09	00	00	00000001
06	00	010	000	9	0000	1	0500006050	0000	2	00	000	0	060	1	000	00	09	00	00	00000001
06	00	010	000	9	0000	1	0500006050	0000	2	00	000	0	060	1	000	00	09	00	00	00000001
06	00	010	000	9	0000	1	0500006050	0000	2	00	000	0	060	1	000	00	09	00	00	00000001
06	00	010	000	9	0000	1	0500006050	0000	2	00	000	0	060	1	000	00	09	00	00	00000001
06	00	010	000	9	0000	1	0500006050	0000	2	00	000	0	060	1	039	00	09	00	00	00000002
06	00	010	000	9	0000	1	0500006050	0000	2	00	000	0	060	1	039	00	09	00	00	00000002
06	00	010	000	9	0000	1	0500006050	0000	2	00	000	0	060	1	039	00	09	00	00	00000002
06	00	010	000	9	0081	1	0499706066	3098	2	00	000	0	062	1	039	00	09	00	00	00000018
06	00	010	000	9	0089	1	0499406068	3096	2	00	000	0	062	1	039	00	09	00	00	00000002
06	00	010	000	9	0067	1	0501306056	3095	2	00	000	0	062	1	039	00	09	00	00	00000255
06	00	010	000	9	0000	1	0500006050	0000	2	00	000	0	062	1	039	00	09	00	00	00000006
06	00	010	000	9	0063	1	0501206048	3095	2	00	000	0	062	1	039	00	09	00	00	00000073
06	00	010	000	9	0000	1	0500006050	0000	2	00	000	0	062	1	039	37	09	00	00	00000011
06	00	010	000	9	0000	1	0500006050	0000	2	00	000	0	062	1	039	37	09	00	00	00000002
06	00	010	000	9	0000	1	0500006050	0000	2	00	000	0	062	1	039	00	09	00	00	00000005
06	00	010	000	9	0000	1	0500006050	0000	2	00	000	0	062	1	039	00	09	00	00	00000002
06	00	010	000	9	0000	1	0500006050	0000	2	00	000	0	062	1	039	00	09	00	00	00000004
06	00	010	000	9	0000	1	0500006050	0000	2	00	000	0	062	1	039	00	09	00	00	00000004
06	00	010	000	9	0000	1	0500006050	0000	2	00	000	0	062	1	039	00	09	00	00	00000003
06	00	010	000	9	0000	1	0500006050	0000	2	00	000	0	062	1	039	00	09	00	00	00000002
06	00	010	000	9	0000	1	0500006050	0000	2	00	000	0	062	1	039	00	09	00	00	00000005
06	00	010	000	9	0000	1	0500006050	0000	2	00	000	0	062	1	039	00	09	00	00	00000014
06	00	010	000	9	0090	1	0499306069	3096	2	00	000	0	063	1	039	00	09	00	00	00000002
06	00	010	000	9	0000	1	0500006050	0000	2	00	000	0	063	1	039	00	09	00	00	00000005
06	00	010	000	9	0000	1	0500006050	0000	2	00	000	0	063	1	039	00	09	00	00	00000001
06	00	010	000	9	0000	1	0500006050	0000	2	00	000	0	063	1	039	00	09	00	00	00000001
06	00	010	000	9	0000	1	0500006050	0000	2	00	000	0	063	1	039	00	09	00	00	00000006
06	00	010	000	9	0079	1	0499206057	3096	2	00	000	0	065	1	039	00	09	00	00	00000539
06	00	010	000	9	0091	1	0499606050	3097	2	00	000	0	065	1	039	00	09	00	00	00000005
06	00	010	000	9	0070	1	0501906066	3096	2	00	000	0	065	1	039	00	09	00	00	00000011
06	00	010	000	9	0095	1	0500606050	3096	2	00	000	0	065	1	039	00	09	00	00	00000521
06	00	010	000	9	0064	1	0502006049	3098	2	00	000	0	065	1	039	00	09	00	00	00002486
06	00	010	000	9	0000	1	0500006050	0000	2	00	000	0	065	1	039	00	09	00	00	00000001
06	00	010	000	9	0000	1	0500006050	0000	2	00	000	0	065	1	039	00	09	00	00	00000006
06	00	010	000	9	0000	1	0500006050	0000	2	00	000	0	065	1	039	00	09	00	00	00000003
06	00	010	000	9	0000	1	0500006050	0000	2	00	000	0	065	1	039	00	09	00	00	00000002
06	00	010	000	9	0000	1	0500006050	0000	2	00	000	0	065	1	039	00	09	00	00	00000003
06	00	010	000	9	0000	1	0500006050	0000	2	00	000	0	065	1	039	00	09	00	00	00000004
06	00	010	000	9	0000	1	0500006050	0000	2	00	000	0	082	1	039	00	09	00	00	00000009
06	00	010	000	9	0000	1	0500006050	0000	2	00	000	0	082	1	039	00	09	00	00	00000040
06	00	010	000	9	0000	1	0500006050	0000	2	00	000	0	082	1	039	00	09	00	00	00000042
06	00	010	000	9	0096	1	0501806050	3098	1	00	000	0	062	1	039	00	09	00	00	00000111
06	00	010	000	9	0083	1	0499406071	3095	1	00	000	0	082	1	039	00	09	00	00	00000286
06	00	010	000	9	0082	1	0499006062	3097	1	00	000	0	015	1	001	00	09	00	00	00000056
06	00	010	000	9	0088	1	0501906060	3097	1	00	000	0	015	1	001	00	00	00	00	00000018
06	00	010	000	9	0092	1	0499406049	3098	1	00	000	0	015	1	001	00	00	00	00	00000161
06	00	010	000	9	0000	1	0500006050	0000	1	00	000	0	015	1	001	00	00	00	00	00000024
06	00	010	000	9	0000	1	0500006050	0000	1	00	000	0	015	1	001	00	00	00	00	00000022
06	00	010	000	9	0000	1	0500006050	0000	1	00	000	0	038	1	039	00	09	00	00	00000009
06	00	010	000	9	0000	1	0500006050	0000	1	00	000	0	038	1	039	00	00	00	00	00000015
06	00	010	000	9	0000	1	0500006050	0000	3	77	507	0	000	1	039	65	00	00	00	00000061
06	00	010	000	9	0000	1	0500006050	0000	3	81	503	0	000	1	039	65	00	00	00	00000001
06	00	010	000	9	0000	1	0500006050	0000	3	82	510	0	000	7	000	65	00	00	00	00000000
06	00	010	000	9	0000	1	0500006050	0000	3	84	510	0	000	7	000	00	00	00	00	00000000

```
06 00 010 000 9 0000 1 0500006050 0000 3 85 510 0 000 7 000 65 00 00 00 00000000
06 00 010 000 9 0000 1 0500006050 0000 3 91 507 0 000 1 039 65 00 00 00 00000000
         PIT 10 ACTIVITY AREA  DATA BASE
06 00 010 000 9 0000 1 0505006050 0000 2 00 000 0 060 1 039 00 09 00 00 00000005
06 00 010 000 3 0077 1 0498806019 3098 2 00 000 0 060 1 039 00 09 00 00 00000007
06 00 010 000 3 0023 1 0495506012 3099 2 00 000 0 060 1 039 00 09 00 00 00000021
06 00 010 000 3 0018 1 0498406040 3100 2 00 000 0 060 1 039 00 09 00 00 00000001
06 00 010 000 3 0014 1 0499106008 3100 2 00 000 0 060 1 039 00 09 00 00 00000004
06 00 010 000 3 0101 1 0504506040 3099 2 00 000 0 060 1 039 00 09 00 00 00000010
06 00 010 000 3 0099 1 0501706032 3100 2 00 000 0 060 1 039 37 09 00 00 00000001
06 00 010 000 3 0098 1 0501606032 3100 2 00 000 0 060 1 039 00 09 00 00 00000001
06 00 010 000 3 0050 1 0503206030 3098 2 00 000 0 060 1 039 00 09 00 00 00000016
06 00 010 000 3 0049 1 0502306028 3098 2 00 000 0 060 1 039 00 09 00 00 00000006
06 00 010 000 3 0044 1 0504206023 3098 2 00 000 0 060 1 039 00 09 00 00 00000009
06 00 010 000 3 0043 1 0502306021 3099 2 00 000 0 060 1 039 00 09 00 00 00000009
06 00 010 000 9 0004 1 0501806048 3099 2 00 000 0 060 1 039 00 09 00 00 00000017
06 00 010 000 3 0010 1 0506506015 3099 2 00 000 0 060 1 039 00 09 00 00 00000130
06 00 010 000 3 0080 1 0497606054 3098 2 00 000 0 060 1 039 00 09 00 00 00000001
06 00 010 000 3 0000 1 0500006050 0000 2 00 000 0 060 1 039 35 09 00 00 00000006
06 00 010 000 3 0071 1 0502706067 3098 2 00 000 0 060 1 039 00 09 00 00 00000006
06 00 010 000 3 0000 1 0505006050 0000 2 00 000 0 060 1 039 00 09 00 00 00000007
06 00 010 000 3 0000 1 0505006050 0000 2 00 000 0 060 1 039 37 09 00 00 00000005
06 00 010 000 3 0000 1 0505006050 0000 2 00 000 0 060 1 039 00 09 00 00 00000002
06 00 010 000 3 0032 1 0508706091 3098 2 00 000 0 060 1 039 00 09 00 00 00000014
06 00 010 000 3 0025 1 0506406052 3099 2 00 000 0 060 1 039 00 09 00 00 00000131
06 00 010 000 3 0100 1 0503006005 3100 2 00 000 0 062 1 039 00 09 00 00 00000027
06 00 010 000 3 0060 1 0502606042 3098 2 00 000 0 062 1 039 00 09 00 00 00000011
06 00 010 000 3 0059 1 0504606040 3098 2 00 000 0 062 1 039 00 09 00 00 00000009
06 00 010 000 3 0054 1 0503306035 3098 2 00 000 0 062 1 039 00 09 00 00 00000073
06 00 010 000 3 0046 1 0502506026 3099 2 00 000 0 062 1 039 00 09 00 00 00000044
06 00 010 000 3 0040 1 0503706015 3098 2 00 000 0 062 1 039 37 09 00 00 00000186
06 00 010 000 3 0036 1 0504806008 3098 2 00 000 0 062 1 039 00 09 00 00 00000127
06 00 010 000 3 0002 1 0501506035 3099 2 00 000 0 062 1 039 00 09 00 00 00000193
06 00 010 000 3 0000 1 0505006050 0000 2 00 000 0 062 1 039 00 09 00 00 00000006
06 00 010 000 3 0015 1 0499406008 3100 2 00 000 0 063 1 039 00 09 00 00 00000072
06 00 010 000 3 0061 1 0504106041 3098 2 00 000 0 063 1 039 00 09 00 00 00000085
06 00 010 000 3 0052 1 0501006033 3098 2 00 000 0 063 1 039 00 09 00 00 00000007
06 00 010 000 3 0075 1 0504706061 3098 2 00 000 0 063 1 039 00 09 00 00 00000022
06 00 010 000 3 0042 1 0504606018 3099 2 00 000 0 065 1 039 00 09 00 00 00000006
06 00 010 000 3 0008 1 0505006027 3099 2 00 000 0 065 1 039 00 09 00 00 00000447
06 00 010 000 3 0012 1 0500206031 3098 2 00 000 0 065 1 039 00 09 00 00 00000001
06 00 010 000 3 0000 1 0500006050 0000 2 00 000 0 065 1 039 00 09 00 00 00000015
06 00 010 000 3 0076 1 0504706067 3099 2 00 000 0 065 1 039 00 09 00 00 00000045
06 00 010 000 3 0074 1 0503906062 3098 2 00 000 0 065 1 039 00 09 00 00 00000112
06 00 010 000 3 0030 1 0505106067 3099 2 00 000 0 065 1 039 00 09 00 00 00000034
06 00 010 000 3 0024 1 0495406019 3100 2 00 000 0 082 1 039 00 09 00 00 00000014
06 00 010 000 3 0017 1 0499006031 3098 2 00 000 0 082 1 039 00 09 00 00 00000034
06 00 010 000 3 0053 1 0501406034 3099 2 00 000 0 082 1 039 00 09 00 00 00000226
06 00 010 000 3 0035 1 0503206009 3100 2 00 000 0 082 1 039 00 09 00 00 00000044
06 00 010 000 3 0007 1 0503106024 3100 2 00 000 0 082 1 039 00 09 00 00 00000012
06 00 010 000 3 0004 1 0497506055 3099 2 00 000 0 082 1 039 00 09 00 00 00000021
06 00 010 000 3 0027 1 0498806063 3098 2 00 000 0 082 1 039 37 09 00 00 00001203
06 00 010 000 3 0008 1 0497506090 3100 2 00 000 0 048 1 039 37 09 00 00 00002460
06 00 010 000 3 0094 1 0500006098 3098 2 00 000 0 050 1 018 00 09 00 00 00000116
06 00 010 000 3 0097 1 0501406032 3100 2 00 000 0 051 1 020 00 09 00 00 00000001
06 00 010 000 3 0000 1 0505006050 0000 2 00 000 0 059 1 039 00 09 00 00 00000031
06 00 010 000 3 0000 1 0500006050 0000 2 00 000 0 099 7 038 00 09 00 00 00000010
06 00 010 000 3 0000 1 0505006050 0000 2 00 000 0 099 7 038 00 09 00 00 00000005
06 00 010 000 3 0058 1 0502006040 3098 2 00 000 0 099 1 039 00 09 00 00 00000041
06 00 010 000 3 0055 1 0502406038 3098 2 00 000 0 099 1 039 00 09 00 00 00000020
06 00 010 000 3 0034 1 0501706005 3099 2 00 000 0 099 7 038 00 09 00 00 00000001
06 00 010 000 3 0086 1 0497506055 3099 1 00 000 0 060 1 039 00 09 00 00 00000014
06 00 010 000 3 0039 1 0502406014 3099 1 00 000 0 003 1 002 00 00 00 03 00001365
06 00 010 000 3 0006 1 0502906026 3100 1 00 000 0 003 1 002 00 00 00 00 00000240
06 00 010 000 3 0048 1 0502906028 3099 1 00 000 0 003 1 002 00 00 00 00 00000000
06 00 010 000 3 0051 1 0502506031 3100 1 00 000 0 003 1 002 00 00 00 02 00000500
06 00 010 000 3 0026 1 0509006056 3099 1 00 000 0 003 1 002 00 00 00 00 00000028
06 00 010 000 3 0022 1 0496306025 3100 1 00 000 0 015 1 001 00 00 00 00 00000003
06 00 010 000 3 0104 1 0498606049 3100 1 00 000 0 015 1 001 65 00 00 00 00000056
06 00 010 000 3 0047 1 0504606017 3098 1 00 000 0 015 1 001 00 00 00 00 00000015
06 00 010 000 3 0038 1 0502406014 3099 1 00 000 0 015 1 001 00 00 00 00 00000150
06 00 010 000 3 0037 1 0502006015 3099 1 00 000 0 015 1 001 00 00 00 00 00000002
06 00 010 000 3 0003 1 0501606034 3099 1 00 000 0 015 1 001 00 00 00 00 00000118
06 00 010 000 3 0001 1 0500906032 3099 1 00 000 0 015 1 001 00 00 00 00 0000051E
06 00 010 000 3 0103 1 0504706020 3090 1 00 000 0 015 1 001 00 00 00 00 00000020
06 00 010 000 3 0102 1 0504706017 3100 1 00 000 0 015 1 001 00 00 00 00 00000072
```

```
06  00  010  000  3  0066  1  0504406053  3098  1  00  000  0  015  1  001  00  00  00  00  00000048
06  00  010  000  3  0072  1  0503306063  3098  1  00  000  0  015  1  001  00  00  00  00  00000015
06  00  010  000  3  0073  1  0503706062  3099  1  00  000  0  015  1  001  00  00  00  00  00000005
06  00  010  000  3  0087  1  0498506064  3099  1  00  000  0  037  1  001  00  09  00  00  00000067
06  00  010  000  3  0029  1  0505406064  3097  1  00  000  0  037  1  001  00  00  00  00  00000092
06  00  010  000  3  0028  1  0507506065  3097  1  00  000  0  037  1  001  00  00  00  00  00000014
06  00  010  000  3  0057  1  0503706038  3098  1  00  000  0  038  1  039  00  00  00  00  00000665
06  00  010  000  3  0011  1  0505306015  3098  1  00  000  0  038  1  039  00  00  00  00  00000085
06  00  010  000  3  0085  1  0497406058  3098  1  00  000  0  038  1  039  00  00  00  00  00000011
06  00  010  000  3  0065  1  0504706052  3098  1  00  000  0  038  1  039  00  00  00  00  00000154
06  00  010  000  3  0031  1  0505706072  3099  1  00  000  0  038  1  039  00  00  00  00  00000031
06  00  010  000  3  0013  1  0499306007  3100  4  01  000  0  000  1  033  00  00  00  00  00000039
06  00  010  000  3  0016  1  0498806030  3099  4  01  000  0  000  1  033  00  00  00  00  00000043
06  00  010  000  3  0078  1  0498406045  3098  4  01  001  1  000  1  035  00  00  00  00  00000036
06  00  010  000  3  0000  1  0500006000  0000  3  77  507  0  000  1  039  65  00  00  00  00000251
06  00  010  000  3  0000  1  0500006050  0000  3  77  507  0  000  1  039  65  00  00  00  00000110
06  00  010  000  3  0000  1  0500006050  0000  3  81  506  0  000  1  039  65  00  00  00  00000000
06  00  010  000  3  0000  1  0500006050  0000  3  82  510  0  000  7  000  65  00  00  00  00000000
06  00  010  000  3  0000  1  0500006000  0000  3  83  510  0  000  7  000  65  00  00  00  00000001
06  00  010  000  3  0000  1  0500006050  0000  3  84  510  0  000  7  000  00  00  00  00  00000001
06  00  010  000  3  0000  1  0500006050  0000  3  85  510  0  000  7  000  65  00  00  00  00000000
06  00  010  000  3  0000  1  0500006050  0000  3  86  512  0  000  7  000  00  00  00  00  00000001
06  00  010  000  3  0000  1  0500006050  0000  3  86  512  0  000  7  000  00  00  00  00  00000000
06  00  010  000  3  0000  1  0500006000  0000  3  91  507  0  000  1  039  65  00  00  00  00000004
06  00  010  000  3  0000  1  0500006050  0000  3  91  507  0  000  1  039  65  00  00  00  00000000
06  00  010  000  3  0000  1  0500006000  0000  3  92  510  0  000  7  000  65  00  00  00  00000000
```

Appendix M

```
        EXCAVATION SURFACE OUTSIDE OF FEATURES  DATA BASE
06  00  000  000  3  0000  1  0560005850  0000  2  00  000  0  050  7  038  00  09  00  00  00000088
06  00  000  000  3  0000  1  0560005850  0000  2  00  000  0  082  1  039  00  09  00  00  00000263
06  00  000  000  3  0000  1  0560005850  0000  2  00  000  0  062  1  039  00  09  00  00  00000015
06  00  000  000  3  0000  1  0555005700  0000  2  00  000  0  062  1  039  00  09  00  00  00000240
06  00  000  000  3  0000  1  0555005700  0000  2  00  000  0  060  1  039  38  09  00  00  00000035
06  00  000  000  3  0000  1  0555005700  0000  2  00  000  0  060  1  039  00  09  00  00  00000002
06  00  000  000  3  0000  1  0555006000  0000  2  00  000  0  082  1  039  00  09  00  00  00001375
06  00  000  000  3  0000  1  0555006000  0000  2  00  000  0  060  1  039  00  09  00  00  00000002
06  00  000  000  3  0000  1  0550005750  0000  2  00  000  0  082  1  039  00  09  00  00  00000183
06  00  000  000  3  0000  1  0550005750  0000  2  00  000  0  060  1  039  00  09  00  00  00000023
06  00  000  000  3  0000  1  0550005750  0000  2  00  000  0  065  1  039  00  09  00  00  00000919
06  00  000  000  3  0000  1  0550005750  0000  2  00  000  0  065  1  039  00  09  00  00  00000301
06  00  000  000  3  0000  1  0550005750  0000  2  00  000  0  065  1  039  00  09  00  00  00000155
06  00  000  000  3  0000  1  0550005750  0000  2  00  000  0  062  1  039  00  09  00  00  00000058
06  00  000  000  3  0000  1  0550005850  0000  2  00  000  0  082  1  039  00  09  00  00  00000087
06  00  000  000  3  0000  1  0550005850  0000  2  00  000  0  062  1  039  00  09  00  00  00000077
06  00  000  000  3  0000  1  0550005900  0000  5  00  000  0  105  7  038  00  09  00  00  00000139
06  00  000  000  3  0000  1  0550005900  0000  2  00  000  0  015  1  001  00  00  00  00  00000036
06  00  000  000  3  0000  1  0550005900  0000  2  00  000  0  060  1  039  38  09  00  00  00000005
06  00  000  000  3  0000  1  0550005900  0000  2  00  000  0  065  1  039  00  09  00  00  00000012
06  00  000  000  3  0000  1  0550005900  0000  2  00  000  0  060  1  039  36  09  00  00  00000047
06  00  000  000  3  0000  1  0550005900  0000  2  00  000  0  062  1  039  00  09  00  00  00000207
06  00  000  000  3  0000  1  0550005900  0000  2  00  000  0  062  1  039  00  09  00  00  00000157
06  00  000  000  3  0000  1  0550005900  0000  2  00  000  0  062  1  039  00  09  00  00  00000072
06  00  000  000  3  0000  1  0550005900  0000  2  00  000  0  062  1  039  00  09  00  00  00000026
06  00  000  000  3  0000  1  0550005900  0000  2  00  000  0  062  1  039  00  09  00  00  00000035
06  00  000  000  3  0000  1  0550005950  0000  2  00  000  0  060  1  039  38  09  00  00  00000004
06  00  000  000  3  0000  1  0550005950  0000  2  00  000  0  060  1  039  00  09  00  00  00000068
06  00  000  000  3  0000  1  0550005950  0000  2  00  000  0  060  1  039  00  09  00  00  00000005
06  00  000  000  3  0000  1  0550005950  0000  2  00  000  0  060  1  039  00  09  00  00  00000005
06  00  000  000  3  0000  1  0550006000  0000  1  00  000  0  037  1  001  00  00  00  00  00000050
06  00  000  000  3  0000  1  0545005550  0000  2  00  000  0  059  7  038  00  09  00  00  00000107
06  00  000  000  3  0000  1  0545005600  0000  2  00  000  0  061  1  039  00  09  00  00  00002414
06  00  000  000  3  0000  1  0545005600  0000  1  00  000  0  015  1  001  00  00  00  00  00000058
06  00  000  000  3  0000  1  0545005650  0000  1  00  000  0  015  1  001  00  00  00  00  00000572
06  00  000  000  3  0000  1  0545005650  0000  1  00  000  0  015  1  001  00  00  00  00  00000101
06  00  000  000  3  0000  1  0545005650  0000  2  00  000  0  062  1  039  00   9  00  00  00001144
06  00  000  000  3  0000  1  0545005650  0000  2  00  000  0  062  1  039  00   9  00  00  00000162
06  00  000  000  3  0000  1  0545005650  0000  2  00  000  0  060  1  039  38  09  00  00  00000046
06  00  000  000  3  0000  1  0545005650  0000  2  00  000  0  050  1  027  00  09  00  00  00000025
06  00  000  000  3  0000  1  0545005650  0000  2  00  000  0  082  1  039  00  09  00  00  00000665
06  00  000  000  3  0000  1  0545005700  0000  2  00  000  0  060  1  039  00  09  00  00  00000016
06  00  000  000  3  0000  1  0545005700  0000  2  00  000  0  082  1  039  00  09  00  00  00000307
06  00  000  000  3  0000  1  0545005850  0000  1  00  000  0  015  1  001  00  00  00  00  00000062
06  00  000  000  3  0000  1  0545005850  0000  2  00  000  0  064  1  039  00  09  00  00  00000715
06  00  000  000  3  0000  1  0545005850  0000  2  00  000  0  082  1  039  00  09  00  00  00000013
06  00  000  000  3  0000  1  0545005850  0000  2  00  000  0  062  1  039  00  09  00  00  00000040
06  00  000  000  3  0000  1  0545005850  0000  2  00  000  0  062  1  039  00  09  00  00  00000077
06  00  000  000  3  0000  1  0545005850  0000  2  00  000  0  062  1  039  00  09  00  00  00000412
06  00  000  000  3  0000  1  0545005850  0000  2  00  000  0  082  1  039  00  09  00  00  00000066
06  00  000  000  3  0000  1  0545005850  0000  1  00  000  0  038  1  039  00  00  00  00  00000088
06  00  000  000  3  0000  1  0545005900  0000  1  00  000  0  038  1  039  00  00  00  00  00000041
06  00  000  000  3  0000  1  0545005900  0000  2  00  000  0  065  1  039  00  09  00  00  00000362
06  00  000  000  3  0000  1  0545005900  0000  2  00  000  0  075  1  039  00  09  00  00  00005318
06  00  000  000  3  0000  1  0545005850  0000  2  00  000  0  082  1  039  00  09  00  00  00000233
06  00  000  000  3  0000  1  0545005850  0000  2  00  000  0  082  1  039  00  09  00  00  00000232
06  00  000  000  3  0000  1  0545005850  0000  2  00  000  0  065  1  039  00  09  00  00  00000123
06  00  000  000  3  0000  1  0545005950  0000  1  00  000  0  037  1  001  00  00  00  00  00000003
06  00  000  000  3  0000  1  0545005950  0000  1  00  000  0  015  1  001  00  00  00  00  00000094
06  00  000  000  3  0000  1  0545005950  0000  2  00  000  0  060  1  039  00  00  00  00  00000018
06  00  000  000  3  0000  1  0545005950  0000  2  00  000  0  060  1  039  00  00  00  00  00000028
06  00  000  000  3  0000  1  0545005950  0000  2  00  000  0  062  1  039  00  00  00  00  00000193
06  00  000  000  3  0000  1  0545005950  0000  2  00  000  0  063  1  039  00  00  00  00  00000020
06  00  000  000  3  0000  1  0540005550  0000  2  00  000  0  060  1  039  00  09  00  00  00000030
06  00  000  000  3  0000  1  0540005650  0000  1  00  000  0  015  1  001  00  00  00  00  00000257
06  00  000  000  3  0000  1  0540005650  0000  1  00  000  0  015  1  001  00  09  00  00  00000267
06  00  000  000  3  0000  1  0540005650  0000  2  00  000  0  082  1  039  00  09  00  00  00000807
06  00  000  000  3  0000  1  0540005650  0000  2  00  000  0  060  1  039  00  09  00  00  00000016
06  00  000  000  3  0000  1  0540005650  0000  2  00  000  0  062  1  039  00  09  00  00  00000010
06  00  000  000  3  0000  1  0540005750  0000  2  00  000  0  082  1  039  00  09  00  00  00000080
06  00  000  000  3  0000  1  0540005750  0000  2  00  000  0  062  1  039  00  09  00  00  00000557
06  00  000  000  3  0000  1  0540005750  0000  2  00  000  0  062  1  039  00  09  00  00  00000701
06  00  000  000  3  0000  1  0540005800  0000  2  00  000  0  075  1  039  00  09  00  00  00003749
06  00  000  000  3  0000  1  0540005800  0000  2  00  000  0  060  1  039  38  09  00  00  00000013
```

```
06 00 000 000 3 0000 1 0540005800 0000 2 00 000 0 060 1 039 00 09 00 00 00000005
06 00 000 000 3 0000 1 0540005800 0000 2 00 000 0 062 1 039 00 09 00 00 00000122
06 00 000 000 3 0000 1 0540005800 0000 2 00 000 0 060 1 039 38 09 00 00 00000025
06 00 000 000 3 0000 1 0540005800 0000 2 00 000 0 062 1 039 00 09 00 00 0000012C
06 00 000 000 3 0000 1 0540005800 0000 2 00 000 0 062 1 039 00 09 00 00 00000018
06 00 000 000 3 0000 1 0540005900 0000 2 00 000 0 060 1 039 00 09 00 00 00000001
06 00 000 000 3 0000 1 0540005900 0000 2 00 000 0 060 1 039 00 09 00 00 00000001
06 00 000 000 3 0000 1 0540005950 0000 1 00 000 0 015 1 001 00 00 00 00 00000057
06 00 000 000 3 0000 1 0540005950 0000 2 00 000 0 060 1 039 36 09 00 00 00000008
06 00 000 000 3 0000 1 0540006000 0000 2 00 000 0 063 1 039 00 09 00 00 0000005C
06 00 000 000 3 0000 1 0540006000 0000 2 00 000 0 060 1 039 00 09 00 00 00000002
06 00 000 000 3 0000 1 0535005550 0000 2 00 000 0 060 1 039 00 09 00 00 00000002
06 00 000 000 3 0000 1 0535005600 0000 2 00 000 0 050 7 038 00 09 00 00 00000076
06 00 000 000 3 0000 1 0535005600 0000 1 00 000 0 015 1 001 00 09 00 00 00000069
06 00 000 000 3 0000 1 0535005700 0000 2 00 000 0 060 1 039 00 09 00 00 00000007
06 00 000 000 3 0000 1 0535005700 0000 2 00 000 0 062 1 039 00 09 00 00 00000199
06 00 000 000 3 0000 1 0535005750 0000 2 00 000 0 060 1 039 00 09 00 00 00000018
06 00 000 000 3 0000 1 0535005750 0000 2 00 000 0 060 1 039 00 09 00 00 00000025
06 00 000 000 3 0000 1 0535005950 0000 1 00 000 0 015 1 001 00 09 00 00 00000037
06 00 000 000 3 0000 1 0535005950 0000 2 00 000 0 062 1 039 00 09 00 00 00000064
06 00 000 000 3 0000 1 0535006000 0000 1 00 000 0 015 1 001 00 09 00 00 00000031
06 00 000 000 3 0000 1 0535006100 0000 1 00 000 0 015 1 001 00 00 00 00 00000020
06 00 000 000 3 0000 1 0535006250 0000 2 00 000 0 060 1 039 00 09 00 00 00000001
06 00 000 000 3 0000 1 0530005500 0000 2 00 000 0 060 1 039 00 09 00 00 00000002
06 00 000 000 3 0000 1 0530005650 0000 2 00 000 0 060 1 039 00 09 00 00 00000044
06 00 000 000 3 0000 1 0530005650 0000 2 00 000 0 060 1 039 00 09 00 00 00000007
06 00 000 000 3 0000 1 0530005750 0000 2 00 000 0 060 1 039 00 09 00 00 00000004
06 00 000 000 3 0000 1 0530005750 0000 2 00 000 0 063 1 039 00 09 00 00 00000013
06 00 000 000 3 0000 1 0530005950 0000 1 00 000 0 037 1 001 00 00 00 00 00000051
06 00 000 000 3 0000 1 0530005950 0000 2 00 000 0 099 7 038 00 09 00 00 00000029
06 00 000 000 3 0000 1 0530006050 0000 2 00 000 0 050 7 038 00 09 00 00 00000031
06 00 000 000 3 0000 1 0530006200 0000 2 00 000 0 060 1 039 00 09 00 00 00000041
06 00 000 000 3 0000 1 0530006200 0000 2 00 000 0 060 1 039 38 09 00 00 00000018
06 00 000 000 3 0000 1 0525005700 0000 1 00 000 0 015 1 001 00 00 00 00 00000010
06 00 000 000 3 0000 1 0525005700 0000 1 00 000 0 015 1 001 00 00 00 00 00000052
06 00 000 000 3 0000 1 0525005700 0000 1 00 000 0 015 1 001 00 00 00 00 0000003C
06 00 000 000 3 0000 1 0525005700 0000 1 00 000 0 015 1 001 00 00 00 00 00000094
06 00 000 000 3 0000 1 0525005700 0000 2 00 000 0 062 1 039 00 09 00 00 00000102
06 00 000 000 3 0000 1 0525005700 0000 2 00 000 0 062 1 039 00 09 00 00 00000575
06 00 000 000 3 0000 1 0525005700 0000 2 00 000 0 062 1 039 00 09 00 00 00000099
06 00 000 000 3 0000 1 0525005700 0000 2 00 000 0 060 1 039 00 09 00 00 000000C5
06 00 000 000 3 0000 1 0525005700 0000 2 00 000 0 060 1 039 00 09 00 00 00000006
06 00 000 000 3 0000 1 0525005700 0000 2 00 000 0 060 1 039 00 09 00 00 00000009
06 00 000 000 3 0000 1 0525005700 0000 2 00 000 0 060 1 039 00 09 00 00 00000003
06 00 000 000 3 0000 1 0500005900 0000 1 00 000 0 015 1 001 00 00 00 00 00000008
06 00 000 000 3 0000 1 0525005850 0000 2 00 000 0 061 1 039 00 09 00 00 0000069C
06 00 000 000 3 0000 1 0525005850 0000 1 00 000 0 038 1 039 00 00 00 00 00000013
06 00 000 000 3 0000 1 0525005900 0000 1 00 000 0 038 1 039 00 00 00 00 00000013
06 00 000 000 3 0000 1 0525005900 0000 2 00 000 0 082 1 039 00 00 00 00 00000097
06 00 000 000 3 0000 1 0525006150 0000 2 00 000 0 062 1 039 00 00 00 00 00000937
06 00 000 000 3 0000 1 0520005450 0000 1 00 000 0 015 1 039 00 00 00 00 00000157
06 00 000 000 3 0000 1 0520005650 0000 1 00 000 0 015 1 001 00 00 00 00 00000039
06 00 000 000 3 0000 1 0520005650 0000 1 00 000 0 038 1 039 00 00 00 00 00000033
06 00 000 000 3 0000 1 0520005650 0000 2 00 000 0 062 1 039 00 09 00 00 0000C306
06 00 000 000 3 0000 1 0520005700 0000 2 00 000 0 062 1 039 00 09 00 00 00000255
06 00 000 000 3 0000 1 0520005700 0000 2 00 000 0 060 1 039 38 09 00 00 0000009C
06 00 000 000 3 0000 1 0530005950 0000 2 00 000 0 060 1 039 00 09 00 00 00000014
06 00 000 000 3 0000 1 0520006150 0000 2 00 000 0 062 1 039 00 09 00 00 00000019
06 00 000 000 3 0000 1 0515005500 0000 1 00 000 0 015 1 001 00 00 00 00 00003223
06 00 000 000 3 0000 1 0515005600 0000 1 00 000 0 082 1 039 37 09 00 00 00000004
06 00 000 000 3 0000 1 0520005650 0000 1 00 000 0 038 1 039 00 09 00 00 00000327
06 00 000 000 3 0000 1 0515005800 0000 2 00 000 0 076 7 038 35 09 00 00 00004495
06 00 000 000 3 0000 1 0515005800 0000 2 00 000 0 060 7 038 36 09 00 00 00000101
06 00 000 000 3 0000 1 0515005850 0000 2 00 000 0 062 1 039 00 09 00 00 00000056
06 00 000 000 3 0000 1 0515005850 0000 2 00 000 0 062 1 039 00 09 00 00 00000040
06 00 000 000 3 0000 1 0515006100 0000 2 00 000 0 082 1 039 00 09 00 00 0000C344
06 00 000 000 3 0000 1 0515006100 0000 2 00 000 0 082 1 039 00 09 00 00 00000257
06 00 000 000 3 0000 1 0515006100 0000 2 00 000 0 082 1 039 00 09 00 00 00000066
06 00 000 000 3 0000 1 0515006100 0000 2 00 000 0 082 1 039 00 09 00 00 00000134
06 00 000 000 3 0000 1 0515005350 0000 2 00 000 0 062 1 039 00 09 00 00 00000039
06 00 000 000 3 0000 1 0510005400 0000 1 00 000 0 015 1 001 00 09 00 00 00000028
06 00 000 000 3 0000 1 0510005400 0000 2 00 000 0 082 1 039 00 09 00 00 0000C167
06 00 000 000 3 0000 1 0510005450 0000 2 00 000 0 065 1 039 00 09 00 00 000006C2
06 00 000 000 3 0000 1 0510005550 0000 2 00 000 0 062 1 039 00 09 00 00 00000009
```

```
06 00 000 000 3 0000 1 0510005550 0C00 2 00 000 0 060 1 039 00 09 00 00 00000002
06 00 000 000 3 0000 1 0510005950 0000 2 00 000 0 060 1 039 00 09 00 00 00000033
06 00 000 000 3 0000 1 0510006000 0000 2 00 000 0 060 7 038 36 09 00 00 00000012
06 00 000 000 3 0000 1 0510006000 0000 2 00 000 0 060 1 039 00 09 00 00 00000005
06 00 000 000 3 0000 1 0510006050 0000 2 00 000 0 082 1 039 00 09 00 00 00001678
06 00 000 000 3 0000 1 0510006050 0000 2 00 000 0 060 1 039 00 09 00 00 00000006
06 00 000 000 3 0000 1 0515005800 0000 2 00 000 0 060 1 039 00 09 00 00 00000035
06 00 000 000 3 0000 1 0505005250 0000 2 00 000 0 082 1 039 00 09 00 00 00000520
06 00 000 000 3 0000 1 0505005350 0000 2 00 000 0 060 1 039 00 09 00 00 00000001
06 00 000 000 3 0000 1 0490005550 0000 2 00 000 0 060 1 039 00 09 00 00 00000005
06 00 000 000 3 0000 1 0505005450 0000 1 00 000 0 037 1 001 00 00 00 00 00000107
06 00 000 000 3 0000 1 0505005450 0000 2 00 000 0 064 1 039 00 09 00 00 00001333
06 00 000 000 3 0000 1 0540005950 0C00 2 00 000 0 082 1 039 00 09 00 00 00000782
06 00 000 000 3 0000 1 0510005400 0000 2 00 000 0 062 1 039 00 09 00 00 00000073
06 00 000 000 3 0000 1 0510006100 0000 2 00 000 0 075 7 038 00 09 00 00 00004281
06 00 000 000 3 0000 1 0505005350 0000 2 00 000 0 060 1 039 00 09 00 00 00000091
06 00 000 000 3 0000 1 0505005450 CC00 2 00 000 0 060 7 038 36 09 00 00 00000008
06 00 000 000 3 0000 1 0560005850 0000 2 00 000 0 060 7 038 36 09 00 00 00000161
06 00 000 000 3 0000 1 0560005850 0000 2 00 000 0 060 1 039 00 09 00 00 00000032
06 00 000 000 3 0000 1 0555005700 0C00 2 00 000 0 050 7 038 00 09 00 00 00000138
06 00 000 000 3 0000 1 0550005750 0000 2 00 000 0 082 1 039 00 09 00 00 00000275
06 00 000 000 3 0000 1 0550005750 0000 2 00 000 0 082 1 039 00 09 00 00 00000125
06 00 000 000 3 0000 1 0550005850 0000 2 00 000 0 082 1 039 00 09 00 00 00000212
06 00 000 000 3 0000 1 0550005850 0000 2 00 000 0 061 1 039 00 09 00 00 00000143
06 00 000 000 3 0000 1 0545005850 0000 2 00 000 0 060 7 038 35 09 00 00 00000009
06 00 000 000 3 0000 1 0540005950 0000 2 00 000 0 062 1 039 00 09 00 00 00000635
06 00 000 000 3 0000 1 0540005800 0000 2 00 000 0 061 1 039 00 09 00 00 00004876
06 00 000 000 3 0000 1 0505005450 0000 2 00 000 0 060 1 039 00 09 00 00 00000026
06 00 000 000 3 0000 1 0505005450 0CC0 2 00 000 0 062 1 039 00 09 00 00 00000411
06 00 000 000 3 0000 1 0505005450 0000 2 00 000 0 062 1 039 00 09 00 00 00000301
06 00 000 000 3 0000 1 0505005500 0000 1 00 000 0 015 1 001 00 00 00 00 00000061
06 00 000 000 3 0000 1 0505005500 0000 2 00 000 0 060 1 039 00 09 00 00 00000008
06 00 000 000 3 0000 1 0505005500 0000 2 00 000 0 060 1 039 00 09 00 00 00000018
06 00 000 000 3 0000 1 0505005550 0000 2 00 000 0 060 1 039 00 09 00 00 00000014
06 00 000 000 3 0000 1 0505005550 0000 1 00 000 0 015 1 001 00 00 00 00 00000015
06 00 000 000 3 0000 1 0505005550 0000 2 00 000 0 082 1 039 00 09 00 00 00000020
06 00 000 000 3 0000 1 0505005800 0000 2 00 000 0 060 1 039 38 09 00 00 00000025
06 00 000 000 3 0000 1 0505006050 0000 2 00 000 0 060 1 039 00 09 00 00 00000001
06 00 000 000 3 0000 1 0500005300 0000 2 00 000 0 064 1 039 00 09 00 00 00002790
06 00 000 000 3 0000 1 0500005300 00C0 2 00 000 0 062 1 039 00 09 00 00 00000061
06 00 000 000 3 0000 1 0500005350 00C0 2 00 000 0 063 1 039 00 09 00 00 00000082
06 00 000 000 3 0000 1 0500005350 00C0 2 00 000 0 060 1 039 00 09 00 00 00000005
06 00 000 000 3 0000 1 0500005500 0000 2 00 000 0 060 1 039 38 09 00 00 00000144
06 00 000 000 3 0000 1 0500005500 0000 2 00 000 0 060 1 039 00 09 00 00 00000031
06 00 000 000 3 0000 1 0500005500 0000 2 00 000 0 063 1 039 00 09 00 00 00000031
06 00 000 000 3 0000 1 0500005550 0000 2 00 000 0 061 1 039 00 09 00 00 00001888
06 00 000 000 3 0000 1 0500005550 0000 2 00 000 0 065 1 039 00 09 00 00 00000702
06 00 000 000 3 0000 1 0500005600 0000 1 00 000 0 015 1 001 00 00 00 00 00000139
06 00 000 000 3 0000 1 0500005600 00C0 2 00 000 0 082 1 039 00 09 00 00 00000172
06 00 000 000 3 0000 1 0500005600 00C0 2 00 000 0 060 1 039 00 09 00 00 00000160
06 00 000 000 3 0000 1 0500005600 0000 2 00 000 0 060 1 039 00 09 00 00 00000008
06 00 000 000 3 0000 1 0500005600 0000 2 00 000 0 062 1 039 0 09 00 00 00000080
06 00 000 000 3 0000 1 0500005600 0000 2 00 000 0 062 1 039 00 09 00 00 00000081
06 00 000 000 3 0000 1 0500005600 0000 2 00 000 0 082 1 039 00 09 00 00 00000045
06 00 000 000 3 0000 1 0495005350 0000 1 00 000 0 037 1 001 00 09 00 00 00000168
06 00 000 000 3 0000 1 0495005550 0000 2 00 000 0 060 1 039 00 09 00 00 00000022
06 00 000 000 3 0000 1 0495005600 0000 2 00 000 0 062 1 039 00 09 00 00 00000018
06 00 000 000 3 0000 1 0495005600 0000 2 00 000 0 062 1 039 00 09 00 00 00000034
06 00 000 000 3 0000 1 0495005600 0C00 2 00 000 0 062 1 039 00 09 00 00 00000021
06 00 000 000 3 0000 1 0495005600 0000 2 00 000 0 060 1 039 00 09 00 00 00000005
06 00 000 000 3 0000 1 0495005650 0000 2 00 000 0 062 1 039 00 09 00 00 00000031
06 00 000 000 3 0000 1 0495005650 0000 2 00 000 0 062 1 039 00 09 00 00 00000144
06 00 000 000 3 0000 1 0495005950 0C00 2 00 000 0 090 1 039 00 09 00 00 00013000
06 00 000 000 3 0000 1 0495005950 0000 1 00 000 0 015 1 001 00 00 00 00 00000002
06 00 000 000 3 0000 1 0495006000 0000 2 00 000 0 082 1 039 00 09 00 00 00000602
06 00 000 000 3 0000 1 0490005350 0CC0 2 00 000 0 062 1 039 00 09 00 00 00000155
06 00 000 000 3 0000 1 0490005350 0000 2 00 000 0 082 1 039 00 09 00 00 00000077
06 00 000 000 3 0000 1 0490005450 0000 2 00 000 0 062 1 039 37 09 00 00 00000081
06 00 000 000 3 0000 1 0490005550 00C0 2 00 000 0 062 1 039 00 09 00 00 00000242
06 00 000 000 3 0000 1 0490005450 0000 2 00 000 0 060 1 039 37 09 00 00 00000006
06 00 000 000 3 0000 1 0490005550 0000 2 00 000 0 062 1 039 00 09 00 00 00000151
```

```
06 00 000 000 3 0000 1 0490005550 0000 2 00 000 0 082 1 039 00 09 00 00 00000726
06 00 000 000 3 0000 1 0490005550 0000 2 00 000 0 060 1 039 00 09 00 00 00000012
06 00 000 000 3 0000 1 0490005550 0000 2 00 000 0 060 1 039 00 09 00 00 00000009
06 00 000 000 3 0000 1 0490005550 0000 2 00 000 0 062 1 039 00 09 00 00 00000022
06 00 000 000 3 0000 1 0490005550 0000 2 00 000 0 062 1 039 00 09 00 00 00000013
06 00 000 000 3 0000 1 0490005600 0000 2 00 000 0 060 1 039 00 09 00 00 00000009
06 00 000 000 3 0000 1 0490005600 0000 2 00 000 0 082 1 039 00 09 00 00 00000064
06 00 000 000 3 0000 1 0490005700 0000 1 00 000 0 015 1 001 00 00 00 00 00000075
06 00 000 000 3 0000 1 0490005700 0000 2 00 000 0 052 1 039 00 09 00 00 00000015
06 00 000 000 3 0000 1 0490005700 0000 2 00 000 0 083 1 039 00 09 00 00 00006021
06 00 000 000 3 0000 1 0490005700 0000 2 00 000 0 062 1 039 00 09 00 00 00001452
06 00 000 000 3 0000 1 0490005650 0000 2 00 000 0 090 1 039 31 09 00 00 00004304
06 00 000 000 3 0000 1 0490005650 0000 2 00 000 0 060 1 039 00 09 00 00 00000005
06 00 000 000 3 0000 1 0490005650 0000 2 00 000 0 063 1 039 00 09 00 00 00000339
06 00 000 000 3 0000 1 0490005650 0000 2 00 000 0 082 1 039 00 09 00 00 00000086
06 00 000 000 3 0000 1 0490005650 0000 1 00 000 0 015 1 001 00 00 00 00 00000073
06 00 000 000 3 0000 1 0490005900 0000 2 00 000 0 060 1 039 38 09 00 00 00000056
06 00 000 000 3 0000 1 0490005900 0000 2 00 000 0 063 1 039 00 09 00 00 00000017
06 00 000 000 3 0000 1 0490005900 0000 2 00 000 0 062 1 039 00 09 00 00 00000030
06 00 000 000 3 0000 1 0490005950 0000 1 00 000 0 015 1 001 00 00 00 00 00000021
06 00 000 000 3 0000 1 0490006050 0000 1 00 000 0 037 1 001 00 00 00 00 00000041
06 00 000 000 3 0000 1 0490006200 0000 1 00 000 0 037 1 001 00 00 00 00 00000048
06 00 000 000 3 0000 1 0485005350 0000 2 00 000 0 062 1 039 00 00 00 00 00000226
06 00 000 000 3 0000 1 0485005400 0000 2 00 000 0 082 1 039 00 09 00 00 00000110
06 00 000 000 3 0000 1 0485005400 0000 2 00 000 0 082 1 039 00 09 00 00 00000318
06 00 000 000 3 0000 1 0485005400 0000 2 00 000 0 065 1 039 00 09 00 00 00000155
06 00 000 000 3 0000 1 0485005450 0000 1 00 000 0 015 1 001 00 00 00 00 00000004
06 00 000 000 3 0000 1 0485005500 0000 2 00 000 0 082 1 039 00 09 00 00 00000585
06 00 000 000 3 0000 1 0485005500 0000 2 00 000 0 060 1 039 00 09 00 00 00000007
06 00 000 000 3 0000 1 0485005550 0000 2 00 000 0 062 1 039 00 09 00 00 00000012
06 00 000 000 3 0000 1 0485005550 0000 2 00 000 0 075 1 039 00 09 00 00 00005059
06 00 000 000 3 0000 1 0485005550 0000 2 00 000 0 065 1 039 00 09 00 00 00000269
06 00 000 000 3 0000 1 0485005550 0000 2 00 000 0 062 1 039 00 09 00 00 00000166
06 00 000 000 3 0000 1 0485005600 0000 2 00 000 0 075 1 039 00 09 00 00 00002756
06 00 000 000 3 0000 1 0485005600 0000 2 00 000 0 060 1 039 00 09 00 00 00000020
06 00 000 000 3 0000 1 0485005600 0000 2 00 000 0 048 1 039 00 09 00 00 00000359
06 00 000 000 3 0000 1 0485005700 0000 2 00 000 0 082 1 039 00 09 00 00 00000732
06 00 000 000 3 0000 1 0485005700 0000 2 00 000 0 082 1 039 00 09 00 00 00001451
06 00 000 000 3 0000 1 0485005700 0000 2 00 000 0 082 1 039 00 09 00 00 00000406
06 00 000 000 3 0000 1 0485005900 0000 2 00 000 0 090 1 039 00 09 00 00 00011900
06 00 000 000 3 0000 1 0485005900 0000 2 00 000 0 065 1 039 00 09 00 00 00000927
06 00 000 000 3 0000 1 0485005900 0000 2 00 000 0 082 1 039 00 09 00 00 00000277
06 00 000 000 3 0000 1 0485005900 0000 2 00 000 0 060 1 039 00 09 00 00 00000022
06 00 000 000 3 0000 1 0485005900 0000 2 00 000 0 063 1 039 36 09 00 00 00000051
06 00 000 000 3 0000 1 0485005900 0000 2 00 000 0 082 1 039 00 09 00 00 00000063
06 00 000 000 3 0000 1 0485005950 0000 2 00 000 0 082 1 039 00 09 00 00 00000027
06 00 000 000 3 0000 1 0485006850 0000 1 00 000 0 037 1 001 00 00 00 00 00000064
06 00 000 000 3 0000 1 0485006100 0000 1 00 000 0 037 1 001 00 00 00 00 00000097
06 00 000 000 3 0000 1 0485006200 0000 1 00 000 0 037 1 001 00 00 00 00 00000039
06 00 000 000 3 0000 1 0485006200 0000 1 00 000 0 037 1 001 00 00 00 00 00000046
06 00 000 000 3 0000 1 0485006200 0000 1 00 000 0 015 1 001 00 00 00 00 00000407
06 00 000 000 3 0000 1 0485006250 0000 1 00 000 0 037 1 001 00 00 00 00 00000042
06 00 000 000 3 0000 1 0480005450 0000 1 00 000 0 038 1 039 00 00 00 00 00000004
06 00 000 000 3 0000 1 0480005450 0000 2 00 000 0 065 1 039 00 09 00 00 00000132
06 00 000 000 3 0000 1 0480005500 0000 2 00 000 0 062 1 039 00 09 00 00 00000324
06 00 000 000 3 0000 1 0480005500 0000 2 00 000 0 082 1 039 00 09 00 00 00001057
06 00 000 000 3 0000 1 0480005600 0000 2 00 000 0 060 1 039 00 09 00 00 00000002
06 00 000 000 3 0000 1 0480005600 0000 2 00 000 0 082 1 039 00 09 00 00 00003505
06 00 000 000 3 0000 1 0480005650 0000 2 00 000 0 062 1 039 00 09 00 00 00000073
06 00 000 000 3 0000 1 0480005700 0000 2 00 000 0 062 1 039 00 09 00 00 00000019
06 00 000 000 3 0000 1 0480005700 0000 2 00 000 0 061 1 039 00 09 00 00 00000700
06 00 000 000 3 0000 1 0480005700 0000 2 00 000 0 060 1 039 38 09 00 00 00000002
06 00 000 000 3 0000 1 0480005700 0000 2 00 000 0 060 1 039 00 09 00 00 00000006
06 00 000 000 3 0000 1 0480005750 0000 1 00 000 0 037 1 039 00 00 00 00 00000053
06 00 000 000 3 0000 1 0480005750 0000 2 00 000 0 062 1 039 00 09 00 00 00001302
06 00 000 000 3 0000 1 0480005750 0000 2 00 000 0 062 1 039 00 09 00 00 00000718
06 00 000 000 3 0000 1 0480005750 0000 2 00 000 0 062 1 039 00 09 00 00 00000297
06 00 000 000 3 0000 1 0480005750 0000 2 00 000 0 062 1 039 00 09 00 00 00000020
06 00 000 000 3 0000 1 0480005750 0000 2 00 000 0 062 1 039 00 09 00 00 00000413
06 00 000 000 3 0000 1 0480005800 0000 1 00 000 0 015 1 001 00 00 00 00 00000013
06 00 000 000 3 0000 1 0480005800 0000 2 00 000 0 062 1 039 00 00 00 00 00000177
06 00 000 000 3 0000 1 0480005900 0000 2 00 000 0 015 1 001 00 00 00 00 00000014
```

06	00	000	000	3	0000	1	0480005950	0000	2	00	000	0	082	1	039	00	09	00	00	00000102
06	00	000	000	3	0000	1	0480005950	0000	1	00	000	0	037	1	001	00	00	00	00	00000008
06	00	000	000	3	0000	1	0480005950	0000	2	00	000	0	062	1	039	00	09	00	00	00000293
06	00	000	000	3	0000	1	0480005950	0000	2	00	000	0	060	1	039	00	09	00	00	00000005
06	00	000	000	3	0000	1	0480006000	0000	1	00	000	0	037	1	001	00	00	00	00	00000428
06	00	000	000	3	0000	1	0480006000	0000	2	00	000	0	062	1	039	00	09	00	00	00000004
06	00	000	000	3	0000	1	0480006050	0000	2	00	000	0	083	1	039	31	09	00	00	00003986
06	00	000	000	3	0000	1	0480006050	0000	1	00	000	0	037	1	002	00	00	00	00	00000061
06	00	000	000	3	0000	1	0480006050	0000	1	00	000	0	037	1	001	00	00	00	00	00000033
06	00	000	000	3	0000	1	0480006050	0000	1	00	000	0	037	1	001	00	00	00	00	00000043
06	00	000	000	3	0000	1	0480006050	0000	1	00	000	0	037	1	001	00	00	00	00	00000043
06	00	000	000	3	0000	1	0480006050	0000	1	00	000	0	037	1	001	00	00	00	00	00000015
06	00	000	000	3	0000	1	0480006050	0000	1	00	000	0	037	1	001	00	00	00	00	00000074
06	00	000	000	3	0000	1	0480006050	0000	1	00	000	0	037	1	001	00	00	00	00	00000025
06	00	000	000	3	0000	1	0480006050	0000	1	00	000	0	037	1	001	00	00	00	00	00000033
06	00	000	000	3	0000	1	0475005550	0000	2	00	000	0	062	1	039	00	09	00	00	00000008
06	00	000	000	3	0000	1	0475005550	0000	2	00	000	0	062	1	039	00	09	00	00	00000006
06	00	000	000	3	0000	1	0475005550	0000	2	00	000	0	061	1	039	00	09	00	00	00000469
06	00	000	000	3	0000	1	0475005550	0000	2	00	000	0	060	1	039	38	09	00	00	00000034
06	00	000	000	3	0000	1	0475005550	0000	2	00	000	0	060	1	039	00	09	00	00	00000021
06	00	000	000	3	0000	1	0475005600	0000	2	00	000	0	060	1	039	00	09	00	00	00000007
06	00	000	000	3	0000	1	0475005600	0000	2	00	000	0	062	1	039	00	09	00	00	00000123
06	00	000	000	3	0000	1	0475005600	0000	2	00	000	0	062	1	039	00	09	00	00	00000475
06	00	000	000	3	0000	1	0475005600	0000	2	00	000	0	062	1	039	00	09	00	00	00000129
06	00	000	000	3	0000	1	0475005600	0000	2	00	000	0	062	1	039	00	09	00	00	00000120
06	00	000	000	3	0000	1	0475005600	0000	2	00	000	0	062	1	039	00	09	00	00	00000100
06	00	000	000	3	0000	1	0475005600	0000	2	00	000	0	062	1	039	00	09	00	00	00000162
06	00	000	000	3	0000	1	0475005600	0000	2	00	000	0	063	1	039	00	09	00	00	00000045
06	00	000	000	3	0000	1	0475005650	0000	1	00	000	0	038	1	039	00	00	00	00	00000085
06	00	000	000	3	0000	1	0475005650	0000	2	00	000	0	062	1	039	00	09	00	00	00000214
06	00	000	000	3	0000	1	0475005650	0000	2	00	000	0	062	1	039	00	09	00	00	00000030
06	00	000	000	3	0000	1	0475005650	0000	2	00	000	0	060	1	039	00	09	00	00	00000011
06	00	000	000	3	0000	1	0475005650	0000	2	00	000	0	060	1	039	00	09	00	00	00000004
06	00	000	000	3	0000	1	0475005700	0000	2	00	000	0	062	1	039	00	09	00	00	00000117
06	00	000	000	3	0000	1	0475005700	0000	2	00	000	0	082	1	039	00	09	00	00	00000125
06	00	000	000	3	0000	1	0475005700	0000	2	00	000	0	062	1	039	00	09	00	00	00000028
06	00	000	000	3	0000	1	0475005750	0000	2	00	000	0	082	1	039	00	09	00	00	00000186
06	00	000	000	3	0000	1	0475005750	0000	2	00	000	0	062	1	039	00	09	00	00	00000438
06	00	000	000	3	0000	1	0475005750	0000	2	00	000	0	062	1	039	00	09	00	00	00000503
06	00	000	000	3	0000	1	0475005750	0000	2	00	000	0	062	1	039	00	09	00	00	00000394
06	00	000	000	3	0000	1	0475005750	0000	2	00	000	0	065	1	039	00	09	00	00	00000120
06	00	000	000	3	0000	1	0475005800	0000	1	00	000	0	037	1	001	00	09	00	00	00000021
06	00	000	000	3	0000	1	0475005800	0000	1	00	000	0	037	1	002	00	09	00	00	00000020
06	00	000	000	3	0000	1	0475005800	0000	2	00	000	0	060	1	039	00	09	00	00	00000010
06	00	000	000	3	0000	1	0475005800	0000	2	00	000	0	062	1	039	00	09	00	00	00000009
06	00	000	000	3	0000	1	0475005850	0000	2	00	000	0	082	1	039	00	09	00	00	00000520
06	00	000	000	3	0000	1	0475005850	0000	2	00	000	0	062	1	039	00	09	00	00	00000011
06	00	000	000	3	0000	1	0475005850	0000	2	00	000	0	060	1	039	00	09	00	00	00000015
06	00	000	000	3	0000	1	0475005900	0000	2	00	000	0	050	1	019	00	09	00	00	00000070
06	00	000	000	3	0000	1	0475005900	0000	2	00	000	0	050	1	023	00	09	00	00	00000067
06	00	000	000	3	0000	1	0475005900	0000	2	00	000	0	062	1	039	00	09	00	00	00000138
06	00	000	000	3	0000	1	0475005900	0000	2	00	000	0	062	1	039	00	09	00	00	00000029
06	00	000	000	3	0000	1	0475005900	0000	2	00	000	0	062	1	039	00	09	00	00	00000049
06	00	000	000	3	0000	1	0475005900	0000	2	00	000	0	082	1	039	00	09	00	00	00000066
06	00	000	000	3	0000	1	0475005950	0000	1	00	000	0	037	1	001	00	00	00	00	00000113
06	00	000	000	3	0000	1	0475005950	0000	2	00	000	0	060	1	039	00	09	00	00	00000006
06	00	000	000	3	0000	1	0475005950	0000	2	00	000	0	060	1	039	00	09	00	00	00000006
06	00	000	000	3	0000	1	0475005950	0000	2	00	000	0	060	1	039	00	09	00	00	00000002
06	00	000	000	3	0000	1	0475006050	0000	1	00	000	0	037	1	001	00	00	00	00	00000055
06	00	000	000	3	0000	1	0475006100	0000	2	00	000	0	062	1	039	00	09	00	00	00000127
06	00	000	000	3	0000	1	0475006250	0000	2	00	000	0	065	1	039	00	09	00	00	00006272
06	00	000	000	3	0000	1	0465005700	0000	2	00	000	0	062	1	039	00	09	00	00	00000268
06	00	000	000	3	0000	1	0465005700	0000	2	00	000	0	062	1	039	00	09	00	00	00000074
06	00	000	000	3	0000	1	0465005700	0000	2	00	000	0	062	1	039	00	09	00	00	00000222
06	00	000	000	3	0000	1	0465005700	0000	2	00	000	0	062	1	039	00	09	00	00	00000070
06	00	000	000	3	0000	1	0465005700	0000	2	00	000	0	062	1	039	00	09	00	00	00000023
06	00	000	000	3	0000	1	0465005700	0000	2	00	000	0	062	1	039	00	09	00	00	00000011
06	00	000	000	3	0000	1	0465005700	0000	2	00	000	0	082	1	039	00	09	00	00	00000208
06	00	000	000	3	0000	1	0465005700	0000	2	00	000	0	082	1	039	00	09	00	00	00000114
06	00	000	000	3	0000	1	0510005900	0000	2	00	000	0	090	1	039	00	09	00	00	00000560
06	00	000	000	3	0000	1	0470005700	0000	2	00	000	0	082	1	039	00	09	00	00	00000413
06	00	000	000	3	0000	1	0470005700	0000	2	00	000	0	062	1	039	00	09	00	00	00000068
06	00	000	000	3	0000	1	0470005700	0000	2	00	000	0	062	1	039	00	09	00	00	00000100
06	00	000	000	3	0000	1	0470006150	0000	2	00	000	0	062	1	039	00	09	00	00	00000115
06	00	000	000	3	0000	1	0470006200	0000	2	00	000	0	062	1	039	00	09	00	00	00000142
06	00	000	000	3	0000	1	0470006200	0000	2	00	000	0	062	1	039	00	09	00	00	00001192
06	00	000	000	3	0000	1	0470006200	0000	2	00	000	0	065	1	039	00	09	00	00	00003748

```
06 00 000 000 3 0000 1 0465005650 0000 2 00 000 0 060 1 039 00 09 00 00 00000031
06 00 000 000 3 0000 1 0465005700 0000 2 00 000 0 062 1 039 00 09 00 00 00000161
06 00 000 000 3 0000 1 0465005700 0000 2 00 000 0 062 1 039 00 09 00 00 00000075
06 00 000 000 3 0000 1 0465005700 0000 2 00 000 0 062 1 039 00 09 00 00 00000075
06 00 000 000 3 0000 1 0560005850 0000 2 00 000 0 060 1 039 00 09 00 00 00000025
06 00 000 000 3 0000 1 0560005900 0000 2 00 000 0 062 1 039 00 09 00 00 00000052
06 00 000 000 3 0000 1 0560005900 0000 2 00 000 0 062 1 039 00 09 00 00 00000026
06 00 000 000 3 0000 1 0560005900 0000 2 00 000 0 062 1 039 00 09 00 00 00000128
06 00 000 000 3 0000 1 0560005900 0000 2 00 000 0 065 1 039 00 09 00 00 00000313
06 00 000 000 3 0000 1 0560005900 0000 2 00 000 0 082 1 039 00 09 00 00 00000156
06 00 000 000 3 0000 1 0555005850 0000 2 00 000 0 082 1 039 00 09 00 00 00000066
06 00 000 000 3 0000 1 0555005850 0000 2 00 000 0 082 1 039 00 09 00 00 00000176
06 00 000 000 3 0000 1 0555005850 0000 2 00 000 0 062 1 039 00 09 00 00 00000102
06 00 000 000 3 0000 1 0555005850 0000 1 00 000 0 015 1 001 00 00 00 00 00000090
06 00 000 000 3 0000 1 0555005900 0000 2 00 000 0 060 1 039 00 09 00 00 00000025
06 00 000 000 3 0000 1 0555005900 0000 2 00 000 0 060 1 039 00 09 00 00 00000027
06 00 000 000 3 0000 1 0555005900 0000 2 00 000 0 060 1 039 00 09 00 00 00000008
06 00 000 000 3 0000 1 0555005900 0000 2 00 000 0 065 1 039 00 09 00 00 00000051
06 00 000 000 3 0000 1 0545005650 0000 1 00 000 0 015 1 001 00 00 00 00 00000842
06 00 000 000 3 0000 1 0545005900 0000 1 00 000 0 015 1 001 00 00 00 00 00000009
06 00 000 000 3 0000 1 0545005850 0000 1 00 000 0 015 1 001 00 00 00 00 00000046
```

References

Asch, Nancy B., Richard I. Ford, and David L. Asch
  1972 Paleoethnobotany of the Koster site: The Archaic horizons. *Illinois State Museum Reports of Investigations* 24. Springfield.
Battle, Herbert
  1922 The domestic use of oil among the southern aborigines. *American Anthropologist* 24: 171–182
Binford, Lewis R.
  1970 Archaeology at Hatchery West. *Memoirs of the Society for American Archaeology* 24.
  1972 *An archaeological perspective.* New York: Seminar Press.
Black, Thomas K. III
  1976 The biological and social analysis of a Mississippian cemetery from southeast Missouri: The Turner site, 23 Bu 21A. Paper presented at the Southeastern Archaeological Conference, 4–6 November, Tuscaloosa Alabama.
Bonner, F. T., and L. C. Maisenhelder
  1974 *Carya* Nutt. Hickory. In *Seeds of the woody plants in the United States. Agriculture Handbook* 450. Forest Service, United States Department of Agriculture, pp. 269–272.
Braun, E. Lucy
  1950 *Deciduous forests of eastern North America.* New York: Hafner.
Bray, Robert T.
  1957 Lander shelter no. 1. *The Missouri Archaeologist* 19 (1–2).
Brown, James A.
  1964 The identification of a prehistoric bone tool from the midwest: The deer-jaw sickle. *American Antiquity* 29: 381–386.
Casselberry, Samuel E.
  1974 Further refinement of formulae for determining population from floor area. *World Archaeology* 6(1):117–124.
Casteel, Richard W.
  1975 Estimation of size, minimum numbers of individuals, and seasonal dating by means of fish scales from archaeological sites. In *Archaeozoological Studies*, ed. A. T. Clason. Amsterdam: North Holland Publishing Company.
Chamberlain, Thomas C.
  1965 The method of multiple working hypotheses. *Science* 148:754–759.
Clark, P. J., and F. C. Evans
  1954 Distance to nearest neighbor as a measure of spatial relationships in populations. *Ecology* 35:445–453.
Clarke, S. K.
  1971 A method for the determination of prehistoric pueblo population estimates. Xerographic copy. Center for Man and Environment, Prescott College, Prescott, Arizona.

Cook, S. F.
    1972   *Prehistoric Demography*. Module no. 16. A McCaleb Module in Anthropology.
           Reading, Mass.:Addison-Wesley.
Cook, S. F., and R. F. Heizer
    1965   The quantative approach to the relation between population and settlement
           size. *University of California Archaeological Survey Report* 64. Berkeley,
           California.
Cook, S. F., and A. E. Treganza
    1950   The quantative investigation of Indian mounds. *University of California Publi-
           cations in American Archaeology and Ethnology* 40:223–262. Berkeley,
           California.
Copi, Irving M.
    1972   *Introduction to logic*. New York: MacMillian.
Cutler, Hugh C., and Leonard Blake
    1973   Plants from archaeological sites east of the Rockies. Mimeographed. Missouri
           Botanical Garden: St. Louis, Missouri.
Essex, Burton L., and John S. Spencer, Jr.
    1974   Timber resources of Missouri's eastern Ozarks, 1972. *United States Department
           of Agriculture Forest Service Resource Bulletin* NC-19. North Central Forest
           Experiment Station, St. Paul, Minnesota.
Fish, Suzanne K., and Paul R. Fish
    1976   The small house in a social network. Mimeographed. Department of Anthropol-
           ogy, Univ. of Georgia, Athens, Georgia.
Ford, Richard I.
    1968   An ecological analysis involving San Juan Pueblo, New Mexico. Ph.D. Disserta-
           tion, Department of Anthropology, University of Michigan. Ann Arbor,
           Michigan: University Microfilms.
Fowler, Melvin L.
    1957   Archaic projectile point styles, 7000–2000 B.C. in the central Mississippi valley.
           The Missouri Archaeologist 19 (1–2).
Griffin, James B., ed.
    1952   *Archaeology of eastern United States*. Chicago: Univ. of Chicago Press.
Griffin, James B.
    1967   Eastern North American archaeology: A summary. *Science* 156:175–191.
Harrington, M. R.
    1908   Some Seneca corn-foods and their preparation. *American Anthropologist*
           10:575–590.
Hill, James N.
    1972   The methodological debate in contemporary archaeology: A model. In *Models
           in archaeology,* ed. D. L. Clarke, London: Methuen, pp. 61–108.
Hosner, J. F., and L. S. Minckler
    1963   Bottomland hardwood forests of southern Illinois: Regeneration and succession.
           Ecology 44:29–41
Kaplan, Lawrence
    1956   The cultivated beans of the prehistoric Southwest. *Annals of the Missouri Bo-
           tanical Garden* 43:189–251.
Lawson, John
    1860   *History of Carolina, containing the exact description and natural history of
           that country.* London: Raleigh (reprint of 1714 edition).
Murdock, George P., and Catrina Provost
    1973   Factors in the division of labor by sex: A cross cultural analysis. *Ethnology*
           12(2):203–225.

Naroll, R.
  1962   Floor area and settlement population. *American Antiquity* 27:587–589.
Olson, David F.
  1974   *Quercus* L. Oak. In *Seeds of the woody plants in the United States. Agriculture Handbook* 450. Forest Service, United States Department of Agriculture, pp. 292–703.
Price, James E.
  1969   Analysis of a Middle Mississippian house. *Museum Briefs* 1. Museum of Anthropology. Univ. of Missouri. Columbia, Missouri.
  1973   Settlement planning and artifact distribution on the Snodgrass site and their socio-political implications in the Powers Phase of southeast Missouri. Ph.D. dissertation, Department of Anthropology, Univ. of Michigan. Ann Arbor, Michigan: University Microfilms.
  1974   Mississippian settlement systems of the central Mississippi valley. Paper presented at an advanced seminar on Mississippian development at the School of American Research, 10–15 November, Santa Fe, New Mexico.
Putnam, J. A.
  1951   Management of bottomland hardwoods. Southern Forest Experiment Station. *Occasional Papers* 16.
Putnam, J. A., G. M. Furnival, and J. S. McNight
  1960   Management and inventory of southern hardwoods. *Agriculture Handbook* 181. Forest Service, United States Department of Agriculture.
Ray, Robert H.
  1976   The use of freshwater mussel shells as indicators of seasonal occupation of archaeological sites. Paper presented to the Arkansas Academy of Science, 10 April. Fayetteville, Arkansas.
Roberts, Ralph G.
  1965   Tick Creek Cave: An Archaic site in the Gasconade River valley of Missouri. *The Missouri Archaeologist* 27(2).
Saucier, Roger T.
  1974   Quaternary geology of the lower Mississippi valley. *Arkansas Archaeological Survey Research Series* 6. Fayetteville, Arkansas.
Shelford, Victor E.
  1954   Some lower Mississippi valley flood plain biotic communities: Their age and elevation. *Ecology* 35:126–142.
  1963   *The ecology of North America*. Urbana, Illinois: Univ. of Illinois Press.
Smith, Bruce D.
  1974a Predator–prey relationships in the eastern Ozarks: A.D. 1300. *Human Ecology* 2:31–44.
  1974b Middle Mississippi exploitation of animal populations: A predictive model. *American Antiquity* 29:274–291.
  1975   Middle Mississippi exploitation of animal populations. *Anthropological Papers* 57. Museum of Anthropology, Univ. of Michigan, Ann Arbor, Michigan.
  1976   Determining the selectivity of utilization of animal species by prehistoric human populations. Paper presented at the Annual Meeting, the Society for American Archaeology. 6–8 May. St. Louis, Missouri.
  1977   Archaeological inference and inductive confirmation. *American Anthropologist* 79(3):598–617.
  n.d.   An Archaic burial site east of Neelyville, Butler County Missouri. Xerographic copy. Museum of Anthropology, Univ. of Michigan. Ann Arbor, Michigan.
Speck, Frank G.
  1909   Ethnology of the Yuchi indians. *Anthropological Publications* 1, no. 1. University Museum, Univ. of Pennsylvania. Philadelphia, Pennsylvania.

Steyermark, Julian A.
  1963   *Flora of Missouri*. Ames, Iowa: The Iowa State Press.
Swanton, John R.
  1911   Indian tribes of the lower Mississippi valley. *Bureau of American Ethnology Bulletin* 43. Washington, D.C.
  1946   The Indians of the southeastern United States. *Bureau of American Ethnology Bulletin* 137. Washington, D.C.
Thomas, Cyrus
  1894   Report on the mound explorations of the Bureau of American Ethnology. *Twelfth Annual Report of the Bureau of American Ethnology*. Washington, D.C.
Webb, William S.
  1940   The Wright Mounds. *The University of Kentucky Reports in Anthropology* 5(1). Lexington, Kentucky.
  1941   Mt. Horeb earthworks and the Drake Mound. *The University of Kentucky Reports in Anthropology* 5(2). Lexington, Kentucky.
Wetterstrom, Wilma A.
  1970   An assessment of the nutritional status of San Juan Pueblo, New Mexico. Mimeographed. Univ. of Michigan Museum of Anthropology. Ann Arbor, Michigan.
Whallon, Robert, Jr.
  1974   Spatial analysis of occupation floors II: The application of nearest neighbor analysis. *American Antiquity* 39:16–34.
Woot-Tsuen Wu Leung, and Marina Flores
  1961   *Food composition table for use in Latin America*. Interdepartmental Committee on Nutrition for National Defense, National Institutes of Health. Bethesda, Maryland.
Wright, Muriel
  1958   American indian corn dishes. *The Cronicle of Oklahoma* 36:155–166.
Yarnell, Richard A.
  1972   *Iva annua* var. *Macrocarpa*: Extinct American cultigen? *American Anthropologist* 74:335–341.
  1974   Intestinal contents of the Salts Cave mummy and analysis of the initial Salts Cave flotation series. In *Archaeology of the Mammoth Cave Area*. ed. Patty Jo Watson. pp. 109–112. New York: Academic Press.
Zawacki, April, and Glenn Hausfather
  1969   Early vegetation of the lower Illinois valley. *Illinois State Museum Reports of Investigations* 17. Springfield, Illinois.

Index

Numbers in italics are page numbers of figures.

STUDIES IN ARCHEOLOGY

Consulting Editor: Stuart Struever

Department of Anthropology
Northwestern University
Evanston, Illinois

James N. Hill and Joel Gunn (Eds.). **The Individual in Prehistory: Studies of Variability in Style in Prehistoric Technologies**

Michael B. Schiffer and George J. Gumerman (Eds.). **Conservation Archaeology: A Guide for Cultural Resource Management Studies**

Thomas F. King, Patricia Parker Hickman, and Gary Berg. **Anthropology in Historic Preservation: Caring for Culture's Clutter**

Richard E. Blanton. **Monte Albán: Settlement Patterns at the Ancient Zapotec Capital**

R. E. Taylor and Clement W. Meighan. **Chronologies in New World Archaeology**

Bruce D. Smith. **Prehistoric Patterns of Human Behavior: A Case Study in the Mississippi Valley**

in preparation

Barbara L. Stark and Barbara Voorhies (Eds.). **Prehistoric Coastal Adaptations: The Economy and Ecology of Maritime Middle America**

Lewis R. Binford. **Nunamuit Ethnoarchaeology**

Charles L. Redman (Ed.). **Social Archeology: Beyond Subsistence and Dating**

Bruce D. Smith (Ed.). **Mississippian Settlement Patterns**

Sarunas Milisauskas. **European Prehistory**

J. Barto Arnold III and Robert Weddle. **The Nautical Archeology of Padre Island: The Spanish Shipwrecks of 1554**